DIVINE DOPPELGÄNGERS

Divine Doppelgängers

YHWH's *Ancient Look-Alikes*

EDITED BY COLLIN CORNELL

EISENBRAUNS | University Park, Pennsylvania

This book received two grants: the Judaic Book Fund Grant from the Tam Institute of Jewish Studies at Emory University and a Competitive Research Award from the Professional Development Support Funds program at Emory University's Laney Graduate School.

Library of Congress Cataloging-in-Publication Data

Names: Cornell, Collin, 1988– editor.
Title: Divine doppelgängers : YHWH's ancient look-alikes / edited by Collin Cornell.
Description: University Park, Pennsylvania : Eisenbrauns, [2020] | Includes bibliographical references and index.
Summary: "A collection of essays by scholars of the Hebrew Bible providing recommendations for how Jews and Christians can think theologically about the challenge of similarities between YHWH and other ancient gods"—Provided by publisher.
Identifiers: LCCN 2019055837 | ISBN 9781575067445 (hardback) | ISBN 9781575067469 (paper)
Subjects: LCSH: Chemosh (Moabite deity) | God—Comparative studies. | God (Christianity)
Classification: LCC BL205.D575 2020 | DDC 202/.11—dc23
LC record available at https://lccn.loc.gov/2019055837

Copyright © 2020 The Pennsylvania State University
All rights reserved
Printed in the United States of America
Published by The Pennsylvania State University Press,
University Park, PA 16802-1003

The Pennsylvania State University Press is a member of the Association of University Presses.

It is the policy of The Pennsylvania State University Press to use acid-free paper. Publications on uncoated stock satisfy the minimum requirements of American National Standard for Information Sciences—Permanence of Paper for Printed Library Material, ANSI Z39.48–1992.

CONTENTS

Editor's Preface. vii
Acknowledgments xiii
List of Abbreviations xv

PART 1. THE PROBLEM AT LARGE

Chapter 1. God and the Gods: History of Religion as an Approach
and Context for Biblical Theology 5
Patrick D. Miller Jr.

Chapter 2. Canaan—Israel—Christianity: The Case for a Vertical
Ecumenism 32
Othmar Keel, translated by Armin Siedlecki

Chapter 3. More Than One God? Three Models for Construing the
Relations Between YHWH and the Other Gods 60
Bob Becking

Chapter 4. Who Is Like You Among the Gods? Some Observations
on Configuring YHWH in the Old Testament 77
J. Andrew Dearman

Chapter 5. Why Should the Look-Alikes Be a Problem? 88
Robert Goldenberg

PART 2. CHEMOSH AS A CASE STUDY

Chapter 6. Theological Approaches to the Problem of God's Ancient
Look-Alikes 101
Collin Cornell

Chapter 7. Chemosh Looks Like YHWH, but That's Okay 115
Josey Bridges Snyder

Chapter 8. YHWH and Chemosh: An Investigation of Look-Alike
Gods Using the Moral Foundations Theory 126
M. Patrick Graham

Chapter 9. YHWH, Chemosh, and the Rule of Faith 138
Brent A. Strawn

Chapter 10. Is There a Counterpart in the Hebrew Bible to New
Testament Anti-Semitism? 159
Jon D. Levenson

PART 3. OTHER CASE STUDIES

Chapter 11. *Miqreh* and YHWH: Fate, Chance, Simultaneity, and
Providence 181
Stephen B. Chapman

Chapter 12. "Can a Woman Forget Her Nursing Child?" Divine
Breastfeeding and the God of Israel 201
Christopher B. Hays

Chapter 13. Bulls and Horses, Gods and Goddesses: The Religious
Iconography of Israel's Neighbors 219
P. M. Michèle Daviau

List of Contributors. 239
Index of Authors 243
Index of Scripture. 253
Subject Index 259

EDITOR'S PREFACE

Sooner or later, whether by a note in a study Bible, a religion class, or a seminary course, students bump up against the fact that God—the biblical God—was one among other, comparable gods. Indeed, the ancient world was full of gods: great gods of conquering empires, dynastic gods of petty kingdoms, goddesses of fertility, personal spirit guardians. And, in various ways, these gods looked like the biblical God, and vice versa. Like the God of the Bible, they too controlled the fates of nations, chose kings, gave fecundity and blessing, and cared for their individual human charges. They spoke and acted. They experienced wrath and delight. They inspired praise.

None of this, of course, is problematic in itself. Antiquity was well aware of the biblical God as a single example within a larger class of divine beings. Envoys from the Assyrian king Sennacherib had, for example, according to 2 Chr 32:19, "spoke[n] of the God of Jerusalem as if he were like the gods of the peoples of the earth" (NRSV). Many papyri written in Greek list out magical spells invoking numerous gods; some of them set YHWH, the name of the biblical God, indiscriminately alongside other deity names.[1] Or again: some Christian gnostics understood the god YHWH as one member in a cohort of lesser emanations descending from the transcendent divine One.[2] Plainly, the biblical God could be thought of as belonging to a kind: as a god among gods.

The trouble is that these descriptions arise from outsiders: outsiders to the biblical traditions. Those "on the inside," the ancient and modern communities who receive the Hebrew Bible as a religious norm, would never accept this

---

1. George H. van Kooten, "Moses/Musaeus/Mochos and His God Yahweh, Iao, and Sabaoth, Seen from a Graeco-Roman Perspective," in *Revelation of the Name YHWH to Moses: Perspectives from Judaism, the Pagan Graeco-Roman World, and Early Christianity*, ed. George H. van Kooten, Themes in Biblical Narrative (Leiden: Brill, 2005), 107–83.

2. See, e.g., the second-century *Apocryphon of John*; on its pantheon, see A. J. Welburn, "The Identity of the Archons in the 'Apocryphon Johannis,'" *Vigiliae Christianae* 32 (1978): 241–54.

classification. For them, the biblical God is *sui generis*: without parallel; one of a kind. One standard of faith, though particular to the Reformed branch of the Christian churches, expresses a belief shared by all the inheritors of the Bible: "There is but one only living and true God."[3] The origins of this confession are complex and debated, but they certainly include influence from biblical texts like Isa 45:5a: "I am YHWH, and there is no other; besides me there is no god."[4] Likewise, in the New Testament, the apostle Paul congratulates his gentile addressees for "turn[ing] to God from idols, to serve the living and true God" (1 Thess 1:9b). On this line of thinking, it may be true at a linguistic level that the word used for God ("God") can be applied to other beings ("gods"), but theologically, God alone is God. Assyrian officials, Greek magicians, and Christian gnostics are mistaken in their perception, or so it would seem.

And yet this judgment has changed and grown more difficult in the era since colonizing European powers began to seize artifacts and texts from the ancient Near East and to subject them to serious study. Beginning in the 1700s and continuing into the 1900s, archaeologists, cuneiformists, expert Semitists, and biblical scholars produced a much higher definition picture of the similarities between God and the gods than had theretofore been available. They deciphered hymns of praise to powerful imperial gods, analyzed prayers calling on personal divine guardians, and discovered female figurines designed to catalyze blessing. The biblical hymns and prayers and stories and blessings of YHWH, his affect, his anger and pleasure, all came to be seen within this comparative context. Claims about the uniqueness of the biblical God appeared to suffer erosion.

How then did the heirs, the insiders to the biblical traditions, respond? What did the scholars say who belonged to religious communities centered on the worship of one God? Was there an answer to this problem of God's ancient look-alikes?

In fact, not very much was written that addressed these questions directly. This was due in part to disciplinary specialization. As excavations and expropriations from the Middle East brought troves of artifacts into academic discussion, philologists and historians had their hands full just trying to reach a basic understanding of these new data. Decrypting the ancient materials and making preliminary comparisons with biblical literature occupied the energy of generations. Even if such scholars had received the training to zoom out from the details and to talk more theologically about the significance of God among the gods, there was little professional quarter for doing so. On the other hand, theologians and other intellectuals operating from within the biblical

---

3. *The Westminster Confession of Faith* 2.1.
4. This is an example of the so-called "exclusivity formulae," as in Isa 43:10; 44:6; 45:5–6; 46:9. Here and elsewhere in this preface, quotations are drawn from the NRSV unless otherwise noted.

traditions mostly lacked the interest and preparation to reflect on what it meant that other gods recovered from the archaeological record mirrored the biblical God. Of necessity, they spoke in generalities about the relationship of the living God to God's creation in its manifold forms. The result was and remains a dearth of resources that consider the problem of confessing one God while recognizing this god's profound similarity to many others.

The present volume intends to help fill that gap. The idea for it emerged from my experience as a student in seminary. As I recount in my own chapter contribution, I had to read and translate the Mesha Inscription for a class—an artifact from the Iron Age Levant brought to European attention in 1868.[5] The focus of our class discussion was linguistic and historical; my classmates and I were immersed in the peculiarities of Moabite morphology and the usefulness of the inscription as a historical source. But for me, a theological reality loomed large: here in this text was a god, the Moabite god named Chemosh, who was a divine doppelgänger of the biblical God. Like YHWH, he was angry with his land and handed his people over to oppression by foreigners. Like YHWH, he spoke and issued orders for battle. He loved his chosen king.[6]

There could be no going back from seeing these (and other) theological parallels, and no ducking out of the seeming conflict they pose with the core affirmation of Judaism and Christianity that God is unique. But since I found scant resources at hand to think this dilemma carefully through, the question lay dormant. What I did not know, as I enrolled in Emory University's graduate program in Hebrew Bible, was that I was entering an unusually rich vector of Chemosh-related research, one that would afford me opportunities to study this god, and numerous others, in several dimensions—and also to reflect theologically on their significance vis-à-vis the god YHWH. Unwittingly, I had subscribed to the "Emory Chemosh School."[7]

Insofar as such an entity is identifiable, its obvious first entry is the 1989 edited volume *Studies in the Mesha Inscription and Moab*. This book traces back

---

5. See Collin Cornell, "Theological Approaches to the Problem of God's Ancient Look-Alikes," 101–14. For more on the discovery of this inscription, see especially M. Patrick Graham, "The Discovery and Reconstruction of the Mesha' Inscription," in *Studies in the Mesha Inscription and Moab*, ed. J. Andrew Dearman, ABS 2 (Atlanta: Scholars Press, 1989), 41–92.

6. For a sustained comparison of YHWH and Chemosh, see M. Patrick Graham, "YHWH and Chemosh: An Investigation of Look-Alike Gods Using the Moral Foundations Theory," 126–37.

7. Not to be confused with the "Emory annex to the Fribourg school," on which, see Brent A. Strawn, "The Hebrew Bible and Ancient Near Eastern Iconography: Past and Present Research, Present and Future Trajectories (A Committed Outsider's Perspective)," a lecture given at the University of Zurich on January 20, 2017. A revision, though without reference to the Emory annex, appears in Strawn, "Introduction: Othmar Keel, Iconography, and the Old Testament," in Othmar Keel, *Jerusalem and the One God: A Religious History*, ed. Brent A. Strawn (Minneapolis: Fortress, 2017), xxv–xlii.

to several seasons of the Central Moab Survey.[8] J. Maxwell Miller, professor of Old Testament at Emory, was the director of this survey project "to develop an accumulative and comprehensive gazeteer of the archaeological sites of the [Kerak] plateau."[9] The team that undertook this work included several Emory graduate students. One of them, J. Andrew Dearman, would go on to organize and edit the volume on the Mesha Inscription, enlisting both his former teacher and student colleagues to write chapters.[10] Miller had already penned an important journal article on the literary character of the Mesha Inscription,[11] and the volume to which he and some members of his erstwhile survey team contributed would become a baseline reference for me and others in the study of the Moabite god Chemosh.[12]

The next generation of this "school" emerged in 2010, when Josey Bridges Snyder, then an Emory graduate student, published an article on Chemosh in *Ugarit-Forschungen*. In it, she examines the Moabite personal names preserved on stamp seals (small clay devices to close a letter, often imprinted with artwork and short inscriptions) to determine the population of the Moabite pantheon. Was the god Chemosh worshipped by Moabites as one partner in a divine couple? Or was he a solitary "bachelor god" similar to YHWH in the HB? In the end, Snyder argues for the latter: Chemosh, like YHWH, was a "lonesome god."[13] In collaboration with Brent A. Strawn, then a professor of Old Testament at Emory, Snyder would also write a study on the poetics of the Mesha Inscription.[14] Lastly, I wrote a journal article on the "afterlife" of Chemosh:

---

8. See J. Andrew Dearman, "Introduction," in *Studies in the Mesha Inscription*, viii–x.

9. J. Maxwell Miller, ed., *Archaeological Survey of the Kerak Plateau*, American Schools of Oriental Research Archaeological Reports 1 (Atlanta: Scholars Press, 1991), 18.

10. See J. Andrew Dearman's biographical sketch of Miller, with a select bibliography of Miller's works ("J. Maxwell Miller, Scholar and Teacher: A Sketch," in *The Land that I Will Show You: Essays on the History and Archaeology of the Ancient Near East in Honor of J. Maxwell Miller*, ed. J. Andrew Dearman and M. Patrick Graham, JSOTSup 343 [Sheffield: Sheffield Academic Press, 2001], 16–35).

11. J. Maxwell Miller, "The Moabite Stone as a Memorial Stele," *Palestine Exploration Quarterly* 106 (1974): 9–18.

12. Also deserving mention in connection with the first generation of the Emory Chemosh School is Patrick D. Miller Jr. Though a professor at Princeton Seminary, his works on the Mesha Inscription exerted an important influence on subsequent writings by Emory faculty and graduates: Miller, "A Note on the Mesha Inscription," *Or* 38 (1969): 461–64; Miller, "Moabite Stone," *International Standard Bible Encyclopedia*, ed. George W. Bromiley, 4 vols. (Grand Rapids: Eerdmans, 1979–1988), 3:396. See also Miller, "Psalms and Inscriptions," in *Congress Volume Vienna 1980*, ed. J. A. Emerton, VTSup 32 (Leiden: Brill, 1980), 311–32.

13. Josey Bridges Snyder, "Did Kemosh Have a Consort (or Any Other Friends)? Reassessing the Moabite Pantheon," *UF* 42 (2010): 645–75, at 667. See also Snyder, "Chemosh Looks Like YHWH, but That's Okay," 115–25.

14. Josey Bridges Snyder and Brent A. Strawn, "Reading (in) Moabite Patterns: 'Parallelism' in the Mesha Inscription and Its Implications for Understanding Three Cruxes ('*štr kmš*, line 17; *h/ryt*, line 12; and *'r'l dwdh*, line 12)" (forthcoming).

how the worship of this deity subsisted in the era after Moab's loss of political independence and how Chemosh's profile changed to accommodate these new conditions.[15]

All these entries present a fine-grained historical portrait of one divine look-alike of the biblical God, but they do not yet say anything directly theological about it. They yield the raw materials for reflection, but they tender no guidance to persons "on the inside," to Jews or Christians who acknowledge YHWH as the living and true God. As it happens, this is not for lack of faith commitments on the part of the contributors. Many or most of them teach in theological schools, write for theological journals, and exercise leadership in worshipping communities. And so—it seemed to me—these same people would be ideal commentators on the theological meaning of God and the gods. They are steeped in the ancient materials, textual and archaeological, but also anchored in the continued practice of reading the Bible as a religious norm.

The few helpful essays I encountered on this topic came from scholars who met just that description, chief among them Patrick D. Miller Jr. and Jon D. Levenson. In the lecture he gave at his promotion to full professor at Union Presbyterian Seminary, Miller engaged at length with scholarship on the history of religion, including the history of the god YHWH in both its distinctiveness and its commonality with neighboring religious traditions. But Miller also considers these matters as a Christian: "What I am talking about is finally not just Yahweh and the gods, an interesting analysis of an Iron Age deity. It is God and the gods. Whatever we say about Yahweh as an El figure or in conflict with Baal is conversation about the God we know and worship in Jesus Christ."[16] So, too, Jon Levenson, then teaching at the University of Chicago and now a longtime professor at Harvard Divinity School, wrote a 1985 article about the parallel of New Testament invective against Judaism and the Hebrew Bible's invective against Canaanite religion. Here again, his descriptive observations about these similarities gesture toward constructive theological implications for Judaism and Christianity.[17]

I wanted to read more in that same vein. I also wanted to make these two essays more easily accessible to other persons in their wrestling and deliberation. So it was that the present volume came about. Many members of the Emory Chemosh School agreed to contribute, and this particular god, given his similitude to YHWH, is well-represented in the essays that follow. Miller and Levenson granted permission to reprint their prior publications. I also received generous

---

15. Collin Cornell, "What happened to Kemosh?," *ZAW* 128 (2016): 284–99.
16. Patrick D. Miller Jr., "God and the Gods: History of Religion as an Approach and Context for Biblical Theology," 5–31, at 29.
17. Jon D. Levenson, "Is There A Counterpart in the Hebrew Bible to New Testament Anti-Semitism?," 159–78.

support from the Tam Institute of Jewish Studies at Emory University. Their award of the Judaic Book Fund grant enabled me to purchase reprint permissions and, together with a Competitive Research Award from the Professional Development Support Funds program at Laney Graduate School, to commission Armin Siedlecki to translate a significant theological essay by Othmar Keel.[18] Other scholars well-practiced in reading the Bible in its ancient environments graciously agreed to think theologically about the problem of God's ancient look-alikes. Brent A. Strawn, my *Doktorvater* and a chapter contributor, gave indispensable editorial advice throughout the process of organizing the book.

For those who do bump up against the fact of God's resemblance to other ANE gods, I hope that the present collection furnishes them with stimulation and help for thinking deliberately through the issue, neither denying the presence of such similarities nor, on the other hand, departing too quickly from the long-standing trust of worshipping communities that the Hebrew Scriptures speak of the living God.

Collin Cornell

---

18. Othmar Keel, "Canaan—Israel—Christianity: The Case for a Vertical Ecumenism," 32–59.

ACKNOWLEDGMENTS

Chapter 1 was previously published in *Israelite Religion and Biblical Theology: Collected Essays*, LHBOTS 267 (Sheffield: Sheffield Academic, 2000), 365–96. It is reprinted with permission from Bloomsbury Publishing.

Chapter 2 was previously published as "Kanaan—Israel—Christentum: Plädoyer für eine vertikale Ökumene," in *Interesse am Judentum: die Franz-Delitzsch-Vorlesungen 1989–2008*, ed. J. Cornelis de Vos, Folker Siegert, Münsteraner Judaistische Studien, Wissenschaftliche Beiträge zur christlich-jüdischen Begegnung 23 (Berlin: LIT, 2008), 363–91. It has been translated by Armin Siedlecki with permission from LIT Verlag.

Chapter 3 was previously published as "Only One God: On Possible Implications for Biblical Theology," in *Only One God? Monotheism in Ancient Israel and the Veneration of the Goddess Asherah*, ed. Bob Becking, Meindert Dijkstra, Marjo C. A. Korpel, and Karel J. H. Vriezen (Sheffield: Sheffield Academic, 2001), 189–201. It has been reprinted and revised by Bob Becking with permission from Bloomsbury Publishing.

Chapter 10 was previously published in *Journal of Ecumenical Studies* 22 (1985): 24–60. It is reprinted with permission from the University of Pennsylvania Press.

ABBREVIATIONS

ABS   Archaeology and Biblical Studies
ADAJ   *Annual of the Department of Antiquities of Jordan*
ANET   *Ancient Near Eastern Texts Relating to the Old Testament*. Edited by James B. Pritchard. 3rd ed. Princeton: Princeton University Press, 1969
b.   Babylonian Talmud
BASOR   *Bulletin of the American Schools of Oriental Research*
BK   *Bibel und Kirche*
BZAW   Beihefte zur Zeitschrift für die alttestamentliche Wissenschaft
CAD   *The Assyrian Dictionary of the Oriental Institute of the University of Chicago*. Chicago: The Oriental Institute of the University of Chicago, 1956–2006
CBQ   *Catholic Biblical Quarterly*
CEB   Common English Bible
CHANE   Culture and History of the Ancient Near East
CTU   *The Cuneiform Alphabetic Texts from Ugarit, Ras Ibn Hani, and Other Places*. Edited by Manfried Dietrich, Oswald Loretz, and Joaquín Sanmartín. Münster: Ugarit-Verlag, 1995
DDD   *Dictionary of Deities and Demons in the Bible*. Edited by Karl van der Toorn, Bob Becking, and Pieter W. van der Horst. 2nd rev. ed. Leiden: Brill; Grand Rapids, MI: Eerdmans, 1999
ESV   English Standard Version
FAT   Forschungen zum Alten Testament
FR   *Freiburger Rundbrief*, new series
FRLANT   Forschungen zur Religion und Literatur des Alten und Neuen Testaments
HTR   *Harvard Theological Review*
JBL   *Journal of Biblical Literature*

JNES	*Journal of Near Eastern Studies*
JSem	*Journal of Semitics*
JSOTSup	Journal for the Study of the Old Testament Supplement Series
KAI	*Kanaanäische und Aramäische Inschriften*. Edited by Herbert Donner and Wolfgang Röllig. 2nd ed. Wiesbaden: Harrassowitz, 1966–1969
KJV	King James Version
KTU	*Die keilalphabetischen Texte aus Ugarit*. Edited by Manfried Dietrich, Oswald Loretz, and Joaquín Sanmartín. Münster: Ugarit-Verlag, 2013. 3rd enl. ed. of *CTU*
LHBOTS	The Library of Hebrew Bible/Old Testament Studies
m.	Mishnah
NRSV	New Revised Standard Version
OBO	Orbis biblicus et orientalis
Or	*Orientalia* (NS)
OTL	Old Testament Library
OtSt	*Oudtestamentische Studiën*
RB	*Revue biblique*
SBLDS	Society of Biblical Literature Dissertation Series
SBT	Studies in Biblical Theology
TADAE	*Textbook of Aramaic Documents from Ancient Egypt*. Edited by Bezalel Porten and Ada Yardeni. 4 vols. Jerusalem: Hebrew University, 1986–1993
UF	*Ugarit-Forschungen*
VT	*Vetus Testamentum*
VTSup	Supplements to Vetus Testamentum
ZAW	*Zeitschrift für die alttestamentliche Wissenschaft*
ZDPV	*Zeitschrift des deutschen Palästina-Vereins*

PART I

The Problem at Large

PART I OF THE VOLUME introduces the problem of God's ancient look-alikes, setting forth its basic materials and suggesting some constructive directions. Patrick D. Miller's chapter situates the theological challenge within the discipline of "history of religions." In other words, the kind of scholarship that brought the issue to the fore was developmental and comparative in its profile. After providing a historical retrospective of the history of religions approach, Miller concentrates on the question of God: theological anxieties about God's uniqueness and historical claims about God's inheritance from neighboring traditions meet precisely there. Miller outlines several ways in which the deity YHWH originates in the world of Canaanite religion—and also how the Bible testifies to YHWH's jealousy and exclusivity. Miller then indicates two theological strategies for addressing this seeming tension: first, a christological analogy, and second, a theological vision for all of human history. Miller's chapter is a substantive, indeed foundational, entry for persons seeking to consider YHWH's divine doppelgängers in theological perspective.

The next chapter, by Othmar Keel, raises the problem of ancient look-alikes from a different vantage: not of *contradiction* between the Bible's rhetoric and the history of religions—but of *loss*, the religious loss incurred when Judaism parted from its Canaanite antecedent. Keel's chapter deploys an analogy first drawn by Jon Levenson: just as early Christianity broke away from its mother-religion Judaism through dissociation and defamation, so also did Judaism long before, breaking away from Canaanite religion through the derision and caricature now canonized in Hebrew Scripture. After describing the religious practices that Hebrew Scripture condemns, Keel articulates the religious losses that Judaism (and Christianity) sustained by reviling their Canaanite forebear, including its sense for the sacredness of earth and its celebration of eroticism. Keel suggests that recent efforts by Christian theologians to "heal the break" with Judaism might also then inform another project: a "vertical ecumenism" that would honor the religious contributions of Canaan. Keel thus seeks to recover respect for the truthfulness and value of YHWH's erstwhile Canaanite contexts and divine colleagues. His chapter delivers an impassioned theological provocation.

Bob Becking's chapter identifies three historic approaches to YHWH and his divine look-alikes. The chapter begins from an apparent contradiction: on the one hand, the monotheism of the Christian tradition, following as it does from Judaism, and on the other, the multiple gods that feature in Hebrew Scripture and ancient Israelite religion. In response, Becking sketches three conceptual models to describe the ways that ancient Israelites and Judeans negotiated YHWH and "other gods": intolerant monotheism, amply attested within Hebrew Scripture itself; conditional acceptance of other gods, also found in Hebrew Scripture; and, lastly, unconditional respect for the reality and religious validity of other peoples' gods, which Becking develops on the basis of Aramaic texts recovered from the Nile island of Elephantine. Becking's essay presents indispensable data for working through the problem of YHWH's divine doppelgängers.

Andrew Dearman's chapter surveys the "primary terminology" used of the deity YHWH in Hebrew Scripture. The first part of the chapter pursues basic terms for this god such as *'ēl, 'elōhîm, 'elôah,* and the name YHWH. The second part engages terms for lordship, including *'ādôn* and *ba'al*. Dearman takes up all these terms in developmental and comparative perspective, as evidences of theological convergence or differentiation relative to other ANE gods. In the end, Dearman renders a subtle portrait of a god among the gods—YHWH at once deeply rooted in his originating contexts and yet also named and individual. Dearman's observations help to ground and situate the work of discerning the ongoing theological significance of biblical claims for YHWH's sole sufficiency or covenant partnership.

The final chapter of part I, by Robert Goldenberg, considers the problem of YHWH's ancient look-alikes in two dimensions. First, it engages Second Isaiah's rhetoric about YHWH's uniqueness, and it suggests that such texts reflect exaggeration, whether from fervor or as part of a theological confrontation with religious rivals. Second, it emphasizes the national character of biblical claims about YHWH. The writers of Hebrew Scripture do not make global theological claims; always their expressions address God's covenant partner, Israel, to inspire them to keep God's laws and to worship YHWH alone. With these two points in mind, Goldenberg proposes that rabbinic midrash contains interpretive resources that can enable modern-day readers to negotiate monotheistic language in the Bible in more flexible and non-literal ways. This chapter offers a helpful, textually grounded, and specifically Jewish approach to the theological dilemma of YHWH's divine doppelgängers.

CHAPTER I

God and the Gods: History of Religion as an Approach and Context for Bible and Theology

---

Patrick D. Miller Jr.

A History of Religion Approach to the Old Testament

The particular stance or perspective I want to highlight here is the history of religion. I want therefore to begin with a plea or claim for the continuing importance and validity of this perspective in the study of Scripture, then look at the central issue in the history of the religion of Israel, and finally ask tentatively about the theological character and base of a history of religion approach to the Old Testament.

I do not want to give the impression that I am urging what I consider to be the *only* or even the *primary* way to look at the materials of Scripture. This is of course but *one* dimension—both in method and content of the study of the Old Testament. It exists along with other methodologies and concerns: exegesis, isagogics, theology, hermeneutics. But within traditional theological education as well as to a large extent in the study of theology proper, the history of religion perspective has not been a major one, or if it has, it has been used to reinforce a particular theological point of view (see below) even as the history of religion concern may be neglected for theological reasons. As a general discipline and as a dimension of biblical study, history of religion has been far more popular in university departments of religion or Near Eastern studies where the study of systematic theology is less central than in a seminary and where Scripture is not necessarily studied with a bias toward its normative or canonical character and a primary interest in the continuing relevance.

Certainly this approach is not *new*. As a facet of Old Testament research, it reaches back before this century, but there have been periods of greater and lesser attention to the history of Israel's religion in the world of its time. Even so, within any particular period—and it is possible generally to characterize the movements of Old Testament study—there has been varying interest on the part of individual scholars.

A Historical Retrospect[1]

The study of Israel's religion reaches back a long way in the modern critical study of Scripture. Probably the classic work of the last century was Wilhelm Vatke's treatment of the religion of the Old Testament (1835), heavily under the influence of Hegel and developmental theories about the growth of religious institutions and ideas.[2] This work, which was one of the numerous significant influences on Julius Wellhausen in his reconstruction of the religious history of Israel, contained many insights into the Old Testament but could not finally stand as an adequate reconstruction of that religion. The disintegration of this nineteenth-century reconstruction is perhaps best seen in Karl Marti's work which was translated into English as *The Religion of the Old Testament*.[3] Here one encounters a picture of the movement of Old Testament religion through several stages—nomadic, peasant, prophetic, and legal. The criticism of this and other works is easy to make from our perspective. The nomad religion described by Marti as the first stage in Israel would now have to be pushed back into the Stone Age. The later period is unfortunately and erroneously viewed so negatively and inadequately that Jesus is said to have skipped back behind it to the prophets.

But I do not mention these examples to make easy particular criticism of outdated works but because, in addition to questionable hypotheses about the development of religion, they suffer from a fundamental weakness. They do not take into sufficient consideration the milieu of Israel's religion, the religious world in which the Hebrews lived and of which they were a part.[4] That is true even of such works as those of Wellhausen who acknowledged the significance of this data for understanding Israel.[5] As Werner Klatt has remarked in his major

---

1. For more extensive treatment of the history of the discipline, see Herbert F. Hahn, *The Old Testament in Modern Research* (Philadelphia: Fortress, 1962), 83–118, and H.-J. Kraus, *Geschichte der historisch-kritischen Erforschung des alten Testaments von der Reformation bis zur Gegenwart* (Neukirchen: Verlag der Buchhandlung des Erziehungsvereins, 1956). For New Testament developments, see W. G. Kümmel, *The New Testament: The History of the Investigation of Its Problems*, trans. S. McLean Gilmour and H. C. Kee (New York: Abingdon, 1972), 206–324.

2. Wilhelm Vatke, *Die Religion des alten Testaments nach kanonischer Büchern*, vol. 1 of *Die biblische Theologie wissenschaftlich dargestellt* (Berlin: Bethge, 1835).

3. Karl Marti, *The Religion of the Old Testament: Its Place among the Religions of the Nearer East* (New York: G. P. Putnam's Sons, 1907).

4. Marti makes reference to Phoenician and Arabian religion as well as to general Semitic religion. But these do not play a large role and where used are primarily as a foil to Israelite religion—a common practice even today. Further, the important data from Mesopotamia available at that time are acknowledged and used slightly at the beginning but play no major role in the analysis of Israel's religion.

5. Werner Klatt, *Hermann Gunkel*, FRLANT 100 (Göttingen: Vandenhoeck & Ruprecht, 1969), 49.

study of the work of Hermann Gunkel, Wellhausen stated that Israel was in the center of world history between the two ancient cultural centers of Egypt and Mesopotamia and that its religion was decisively influenced by this world history; but, astonishingly, he drew no consequences out of this recognition. The history of Israel remained for him a history which stood alone and would be comprehended out of its history alone. As a single history of religion parallel to illustrate or illumine the early period of Israel, he used Arab nomadism, a most dubious and remote parallel.[6] While historical methods came more and more into play during this period in the works of leading scholars,[7] the world of the ancient Near East as it was unfolding to modern discovery and investigation played a minor role in many of the studies of the history of Israelite religion.[8] Primary attention was given to pre-Islamic Arabian religion and Canaanite-Phoenician religion.[9] The inclusion of the latter was a step in the right direction even though at that time the principal sources for knowledge of that religion were the Old Testament and later Greek works such as those of Eusebius and Lucian, the reliability of which at that time was uncertain.

The situation did not remain as such for long. The discoveries in the ancient Near East, which had been going on for a century, albeit slowly to that point, began to have an impact. Scholars began to realize more and more that Israel did not have its origins in the misty past of humanity's historical beginnings. Civilizations representing a significant cultural level had risen and fallen before the entity Israel appeared on the stage of history. Thus, around the turn of the century as students of ancient history became increasingly aware of and impressed by this fact, the pan-Babylonian school of Hugo Winckler and A. Jeremias asserted a common culture and pattern of thought throughout the Near East, which was derived essentially from the Babylonians. Friedrich Delitzsch forcefully applied this theory to the Old Testament and stirred up a hornet's nest of controversy with his famous lecture "Babel und Bibel" (1902), in which he declared the Old Testament to be largely a reflection of this Babylonian-Assyrian culture.[10]

The "pan-Babylonians" did not win the day. They did, however, force the issue in a way that could no longer be ignored. Students of the Old Testament or of Israel's religion had to look at its historical and religious setting and ask after both method and significance in handling the ever-increasing data from

---

6. Klatt, *Hermann Gunkel*.
7. On Wellhausen in this regard, see Lothar Perlitt, *Vatke und Wellhausen*, BZAW 94 (Berlin: Töpfelmann, 1965).
8. Georg Fohrer, *History of Israelite Religion*, trans. D. E. Green (New York: Abingdon, 1972), 19, attributes the first use of the designation "history of Israelite religion" to Rudolf Smend in 1893, in his *Lehrbuch der alttestamentlichen Religionsgeschichte*.
9. Fohrer, *History of Israelite Religion*.
10. Cf. Kraus, *Geschichte*, 274–83, and Klatt, *Hermann Gunkel*, 99–103.

the Near East. The context in which Israel's religion took shape and progressed had been pushed backward and outward.[11]

Nowhere was that taken more seriously than in the so-called *Religionsgeschichtliche Schule* ("History of Religion School"), which reaches back into the nineteenth century and has its roots in the work of Albert Eichhorn,[12] but found its mature and greatest exponents, as far as Old Testament studies is concerned, in Hugo Gressmann and Hermann Gunkel.[13] Gressmann in his studies of the origin of eschatology and the Messiah concept found the roots of the Old Testament conceptions in the religious world of Mesopotamia and particularly Egypt. He traced a history of stages of the development of the Messiah idea that reached back into the court style of the ancient Near East. He described the Egyptian "messianic hope" at length and used this as a guide to discern the nuancing of the Israelite development. Whether Gressmann's analysis of either the Near Eastern material or the Old Testament will stand without major corrections is not as important as the fact that he drew upon the data of Israel's religious world to help clarify the Israelite picture all along the way. Yet while he saw dependence on Egyptian and other conceptions, he recognized the particular character and development of Israel's own eschatological conceptions as they grew out of that milieu.

The same is equally true of Gunkel. Probably his most important and representative work in this field was *Schöpfung und Chaos in Urzeit und Endzeit*.[14] In this work Gunkel guarded against some of the dangers and weaknesses of both the pan-Babylonian extreme emphasis on outside influences and the literary-critical ignoring of them as antiquarian curiosities unrelated in any significant way to the history of Israel's religion.[15] He first examined Genesis 1 on its own terms in conscious disregard of the Assyriological parallels. On "inner theological" or inner-biblical grounds he came to the conclusion with regard to the origin

---

11. Fohrer, *History of Israelite Religion*, gives credit to the pan-Babylonian school for drawing attention to certain religious phenomena which were not fully appreciated until later: the connection between myth and cult, the role of the Babylonian king at the New Year festival, and the cultic representation of religious teaching.

12. Cf. Kraus, *Geschichte*, 296ff. Gunkel dedicated his *Schöpfung und Chaos in Urzeit und Endzeit* to Eichhorn.

13. The *Religionsgeschichtliche Schule* had just as much impact on the study of the New Testament as reflected in the works of such persons as Reitzenstein, Bousset, Bultmann, and Gunkel himself. The questions and theological implications are no less important here than in the study of the Old Testament, but the scope and focus of this essay prohibits more than an allusion to this parallel development. See Kümmel, *The New Testament*.

14. Hermann Gunkel, *Schöpfung und Chaos: eine religionsgeschichtliche Untersuchung über Gen 1 und Ap Joh 12* (Göttingen: Vandenhoeck & Ruprecht, 1895).

15. A judgment made of Gunkel's work on *Schöpfung und Chaos* by Wellhausen who is reputed to have judged it "mehr Chaos als Schöpfung" ("more chaos than creation"). See Klatt, *Hermann Gunkel*, 70.

of Genesis 1 that "this tradition could not have arisen in Israel."[16] Then he turned to the comparative data and examined the different dimensions of the Babylonian myth in its various forms and concluded that there is sharp difference between the biblical and Babylonian myths in religious attitude and aesthetic coloration. But Gunkel did not stop with this apparently negative result. He looked at the oral tradition of this material and in an examination of the history of tradition uncovered in many Old Testament and apocryphal texts reflexes and motifs from the myth of the battle of Marduk against Tiamat. This is especially true of poetic texts. Comparison of this Old Testament data and Babylonian creation mythology reveals that Israelite and Babylonian creation reports have all things in common. One cannot speak of two myths but of one myth which comes down in two different recensions—Israelite and Babylonian. Dependency on Babylonian myth cannot be doubted, but it is not a matter of an Israelite scribe or theologian simply copying down the Babylonian myth. The material has been handed down orally and has a long history of tradition. The connecting links from the Babylonian myth, which therefore must have been known in pre-exilic Israel, to the Priestly creation account were these poetic reminiscences of the chaos battle.

Gunkel was not content simply to point out analogies and literary dependence.[17] He sought to uncover the particular character of the different mythological reports and even to see in Israel the developments and changes in the history of the tradition of the material.[18] It was this sensitivity both to the significant outside influences on Israelite thought and religion and to the history and shaping of these traditions and influences within the history of Israel's religion that made Hermann Gunkel the best representative of the *Religionsgeschichtliche Schule* and a continuing example for students of the religion of Israel and the ancient Near East.[19]

Gunkel was not unaware of theological implications in his approach and reflected on them to some degree.[20] He did not see his work as counter to a theological notion of revelation and could even speak of God's revealing himself to Israel "in a special way." But this was for him a historical judgment in the

---

16. Gunkel, *Schöpfung und Chaos*, 15. This summary of Gunkel's approach is heavily indebted to Klatt, *Hermann Gunkel*, 54ff.

17. A purely phenomenological observation of analogies was more clearly characteristic of literary critics and others who cited similarities between Israel and ancient Arabian nomadism.

18. The beginnings of form-critical study and *Überlieferungsgeschichte* are clearly seen in this seminal work by Gunkel. Klatt has pointed this out in some detail.

19. Fohrer, *History of Israelite Religion*, has summarized the work of this school as follows: "The religion of Israel was seen in its relationship to the religions of the surrounding world, particularly Mesopotamia and Egypt: Israelite religion itself was understood as a piece of 'history,' a process taking place according to the 'laws' of intellectual, spiritual, and social life, within which its transforming power was appreciated despite all dependence on pre-existing forms" (20).

20. Klatt, *Hermann Gunkel*, 74ff.

light of comparative data and not derived from prior supernaturalistic notions or a *heilsgeschichtliche* ("History of Salvation") view of Israel's place in history. On the contrary, he saw humanity—and thus human history—as one, and this whole history of humankind as the locus of revelation. Gunkel understood his study of creation and chaos to be a bridge between the people of God and the heathen nations, and for this reason the Babylonian influence on Israel was more than a "curiosity" or an "antiquarian" note, as Harnack and Wellhausen had expressed it. He was in fact genuinely moved at the thought of primeval myths of humankind and the Revelation of John so widely separated in time and thought and still at base the same material or substance.

This did not of course mean, as Klatt has pointed out, that Gunkel would turn Marduk into Christ. He believed that one could genuinely make distinctions between Christian faith and thought and Babylonian and, for that matter, Christian faith over against Israelite. But these appear to have been historical judgments for Gunkel, seen in the light of the whole of history and the long course of Israelite and Christian religion. He would not deny the particularity of Israelite religion nor that "in this history God reveals himself in a special way." Genesis 1 could not be seen as the special revelation of God which somehow had come to the first person, but in the movement of Israelite religion—and apparently history in general—the rule of the living God is revealed. The task of the historian of religion is to show this at those high points in history where it is most clear. Genesis 1 is such a high point.

Yet, because the whole of human history is the sphere of revelation, the foreign, polytheistic myths of Mesopotamia also point, however incompletely, to eternal truth. "The theologian will do well to handle even the Marduk myth with piety; one honors his parents not by thinking less of his ancestors."[21] Or, to put it another way: "We Christians have no basis for the assumption that everything good and worthwhile could stem only from Israel.... The seed of the divine revelation has not been strewn only on Jewish soil."[22] Thus, for Gunkel it was clear: Whoever would engage in a genuine historical understanding of the Israelite or Christian religion must also give to the other religions of the Near East a new theological position.

There are clearly unresolved tensions in such formulations. On the one hand a strong valuation of Near Eastern religions in the history of humankind and the revelation of God, but on the other hand a special way of revelation to Israel that seems to separate it sharply from these neighbors. One is tempted to accuse Gunkel of wanting to have his cake and eat it too, but his effort to maintain a balance or tension was in the right direction.

21. Ibid., 75.
22. Ibid., 75.

The history of religion approach to biblical materials has continued, but from at least 1930, if not before, this emphasis was not to the fore. This was true especially on the continent and in this country. The reason usually cited for the decline in this period is the influence of dialectical theology, and particularly Karl Barth, in Europe and America, together with its outgrowth, at least in part, in the emphasis on biblical theology.[23] While I cannot testify to the full accuracy of such a generalization, I think there is a kernel of truth in the claim. The negative attitude toward religion which appears so strongly in volume 1 of Barth's *Church Dogmatics* contributed to a de-emphasis on the worth of phenomenological and historical analysis of religious movements.[24] At the same time, for many, the *Religionsgeschichtliche Schule* had not opened up the Scriptures for a clearer, more relevant hearing by modern persons. On the contrary both conservative and liberal attempts to dissolve the distance between the Bible and contemporary ideas and perspectives were heavily damaged by the history of religion investigation of Hebrew and Christian religion.

The above remarks should not be interpreted as a critique of these developments but as a description of a general change in mood, a shift in emphasis, a focus on different perspectives. In many respects the shift was healthy and desirable. It is also true that the results of the work of those identified with the history of religion school and others like them were a significant part of the base on which the movements of the 1930s, 1940s, and 1950s were built. Krister Stendahl has described this well in his article on contemporary biblical theology.[25] While the work of the *Religionsgeschichtliche Schule* brought into sharper focus the hiatus between the ancient world and its thought and the contemporary world, that "experience of the distance and strangeness of biblical thought" was turned into a "creative asset rather than ... a destructive and burdensome liability."[26] Further, the comparative data from the ancient Near East was used as a foil to point to the sharp distinctiveness of biblical thought and religion.[27]

---

23. On the history of biblical theology in this period in America and the various influences and forces at work, see Brevard S. Childs, *Biblical Theology in Crisis* (Philadelphia: Westminster, 1970).

24. Barth's own understanding and treatment of religion is, I suspect, more sophisticated, careful, and open than he is sometimes given credit for, but the outcome or influence in general theological thinking is still there.

25. Krister Stendahl, "Biblical Theology, Contemporary," *The Interpreter's Dictionary of the Bible*, ed. George A. Buttrick, 4 vols. (New York: Abingdon, 1962), 1:418–32.

26. Stendahl, "Biblical Theology," 1:420. See also Childs, *Biblical Theology*. G. E. Wright wrote an article for *Interpretation* 3 (1949): 450–59, entitled "The Problem of Archaizing Ourselves," as a response to H. J. Cadbury's liberal protest, "The Peril of Archaizing Ourselves," *Interpretation* 3 (1949): 331–37.

27. The best example of this is G. E. Wright's *The Old Testament Against Its Environment*, SBT 2 (London: SCM Press, 1950), discussed below.

Investigation of the history of Israel's religion and early Christianity in the light of their milieu did go on.[28] Eissfeldt, Baumgartner, and others continued to plow this field in Old Testament as did Bultmann and his students in New Testament, but the dominant emphasis in the work of scholars and of theological students shifted—to biblical theology, then to Old Testament and New Testament theology, then to hermeneutics. The shift was less pronounced in Scandinavia and in the British Isles, but was nevertheless widespread, both here and abroad. As always, the wheel turns and the pendulum shifts, albeit subtly. Thus, beginning in 1962, two years after the publication of Gerhard von Rad's second volume of his *Old Testament Theology*, there appeared a series of articles and debates by two students of von Rad, Klaus Koch and Rolf Rendtorff, and the older scholar Friedrich Baumgärtel. Koch and Rendtorff signaled a renewal of interest in the history of Israel's religion, particularly in light of the large amount of comparative data that have come from Ugarit, Mari, and Hittite culture as well as from other sources in the ancient Near East. They also raised anew the question of distinctiveness, which they regarded as a significant historical issue in light of the increasing indications of Israel's ties with its neighbors, as well as a theological issue. It was in debate on this point that Baumgärtel entered the discussion. At approximately the same time, even as we were seeing the last major Old Testament theology for a while, the first full-scale studies of Israel's religion in several decades appeared in English, a translation of T. Vriezen's *The Religion of Israel*. The same year there appeared the translation of H. Ringgren's *Israelite Religion* and in 1967 Georg Fohrer's *History of Israelite Religion*, just translated into English. Meanwhile, in a series of articles beginning roughly about the same time (1962), the most significant body of work in this area in America has been coming forth from the pen of Frank Cross. A major revision and enlarging of these articles will appear shortly (*Canaanite Myth and Hebrew Epic*). I will say no more at this point about Cross's work because I am too close to it, and it is heavily embodied in part of what follows.

Characteristics of the History of Religion Approach

In connection with this summary historical retrospect, I want now to characterize briefly the history of religion approach to the study of the Old Testament.

---

28. Childs has pointed out how this was especially true of New Testament study (*Biblical Theology*, 73). A brilliant exception to the trend in America was Arthur Darby Nock at Harvard, a fact sharply demonstrated by the recent publication of two volumes of his collected essays, a veritable gold mine of judiciously interpreted data concerning the environment of New Testament Christianity (A. D. Nock, *Essays on Religion and the Ancient World*, ed. Zeph Stewart [Cambridge: Harvard University Press, 1972]).

To begin with, it is *phenomenological* in a general sense though not in the fully technical sense. The historian of the religion of Israel seeks to understand and give meaning to the various phenomena of that religion, to describe and name them, and to uncover their structure and inner relationships. The agenda for a general analysis of the phenomenology of religion is applied as fully as possible to the analysis of a *specific* religion. The categories of the phenomenology of religion provide handles and a framework which function as a useful guide to the historian, although because other concerns are in the picture the resultant description of religion by the historian will take a different shape from that of the phenomenologist. But the phenomenologist's primary aim empathetically to comprehend and clarify religion as it appears and even to some extent the effort to maintain the *epoché*, to "bracket" out the question of what lies "behind" the phenomena though this latter is much more debatable—are attitudes toward the data that ought to come to play in a history of religion investigation.[29]

But a history of religion approach goes beyond the phenomenological level in that it is quite naturally *historical*. The historical question, simply put, is twofold: It is a question of *origins*—how the religious conceptions and practices arise, where they come from, what their earliest form is; it is also a question of the *historical development* of that religion—what it looks like in its long course, what changes take place, what aspects continue fundamentally the same, what tensions and strains arise in the course of that history.

In the attempt to work out this historical development another dimension of the history of religion approach comes into play—*the comparative*. What effect does our knowledge of the religion and culture of the ancient Near East have on our understanding of the history of the religion of Israel, a relatively late comer on that scene? The mushrooming amount of information that continues to come from discoveries in the Middle East forces this question ever more prominently into the forefront of Old Testament studies. As an example, the excavations from one site, Ras Shamra, the ancient city of Ugarit on the coast of Syria, have had as much, or more, impact on and continuing significance for understanding the Old Testament as the famed Dead Sea Scrolls for the New Testament.[30] There is hardly any aspect of Old Testament studies that has not been affected by what has come from this site, which is still not fully excavated.

---

29. For discussion of the relationship between phenomenology of religion and history of religion and the contribution of the former to the latter, see the essays in *Problems and Methods of the History of Religions*, ed. U. Bianchi, C. J. Bleeker, and A. Bausani, Numen Book Series 19 (Leiden: Brill, 1972), especially those by Widengren, Bianchi, and Blecker.

30. One indication of this fact is the work of the Ras Shamra parallels project, one large volume of which (*Ras Shamra Parallels*, vol. 1) has just been published by the Pontifical Biblical Institute (1972).

The comparative analysis whereby Israel is looked at in the context of its environment has two concerns. One is to determine where the religious phenomena of the milieu have *influenced* or affected Israel's religion. The other is to improve our understanding of the phenomena of the religion of Israel in the light of what we have learned about their parallels, where such exist, even if direct influence cannot be demonstrated. The growing awareness that Israel had much in common with its neighbors inevitably raises the question: What then is distinctive or unique about Israel's religion? What is its particularity? That question has been there all along, ever since the parallels between Babylonian myth and the Old Testament were pointed out. It is present in the work of the *Religionsgeschichtliche Schule*. It is the major issue in G. Ernest Wright's monograph, *The Old Testament Against Its Environment*. One finds it again in the programmatic essays of Rendtorff and Baumgärtel as well as in many others along the way.[31] The question may be raised for several reasons. At times the concern for distinctiveness seems to be only a matter of depicting the history of that religion as a whole, as a distinct entity, as is every other religion including Babylonian, Egyptian, and Canaanite. The task is no more nor less than that of a responsible historical treatment of one of these other religions. At other times this issue of particularity rises to the fore because of the apparent difficulty of locating what is peculiar to Israel, or at least out of a sense that that particularity is no longer sharply etched in the light of all that Israel's religion had in common with and in dependence upon the others. Again, the issue of uniqueness may be the historian's way of trying to resolve the question as to why this religion survived when others that were contemporary, similar, and influential upon it did not. Finally, the concern for distinctiveness may be a theological one, usually tied to a particular notion of revelation.

These concerns are not altogether invalid and are certainly understandable. I have some of them working in me. But I want to propose that a preferable way of dealing with Israel's religion, historically and comparatively, is not to focus our concern primarily on the question of distinctiveness, but rather to describe the interplay of *continuity* and *discontinuity* that is always going on. It goes on both synchronically and diachronically, that is, both in relation to contemporary religious expressions outside Israel at any given moment and in relationship to past expressions of Israel's religion. But the effort to give attention to the interaction of those two factors is not only a more helpful way of describing the history of Israel's religion, but may be more useful and valid theologically than a singular focus on an ever-decreasing list of characteristics or elements peculiar to Israel.

---

31. For an earlier discussion of this question that gives some reference to other answers, see Johannes Lindblom, "Zur Frage der Eigenart der alttestamentlichen Religion," in *Werden und Wesen des Alten Testaments: Vorträge gehalten auf der Internationalen Tagung alttestamentlicher Forscher zu Göttingen vom 4.–10. September 1935*, ed. Paul Volz, Friedrich Stummer, and Johannes Hempel, BZAW 66 (Berlin: de Gruyter, 1936), 128–37.

Further Concerns

There are some dangers or problems in a history of religion approach that may explain why it does not always get its due. History of religion appears at times to be an embarrassment to the theologian, whether biblical or systematic. It may seem to undermine the basis for faith by relativizing it. The awareness of commonality with the "pagan religions" of the ancient Near East raises disturbing questions about the absoluteness and revelatory character of Israel's faith. Concentration on the history of religion may also seem, as it did to Gunkel's critics, an antiquarian exercise that says little if anything about the way the stuff of Scripture impinges on the present life of the community of faith. Or perhaps even more seriously, as an examination of the history of biblical study shows, a history of religion approach to the biblical data may work to widen the gap that we already feel between our world and the life and thought of the Bible. It is hard enough to relate to Yahweh, but if Yahweh looks a lot like Marduk, that makes it even tougher, and what do we do with Tiamat and her look-alikes in the Old Testament? The norm for faith (Scripture) may seem less and less able to relate to our present existence.

One who has any familiarity with the present scene in biblical scholarship, or for that matter, past tendencies, cannot be unaware that younger scholars who come out of a theological context into history of religion study (whether ancient or modern) often become disinterested in theology, and even acquire a negative attitude toward it. I am such a younger (?) scholar who finds the history of religion perspective both a valid dimension of my field of study, that is, data and an approach to it that cannot and should not be ignored, and also a part of whatever truth claims may be made about the subject matter under study. But I do not assert the significance of history of religion as a move from theology. Rather, I continue to search for its theological character, its proper place in any theological system, with a growing conviction that it may be theological gain rather than embarrassment.

Yahweh and the Gods

The critical religious question is always about God—who God is, what God does and requires, and how the deity is known, apprehended, or experienced. As an obvious corollary to that, the central concern for history of religion generally, and certainly the religion of Israel in its environment, is God. We are interested in various dimensions of Old Testament religion—sacrifice, feasts, temples, laws, ethics, and others—but the understanding of God remains the critical focus. The other matters may safely remain time-bound for us. The notion of

God presses itself upon us as so fundamental that we cannot regard it simply as antiquarian information from a past and primitive religion. Needless to say, the same is true of Israel's relationship with its neighbors and our assessment of that relationship, that is, the God issue, is the crucial one.

I want therefore to look at the relationship of Yahweh and the gods in Israelite religion both as an example of the interplay of continuity and discontinuity in the history of that religion and as its critical theological issue. Rather than presenting new data or new research in this area, I shall draw heavily on the analyses and constructs of other scholars at this point to show how one can put the material together to sketch the major outlines of that symbiotic and dialectical relationship. I propose to do this under three headings: (1) Yahweh out of the Gods, (2) The Gods in Yahweh, and (3) Yahweh against the Gods.

Yahweh out of the Gods

Let me begin by juxtaposing two ideas, apparently contradictory, but in fact both true, that together express an important theological or religious reality:

1. God[32] has a beginning;
2. God has no beginning.

The combination of those two propositions is a way of expressing what I mean by the phrase "Yahweh out of the gods."

It is now generally accepted in Old Testament study that the god Yahweh whom Israel worshiped as Lord of Israel and Creator of heaven and earth has roots and origins deep in the polytheistic world of Canaanite religion and the tutelary or clan deities of the patriarchs. The most plausible reconstruction of the origins of Yahweh or the worship of Yahweh is, in my judgment, that of Frank Cross. It is a hypothetical reconstruction, but it builds on a broad base of data and in a holistic way makes the best sense of both biblical and extrabiblical materials. Starting with the fundamental work of Albrecht Alt, Cross points out that in the patriarchal traditions in the Pentateuch, the god worshiped by a patriarch is identified by the patriarch's name, for example, "the god of Abraham"

---

32. I am aware of the problem encountered by the double use of the term "God," that is, as generic and proper name. That is unavoidable now. The proper name has fully absorbed the generic, and the generic is known only in the proper name within Christian theology. The issue before us involves how one can hold together in one both proper name and generic noun. Does the proper name maintain its meaning, force, validity, and revelatory content without sliding over into simply the generic, cultural, general phenomenon of deity? Does the content of the generic in its totality apply fully to the proper name? Our task is to look at the proper name in the tradition and the generic noun in the religious world and see what interrelationship they have.

or in another form, the "Bull of Jacob." In Cross's summary of Alt, "the god of the father" is

> not attached to a shrine, but is designated by the name of the Patriarch with whom he has a special relation, or rather, in Alt's view, by the name of the founder of his cult. He is not a local deity, but the patron of the clan, the social group. He may be described as a "historical" god, that is, one who enters into a kinship or covenantal relationship with a clan, and who guides the social group in its peregrinations, its wars, in short through historical vicissitudes to its destiny. The election motif running through the Patriarchal histories was native to the religion of the Fathers, and, though heavily nuanced by later Yahwistic features, was not a theme simply read back into primitive tradition. The special traits of the cult of the Patriarchal gods in fact anticipate at a number of points characteristics of the religion of Yahweh, the lord of covenant and community. These provide continuity between the old religious forms and the new, a historically credible background for emergent Yahwism and an explanation of the development of a religious unity of apparently disparate clans which came together in the Yahwistic league. The gods of the Fathers were *paidagōgoi* to the god Yahweh who later took their place.[33]

Cross provides correction to Alt specifically at the point of his assumption that the gods of the Fathers were nameless. In the light of biblical, Aramaic, Amorite, and Old Akkadian evidence, Cross demonstrates that:

> These clan or "social" gods were high gods and were quickly identified by common traits or by cognate names with gods of the local pantheon [in Canaan]. For example, an Amorite moving from northern Mesopotamia would have no difficulty in identifying Amorite 'Il and Canaanite 'El, Amorite Dagan and Canaanite Dagnu, Amorite Hadad and Canaanite Haddu.[34]

The other element in patriarchal religion that Cross points to is the worship of the high god El as indicated in the divine names in Genesis such as El Olam and El Shaddai. These names do not reflect local numina, as Alt assumed, but are various liturgical or cultic titles for the head of the Canaanite pantheon, El.

---

33. F. M. Cross, *Canaanite Myth and Hebrew Epic: Essays in the History of the Religion of Israel* (Cambridge: Harvard University Press, 1973), 31. Cf. Alt's earlier version, "Yahweh and the God of the Patriarchs," *HTR* 55 (1926): 227–28.

34. Cross, *Canaanite Myth*, 37.

This deity is well known to us now from Canaanite and Amorite sources. He was judge over the council of gods, a patriarchal figure, the primordial father of gods and human beings, sometimes stern, often compassionate, always wise in judgment. He was a social god both in reference to the family of gods as well as to human beings. He frequently plays the role of "god of the Father," the social deity bound to tribe or king with kinship or covenant ties, guiding or leading them. The epic materials from Ugarit regularly show El answering, helping, directing the royal figures. In addition El was the transcendent creator God. As the Genesis narratives reveal, the gods of the Fathers were identified with Canaanite El who bore in his character traits that made the identification natural, particularly in light of the fact that the god of the father, of Abraham, Jacob, and the like, may have been Amorite El.[35]

Then comes the basic question: Whence Yahweh? Where does this new development of which Elohist and Priestly writers speak come from? Both these traditions see the revelation of Yahweh to Moses as a new stage but one clearly understood as tied to both the preceding lines described above, that is, a new manifestation of the god worshiped by the Fathers. Exodus 3:15 says when Moses inquires what he shall tell the people when they ask the name of the God who sent him: "God also said to Moses, 'Say this to the people of Israel, "Yahweh, the God of your fathers, the God of Abraham, the God of Isaac, and the God of Jacob, has sent me to you"'" (E). And in the Priestly account: "God said to Moses, 'I am Yahweh. I appeared to Abraham, to Isaac, and to Jacob as El Shaddai, but by my name Yahweh I did not make myself known to them'" (Exod 6:2–3).

Cross proposes an answer to the question ("Whence Yahweh?") which is hypothetical but which rests on careful analysis of various kinds of data. In a nutshell, he suggests that Yahweh was originally a cultic name of El (*'ēl dū yahwī ṣabaʾōt*, "El who creates the hosts"), perhaps the epithet of El as patron deity of a Midianite (or Kenite?) league in the south. The god Yahweh then would have split off from El in the radical differentiation of his cultus, eventually ousting El from his place in the divine council and condemning the ancient gods to death (Ps 82).[36] Yahweh was thus in origin an El figure and the various El names continued throughout the history of Israel's religion to be acceptable titles for Yahweh.

Cross's analysis, in my judgment the most extensive and far-reaching to date, serves to illuminate and clarify the continuities between the god of the Fathers and Canaanite El and Yahweh, god of Israel.[37] The roots of Yahweh have been

---

35. Ibid., 67–68.
36. Ibid., 85–100, esp. 96–97.
37. Ibid., 100: "Patriarchal religion had special features: the tutelary deity or deities entered into an intimate relationship with a social group expressed in terms of kinship or covenant, established its justice, led its battles, guided its destiny. This strain entered Yahwism. Yahweh was judge and

traced back far (historically) and broadly (geographically) into the religious world of the ancient Near East. Semi-nomadic clan religions, Amorite religion, Canaanite religion—all these are the sources for the origin of the god Yahweh. It is not just a matter of a few similarities between Yahweh and these other divine figures. Yahweh clearly comes out of this religious world. Virtually all of the characteristics of the God of Israel are present in the early stages of Yahwism, and most of them reach back beyond Israel's earliest stage to pre-Israelite religious developments.

We may thus begin to write the history of God at this point. And God as known in the revelation of Yahweh has a beginning. Yet, as the Bible has always maintained, that beginning is only a stage, albeit an important one, in a historical development, and it is fully continuous with religious expressions and developments in the non-Israelite history before it.

The Gods in Yahweh

But if we can legitimately show how Yahweh comes out of the gods, it is also possible to speak of the gods in Yahweh. Some of the same data I have just been speaking of points to this reverse movement. Yahweh is, according to Cross's hypothesis, a split-off from El, and El is now in Yahweh. As Cross correctly says:

> Many of the traits and functions of El appear as traits and functions of Yahweh in the earliest traditions of Israel: Yahweh's role as judge in the court of 'El (Psalm 82; Psalm 89:6–8) and in the general picture of Yahweh at the head of the Divine council: Yahweh's kingship (Exodus 15:18; Deuteronomy 33:15; Numbers 24:21); Yahweh's wisdom, age, and compassion (*yahweh 'ēl raḥūm we-ḥannūn*) and above all, Yahweh as creator and father (Genesis 49:25; Deuteronomy 32:6).
>
> The early cultic establishment of Yahweh and its appurtenances—the Tabernacle, its structure of *qerašim*, its curtains embroidered with cherubim and its cherubim throne, and its proportions according to the pattern (*tabnīt*) of the cosmic shrine—all reflect Canaanite models, and specifically the Tent of El and his cherubim throne.[38]

---

war leader of the historical community. He revealed himself to the Patriarch Moses, led Israel in the Conquest; he was the god who brought Israel up from the land of Egypt, her savior. There is also the second strain which entered Israel's primitive religion, that of the high and eternal one, El the creator of heaven and earth, father of all." Fohrer in his *History of Israelite Religion* says: "Thus El, the god identified with the clan gods, was conceived as a past revelation of the God who later made himself known as Yahweh" (cited in ibid., 104–5).

38. Ibid., 97.

One can add to that the fact that his characteristic mode of manifestation appears to be the vision or audition, often in dreams. There are of course clearly dimensions and functions of El that are not carried over into the character of Yahweh. Yahweh's creative activity is not theogonic and procreative (though, remnants of such mythopoeic ideas survive in highly transformed fashion in the Old Testament). He has no consort or sexual relations as does El.

In similar fashion one can also speak of Yahwism's "debt to the myths of Baal"[39] in Canaanite religion, a debt larger than simply the preservation of a few mythological fragments about Yahweh's slaying the dragon (e.g. Isa 27:1; 51:9, and so on). Once again Yahweh stands in continuity and discontinuity with Baal, though the latter is sharper than in regard to El because a genuine conflict develops in Israel between Yahweh and Baal or between the worship of Yahweh and worship of El. That conflict is not sharply present in the early stage of Israel's history but comes later. An accounting of the growing discontinuity with Baal is a task for "the history of the religion of Israel."[40] I shall only point to one or two fundamental dimensions of the Baal figure that are basic also to Yahweh. The patterns and motifs of Baal as storm god who rides the clouds and whose theophany has such powerful effects on the natural world are all present in the numerous hymnic and prose traditions of the theophany of Yahweh, whether it be in the Sinai traditions of Exodus or a hymn like Ps 29, which is now generally regarded as a Canaanite hymn only slightly modified for use in the early cultus of Yahweh.[41] Similarly the imagery of Yahweh as the Divine Warrior, which runs throughout the Old Testament and is basic to any theology proper of that part of Scripture, reflects the Divine Warrior character of El and other gods and goddesses but most particularly of Baal, who is frequently depicted both in his march accompanied by his entourage to battle the enemy and in his return from battle to take his place in his new temple on his holy mountain. The reflections in the Old Testament of the march and battle with both historical and cosmic effects are numerous.[42] Although they are transformed in the service of Yahwism, and Yahweh is not Baal, these reflexes and elements from the Near Eastern mythological world of the gods are there in Yahweh, and that is the point I wish to underscore here.

Let me suggest another way of putting the matter that points to the appropriateness of the rubric: the gods in Yahweh. Paul Riemann of Drew University has suggested that while it may be impossible to avoid completely some use of the term "monotheism" in speaking of Yahwism, the term is problematic in

---

39. Ibid., 109.
40. See Norman Habel, *Yahweh Versus Baal* (New York: Bookman Associates, 1964).
41. Cross, *Canaanite Myth*, 173ff.
42. See Patrick D. Miller Jr., *The Divine Warrior in Early Israel*, Harvard Semitic Monographs 5 (Cambridge: Harvard University Press, 1973).

that it always requires some qualifying adjective or explanation and is not in itself accurately descriptive of the worship of Yahweh.[43] He proposes instead to speak of a centralization or integration of divine power and authority, perceived as the supremacy of one single deity to whom all other divine beings are subordinate. A similar tendency may be discerned in Mesopotamian religion, particularly, in the two national gods, Marduk and Aššur.[44] In what Thorkild Jacobsen calls the last phase of ancient Mesopotamian religion beginning in the Old Babylonian period and lasting until the end of Babylonian and Assyrian civilization, these two gods rise to supreme power in the divine realm, Marduk for the Babylonians and Aššur for the Assyrians. Other gods act as agents or intercessors. There is a strong feeling of unified central power in the divine world. Various gods are seen as in essence *one* with aspects of a supreme god. Enlil, for example, is Marduk (as god) of lordship and council. The gods are either identified with the supreme god (as in the ascription of 50 divine names to Marduk in the Creation Epic) or reinterpreted as manifestations of the supreme god. The polytheistic framework is never abandoned. "The old pantheon and religious framework remained generally unchanged.[45] But "the emphasis had subtly shifted; power and decision were now centered in Marduk or in Ashur";[46] national and political deities closely tied to their people, divine powers active in human affairs as well as nature. Looking at this effective integration of divine power, Jacobsen concludes: "There is a recognizable drive to see the forces that govern the cosmos as basically one and unified."[47]

Obviously one cannot transfer the process that leads to this point in Babylonia and Assyria to Israel. That would violate any serious historical approach to the study of these religions. Yet it may be that this integrative dimension, this drive to see the cosmic forces as unified, is reflected in Yahweh. Riemann argues: "One could go no further along this path than the Old Testament does in the claims it makes for Yahweh."

A number of factors make sense in this framework. Only one or two can be mentioned here. This integration of the divine world is probably best reflected in the numerous references and allusions to the divine council or heavenly assembly in the Old Testament, a phenomenon fully familiar from the polytheistic

---

43. In an unpublished essay read to the Colloquium for Old Testament Research, Cambridge, 1972.

44. Here Riemann is heavily dependent upon various articles by Thorkild Jacobsen, reprinted in his volume of essays, *Toward the Image of Tammuz and Other Essays in Mesopotamian History and Culture*, ed. William L. Moran, Harvard Semitic Series 21 (Cambridge: Harvard University Press, 1970), especially "Mesopotamian Gods and Pantheons" and "Ancient Mesopotamian Religion: The Central Concerns."

45. Jacobsen, *Toward the Image*, 20.

46. Ibid., 20.

47. Ibid., 21.

world of Near Eastern religions. Yahweh is envisioned as seated upon his throne of kingship in his temple or palace surrounded by a nameless host of divine beings who serve him, whom he commissions with certain tasks, with whom he takes counsel, and who often sit as a court to judge a case and pronounce the verdict. The gods may also go from the assembly to accompany Yahweh into battle. In either case:

> The scene resembles those of divine assemblies elsewhere, except that all power and authority clearly reside in Yahweh alone, the attendant beings have virtually no independent role, and the matter before the council is never a conflict of power and authority among the gods.[48]

Riemann notes further that the radical integration of divine power accounts for the ease with which Yahweh has absorbed or manifests characteristics and epithets of other gods, such as I have described above, and the difficulty of articulating his peculiar character as a deity.

Attempts to account for Yahweh as in origin a storm god, a mountain god, a sky god, a national god, a warrior god, among others, have never succeeded. "The possibilities are too numerous, for the reason that there are few aspects of the cosmos which are not explicitly associated with him, and none seem to be excluded in principle."[49]

The familiar fact of the absence of myth in the proper sense in the Old Testament reflects this centralization of divine authority and rule (there are a few fragments such as Ps 82 that come close to being myths of the divine world). "The radical subordination of all other divine powers has radically reduced the role of the heavenly realm as the locus of drama and conflict."[50]

The neglect or obliteration in Israelite religion of the feminine dimension in the divine world is one of the more obvious, oft-noted peculiarities of Yahwism over against neighboring religions. Is this characteristic originally anti-Canaanite or anti-mythological? Or is it that in the extreme integration of divine characteristics and power in Yahweh the feminine element is absorbed also? That would mean in effect its disappearance because most of the characteristics of goddesses in the ancient Near East except childbearing are characteristics shared by male deities also. Perhaps more plausible is the assumption that in the integration process centering in the male deity Yahweh, a choice has been made and the feminine element drops out. In any event, there are various signs

---

48. Riemann, essay for the Colloquium for Old Testament Research (Cambridge).

49. Ibid. Jacobsen has pointed out that Marduk and Aššur in the later period became hard to identify as particular kinds of deities though in origin they were such.

50. Ibid.

in Israelite and later Jewish religion of compensation for neglect of the feminine. One may cite the large number of female (not male) figurines found in Israelite cities as well as a tendency in later times toward hypostatization of certain elements that are characterized as feminine such as *ḥokmâ* ("wisdom") and *šəkînâ* ("presence").[51]

When one examines the whole history of Israelite religion, it becomes clear that a counter-move to this integration of the divine world in Yahweh developed in the later period, that is, a tendency toward disintegration, the renewal of conflict in the divine world, the telling of stories about a heavenly realm—a move, if not toward polytheism, toward dualism (of course never realized in full-bodied fashion). In ancient Near Eastern religions catastrophes are usually god-caused and may arise out of conflict in the divine world over which human beings have no control.[52] In Israelite religion, however, the burden of responsibility is human, that is, trouble and catastrophe—even in nature, if I read Gen 3 correctly—are tied to human sin. If not, then there is an almost unbearable arbitrariness in the deity, a situation intolerable for a religion of the ethical nature of Yahwism and one where righteousness is the character of the divinely willed order. But the assumption of human responsibility for the evil of the world is also an almost intolerable point of view. It begins to break down, and with it the radical integration of the divine powers in one deity breaks down. The disintegration, however, is at a secondary level. In the later period, particularly apocalyptic but not alone there, there is a return to stories of the gods and some of the formerly nameless divine beings bear names, for example, Michael, Gabriel. This is an unusual though not unprecedented development in Israelite religion but in clear continuity with the character of the divine world in Canaanite and Mesopotamian religion. These named beings are clearly subordinate semi-divine beings, either helper gods as one sees, for example, around Marduk and Tiamat, or messenger gods as one sees, for example, in association with Baal and Yamm. The problem of theodicy, which cannot be adequately handled by laying responsibility for evil at the foot of human beings, or satisfactorily resolved by attributing arbitrariness to the deity, begins to be dealt with in terms of conflict in the divine realm. That leads to disintegration, a move away from

---

51. A number of scholars have argued strongly that in the light of biblical and archaeological evidence goddess worship was common in Israelite religion and that the Old Testament rejection of goddess worship represents a minority opinion in regard to the actual practice of Israelite religion. See, e.g., Raphael Patai, *The Hebrew Goddess* (New York: Ktav, 1967), and Gösta W. Ahlström, *Aspects of Syncretism in Israelite Religion*, trans. Eric J. Sharpe, Horae Soederblomianae 5 (Lund: Gleerup, 1963), 46–57. See now Patrick D. Miller Jr., "The Absence of the Goddess in Israelite Religion," in *Israelite Religion and Biblical Theology: Collected Essays*, LHBOTS 267 (Sheffield: Sheffield Academic, 2000), 197–207.

52. See Jacob J. Finkelstein, "Bible and Babel: A Comparative Study of the Hebrew and Babylonian Religious Spirit," *Commentary* 26 (1958): 431–44.

unity and oneness in the deity, as Yahweh encounters opposing forces. These forces get certain identities and thus function in a way as subordinate deities. "Satan" in Job is a step on that way. It is *haśśāṭān*, "the adversary," becoming Satan, who challenges Yahweh.

Yahweh Against the Gods

What has been said in the preceding section about the integration of the divine world in Yahweh should not be interpreted as implying a gradual evolution from polytheism to monotheism.[53] Such an interpretation would not conform to the complexity of the origins of Yahwism, nor would it account for the fact that this radical centralization of divine power and authority in Yahweh is present from the earliest stages. From the beginning also, insofar as we can press the question of origins, there is present what might be called a counter-theme: Yahweh against the gods. The God of Israel, who comes out of the gods and in whom the world of the gods may be discerned, stands over against all other gods, claiming a unity and exclusiveness that rules them out. Such a claim is not primarily an ontological assertion but a claim on Israel, the worshipers of Yahweh. It nevertheless carries with it a theological perspective on the nature of the divine reality that is of far-reaching significance in the history of Israelite religion.

The conception of Yahweh over against the gods of the Near Eastern religions permeates much of Old Testament literature and is expressed in legal formulations, prophetic indictments, psalms, mythopoeic stories, historical narratives, and elsewhere. I shall mention only a few of the many places where Israelite religion asserts in a particularly vigorous way Yahweh's conflict with all other deities.

One of the clearest and most interesting is Psalm 82, highly mythological in character. Its setting is the divine council[54] with the gods seated all about. In some obvious ways the psalm looks as if it could have come straight out of Canaanite mythology—the heavenly assembly, the technical language, the casual acknowledgment of the gods, the theme of conflict in the cosmic realm. But in significant ways it departs from that typical mythological context. There are no other named deities here, no battle between Baal and Yamm, Marduk and

---

53. The same is true for the analysis of Mesopotamian religion taken from Jacobsen. I leave open the debated question as to whether such a movement (polytheism to monotheism) can happen or has happened.

54. Of course, *'ădat-'ēl* (v. 1) is technical terminology for the heavenly assembly, well known also from the Ugaritic literature. On Ps 82, see Wright, *The Old Testament*, 30–41; James S. Ackerman, "An Exegetical Study of Psalm 82" (ThD diss., Harvard Divinity School, 1966); and Hans-Winfried Jüngling, *Der Tod der Götter: eine Untersuchung zu Psalm 82*, Stuttgarter Bibelstudien 38 (Stuttgart: Katholisches Bibelwerk, 1969).

Tiamat. The gods are nameless, colorless, silent. They have no autonomy and independence apart from Yahweh. In the midst of this assembly, according to the psalm, Yahweh rises and in explicit and, to my knowledge, unprecedented fashion condemns all the other deities to death for their failure to carry out justice in the social realm. Justice in the human realm is a concern of all Near Eastern religions, but here it is claimed that the cosmic realm also depends upon justice in the social order. This psalm is therefore a story of the death of the gods. The immortals are condemned to mortality. Only Yahweh has any power in the divine realm.

With the increasing popularity in the ninth century of the cult of Baal, the conflict between Yahweh and the gods becomes most explicit and indeed apparently a life-and-death conflict. The issue was not that Yahweh could be forgotten or ignored, but that he would become simply another god alongside the other great gods and goddesses of Canaanite religion.[55] The central figure in this conflict is Elijah; the central moment, the contest between Elijah and the prophets of Baal on Mount Carmel and its sequel in Yahweh's revelation to Elijah at Horeb (1 Kgs 18–19), which in a sense is a recapitulation of the first revelation to Moses. Then Yahweh had come in the full form of the storm theophany, a tradition heavily shaped by Canaanite theophanic imagery and traditions clustered around the storm god Baal, but in this second revelation the storm imagery that was so clearly associated with Baal is rejected emphatically. Wind, quaking, and fire—typical elements in the theophany of the storm god—come upon Sinai again. But three times the story makes the point: "Yahweh was not in the wind.... Yahweh was not in the earthquake.... Yahweh was not in the fire." Instead, he comes in "the sound of a low whisper." The passage is clearly a polemic against Baal, the Canaanite storm god. Imagery and mode of revelation from the world of Canaanite religion that were once acceptable as a vehicle for Yahweh are here rejected.[56]

In an almost reverse manner the prophecy of Hosea sets forth the polemic against Baal in terms not of Yahweh's rejection of Baal imagery, but his appropriation in transformed fashion of Canaanite language and thought. Yahweh preempts the role of Baal by his promise to bestow fertility upon a faithful people and their land.[57]

These moments just described belong to a particular conflict that arose in the history of Israel's religion when in fact Yahweh's rule and power as the

---

55. See Cross, *Canaanite Myth*, 213.

56. Cross argues that the rejection of Baal's mode of revelation followed by the oracle to Elijah implies support for the mode of revelation associated with El and the council of El, that is, the prophetic language of the "word" or judgment of Yahweh (ibid., 216). See his whole discussion of this passage and its background.

57. See in this regard James L. Mays, *Hosea*, OTL (Philadelphia: Westminster, 1969), 7–15 and 45–53.

sole object of Israel's loyalty was severely threatened. But the point at which Yahweh's place and claim over against the divine world is most clear is in the presence and influence of the first and second commandments of the Decalogue, forbidding the worship of other gods and the making of divine images. To rehearse the role and influence particularly of the first commandment would go far beyond the scope of this essay.[58] Let me simply indicate some of the ways in which the intention of this commandment comes to expression. It goes without saying, I should think, that its place at the beginning of this list of fundamental norms and instructions for Israel's existence underscores its preeminence as a basic tenet of Yahwism. Various other legal formulations which grow out of the first commandment or are analogous to it may be found in the Hexateuch, the historical books, the Psalms, and the prophets. The frequent characterization of Yahweh as "jealous," which is not characteristic of the gods of the Near East, reflects the demand upon Israel to worship no other gods.

Especially significant in this regard is the Shema in Deut 6:4–5. I will confess that along with many others I am uncertain how to translate what appears, deceptively, to be simple and is translated by the RSV as "The Lord our God is one Lord."[59] Specifically, does *yahweh 'eḥād* mean "Yahweh is one" or "Yahweh alone"? I do not think it necessary in this connection to make a final choice. I incline toward the translation "Yahweh is one," which affirms the unity of the deity over against the multiplicity of other gods and powers. The term "one" may signify inclusiveness, comprehensiveness, all-in-oneness, but Yahweh is no pantheon of gods and the notion of radical integration mentioned previously cannot mean that. The less likely translation, "Yahweh alone" is our God, would affirm what the first commandment enjoins. Yahweh is the sole recipient of Israel's worship and obedience. Both interpretations reflect Deuteronomic theology as well as the intention of the first commandment. The appropriate corollary of this injunction-affirmation follows in verse 5. The one all-inclusive God requires one, all-inclusive, total love and obedience.

The great commandment given as an interpretation or outgrowth of the first commandment dominates the book of Deuteronomy, especially chapters 6–11. In various formulations this exclusive claim of Yahweh on Israel and over against all other gods comes to expression in these chapters and elsewhere in the book.[60] But one would have to go through the whole Old Testament to

---

58. See the recent monograph by Werner Schmidt, *Das erste Gebot: seine Bedeutung für das Alte Testament*, Theologische Existenz heute 165 (Munich: Chr. Kaiser Verlag, 1969).

59. The RSV gives three alternate readings in a footnote.

60. See Nobert Lohfink, *Das Hauptgebot*, Biblica 20 (Rome: Pontifical Biblical Institute, 1963), and his essay "The Great Commandment," in *The Christian Meaning of the Old Testament*, trans. R.A. Wilson (Milwaukee: Bruce, 1968), 87–102. Note the very expression "other gods" is particularly characteristic of Deuteronomy and the Deuteronomistic History.

give adequate account of the impact of the first (and second) commandment on Israelite religion, although it is often the breach of these commandments that is at issue. Here is a touchstone of that religion, and perhaps it is as close as we can come to marking the particularity, or uniqueness, of Israel's religion. One can say that for two reasons: (1) the intention of the first commandment is spelled out in various ways throughout the documents which are our basic source for understanding that religion, and in a way that indicates they are basic for understanding Israel's religion throughout its course; and (2) we know no genuine analogies in the ancient Near East to this exclusive, imageless worship of one deity.[61] Thus in the first commandment we encounter a basic principle that reflects both the radical integration or centralization of the divine realm in Yahweh and also his exclusive claim over against all other gods.[62]

Theological Reflections

I would not want what I have said about the role and significance of the first commandment to be misconstrued as implying that the last point—Yahweh against the gods—is where I have been heading, that is, to come down on the discontinuity as the significant and crucial issue. It is not uncommon to make that the focus or base for talking about the revelatory character of Israel's religion over against all others, the proof or basis for truth claims, or the basis of survival. An excellent example of such an approach is Wright's *The Old Testament Against Its Environment*.[63] In many ways that small volume is still a masterpiece as a holistic examination of the interrelationships between the Old Testament and the religious world of which it was a part. But the emphasis is heavily on the differences. Similarities and influences are clearly acknowledged (Wright was well aware of them), but they are given brief treatment and little significance, or relegated to footnotes.[64] The general tone or focus of the book is reflected in such statements as: "Israel's religious literature was utterly

---

61. See Schmidt, *Das erste Gebot*, 14, and Gerhard von Rad, *Deuteronomy*, trans. Dorothea Barton, OTL (Philadelphia: Westminster, 1966), 56.
62. A full treatment of the later theme, Yahweh against the gods, would have to include discussion of such matters as the incomparability declarations, for example, "Who is like thee among the gods?" or "There is no god like the God of Jeshurun," which are drawn from the language of the Near Eastern religions but used to make Yahweh's claim against the gods, as well as Deutero-Isaiah's extensive attention to Yahweh's relation to other gods and idols. These are, however, simply further—albeit not unimportant—examples of the point elaborated above.
63. Wright, *The Old Testament*. It should be acknowledged that Wright might not frame his treatment of that subject in exactly the same manner if he were writing the monograph now. The point of view expressed so well there has, however, been widely influential in the intervening years.
64. See, for example, his short footnote on the religion of the patriarchs, ibid., 28n33.

different from that of its environment" (p. 28), or "The religion of Israel suddenly appears in history, breaking radically with the mythopoeic approach to reality" (p. 29). At one point Wright specifically raises the question of revelation and approaches it in the following way:

> Finally, in what sense can the Old Testament be considered revelation? The Christian is one who has committed himself; accordingly he does not stand on neutral ground. For him the unique, the discontinuous, the extraordinary nature of the Old Testament can only be explained as the dramatic, purposeful intervention of God—who here was inaugurating a special revelation of himself, one which culminated in Christ.... One ... can single out point after point where the Old Testament was a part of its world. Yet the astonishing thing is that far more basic resemblances exist between the religions of the ancient world than exist between the Bible and any one of them. *What Israel borrowed was the least significant*; it was fitted into an entirely new context of faith. Consequently, the Christian and the Jew as well look upon this distinctiveness of the Old Testament as proof of its claim for special revelation.[65]

More recently Baumgärtel has put the issue in a different way. He maintains that for the theologian or dogmatician the history of religion comparative study is of service by separating out definite ancient Near Eastern materials from the genuine, fundamental, basic conceptions of the Old Testament.[66]

This approach, which places weight and value essentially on those dimensions of Israelite religion and its view of God which are discontinuous with the religions of the Near East, is one that I have taken in the past both self-consciously and, I am sure, often unconsciously. In part I would still affirm the significance of the element of discontinuity. But a sole or primary focus on Israel's break with its religious world is not really satisfactory either as a proper handling of the material from a history of religion perspective or as a theologically meaningful or legitimate approach. In the first instance the claim that distinctiveness and uniqueness are the central conclusions of the study of Israelite religion involves an explicit use of history of religion data, but that use may include only part of the data or it may interpret them in a somewhat loaded fashion. In the second instance I think a questionable theological weight has been given to the notion of uniqueness.

---

65. Ibid., 73–74 (my italics).
66. Friedrich Baumgärtel, "Das Offenbarungszeugnis des Alten Testaments im Lichte der religionsgeschichtlich-vergleichenden Forschung," *Zeitschrift für Theologie und Kirche* 63 (1966): 393–422, at 422.

I would argue, therefore, that the focus of concern properly belongs on the interplay of discontinuity *and continuity*. The careful investigation of the history of Israel's religion impresses one with both realities, as I have tried to indicate in the preceding section. And although various interpreters may come down more strongly on one side or the other, no true analysis of that religion can ignore either element or set it aside. While Israel's understanding of its God is distinctive, the tendency to regard it as utterly unique and *sui generis* is misleading in that it fails to take account of the way in which that conception is similar to or shaped by the religious environment. It is not simply a matter of a few metaphors or epithets which are paralleled elsewhere, but of basic language, thought forms, and relationships between deity and nature, history, tribe, state, and individual. The claim of Yahweh to the exclusive worship of Israel is represented with such flexibility and creativity that it may at one time involve explicit rejection of language or forms associated with another deity while at another time appropriating them openly. Association with one deity (Baal) may be rejected at an early stage, while association with another deity (El) may be implicitly accepted for a long period of time.[67] To seek to discard all this as form and not content, to disregard all the complex associations of Yahweh and the gods is to throw the baby out with the bathwater. Commonality, therefore, or continuity, both synchronically and diachronically, is just as strong and significant a history of religion conclusion as is discontinuity.

It is also a theological datum. And here the historian of religion moves beyond the historical stance. What I am talking about is finally not just Yahweh and the gods, an interesting analysis of an Iron Age deity. It is God and the gods. Whatever we say about Yahweh as an El figure or in conflict with Baal is conversation about the God we know and worship in Jesus Christ. How do we handle that? The focus upon discontinuity and distinctiveness is one way. The God who reveals himself in Jesus Christ is totally different from these gods who inhabit the divine world of Near Eastern religions. But any systematic theology that seeks to exploit the conceptions, language, and imagery for God in the Old Testament will quickly find itself speaking out of a continuity with the gods of Canaan, Mesopotamia, and Egypt, whether aware of it or not.[68] This should not, however, be surprising or unexpected. The revelation of God is not confined to acts, events, moments, or insights that break into or erupt out of the historical context isolated from and undetermined by that context. Theological meaning and reality are to be found in the interrelation of continuity and discontinuity not only where Israel's religion seems to differ from the understanding of reality

---

67. See Cross's discussion of the relation between Yahweh and El, *Canaanite Myth*, 96–100.
68. One of the more recent systematic theologies demonstrates this quite clearly. See Gordon Kaufman, *Systematic Theology: A Historicist Perspective* (New York: Scribner, 1968), esp. 134–47.

shared by her neighbors, but also where these religions touch, interact, develop out of, and affect one another.

I would see at least two theological bases for such an interpretation of Israel's religion as a pointer to that which we know and speak of as God. One base would be a christological analogy, I think not unlike the *analogia fidei* (analogy of faith) or perhaps more nearly the *analogia Christi* (analogy of Christ) which Gordon Kaufman has recently set forth in his *Systematic Theology* as a fundamental theological and methodological criterion and which of course has much deeper roots in the history of Christian doctrine.[69] Our understanding of the revelation of God in Jesus Christ can serve as an analogy for understanding Israel's religion, in continuity and discontinuity with its world, as the revelation of God. That is, the Messiah, whom the New Testament identifies as Jesus Christ, was one who came out of our world and was fully continuous with it yet not fully explicable as a part of our world and us, therefore also discontinuous. The interplay of continuity and discontinuity is revealed from beginning to end, and it is in the whole of that that the revelation of the nature and purpose of God was manifest. It is when we lay hold of only one of these poles in our Christology—whether as laypersons or sophisticated theologians that we move toward heresy (or, perhaps in more palatable terms, away from the truth content of God's revelation in Christ)—that is, when all we can or will say is "Jesus was one of us," and he is understood simply as another human being, completely and totally continuous with our world and life, or when all we can and will say is "Jesus was (or is) God with us," and we see him as a divine phenomenon that interrupts or intervenes in our human life from beyond, totally discontinuous with our existence and therefore ultimately inexplicable in any human framework or without point of contact with our life. Thus analogously the revelation of God in Israel's religion is manifest both in those complex ways by which it shows its common ground with its religious world and in its equally complex differentiation from it.

The *analogia Christi* means also that Jesus Christ as the revelation of God stands in judgment on the whole of Israel's religion—that which is common and that which is uncommon. Insofar as in the totality of that religious expression one claims to learn of God and his will for the world, Jesus is the criterion for weighing and validating that claim as a whole or in any of its parts.

This leads into a second theological base for understanding the whole of Israel's religion, including its continuity with the other religions, as datum for

---

69. What follows may be seen secondarily as an attempt to respond to Baumgärtel's question: "Und was hat dieses in seiner Umwelt einzigartige Gottbegreifen zu tun mit der 'Offenbarung,' d.h. für die Theologie mit dem *ho logos sarx egeneto*?" ("And what does this understanding of God, unique in its environment, have to do with the 'revelation,' i.e. for theology, with the word become flesh?"); "Der Tod des Religionsstifters," *Kerygma und Dogma* 9 (1963): 223–33, at 231.

our understanding and reflection on God. That base is a theological understanding of history as a whole, as the one work of God with Jesus Christ, as the center and the one who illumines the mystery of the divine reality and judges all human perceptions or expressions about that reality. But the whole process is, to use John Dillenberger's apt phrase, God's opportunity.[70] I do not think it accidental that one sees an openness to the history of religion perspective as theologically significant in certain contemporary efforts to work out a systematic theology where history as a unity is taken seriously as the locus of God's presence and activity and thus of God's self-disclosure, that is, the systematic constructions of Wolfhart Pannenberg and Gordon Kaufman.[71] History is meaningful and moving toward a definite goal intended from the beginning by God.[72] The history of religion is a central dimension of that whole within which or behind which God is present "not only as the author of historical change ... but also as the power for altering his own previous manifestations."[73] Israel spoke in just such a manner of its God and in so doing affirmed the prior history of religion as also the sphere of God's revelation (Exod 6:2–3). The mystery of the divine reality is there however we qualify it or qualify and judge the various human apprehensions and expressions of it. Furthermore, that revelatory history we see in Israel's experience was indebted to and a part of that religious world even as it stood in judgment upon the other religions. As Pannenberg has stated:

> Even looking back at it from the standpoint of Jesus, the history of religions permits of being understood as the appearance of the God revealed by him. The alien religions cannot be adequately interpreted as mere fabrications of man's striving after the true God. Ultimately, they have to do with the same divine reality as the message of Jesus.[74]

Perhaps all I have been saying can be summed up as a reminder to myself that from a religious perspective the Canaanites were Israel's enemies. But they were also their kinfolk. Both aspects of that relationship must be kept in mind as we study the Old Testament and appropriate it for theological reflection and insight.

---

70. John Dillenberger, "Revelational Discernment and the Problem of the Two Testaments," in *The Old Testament and Christian Faith*, ed. Bernhard W. Anderson (New York: Harper & Row, 1963), 159–75, at 164.

71. Wolfhart Pannenberg, "Toward a Theology of the History of Religions," in *Basic Questions in Theology*, trans. George H. Kehm, 2 vols. (Philadelphia: Fortress, 1961), 2:65–118; Gordon Kaufman, "Revelation and Cultural History," in *God the Problem* (Cambridge: Harvard University Press, 1972), 148–70.

72. Kaufman, "Revelation," 162.

73. Pannenberg, "Toward a Theology," 114.

74. Ibid., 115.

CHAPTER 2

Canaan—Israel—Christianity: The Case for a Vertical Ecumenism

Othmar Keel
Translated by Armin Siedlecki

CHRISTIANITY PARTED FROM ITS MOTHER Judaism in a bitter quarrel. More than fifty years after Auschwitz, this is widely acknowledged. Not as well-known is the fact that, like Christianity, Judaism also separated violently from its source in the seventh/sixth century BCE, albeit with different results. To become whole, the heirs of the ancient Near Eastern, Israelite/Jewish, and Christian tradition must acknowledge their injuries and losses. They must reunite that which has been wrongly divided and integrate the values lost to them, or at least recognize them along with their own as belonging to their siblings.

Healing the Break Between "Canaanite" and "Israelite" Culture

Edna Brocke carefully articulated the break between Canaanite and Jewish culture in her lecture "Judentum ist mehr als nur eine Religion" ("Judaism Is More Than Just a Religion"), presented on October 19, 2001, in Heidelberg during the Gerhard von Rad symposium. According to Brocke, Israel came into being by deliberately separating from groups that immanently materialized their deities by cutting them from wood or hewing them into stone. Israel as a people distanced itself from this understanding of tangible deities. It developed an abstract concept of deity and developed a dialectical relationship between this sole, invisible deity and itself.[1]

The texts where this is found and became normative are Deuteronomy and the writings that it influenced, in particular the so-called Deuteronomistic History, including the books of Deuteronomy through Kings, the prophetic book of Hosea, and other prophetic texts influenced by it such as parts of Jeremiah. In the fashion of the loyalty obligations owed to the Assyrian king,[2] Deuteronomy

---

1. Page 3 of an unpublished manuscript, kindly provided to me by the author.
2. Moshe Weinfeld, *Deuteronomy and the Deuteronomic School* (Oxford: Clarendon, 1972), 59–157; Hans Ulrich Steymans, *Deuteronomium 28 und die* adê *zur Thronfolgeregelung*

proposes an exclusive loyalty ("love") for Israel with respect to YHWH; dependence on him and disregard for all "other gods" are made obligatory. Deviations from these obligations on the human social level (Deut 13) and on the divine level (Deut 28:15–68) are severely and even violently penalized. Parallel to this is a socially consequential differentiation between the "brother"—who is of the same people and religion—and the stranger. The particularities that provide a people with an identity, from food preparation or the organization of sexuality to the handling of sickness and death, receive theological dignity in Deuteronomy. This development, which Brocke evoked with her statement that "Judaism is more than just a religion" has produced a characteristic that has often been caricatured and perceived negatively from the outside, as for example in Tacitus's claim in the early second century CE that the cause of the Jews is furthered among other things by the fact that:

> The Jews are extremely loyal toward one another, and always ready to show compassion, but toward every other people they feel only hate and enmity.... Those who are converted to their ways follow the same practice, and the earliest lesson they receive is to despise the gods, to disown their country, and to regard their parents, children, and brothers as of little account. However, they take thought to increase their numbers; for they regard it as a crime to kill any late-born child. (*Histories* 5.55)[3]

In addition to individual strangers or foreigners, Deuteronomy includes entire peoples who are presented as alien. These nations had supposedly lived in the land prior to Israel and had to be, or at least should have been, exterminated, "so that they do not teach you to imitate all the abominations they committed when they served their gods, and so that you do not sin against YHWH, your God" (Deut 20:18). No treaties are to be made with them, and no mixed marriages should be entered into, so that they do not entice Israel to serve other gods (*'ĕlōhîm 'aḥērîm*), and the wrath of YHWH then destroy them. "This is how you shall deal with them: you shall tear down their altars, smash their standing stones [*maṣṣēbôt*], cut down their cultic pillars ['*ašērîm*] and burn their idol images [*pĕsilîm*] with fire" (Deut 7:5; cf. Deut 12:2–3 and 20:16–18). The Deuteronomic/Deuteronomistic texts construct a foreign, preexisting population from which Israel is substantially different. The names are derived from the traditional school knowledge of "historical geography" (Gen 10:6–20; cf. 15:19–21;

Asarhaddons: Segen und Fluch im Alten Orient und in Israel, OBO 145 (Fribourg: Academic Press; Göttingen: Vandenhoeck & Ruprecht, 1995); Eckart Otto, *Das Deuteronomium: politische Theologie und Rechtsreform in Juda und Assyrien*, BZAW 284 (Berlin: de Gruyter, 1999), 1–90.

3. In *Greek and Latin Authors on Jews and Judaism*, ed. Menahem Stern, 3 vols. (Jerusalem: Israel Academy of Sciences and Humanities, 1980), 2:19, 26.

Exod 23:23, 28–9). In most passages, the list of peoples is limited to six names. Never missing and usually named first are the Canaanites.[4]

It does not require much knowledge of the Bible to see that the abominations of these peoples, the altars and standing stones that are to be destroyed, were once part of the religion of Israel and not of some wicked peoples.[5] The same is true of cultic pillars or sacred trees.

In their apologetic stance, articles and books about the relation between Judaism and Christianity unfortunately overlook this violent disengagement, and thereby, like all apologetic literature, create new boundaries instead of contributing to a comprehensive engagement that respects each in its own, delimited way.[6] Just as Christianity later believed it could find its identity only by establishing a caricature of its origin and by outlining a dark foil in contrast to its enlightenment, so Judaism has also done. In doing so, Judaism has, like Christianity, suppressed or at least set aside important aspects of being human. The origin that Judaism has treated in this way shall be referred to as Canaan: a *pars pro toto* for the peoples who lived in Palestine before and together with Israel, and from which Israel emerged.[7] Jon D. Levenson raised this issue in 1985 in a groundbreaking essay,[8] noting that Judaism does not know the problem of an elder brother and also never appropriated a book—an "Old Testament"—that it had to justify as its own.

However, Israel does know a brother who is cursed and from whom it received an inheritance. Because Canaan's father Ham sexually abused his father Noah according to Gen 9:25–6, his son Canaan and all his descendants are cursed and destined to be the lowest servants of Shem, the ancestor of Abraham (Gen 11:10–26). This curse of Canaan is only one of the reasons given to justify Israel's treatment of "Canaan." There are others, as we shall see, all of

---

4. Exod 3:8, 17; 13:5; 23:23, 28; 33:2; 34:11; Deut 7:1; 20:17; Josh 3:10; 9:1; 11:3; 12:8; 24:11; Judg 3:5; 1 Kgs 9:20.

5. Gen 28:10–22; 31:13; Exod 24:3–8; Hos 3:4; 10:1.

6. See, e.g., the following books, which are very instructive in general: Erich Zenger, *Das erste Testament: die jüdische Bibel und die Christen* (Düsseldorf: Patmos, 1993); Walter Dietrich and Christian Link, *Die dunklen Seiten Gottes*, 2 vols. (Neukirchen-Vluyn: Neukirchener, 1997). In their paraphrase of Deut 7:1–11, Dietrich and Link omit the strongest statement, the extermination of the peoples who previously inhabited the land (1:105). The equally strong, inwardly directed Deut 13:7–12 does not even appear in their index of Bible passages (2:229). The same applies to Exod 22:17: "You shall not let a witch live," a passage that has had disastrous consequences in the history of reception.

7. Regarding the terminology, see Othmar Keel, Max Küchler, and Christoph Uehlinger, *Orte und Landschaften der Bibel: ein Handbuch und Studien-Reiseführer zum Heiligen Land*, 4 vols. (Göttingen: Vandenhoeck & Ruprecht 1984), 1:250–53, and Christoph Uehlinger, "The 'Canaanites' and Other 'Pre-Israelite' Peoples in Story and History," *Freiburger Zeitschrift für Philosophie und Theologie* 46 (1999): 546–78; and 47 (2000): 173–98.

8. Jon D. Levenson, "Is There a Counterpart in the Hebrew Bible to New Testament Anti-Semitism?," *Journal of Ecumenical Studies* 22 (1985): 242–60; reprinted in the present volume 159–78.

which had disastrous consequences, although they are in no way to be used as an accusation against Judaism.[9]

Israel and Canaan were in fact not two mutually exclusive cultures, but different phases of one and the same culture. It is said even of the Jewish colonies in Egypt that they spoke the language of Canaan (Isa 19:18). The prophet Ezekiel notes as late as the sixth century BCE that Jerusalem has her origins in the land of Canaan and that her father and mother are descendants of Canaan (cf. Ezek 16:3 and Gen 10:15–6). We now know that most of what was to become Israel had always lived in the land,[10] even if its culture was seminomadic and rural rather than urban[11] like the culture which we now too simply call Canaanite.

Just as the childhood stories of Jesus refer to a physically supernatural origin, the patriarchal and exodus narratives posit a geographical origin outside Canaan for Israel. Deuteronomy in particular, which came into being during a time of national restoration, asserted—under the influence of the prophet Hosea—the total distinctness of Israel from other peoples.

One could argue that the horrendous passages from Deuteronomy cited in connection with this process remained theoretical, while the Christian hatred of Jews led to atrocious consequences. This cannot and shall not be denied. It is also important to note that theories and their consequences are two different things. Those who conceived of the curse of Canaan did not have the horrific acts in mind for which it was used in justification. Theories are to be compared to other theories and as such can be deemed acceptable or objectionable. Their nonrealization or actualization in practice does not make them any better or worse. Both are usually contingent on many factors inaccessible to those who formulated the theory. Judaism was not always immune from putting into practice the above-mentioned ideas or others like it. Perhaps the murder of the priests of the high places in 2 Kgs 23:20 attributed to Josiah is not historical. It is, however, historical that John Hyrcanus, after the conquest of Idumean territory around 125 BCE, forced the population to be circumcised or to leave the land

---

9. Since Ham is identified in Gen 10 as the father not only of Canaan but also of Cush and of all black people, whites have repeatedly used this curse as a justification to enslave blacks, as was done by the initiators of black slave trade to North America or by some Boer churches in South Africa, who based their legitimization of apartheid primarily on Deut 7:1–5 and its prohibition of intermarriage. See Ferdinand Deist, "The Dangers of Deuteronomy: A Page from the Reception History of the Book," in *Studies in Deuteronomy: In Honour of C. J. Labuschagne on the Occasion of his 65th Birthday*, ed. Florentino García Martínez, VTSup 53 (Leiden: Brill, 1994), 13–29; Deist, "Post-Modernism and the Use of Scripture in Theological Argument: Footnotes to the Apartheid Theology Debate," *Neotestamentica* 28 (1994): 253–63.

10. See Baruch Halpern, *The Emergence of Israel in Canaan*, Society of Biblical Literature Monograph Series 29 (Chico: Scholars Press, 1983); Israel Finkelstein, *The Archaeology of the Israelite Settlement* (Jerusalem: Israel Exploration Society, 1988).

11. Aharon Kempinski, "How Profoundly Canaanized Were the Early Israelites?," *ZDPV* 108 (1992): 1–7.

(see Josephus, *Jewish Antiquities* 13.257–58 and 13.318), as Catholic Spain was to force Jews fifteen hundred years later to be baptized or go into exile.

As the physical removal of adherents to another religion was not usually possible, their religion was dealt with through caricatures and ridicule and neutralized as a temptation in order to turn it into a dark foil for one's own religion. The First Testament is interspersed with severe and subjective derision of non-Jewish or non-Israelite religions.[12] Horst Dietrich Preuss deserves credit for compiling and commenting on the pertinent passages,[13] although I do not follow his explanation and especially his justification of these texts by referring to "YHWH-certainty."[14] A certainty that cannot be justified rationally, and therefore communicated in the human realm, possesses no objective value and yields no reason for superiority. Neither the conviction and certainty of numerous inquisitors and witch hunters that their cause was sacred nor the conviction and certainty of numerous Germans that the fateful war against Russia was the salvation of Europe changed the criminal nature of their undertakings. Insofar as the newly found conviction and certainty of the Deuteronomists about God's supremacy in the world, or of Christians about the triumph over this (evil) world through the death and resurrection of Christ, were mature and communicable insights and convictions, they could do without violence. However, insofar as they were only deeply vulnerable suppositions and assumptions, they responded to "temptation" with defamation and violence.

The "Abominations of the Canaanites"

As already briefly suggested above, the accusations leveled against the Canaanites, or rather the peoples who (according to the OT) had lived in the land before Israel, include:

1. loose sexual morals that tolerate very diverse practices (Lev 18),
2. child sacrifice (Deut 12:31),
3. the worship of sacred stones and trees (Deut 7:5; 12:3),
4. astral worship (Deut 4:19),
5. and divinatory practices of all kinds (Deut 18:9–12, 14).

The accusations leveled against the Canaanites, or rather the peoples against whom Israel is warned, are largely—as suggested above—domestic problems in Israel.[15]

---

12. Levenson, "Is There a Counterpart?," 252–55 (present volume, 170–73).
13. Horst Dietrich Preuss, *Verspottung fremder Religionen im Alten Testament*, Beiträge zur Wissenschaft vom Alten Testament 92 (Stuttgart: Kohlhammer, 1971).
14. German: "JHWHgewissheit" (ibid., 289).
15. See Karl Jaroš, *Die Stellung des Elohisten zur kanaanäischen Religion*, OBO 4 (Fribourg: Academic Press; Göttingen: Vandenhoeck & Ruprecht, 1982).

Concerning sexual behavior, the rules listed in Lev 18:6–18 are those that regulate sexual relationships in Israel within the extended family. In the introduction and in the postscript (Lev 18:3 and 24–30), the condemned transgressions are identified as typically Canaanite or Egyptian. There is no evidence that, for instance, homosexuality was more widespread among Canaanites or Egyptians than among Israelites, and it is very unlikely. By characterizing it as typically Canaanite or Egyptian, homosexuality and the Canaanites are both dismissed at the same time. The Israelites living in extended family units may have had stricter social norms in some areas than the city dwellers, but some OT stories reject this assumption as false (see Gen 20) or hypocritical, since rigorous rules in the area of sexual morality often lead to a double standard, as in the case of Judah and his daughter-in-law Tamar (Gen 38).[16]

Concerning child sacrifice, it is possible that the overpopulated Phoenician (and Punic) cities may have had different practices than the rural regions of Israel, which were dependent on having many children. But stories like the sacrifice of Isaac show that child sacrifice was not entirely unheard-of in some Jewish circles (see Mic 6:7). Furthermore, it has been questioned whether children were indeed sacrificed at the burial sites of Phoenician and Punic settlements, called Topheth according to Jer 7:31 (cf. 19:6), or instead the many victims of a high child-mortality rate were only cremated here. The cremation of dead children was strange and abhorrent to the Greeks (and Jews), and perhaps it was this aversion during the tension-filled atmosphere of the Roman–Punic wars that gave rise to horror stories about child sacrifice.[17] Or perhaps the practices involving children mentioned in a few biblical texts that may refer to a certain type of consecration of children have nothing at all to do with the evidence found exclusively at archaeological sites in the western Mediterranean; perhaps these sites have been interpreted as places of child sacrifice as a result of polemical texts by Greek and Roman authors.

The erection of sacred pillars or the planting of sacred trees is a well-accepted practice in the patriarchal narratives. The oak of Mamre was venerated because God appeared there (Gen 18). The tamarisks at Beersheba were associated with Abraham (Gen 21:33). The pillar at Bethel was said to have been erected and consecrated by Jacob (Gen 28). Israelites were still celebrating sacrificial feasts under sacred trees (Hos 4:13). Even in the late seventh century, Jeremiah accuses his compatriots—not the Canaanites—of worshipping "wood and stone" (Jer 2:27; 3:9).

---

16. Thomas Krüger, "Genesis 38—ein 'Lehrstück' alttestamentlicher Ethik," in *Konsequente Traditionsgeschichte: Festschrift für Klaus Baltzer zum 65 Geburtstag*, ed. Rüdiger Bartelmus, Thomas Krüger, and Helmut Utzschneider, OBO 126 (Fribourg: Academic Press; Göttingen: Vandenhoeck & Ruprecht, 1993), 205–26.

17. Michel Gras, Pierre Rouillard, and Javier Teixidor, "The Phoenicians and Death," *Berytus* 39 (1991): 127–76.

With regard to astral worship, the story of Sodom and Gomorrah (Gen 19, esp. vv. 24-5), may have originally been a story about a sun god who appears every morning to drive out nocturnal demons and who passes judgment on crimes committed during the night. The two messengers that come to Sodom are Justice and Righteousness. Only Lot receives them, but they cannot stay there for the night without being molested. In comparing Jerusalem with Sodom (Isa 1:7, 9), Isaiah states that justice and righteousness were once able to spend the night in Jerusalem unmolested, but (as is the case in Sodom) that this is no longer possible (Isa 1:21).[18] Justice and Righteousness lead Lot and his family out of the condemned Sodom, and they urge him to hurry as dawn approaches, for as the sun rises, fire and sulfur rain on Sodom. Later, the Israelites inserted the name of their God in place of the sun god.[19] The beautiful Ps 104 is, by Hebrew standards, uncharacteristically detailed and tender in its descriptions of flora and fauna. But even it is originally, at least in part, a hymn to the sun.[20] The celebration of the new moon still exists in Judaism today, albeit not in the form of divine worship.[21]

Divination by consulting the dead and by other means was also well-known in Israel, as seen in the story of the woman whom Saul consults to find out the outcome of the battle (1 Sam 28). The polemical rejection of divinatory and magical practices had disastrous consequences at the time. The command not to allow a witch to live (Exod 22:17) is cited in two crucial passages in the "Bible of Witch Hunters," the *Malleus Maleficarum* ("Hammer of Witches"), and it allows the persecutors of witches to maintain a good conscience.[22]

The Significance of the Losses for Judaism (and Christianity) Caused by the Defamation of Canaanite Religion

There can be no doubt that supersession and dissociation from these domains and focusing on the workings of God in history, on human coresponsibility, and

---

18. This detail was pointed out to me by Bernd Janowski in Tübingen.
19. See Othmar Keel, "Wer zerstörte Sodom?," *Theologische Zeitschrift* 35 (1979): 10–17.
20. See Willy Staerk, "Lyrik (Psalmen, Hoheslied und Verwandtes)," in *Die Schriften des Alten Testaments in Auswahl*, 7 vols., 2nd ed. (Göttingen: Vandenhoeck & Ruprecht, 1910–1915), 3/1:82 (26*–28*); Jan Assmann, "Akhanyati's Theology of Light and Time," *Proceedings of the Israel Academy of Sciences and Humanities* 7 (1992): 143–76.
21. See Othmar Keel, *Goddesses and Trees, New Moon and Yahweh: Ancient Near Eastern Art and the Hebrew Bible*, JSOTSup 261 (Sheffield: Sheffield Academic, 1998), 102–9; Gabriele Theuer, *Der Mondgott in den Religionen Syrien-Palästinas: unter besonderer Berücksichtigung von KTU 1.24*, OBO 173 (Fribourg: Academic Press; Göttingen: Vandenhoeck & Ruprecht, 2000), esp. 439–560.
22. Othmar Keel, "Leben aus dem Wort Gottes: vom Anspruch und vom Umgang mit den Schriften des Alten und Neuen Testaments," in *Pfarrei in der Postmoderne Gemeindebildung in nachchristlicher Zeit: für Leo Karre*, ed. Alois Schifferle (Freiburg im Breisgau: Herder, 1997), 95–109, esp. 102–4.

on establishing social justice have imparted a very special character and value to Judaism. But as every transition from one age to another, such as from childhood to youth and from youth to maturity, constitutes both a gain and a loss, so the transition not only from Judaism to Christianity but also from Canaanite to Jewish religion brought with it both gain and loss.

While the de-divinization of the social and natural world does not imply its unrestrained exploitation, as is often claimed, it did lead to a reduced sensitivity to the demands and the life of nature. The loss brought about by the suppression of Canaanite religion was powerfully and accurately perceived by authors like Heide Göttner-Abendroth[23] and Gerda Weiler,[24] even if their own historical reconstructions are largely untenable.

Canaanite religion, or rather Canaanite religions, had a strong and profound sense of the forces of nature, the rustling of trees, the groaning of sky and earth, and vast multitude of stars.[25] When I was young, there was a certain category of people who sought God in nature rather than in church, and instead of attending mass on Sunday, they would go for hikes in the woods or in the mountains. There is no question that, in Catholic circles (and probably also Protestant), such people were spoken of in the most disapproving terms. They were neopagans. The caricature drawn by biblical prophecy of Canaanites worshipping stone and wood was transferred onto them. But the doctor who told me that, after a week of sickness and decay, he needed the healthy smell of wood and hard feeling of stone did not worship wood and stone, but the creator who infused these forces into creation. After stone and tree worship in Israel had been classified as typically Canaanite and proscribed as such, rejection took on increasingly radical forms. The walls of the sanctuary in the preexilic temple were adorned with palm trees, and there were apparently living palm trees in the courts, marking the temple complex as a paradisiac place of life (see Pss 52:10; 92:13-4). At some point in the postexilic period, the trees in the temple courts were cut down, as attested by a text written around 100 BCE and attributed to the Greek author Hecataeus of Abdera. There was no trace of any plant or sacred grove, as Flavius Josephus proudly reports (*Against Apion* 1.199). This process may seem strange to us, if not repugnant. The fear of being seen as worshippers of wood or the like often led to a completely insensitive relationship with nature.

Similar to the treatment of trees, the anti-Canaanitism of the First Testament also had implications for sexuality. On numerous Canaanite seals we can see, for instance, the earth goddess who confidently presents her genitalia before

23. Heide Göttner-Abendroth, *The Goddess and Her Heroes*, trans. Lilian Friedberg, 10th ed. (Stow, MA: Anthony, 1995).
24. Gerda Weiler, *Das Matriarchat im alten Israel* (Stuttgart: Kohlhammer, 1989).
25. Manfred Dietrich and Oswald Loretz, *Texte aus der Umwelt des Alten Testaments*, 3 vols. (Gütersloh: Mohn, 1997), 3/6:1141 (*KTU* 1.3.3.22-25); cf. 3/6:1144 (*KTU* 1.3.4.15-17).

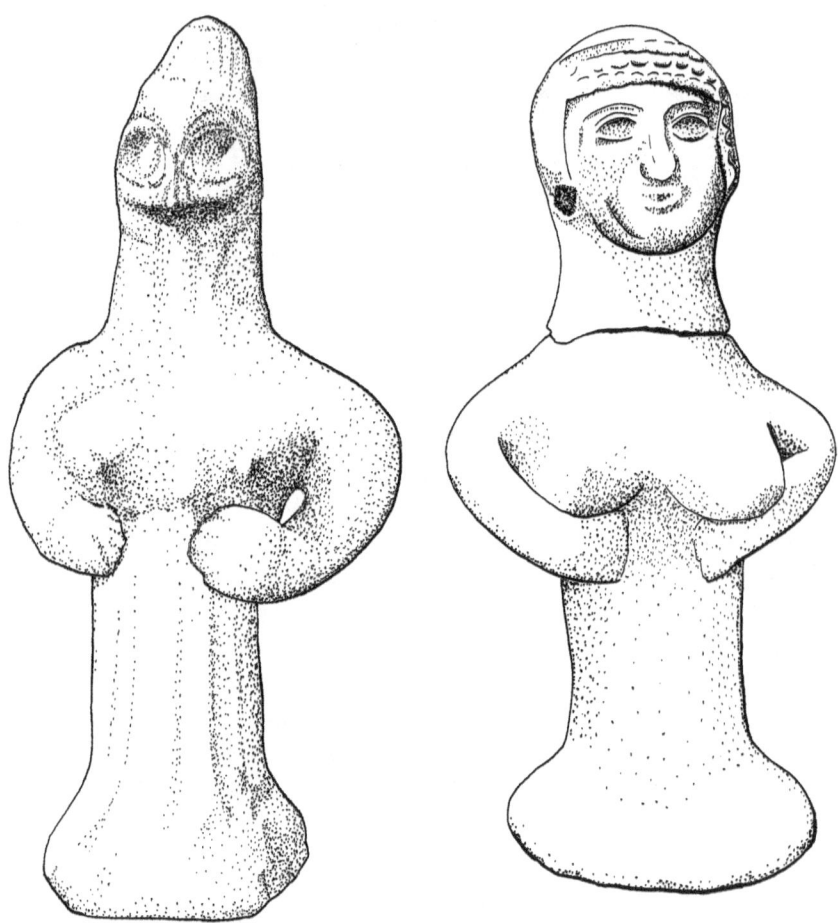

FIGURES 2.1–2.2. Pillar figurines from the "Bibel und Orient" collection at the University of Fribourg (Switzerland), nos. 1998.3 and 1998.12. Drawings by Hildi Keel-Leu.

the weather god in order receive from him the seed of rain. Countless terracotta figurines depict goddesses who exhibit their breasts, sometimes with a smile that was carefully sculpted onto the model, at other times with a stylized head resulting from a pinch of the fingers (see figs. 2.1 and 2.2). In the Canaanite world of the thirteenth century BCE, the representation of a nude female standing on top of a lion with lotus flowers and snakes in her hands (see fig. 2.3) could be seen as the image of a sacred figure (qədešat) or of sacredness (qudšu). Are the Judean pillar figurines of the eighth/seventh century BCE only a pale survival of this "paganism"? In many part of the biblical tradition, with its accent on social order, nude women like Eve, Bathsheba, and Susanna appear almost exclusively

FIGURE 2.3. Limestone stele in the Museo Egizio, Turin. Drawing in Othmar Keel, *Das Hohelied*, Zürcher Bibelkommentare 18 (Zürich: Theologischer Verlag, 1992), 149, fig. 88a.

as dangerous seductresses.[26] The Christian tradition, by shifting toward an immanent expectation of the kingdom of God, intensified this tendency into a deeply neurotic stance. I became abruptly aware of this issue when I saw a young woman who had difficulties accepting her own womanhood and consequently suffered from anorexia; she placed on her bedside table a copy of one of these pillar goddesses proudly exhibiting her breasts. She attributed a healing quality to this "pagan" figurine, which helped her to accept her womanhood. The Scriptures of the Old or First Testament are, however, in some ways not nearly as body-phobic as they were later perceived to be, especially by Christianity. A careful correlation of Iron Age images like the Judean pillar figurines with biblical texts shows this clearly and may help to turn the OT upright, from its head back to its feet.

26. On the subject of sexuality in Judaism, see Judith Plaskow, *Standing Again at Sinai: Judaism from a Feminist Perspective* (San Francisco: Harper & Row, 1990), 170–210.

In interpretations of OT theology published in the past few decades,[27] aside from that of Claus Westermann,[28] the great themes of the Hebrew Bible are God's covenant with human beings, especially Noah, Abraham, Moses, and David, the election of Israel, YHWH's presence in history, the law, sin and forgiveness, and justice and wisdom. Blessing is immaterial or marginal. How do these prioritizations relate to the fact that archaeologists have found female figurines proudly exhibiting their breasts in almost every Jewish house of the eighth or seventh century?[29] Are they representations of the infamous goddess Asherah? Are they erotic figurines? Even then, breasts were of interest not only to infants. The book of Proverbs, aimed at young men, calls on them not to be unfaithful: to rejoice in the wife of their youth and to find delight in her breasts (Prov 5:18–19). Song of Songs evokes the significance of breasts with an array of similes and metaphors. They invigorate like clusters of dates or grapes; they beguile like myrrh; they are lively like fawns of a gazelle. In addition, the importance of breasts for raising infants must not be overlooked. They were more essential than today. Baby formula was not yet available. Dry breasts were a curse (Hos 9:14; Lam 4:3); full breasts and an open womb were a blessing (Gen 49:25), a life-giving gift from God.

If we follow the direction suggested by the omnipresent pillar figurines, we discover that, while the covenants, the election of Israel, YHWH's presence in history, the law, sin and forgiveness, and justice and wisdom may be important, they nevertheless represent secondary themes. What the grand compositions of the First Testament point to—whether it is the so-called primordial history, the patriarchal narratives, Deuteronomy, or the Holiness Code—is blessing: blessing for individuals, for families, for tribes, for the people (Gen 9:1–7; 49:1–28; Lev 26:3–13; Deut 28:1–14, 33). The primary and often exclusive interests of exegetes (covenant, law, etc.) are only means to an end, means and ways of obtaining a blessing that guarantees vitality, fertility, and survival. The pillar figurines set the overly cerebral world of the exegetes back on its feet. The pillar figurines did not only evoke a blessing of breasts, just as a menorah does not

---

27. Walther Eichrodt, *Theologie des Alten Testaments*, 2 vols. (Stuttgart: Klotz, 1959); Gerhard von Rad, *Theologie des Alten Testaments*, 2 vols. (München: Chr. Kaiser, 1957–1960); Ludwig Köhler, *Theologie des Alten Testaments*, Neue theologische Grundrisse (Tübingen: Mohr Siebeck, 1966); Alfons Deissler, *Die Grundbotschaft des Alten Testaments: ein theologischer Durchblick* (Freiburg im Breisgau: Herder, 1972); Georg Fohrer, *Theologische Grundstrukturen des Alten Testaments* (Berlin: de Gruyter, 1972); Walther Zimmerli, *Grundriss der alttestamentlichen Theologie* (Stuttgart: Kohlhammer, 1972); Otto Kaiser, *Der Gott des Alten Testaments: Theologie des Alten Testaments* (Göttingen: Vandenhoeck & Ruprecht, 1993).

28. Claus Westermann, *Theologie des alten Testaments in Grundzügen*, Grundrisse zum Alten Testament 6 (Göttingen: Vandenhoeck & Ruprecht, 1978).

29. Raz Kletter, *The Judean Pillar-Figurines and the Archaeology of Asherah*, British Archeological Reports International Series 636 (Oxford: Tempus Reparatum, 1996).

only represent a lampstand, the cross does not only stand for the crucifixion, and the Kaaba denotes more than just that particular sanctuary. All signs of this kind stand for entire symbol systems. The "blessings of breasts and womb" are also parts representing the whole, but as is always the case, the whole is signified by essential parts.

Israel's view of the power and joys of eroticism was not always and everywhere equally restrictive. The poetry of the Song of Songs celebrates erotic love as a spontaneous response to a unique physical and spiritual attraction that one specific person has toward another, without considering family politics, economic issues, or problems of faithfulness.[30] The limitation of erotic feelings to the context of marriage (see Prov 5:15–23)[31] and the reception of "classical" Hebrew literature as religious literature had become so strong by the time of the first century CE, that Song of Songs, without a clear connection to the eroticism of marriage, could remain tenable only allegorically. Marital sexuality, however, was and continues to be for Judaism a participation in the creative work of God, and therefore completely legitimate and enjoyable. Early Christianity with its imminent eschatological expectations, as mentioned above, also devalued marriage in addition to eroticism (1 Cor 7:7).[32]

Astrology and divination, which are often linked, can be seen as an attempt to understand the world as a text that can be read as a divine message. Of course, this approach has the danger of becoming slavishly dependent on the "elementary principles of the world" (Gal 4:3; Col 2:8, 20). However, the polemic against it often led to a concerning cosmic neglect. The knowledge of cosmic connections, the respect for natural orders and seasons, can provide a home for us that has largely been lost to the modern world.

In our book *Gods, Goddesses, and Images of God in Ancient Israel*,[33] Christoph Uehlinger and I have tried to make the Canaanite roots of the OT more visible. One critic of the book asked uneasily whether we were trying to remythologize the OT image of God and whether YHWH was to lose his absolute transcendence of the world and of gender—and to become a nature god again.[34] He need not be concerned. The rediscovery of Judaism and a regained respect for its values (see below) do not require Christians to return to Judaism; and

---

30. Cf. Othmar Keel, *Das Hohelied*, Zürcher Bibelkommentare 18 (Zürich: Theologischer Verlag, 1992). On the subject of erotic fantasies in patriarchal societies, see David McLain Carr, "Gender and the Shaping of Desire in the Song of Songs and its Interpretation," *JBL* 119 (2000): 233–48.

31. Robert B. Chisholm Jr., "'Drink Water from Your Own Cistern': A Literary Study of Proverbs 5:15–23," *Bibliotheca Sacra* 157 (2000): 397–409.

32. See the section below entitled "The Salvific Functions of Judaism *Post Christum*."

33. Othmar Keel and Christoph Uehlinger, *Gods, Goddesses, and Images of God in Ancient Israel*, trans. Thomas A. Trapp, 2nd ed. (Minneapolis: Fortress, 2012).

34. Franz Courth, Review of *Göttinnen, Götter und Gottessymbole* by Keel and Uehlinger, *Lebendiges Zeugnis* 4 (1992): 308.

the rediscovery of Canaanite religion and a regained respect for its positive values do not demand a return to "paganism." It does, however, demand—and this *should* concern this critic—a willingness toward healthy repentance. Many people seek to heal the suffering caused by repression, restriction, and desensitization in their own lives through the painfully liberating recovery of memories with the help of psychotherapy. The collective spiritual recovery of memories stands inescapably as a challenge before Judaism and Christianity. It is no accident that Jewish and Christian feminist theologians alike have called for a decisive paradigm shift.

Healing the Break Between Judaism and Christianity

Like Judaism with regard to the religion that preceded it, Christianity also underwent a process of detachment, disengagement, separation, and differentiation. However, the consequences for the "mother" were incomparably more severe in this case.

Anti-Judaism in the New Testament...

The shock caused by the Shoah prompted a wave—initially progressing only in slow-motion—of reflections, lectures, statements, articles, and books dealing with the relationship between Christianity and Judaism, and especially with what went awry in this relationship. Distinctions were made between racial and cultural anti-Semitism, which in turn was distinguished from anti-Judaism. There was a tendency to try to escape the horrific realization that the "religion of love" was at the very least vastly complicit in the persecution of Jews, who came to be viewed as subhuman and eventually as a type of vermin destroyed in the gas chambers of Auschwitz.

Some twenty years after the ovens ceased smoking, Pope Paul VI signed, in October of 1965, the Second Vatican Council's *Nostra aetate* (the "Declaration on the Relation of the Church to non-Christian Religions"). Paragraph 4 of this decree identifies and condemns two ideas that have contributed to the vilification of Jews. First, the events surrounding the death of Jesus "cannot be charged against all the Jews, without distinction, then alive, nor against the Jews of today," and second: "The Jews should not be presented as rejected or accursed by God, as if this followed from the Holy Scriptures. All should see to it, then, that in catechetical work or in the preaching of the word of God they do not teach anything that does not conform to the truth of the Gospel and the spirit of Christ. Furthermore, in her rejection of every persecution against any man, the Church, ... moved ... by the Gospel's spiritual love, decries hatred, persecutions, displays of anti-Semitism, directed against Jews at any time and by anyone."[35]

For the church, this may have been a significant step, but viewed from a distance and in light of the horrors of Auschwitz, the insignificance of this reaction is appalling. On the whole, it gives the impression that anti-Semitism was one of many atrocities and failures that periodically afflict humanity and whose origin was unrelated either to the Church or to the Gospel.

Some church leaders persisted long after in this complacent self-characterization and self-deception. Historians asking the question of how it could have gone so far soon arrived at different assessments. Considering the hatred and persecution of the Jews by Reformers and church fathers, they found that the roots of the Christian faith were also the roots of Christian anti-Judaism. Two years after the conciliar decree, a collection of essays was published under the title *Anti-Judaism in the New Testament?*[36] There were attempts to understand a good portion of what could be considered anti-Jewish in the NT, such as the antitheses of the Sermon on the Mount, as part of an internal Jewish debate. The exclusivity statements about Jesus as the only way to God were interpreted as a Christian self-commitment.

Such attempts may have been successful in getting a better and more appropriate understanding of some NT passages, but a hard, insoluble remainder endures. At least three passages[37] can be identified in this context. The first is the speech attributed to Stephen by the book of Acts before his stoning, in which the first Christian martyr traces the malice of his opponents back to their forefathers who had also always resisted the Holy Spirit (Acts 7:51–2). This charge

---

35. The text of *Nostra aetate* can be found in Latin and German in *Das Zweite Vatikanische Konzil: Dokumente und Kommentare*, Supplement to *Lexikon für Theologie und Kirche*, 3 vols. (Freiburg: Herder, 1966–68), 2:488–95. The dramatic story of the development of this text is described by John Oesterreicher in ibid., 2:406–478.

36. Willehad Paul Eckert, Nathan Peter Levinson, and Martin Stöhr, eds., *Antijudaismus im Neuen Testament? exegetische und systematische Beiträge*, Abhandlungen zum christlich-jüdischen Dialog 2 (Munich: Kaiser, 1967). Since then, a barely assessable number of publications have appeared on this subject. It is significant that, in one recent publication, the question mark has disappeared: Samuel Vollenweider, "Antijudaismus in Neuen Testament: der Anfang einer unseligen Tradition," in *Antijudaismus—christliche Erblast?*, ed. Walter Dietrich, Martin George, and Ulrich Luz (Stuttgart: Kohlhammer, 1999), 40–55. Even in cases where the title offers a slight variation, the main focus tends to be on anti-Judaism in the New Testament; see Herbert Frohnhofen and Maurus-Akademie Rabanus, *Christlicher Antijudaismus und jüdischer Antipaganismus: ihre Motive und Hintergründe in den ersten drei Jahrhunderten*, Hamburger theologische Studien 3 (Hamburg: Steinmann & Steinmann, 1990).

37. See Gerd Theissen, "Aporien im Umgang mit den Antijudaismen des Neuen Testaments," in *Hebräische Bibel und ihre zweifache Nachgeschichte: Festschrift für Rolf Rendtorff zum 65 Geburtstag*, ed. Erhard Blum, Christian Macholz, and Ekkehard W. Stegemann (Neukirchen-Vluyn: Neukirchener Verlag, 1990). Theissen also names three passages, but instead of Acts 7:51–52, he includes Matt 27:24–5: "Let his blood be on us and on our children."

casts them as representatives of a people and of a history that has always been sinful and cannot be forgiven (cf. Luke 12:10 and its parallels). Second, there are several lines by Paul. In 1 Thess 2:14–16, the Jews are characterized not only as murderers of a just person, as in Acts 7:52, but as murderers of the Lord, *Kyrios*—of God. The enmity against all people whom Paul accuses is a line from the repertoire of gentile hatred of Jews. It is not entirely clear what he means by the wrath that has come upon them. The third and most extreme passage is found in the Gospel of John. Here Jesus himself is presented as saying that the father of the Jews was the devil, a liar and murderer from the beginning (John 8:39–44). In spite of these and similar defamations in the Gospel of John, one NT scholar concluded after a careful analysis of anti-Judaism in John that "the writer of the fourth Gospel was certainly no anti-Semite."[38] Although the term anti-Semite is anachronistic, the inhabitants of the Franconian village that erected a large tablet at their town entrance during the Nazi era with the inscription "the father of the Jews is the devil"[39] apparently found more common ground than differences between Johannine hatred of Jews and anti-Semitism, especially since leading church figures like Ambrose of Milan or Martin Luther had repeatedly called for the burning of synagogues and similar atrocities.

... *And Some Attempts to Overcome It*

Gerd Theissen has sketched out three strategies[40] that can help to neutralize the anti-Judaism of the NT:

1. The relativization of anti-Jewish passages within the text itself. Paul places the Jews under the eternal wrath of God (1 Thess 2:16), but he also emphatically negates their rejection in Rom 11. The Gospel of John has Jesus refer to the Jews as descendants of the devil, but it also proclaims that salvation comes from the Jews (John 4:22). "The problem is not a categorical rejection of the Jews, but the ambivalence of a newly developing religion with regard to its mother-religion, which also implies a strong bond with this religion."[41]

2. The historical relativization of anti-Jewish statements. This strategy begins with these questions: Who makes these statements that are considered offensive? To whom are they addressed and in what situation? "Accusations against Jews in the New Testament are also found as accusations by some Jewish groups against others. An example of this is Matt 27:24–5. The Jewish historian Josephus assigns responsibility for the destruction of the temple to the Zealots,

---

38. Felix Porsch, "'Ihr habt den Teufel zum Vater' (Joh 8,44): Antijudaismus im Johannesevangelium?," *BK* 44 (1989): 50–57, at 57.
39. Ibid., 50.
40. Theissen, "Aporien im Umgang mit den Antijudaismen," 540–49.
41. Ibid., 541.

who occupied the temple during the Jewish War and instituted a radical temple reform, in process of which they did not shy away from executions. According to Josephus, the destruction of the temple was God's punishment for these illegal executions (Josephus, *Jewish War* 6.109–10 and 6.124–26). At about the same time as Josephus, the Gospel of Matthew claims that the destruction of the temple was God's punishment for the execution of Jesus. The interpretative logic is the same in both passages."[42] Even the accusation of descent from the devil has a Jewish counterpart. The book of Jubilees calls Jews who do not circumcise their children "sons of Beliar" (15:33). Theissen also shows that similarly grave accusations, like being guilty concerning the body and blood of the Lord or being descended from the devil, also have Christian counterparts (1 Cor 11:27; 1 John 3:8).[43]

Despite all these attempts to explain this polemic as an inner-Jewish or inner-Christian, one cannot escape the conclusion: "The anti-Jewish statements in the New Testament are certainly part of the separation-process between Jews and Christians, which did not take place without bitterness and hurt."[44] For some NT examples, it is no longer a case of sibling rivalry, but rather polemic against strangers. In 1 Thess 2:14–16, the accusations of godlessness and human enmity clearly display elements of gentile hatred toward Jews.[45] A fundamental separation is especially visible in the Gospel of John. While the Synoptic Gospels have Jesus arguing with Pharisees and Sadducees, thereby arguing as a Jew with other religious groups within Judaism, the Gospel of John has him consistently confronting the Jews as if he himself was not one of them. For John, "οἱ Ἰουδαῖοι are the enemies of Jesus *per se*."[46]

> Reasons for the separation between Jews and Christians were: 1. the position with regard to the temple, 2. criticism of the law and 3. the development of a "high Christology." ... The Christians thereby violated precisely the values and convictions through which Jewish identity found expression: love for the temple, separation from the way of life of the Gentiles, and strict monotheism. At the same time, through these positions Christianity opened itself up to Gentiles, which led to a further estrangement from Judaism. Within this process of estrangement, three stages can be defined. Criticism of the temple extends back to the time of Jesus, when

---

42. Ibid., 543.
43. Ibid., 544.
44. Ibid.
45. Klaus Haacker, "Elemente des heidnischen Antijudaismus im Neuen Testament," *Evangelische Theologie* 48 (1988): 404–18.
46. Walter Bauer, *Wörterbuch zum Neuen Testament* (Berlin: Töpelmann, 1958), 750. See John 1:19; 2:18, 20; 5:10, 15–16; 6:41, 42; etc. See also Ulrich Luz, "Das 'Auseinandergehen der Wege': über die Trennung des Christentums vom Judentum," in Dietrich, George, and Luz, *Antijudaismus*, 56–73.

he and his followers formed an "inner-Jewish reform movement." In the second generation, a fundamental critique of the law was developed by Paul while this earliest form of Christianity was still a Jewish sect, since everyone still hoped to win over all Jews eventually (Rom 11). In the third generation (especially in the Gospel of John), a "high Christology" emerges as a dividing factor. The sectarian split becomes a persistent schism, which is experienced as final by both sides.[47]

Statements by Paul or the Gospel of John can be understood as a reaction to the persecution of heretics and schismatics by the Jews, as a complication in the separation process of the young Christian movement from Judaism,[48] as a symptom of puberty, so to speak, and a projection onto the Jews of its own insecurities and unbelief. All this does not change the fact that they express a reprehensible position that had disastrous historical consequences.

3. The symbolic relativization of NT anti-Judaism. In the end, the separation of Christianity and Judaism reflects not only a historical process but also different understandings of God, the world, and religion. Theological exegesis tends to understand the conflict not historically, but symbolically. When viewed in this way, the Jews in the Gospel of John are not historically empirical Jews, but rather a cipher for godless unbelievers in general. Theissen correctly criticized this rationalization for merely adopting the same logic as the prejudice of "ascribing qualities that are considered negative to a specific group without having any empirical basis in reality."[49]

The most fundamental reason for NT enmity against the Jews is the fact that the young Christian movement is most closely tied to Judaism through the Old or First Testament as common Scripture,[50] through the hope for the coming kingdom of God, and through the belief in the one God, while Judaism as the mother-religion never accepted the Christian understanding of these ideas. Christianity shattered the law—which organized and defined Israel as the people of YHWH through circumcision, dietary laws, and sacred times—and thereby ignored the dignity of the community and of the people. It made the salvation of God independent of the law and universalized it. It saw the coming of the kingdom of God realized through the appearance of the "Son" beloved by the "Father," and so perceived a dynamic within the one God that revealed love as the essence of God, but it did not forgive Judaism for not sharing these

---

47. Theissen, "Aporien im Umgang mit den Antijudaismen," 544–46.
48. Ibid., 538–39.
49. Ibid., 548. There is no way to escape the conclusion that anti-Judaism had its beginning in the New Testament. See also Vollenweider, "Antijudaismus in Neuen Testament,"
50. Erich Zenger, "Die Bibel Israels—Wurzel der Gemeinsamkeit für Juden und Christen," *FR* 9 (2002): 81–93.

enthusiastic insights. These insights are no doubt a gain and an increase in religious experience. But Christians overlook the fact that, like any other gain, it also implies a loss. Christianity has failed to see this in its triumphalism. Only Auschwitz compelled it to rethink this seriously.

According to Johann Baptist Metz, Christian theology is challenged to view "the messianic tradition of Judaism in its unsurpassed autonomy; as it were, in its enduring messianic dignity, without Christianity betraying or playing down the christological mystery it proclaims."[51] The problem identified by Metz is reminiscent of fitting a square peg into a round hole, and its solubility depends on one's understanding of "betraying" and "playing down." Rosemary Radford Ruether recognizes clearly that there cannot be respect for Jewish perspectives without a certain relativization of the Christian claim to absoluteness. "The fratricidal side of Christian faith can be overcome only through genuine encounter with Jewish identity."[52] Genuine encounter, however, demands as much respect for the other as for oneself. It demands a self-relativization. Erich Zenger speaks of the "relational sovereignty" (*relationaler Eigenwert*) of the Jewish Bible (Tanak) and of the Bible adopted by Christianity and interpreted in reference to Jesus Christ, always using quotation marks around "relational."[53] A German Catholic working group examined all relevant doctrinal documents and stated more explicitly—fifty years after the Shoah—"The future relationship between Christians and Jews is largely dependent on the Christian recognition of Jewish traditions in their own right and with their own specific theological dignity, or a renunciation in the spirit of the Bible (cf. Rom 11:17–24) of Christian claims of absoluteness with regard to Judaism."[54] This is done—without being openly stated—by someone like Cardinal Walter Kasper when he characterizes the relationship using Franz Rosenzweig's expression "mutual supplementation" (*gegenseitige Ergänzung*).[55] Once the sovereignty of each path is fundamentally recognized, one can ask questions without embarrassment about the advantages and disadvantages of one position or the other.

An encounter without embarrassment typically begins with a recognition of common ground before noting differences. The following anecdote is good illustration of this. When I, after having been raised in a strictly Catholic environment, had the opportunity in 1960 to meet Jews in person and to visit Jewish

---

51. Johann Baptist Metz, *The Emergent Church: The Future of Christianity in a Post-Bourgeois World*, trans. Peter Mann (New York: Crossroad, 1981), 23.
52. Rosemary Radford Ruether, *Faith and Fratricide: The Theological Roots of Anti-Semitism* (New York: Seabury, 1974), 261.
53. Zenger, *Das erste Testament*, esp. 155.
54. Willehad Paul Eckert et al., "Antisemitismus, Schoa und Kirche: Studien eines theologischen Arbeitskreises," *FR* 6 (1999): 262–79.
55. Walter Kasper, "Juden und Christen—Schulter an Schulter," *FR* 9 (2002): 250–56.

communities in Jerusalem, many clichés and caricatures in my mind collapsed like a house of cards. This was the case at a celebration of *Simḥat Torah*, the "Joy of the Law," at which gratitude is expressed before God for the orientation and direction that the "law" provides. The atmosphere at the celebration was like Christmas and Easter together. People danced with the Torah scroll and the Pauline curse of the law could not be felt (anymore). Likewise, the notorious works righteousness did not exist when the song *Avinu Malkeinu* was sung in the great Yeshurun Synagogue in Jerusalem—"Our father, our king, have mercy on us ... for we have no works (accomplished)." When I had the opportunity to discuss with Shalom Ben-Chorin, still unknown at that time, the differences between Judaism and Christianity, I made reference to the Christian Messiah who had already come; he asked me to look out the window and to look at the houses that were destroyed in the war of 1948. To salvage my own dogmatic position, I naively proposed to compare Judaism and Christianity to bare fields, of which one was already seeded, while the other was unseeded. Shalom Ben-Chorin was kind enough to overlook the discrimination and pointed out that in any case, both were eagerly awaiting the sun and its warmth, regardless of whether messiah were to come for the first time or the second.

The divide is more easily overcome by the fact, which has been increasingly emphasized in recent years and strongly supported by historical facts, that Jesus was a Jew in his whole feeling and thinking[56] and that Christian theology has Jewish roots.[57] It would be best to emphasize common ground very strongly, but respect for the other also demands a recognition of differences.

The "Salvific Function" of Judaism Post Christum

People with relevant historical expertise who make a deliberate attempt to view Judaism positively, as for example Franz Mußner, point to the difficulty of formulating a sound, thoughtful, and comprehensive appreciation of the long-shunned counterpart that is not just an emotional response to individual aspects. In his *Tractate on the Jews*, Mußner states that the question of whether Judaism still has a "salvific function" (*Heilsfunktion*) *post Christum* is uncommonly difficult. He is aware that many Christians reject even the question itself, and he considers his response merely as an attempt.[58] He goes on to list eight points, which can be grouped into two large themes.

---

56. Friedrich-Wilhelm Marquardt, *Das christliche Bekenntnis zu Jesu, dem Juden: eine Christologie*, 2 vols. (Munich: Kaiser, 1990–1991); Géza Vermès, *Jesus the Jew: A Historian's Reading of the Gospels* (Philadelphia: Fortress, 1981).

57. Hubert Frankemölle, *Jüdische Wurzeln christlicher Theologie: Studien zum biblischen Kontext neutestamentlicher Texte* (Bodenheim: Philo, 1998), 13–24; see also Rom 11:13–24.

58. Franz Mußner, *Tractate on the Jews: The Significance of Judaism for Christian Faith*, trans. Leonard Swidler (Philadelphia: Fortress, 1984), 45.

The first theme is the witness of the Jewish people to what Mußner calls the "concreteness of 'salvation history.'" The continued existence under the most adverse conditions and the harshest persecutions suggests a call and guidance that goes far beyond what can be seen with regard to other peoples. Furthermore, the persistence with which this community has struggled in its particular way to find familial solutions to social problems is much more realistic and concrete than anything achieved by most Christian churches. As a result of strong apocalyptic and Hellenistic components, Christians have always had a broken relationship with history, earthly matters, and especially the body. To be concerned with earthly matters meant to be an enemy of the cross and to resist what the cross stood for—the end of all earthly matters. To be concerned with earthly things was contrary to the idea of heaven as the true home (Phil 3:18–20). This focus on the eschaton could in itself have been immensely liberating, as can be seen in axiomatic statements. Paul teaches that before God there is neither Greek (gentile) nor Jew, neither slave nor free, neither male nor female (Gal 3:28). But in many areas, orthodoxy remained separate from orthopraxis. In practice, these beautiful maxims remained ineffective because earthly things were neglected as secondary to the ultimate goal. Thus, Paul can warn slaves—contrary to all theoretical insights—"Were you a bondservant when called? Do not be concerned about it. But if you can gain your freedom, avail yourself of the opportunity. For he who was called in the Lord as a bondservant is a freedman of the Lord. Likewise he who was free when called is a bondservant of Christ" (1 Cor 7:21–22; ESV).[59] In contrast to such beautiful but ineffective declarations, Judaism has repeatedly tried with realistic solutions to alleviate the suffering of Jewish slaves in concrete and genuine ways.[60] In view of the Christian indifference toward social injustice, or because the clergy was decidedly on side of the oppressor, the protagonists of the French Revolution rejected the official guardians of the biblical tradition and invoked pagan antiquity; their ideals of *liberté*, *égalité*, and *fraternité* in fact had much stronger affinity with the impulses of the OT than with Greco-Roman antiquity. Judaism has remained faithful to these impulses of the OT to a much higher degree. Even the secular Jew Karl Marx wanted not only to interpret the world, as his predecessors had done, but to change it. Bertold Brecht also took up the Jewish tradition of the "First Testament" in his critique of escapism.[61] Erich Zenger accurately points to the corrective value of

---

59. Even more extreme is 1 Tim 6:1–2, where slaves belonging to Christian owners are called to be more submissive to them than they would be to gentiles. However, cf. the letter to Philemon.

60. See Exod 21:2–11; Lev 25:2–38; Deut 15:1–18; 23:16–17; Jer 34:8–22; Neh 5:1–13. On these passages see Eckart Otto, "Der eine Gott—die eine Welt: biblische Fundamente politischer Einigungsprozesse in der Moderne," *Informationes theologiae Europae: Internationales ökumenisches Jahrbuch für Theologie* 1 (1992): 45–57.

61. Othmar Keel, "Bertolt Brecht und das Erste Testament: Politik, Welthaftigkeit und Ideologie," *BK* 50 (1995): 12–19.

Jewish readings of the First, or Old, Testament with regard to self-centered and escapist varieties of Christianity.[62] It is no coincidence that the base communities in South America looking for a religious model in light of their degrading living conditions did not want to read the NT without the OT. Even if they did not perceive it as Jewish, the Jewish exodus model of the Old or First Testament was so significant for them because they wanted to be not only a community focused on the hereafter but also a people on the way forward.

On the other hand, this model is also based on dualistic worldview, that of an evil Pharaoh on the one hand and the good Israelites on the other. Therefore, some groups have turned away from this model and have embraced another model of creation-focused theology—also based on the OT—that puts a stronger emphasis on the shared responsibility of all human beings rather than pitting one group against another.[63]

However, it is not only in emergency or crisis situations but also in everyday life that the Jewish First Testament offers more tangible and practical direction than the New or Second Testament. One may think for example of sexuality and eroticism, in regard to which the Second Testament has little of value to offer with its orientation toward a heaven without marriage where people live (sexless) like the angels (see Mark 12:25). Marriage implies earthly concerns, which Paul wants to spare the faithful (1 Cor 7:28). At best, marriage is a necessary evil, and even when it is celebrated as a kind of sacrament (following texts like Eph 5:21–33), a vibrant and positive view is difficult to discern. I remember arguing as a university student with the Dominican professor Norbert Luyten, who was of the opinion that it was normal for a Christian not to marry. Marriage demanded justification. To value eroticism and marriage in their own right, as one can see in Gen 2, the Song of Songs, or the book of Ruth, for example, is impossible for the NT.[64] The few married women who were canonized—usually women of nobility—are defined in exclusively negative terms as *nec virgo, nec martyr*. To this day, Roman Catholic priests as religious humans par excellence are obliged to remain celibate. In the Greek Orthodox Church, this expectation is limited to bishops. To be sure, the NT is not always equally otherworldly and focused on the hereafter. While the Lord's Prayer humbly asks for daily bread, the Gospel of John advises somewhat naively that one ought not to worry about food that perishes (John 6:27). This general observation could be easily dismissed as a caricature, but even such a dismissal must ask whether such a caricature does not capture some essential characteristics.

---

62. Zenger, *Das erste Testament*, 194n119.

63. Othmar Keel and Sylvia Schroer, *Creation: Biblical Theologies in the Context of the Ancient Near East*, trans. Peter T. Daniels (Winona Lake, IN: Eisenbrauns, 2015).

64. For a nuanced discussion, see Peter Brown, *The Body and Society: Men, Women, and Sexual Renunciation in Early Christianity* (New York: Columbia University Press, 1988).

The second theological benefit ascribed to Judaism by Mußner and other authors is its prospect of a better world, or expressed negatively, its eschatological reluctance: the knowledge that, despite all salvific evidence, for example in the sacraments, the salvation promised by God is still to come. Israel and the Jews have tenaciously refused to recognize any plant, tree, animal, constellation, or human being as the full manifestation of God. They often paid for this refusal with their possessions or with life and limb, for with this refusal they fought for the human freedom not to have to recognize something penultimate as the ultimate. The first reported attempt to eradicate the Jews was formulated because the Jew Mordecai was unwilling to bend the knee before the Persian courtier Haman (Esth 3:1–6). The courtier justifies his proposed genocide by reminding the Persian king that the Jews do not keep the king's laws (to honor the courtiers), and he points to the economic benefits that an extermination of the Jews would bring (Esth 3:7–11). Even though the story told in the book of Esther is not historical, the reasons cited for the extermination have been successfully used numerous times.

From their own kings, Saul, David, and Solomon, to the Roman emperors, Judaism has always refused to see these rulers as infallible, godlike, or even divine beings. This honor was reserved for God alone. Tacitus made the often repeated statement, "Among the Jews all things are profane that we hold sacred" (*Histories* 5.4). Whenever Christian communities had the delusion that their own government realized the rule of Christ—whether in Byzantium, under the Catholic kings and queens of the fifteenth and sixteenth century, or under the czarist Russia of the nineteenth century—Judaism was subjected to particularly fierce hostilities and persecutions. Its mere existence disproved the blasphemous illusion that the kingdom of God had been realized. This persistent witness—often sealed with blood—to the divinity of God and the freedom of human beings from any kind of idolatry has repeatedly earned the Jews the accusation of fomenting sedition. This was also one of the main charges made by the Nazis who so fervently believed in their Führer.[65] I would suggest that another variation of this historical idea underscoring the profaneness of the world is the work of Sigmund Freud. He revealed the dark recesses of the human psyche borne in the soul, which had often been celebrated as a divine spark in gnostic-romantic contradiction to the "flesh." Such dualistic anthropology was foreign to the OT.[66]

---

65. The largely secular state of Israel has long been and continues to be rejected as illegitimate by strict religious groups. In spite of all intentions to absolutize this state and especially its security, one is hard pressed to find another community that faces and tolerates as much self-criticism in light of real, physical threats. Nothing comparable existed in the former Yugoslavia nor in any Arab state.

66. See Silvia Schroer and Thomas Staubli, *Body Symbolism in the Bible*, trans. Linda M. Maloney (Collegeville, MN: Liturgical, 2001).

Another aspect of the eschatological proviso besides the de-divinization (*Entgöttlichung*) of the polis and the individual is the de-divinization of the world, especially as seen in Gen 1. Already Friedrich Schiller in his famous poem "The Gods of Greece" (ca. 1790) lamented the de-divinization of nature in favor of the one, transcendent God. This view has since been invoked on various occasions. The current monotheism debate, prompted by a number of novels,[67] and especially by Jan Assmann's widely reviewed book *Moses the Egyptian*,[68] echoes Schiller's criticism. The basic point is the imaginative void between true and false religion that the "Mosaic distinction" supposedly introduced, and the intolerant arrogance of the former toward the latter. The faith that came out of the desert has turned the world into a desert.[69] Is it appropriate to see monotheism as the scapegoat in this sense? Klaus Koch has good reasons to call this into question.[70] A consistent understanding of monotheism in the sense of the Wisdom of Solomon calls for the love of all creatures and, like Francis of Assisi's "Canticle of the Sun," views them all as sisters and brothers. The cause of numerous crimes is the perversity of monotheists who identify themselves with the one God; in their iniquitous self-divinization, they see their own visions, feelings, and thoughts as those of God. Polytheists are no less reluctant than monotheists to legitimize and justify their wars and crimes, for example through conflicts among the deities. Indeed, the practice of declaring the factual as the normative is particularly common in polytheism. It is also not true that biblical monotheism and its de-divinization of the world has turned the world into the object of human capriciousness or arbitrariness. The Scriptures see creation as the work of the God's hand, an admirable "work of art" that is in itself not God but, as God's handiwork, possesses a numinous radiance.[71] The two aspects

---

67. E.g.: Peter Handke, *Crossing the Sierra de Gredos*, trans. Krishna Winston (New York: Farrar, Straus, and Giroux, 2007); Michel Houellebecq, *Platform*, trans. Frank Wynne (London: Heinemann, 2002); Philip Roth, *The Human Stain* (Boston: Houghton Mifflin, 2000); Martin Walser, *Tod eines Kritikers: Roman* (Frankfurt am Main: List Taschenbuch, 2004). See also Thomas Assheuer, "Macht euch die Erde untertan: nach dem Streit um Walser: Warum Schriftsteller die monotheistischen Religionen für die Sinnkrise verantwortlich machen," *Die Zeit* 30 (2002): 33.

68. Jan Assmann, *Moses the Egyptian: The Memory of Egypt in Western Monotheism* (Cambridge: Harvard University Press, 1998).

69. The idea that biblical monotheism has its origin in the desert is based on the biblical Sinai tradition. Historically, it developed in the cities, in Jerusalem and Babylon in the seventh and sixth centuries. This does not stop cultural philosophers and authors from imagining a desert origin of monotheism. See e.g., George Steiner, *In Bluebeard's Castle: Some Notes Towards the Redefinition of Culture* (New Haven: Yale University Press, 1971); Friedrich Dürrenmatt, *Zusammenhänge: Essay über Israel, eine Konzeption: Nachgedanken unter anderem über Freiheit, Gleichheit und Bruderlichkeit in Judentum, Christentum, Islam und Marxismus und über zwei alte Mythen*, ed. Friedrich Dürrenmatt (Zürich: Diogenes, 1985), 186–87.

70. Klaus Koch, "Monotheismus als Sündenbock?," *Theologische Literaturzeitung* 124 (1999): 874–84.

71. See Keel and Schroer, *Creation*.

of Jewish mission—respect for the concrete world and the preservation of its profaneness and, thus, the preservation of human freedom—can be summed up under the heading "historical existence." However, history also implies contingency, process, freedom, and responsibility of human beings with regard to a God whose passions are justice and righteousness. This makes it very clear, in my opinion, that Christianity—even after Christ—cannot dispense with the witness of Judaism. Though Christianity claims the inheritance of Judaism for itself, it has allowed this witness to waste away and has concerned itself only with the otherworldly emphasis of its own message, that the kingdom of God has come with Christ.

Continued Distortion of Judaism and Its Limitations

Unfortunately, such ideas are still largely ignored in Christian circles, and Judaism continues to be perceived with historical amnesia despite Auschwitz and the resulting self-reflection. It functions for Christians merely as a negative foil to intensify the radiance of Jesus. In such caricatures, whose origins also reach back to the NT (Matt 23; Gal 3:10–11), Judaism is depicted as a religion characterized by painstaking observance of countless petty laws motivated by fear of a patriarchal God whose intention may not be questioned. Particularly crass failures in this regard are the two widely read books by Christa Mulack[72] and Franz Alt.[73]

Such distortions of Judaism are admittedly based on numerous well-intentioned depictions and even certain forms of Jewish self-understanding. An example of this was a documentary hosted by H. Vögeli on Swiss television on March 10, 1993, during prime-time. The program focused largely on depictions of folkloristic customs related to Jewish festivals, on married women replacing head-scarves with wigs, or on the painstaking observance of certain dietary taboos. Nothing was said in this documentary about human freedom and responsibility, the eschatological proviso, or other historically significant achievements of Judaism. The religious dignity that has come to be associated with dietary and other regulations in Judaism is based on the significance that Judaism ascribes to its group identity (compare the Israeli definition of a Jew

---

72. Christa Mulack, *Jesus, der Gesalbte der Frauen: Weiblichkeit als Grundlage christlicher Ethik* (Stuttgart: Kreuz, 1987); see also Susannah Heschel, "Jüdisch-feministische Theologie und Antijudaismus in christlich-feministischer Theologie," in *Verdrängte Vergangheit, die uns bedrängt: feministische Theologie in der Verantwortung für die Geschichte*, ed. Leonore Siegele-Wenschkewitz (Munich: Kaiser, 1988), 86–88, and Silvia Schroer, "Feminismus und Antijudaismus: zur Geschichte eines konstruktiven Streites," in Dietrich, George, and Luz, *Antijudaismus—christliche Erblast?*, 28–39.

73. Franz Alt, *Jesus—der erste neue Mann* (Munich: Piper, 1989). See also Micha Brumlik, *Der Anti-Alt* (Frankfurt am Main: Eichborn, 1991), and Daniel Kosch, "Neue Jesusliteratur: eine Umschau," *BK* 48 (1993): 40–45.

as someone who has a Jewish mother and who has not converted to another religion). In her "Judaism Is More Than Just a Religion" lecture mentioned at the beginning of the present essay, Brocke points out that a Jew is at the same time the member of a people and of a religious group. Similarly, a Muslim is at the same time a member of the *umma* (a type of social community) and of Islam (a religious entity). Every social community has dietary taboos. For example, the Swiss, unlike the Chinese, reject the consumption of dog meat, and unlike the Italians, they reject the eating of songbirds. However, unlike Jewish or Muslim communities, they permit the consumption of pork.[74] It can hardly be denied that the religious dignity associated with such taboos reflects the intended preservation of certain aspects of a tribal religion. Jews like Philo of Alexandria or the great Moses Maimonides, who felt the need to justify themselves before the world, tried with moderate success to explain these taboos on the basis of hygiene or as attempts to draw a distinction from certain Canaanite practices.

The orthodox theological justification that God has the right to demand whatever God wants from human beings, even if it is entirely irrational, is unsatisfactory: it does not sufficiently account for the human responsibility so heavily emphasized by Judaism. It also deflects the central question of whether meat should be eaten at all to focus on side issues like the question of whether any blood is left in the meat or not. To be sure, every existing religion has taboos like this, but we do not do justice to Judaism (or any other religion) as a whole if we consider certain expressions of orthodoxy, practiced by perhaps 10 percent of Jews, as the one and only Judaism. Likewise, we misrepresent Islam or Christianity if we consider only certain fundamentalist variations as the "true Islam," the "true Christianity," or the "true Catholicism." Of course, such groups always claim to be the true guardians and keepers of identity. But what is this identity? Such characterizations must be seen as grossly negligent, just as intellectuals often approach the problem of identity in the most trite and banal ways.

Vertical Ecumenism

Unlike the palace archives of Nineveh and the temple libraries of Egypt, the ANE texts from Israel were not buried (or even destroyed) to be rediscovered

---

74. On the subject of food taboos, see Marvin Harris, *Good to Eat: Riddles of Food and Culture* (New York: Simon and Schuster, 1985), although the author exaggerates the economic and rational aspects of such restrictions. See also Thomas Staubli, *Die Bücher Levitikus, Numeri* (Stuttgart: Katholisches Bibelwerk, 1996), 95–105. The arbitrariness of such restrictions is well exemplified by Herodotus, *Histories* 2.42: "All that have a temple of Zeus of Thebes or are of the Theban district sacrifice goats, but will not touch sheep.... Those who have a temple of Mendes or are of the Mendesian district sacrifice sheep, but will not touch goats" (in Herodotus, *The Persian Wars*, ed. A. D. Godley, 4 vols., Loeb Classical Library [Cambridge: Harvard University Press, 1920–1925]).

and deciphered in the nineteenth and twentieth centuries. The biblical texts were handed down without interruption by living communities, translated first into Greek and then into virtually all existing languages and distributed throughout the entire world. This enormous universalization led to the transfer of many ANE motifs into numerous different cultural memories (art, literature), with the result that, even now, the interpretation of Mesopotamian cities and temple towers is influenced more strongly by the story of the "tower of Babel" (Gen 11) than by the scholarly work on Mesopotamian ziggurats. This reception of Gen 11 has led to several interesting interactions between high-rise architecture and a Near Eastern biblical tradition,[75] culminating in a bloody climax in the destruction of the World Trade Center towers on September 11, 2001, by Al-Qaeda jihadists.[76] The Hebrew and Aramaic Scriptures of the Jewish Bible are the collecting pool of ANE traditions and the reservoir running into channels of different directions. In their interpretation through the Mishnah and Talmud, they represent the essential legacy of various forms of Judaism. Through the interpretation and supplementation of the NT, they constitute the canonical Scriptures of a wide array of Christian religious traditions.[77] Central statements, traditions, figures, and axioms of these traditions have found their way into the Qur'an. The ANE cultures and the biblical Scriptures are a vast river of traditions (*Traditionsstrom*) that has its source in the deep fountain of antiquity. They continue to flow in the Scriptures of Christianity and Islam. We need to be cognizant of the fact that the "Canaanite," Israelite-Jewish, and Christian religions and cultures represent a long chain of traditions. Each generation owes crucial elements to the preceding generation. But the term "generation" is—like the concept of a "river of traditions"—only a simile, a metaphor or a model that does only partial justice to the idea it describes. Generations are connected, and younger generations are dependent on older ones. So far the model holds up. However, generations come and go, and here it is that the model breaks down. Judaism did not disappear after Christianity appeared on the scene and—although this is less obvious—the "Canaanite" pagan world did not disappear after Judaism came into being. Thank God this is not the case.

---

75. Friedrich Dürrenmatt, *Bilder und Zeichnungen: ein Querschnitt durch das gesamte graphische Werk*, ed. Christian Strich (Zürich: Diogenes, 1978), 13–17; Brigitte Pedde, "Das 'neue Babylon': Alter Orient und Hochhausarchitektur in den USA," *Alter Orient aktuell* 2 (2001): 8–12.

76. On the Islamic tradition of Nimrod's heaven-storming tower and its destruction, see Christoph Uehlinger, *Weltreich und 'eine Rede': eine neue Deutung der sogenannten Turmbauerzählung (Gen 11, 1–9)*, OBO 101 (Fribourg: Academic Press; Göttingen: Vandenhoeck & Ruprecht, 1990), 191–94.

77. Blum, Macholz, and Stegemann, *Hebräische Bibel und ihre zweifache Nachgeschichte*.

"For you love all things that exist, and detest none of the things that you have made, for you would not have made anything if you had hated it. How would anything have endured if you had not willed it? Or how would anything not called forth by you have been preserved? You spare all things, for they are yours, O Lord, you who love the living" (Wis 11:24–26; NRSV). This axiom is the basis for the recommendation to the Jewish high council by the Pharisee Gamaliel: "Keep away from these men and let them alone, for if this plan or this undertaking is of man, it will fail; but if it is of God, you will not be able to overthrow them. You might even be found opposing God!" (Acts 5:38–9; ESV)

Each of the three groups or phases has its strengths and weaknesses, which I have presented here in a simplified, even caricatured way. To sum up: the Canaanite-pagan world has generally had a greater sensitivity for the numinous in creation than Judaism and Christianity. Like Baal in the Ugaritic epics, the Canaanites still heard and understood the "word of tree and whisper of stone, converse or Heaven with Earth, of Deeps with Stars, ... the lightning which the Heavens do not know ... and earth's masses do not understand."[78] The Wisdom of Solomon suggests that this sensitivity of the pagan world confuses creation with the creator to some extent (Wis 13:1–7). In contrast to, for instance, the Roman disregard for humanity in slavery, gladiator games, or the exposure of infants, Judaism exhibits respect for all human beings and especially for small social units like nuclear or extended families; it has raised up the idea of social justice. In opposition to the worship of any kind of worldly greatness, especially the emperor, it placed the worship of the one invisible God at the center. Christianity has largely neglected the pagan sensitivity toward nature as well as the struggle for more justice in the world; instead it has focused on eternal life and a heavenly homeland untouched by worldly needs and pains. This orientation finds its realization in a universal compassion and love that is not directed at any single group of people, as was practiced by Francis of Assisi, Albert Schweitzer, or Mother Theresa. The current ecumenical movement tries to gather the various Christian denominations around one table and to foster a dialogue among them that seeks and strengthens the elements that unite them. An extended version includes the other Abrahamic religions[79]—Judaism and Islam[80]—in this

---

78. *Corpus des tablettes en cunéiformes alphabétiques découvertes à Ras Shamra-Ugarit de 1929 à 1939*, ed. Andree Herdner (Paris: Geuthner, 1963), 1.3.3.22–28; Mark S. Smith, *The Ugaritic Baal Cycle* (Leiden: Brill, 1994), 202–3.

79. See Manfred Görg, *In Abraham's Bosom: Christianity without the New Testament*, trans. Linda M. Maloney (Collegeville, MN: Liturgical, 1999), esp. 129–39.

80. Like the birth of Judaism from ANE religions and of Christianity from Judaism, so, too, the birth of Islam from Judaism and Christianity did not occur without violence and injuries. Muhammad initially showed respect for Jews and Christians, the *Ahl al-Kitāb* ("possessors of Scriptures" or "people of the Book") and hoped to be recognized by them. However, after they rejected and even mocked him, he turned against them and threatened them with curses and condemnations (Georges

conversation. This kind of ecumenism can be called horizontal ecumenism. Its efforts often result in noncommittal cordialities or in positional warfare. It should be supplemented by a kind of *vertical ecumenism* that encourages and cultivates an awareness of the genealogical relations between these various groups. They can be seen as relatives, even as a kind of family whose tensions and hostilities must be healed through anamnesis or therapy, for the sake of the creator and father and for every single member of the family. No creator worthy of the name wants that his creation, which is a part of him, should suffer damage or perish. The various groups of creatures, however, are related to each other in many different ways, at least in the Mediterranean cultural context. It is problematic if there is, for example, a recurring Jewish emphasis that Judaism does not need Christianity in order to know itself better and to define itself. To illustrate this problem metaphorically, it is as if parents were to say they did not need their children in order to understand themselves better. Children often draw attention to a potential in their parents, and they bring to light possibilities and weaknesses latent in them. It is well-known that children can see themselves reflected in their parents, even if some children say they are completely different from their parents in order to avoid looking themselves in the face. The same is true of parents and children.

Vajda, "Ahl al-Kitāb," in *The Encyclopedia of Islam*, vol. 1, ed. H. A. R. Gibb et al [Leiden: Brill, 1960], 272–74). This disengagement and dissociation also deserves closer examination, which is not possible here for lack of space, time, and competence.

CHAPTER 3

More Than One God? Three Models for Construing the Relations Between YHWH and the Other Gods

---

Bob Becking

The Christian tradition presents itself, in imitation of Judaism and like Islam, as a monotheistic religion. This implies that believers accept the existence of only one God. Other deities either do not exist, or are seen as the product of human imagination; or they are dismissed as remnants of a persistent paganism. In Christian systematic theology, monotheism is taken for granted. Alister McGrath, for example, opens his section on "God" with a discussion of the gender of God, followed by various remarks on the divine attributes.[1] The proposition that there is only one God receives no consideration from him, because it is accepted. Monotheism is a problem in Christian faith and theology only when it comes to the concept of the Trinity: How can the conviction that there is only one God be reconciled with belief in the divinity of Jesus and of the Holy Spirit? Here too, McGrath exemplifies many dogmatic and systematic positions. The growing identification of Jesus of Nazareth with God in the early church conflicted with biblical monotheism, and the concept of tritheism was proposed.[2] For many Christians and theologians, biblical monotheism is an apparent and clear proposition that needs no discussion or clarification. This conviction is not, however, groundless. It is supported by many centuries of Christian belief and practice, and it can be supported by a passage from the Hebrew Bible. In Deut 6:4 we read the well-known *šəmaʿ yiśrāʾēl*, "Hear, O Israel." There it is confessed: "YHWH is our God, YHWH is one!"[3]

---

1. Alister E. McGrath, *Christian Theology: An Introduction* (Oxford: Blackwell, 1994), 205–46.
2. McGrath, *Christian Theology*, 246–69; see also Veli-Matti Kärkkäinen, *Trinity and Religious Pluralism: The Doctrine of the Trinity in Christian Theology of Religions* (London: Routledge, 2004).
3. On this text and its various interpretations, see now Oswald Loretz, *Des Gottes Einzigkeit: ein altorientalisches Argumentationsmodell zum 'Schma Jisrael'* (Darmstadt: Wissenschaftliche Buchgesellschaft, 1997); Nathan MacDonald, "The Date of the Shema (Deuteronomy 6: 4–5)," *JBL* 136 (2017): 765–82.

A Problem

The HB is not an unambiguously monotheistic book, and neither is the religion in ancient Israel to be seen as fully monotheistic. The HB refers to a variety of "other deities." In the book of Exodus, monotheism as such is not taught by Moses. A reading of the text suggests that Moses did not want to preach a particular idea about God to his people, but he wanted to witness his encounter with a liberating God acting in history. Moses preached about YHWH as a living divine being who saves his people and wants to live in a relationship with them. In other words, Moses wanted to witness about his encounter with God-the-Savior. He did not elaborate on the question of whether this was the only divine being in the whole universe. A few glimpses of other divine beings can be seen, especially in the book of Psalms. The Psalms in the HB strongly imply a symbol system in which only one God should be venerated. Here too, the "forces of nature" have been partly secularized, as can be inferred from the role of the "sun" in Pss 19 and 72.[4]

Some Psalms, however, relate to a symbol system in which more than one god *is* venerated. Psalms 58 and 82 contain the concept that YHWH stands among or above the other deities. Here YHWH is part of a heavenly council.[5] Of special interest is Ps 91. This hymn on trust among the dangers and threats of life mentions YHWH:

> He will cover you with his wings
> > You will be safe in his care
> His faithfulness will protect
> > And defend you.

But in verses 5 and 6 we read:

> You need not fear for the terror of the night
> > For the arrow that flies at daytime
> For the pestilence that goes around in the dark
> > Or the demon that destroys at midday.

---

4. See Martin Arneth, *"Sonne der Gerechtigkeit": Studien zur Solarisierung der Jahwe-Religion im Lichte von Psalm 72*, Beihefte zur Zeitschrift für altorientalische und biblische Rechtsgeschichte 1 (Wiesbaden: Harrassowitz, 2000).

5. Herbert Niehr, *Religionen in Israels Umwelt*, Neue Echter Bibel: Ergänzungsband zum Alten Testament 5 (Würzburg: Echter, 1998), 39; Martti Nissinen, "Prophets and the Divine Council," in *Kein Land für sich allein: Studien zum Kulturkontakt in Kanaan, Israel/Palästina und Ebirnâri für Manfred Weippert zum 65. Geburtstag*, ed. Ernst Axel Knauf and Ulrich Hübner, OBO 186 (Fribourg: Academic Press; Göttingen: Vandenhoeck & Ruprecht, 2002), 4–19.

These four nouns, "terror of the night," "arrow," "pestilence," and "midday demon," refer to threatening demons. Despite the partial secularization of the forces of nature that took place in the religion at state level in ancient Israel, these forces will still have been seen as demons at the level of personal life.[6] Life was not completely disenchanted in ancient Israel.

Another text to be mentioned in this connection is Ruth 1. During the well-known encounter at the border, when Naomi wants Ruth to return to her home country, Ruth declares (Ruth 1:16–17):

> But Ruth answered: "Do not ask me to leave you!
>   Let me go with you!
> Wherever you go,
>   I will go.
> Wherever you live,
>   I will live.
> Your people will be my people
>   And your *'elōhîm* will be my *'elōhîm*."[7]

I deliberately left the Hebrew word *'elōhîm* untranslated. The word can be construed as a singular form, "God," or as a plural, "gods." Most translations render with: "Your God will be my God," taking Ruth's vow as a monotheistic or at least a monolatrous confession. At the end of Ruth 1, however, two gods are mentioned. On return in Bethlehem, Naomi bewails her fate:

> YHWH has witnessed against me
>   And Shadday has made my life bitter.

Traditionally Shadday is rendered with "the Almighty," taking the name as a qualification or an attribute of YHWH. Religio-historical research, however, has made clear that Shadday is the name of a divine being that had been venerated at the fringes of ancient Near Eastern agricultural societies.[8] For Naomi, Shadday has left her with her bitterness instead of protecting her against the evils of time.

---

6. G. J. Riley, "Midday Demon," in *DDD*, 572–73; Meir Malul, "Terror of the Night," in *DDD*, 850–55; Erhard Gerstenberger, *Theologies in the Old Testament*, trans. John Bowden (Minneapolis: Fortress, 2002), 36. For the contrary opinion, see Judit M. Blair, *De-Demonising the Old Testament: An Investigation of Azazel, Lilith, Deber, Qeteb and Reshef in the Hebrew Bible*, FAT 2.37 (Tübingen: Mohr Siebeck, 2009).

7. On Ruth 1:16–7, see, e.g., Kirsten Nielsen, *Ruth*, OTL (London: SCM, 1997), 49–50; Marjo C. A. Korpel, *The Structure of the Book of Ruth*, Pericope 2 (Assen: Gorcum, 2001), 48–90; Anne-Mareike Wetter, *"On Her Account": Reconfiguring Israel in Ruth, Esther, and Judith*, LHBOTS 623 (London: Bloomsbury, 2015), 56–60.

8. See Ernst Axel Knauf, "Shadday," in *DDD*, 749–53; Wetter, *"On Her Account,"* 56–60; Norman Habel, "The *deus absconditus* of Elihu," *Lutheran Theological Journal* 50 (2016): 96–105.

More Than One God? 63

I would like to round off this short tour through personal religion by referring to the "teraphim" (תרפים). They are mentioned in stories that play in the private sphere of life[9] and most probably were ancestor deities that were believed to protect against all threats.[10]

The Aramaic documents from Elephantine make clear that the local Yehudite community venerated other deities next to YHWH. In Elephantine a very interesting document was found dating to the year 419 BCE.[11] This document lists donations for the temple. After the date, the text starts as follows:

These are the names of the Yehud Garrison, who gave silver for the god Yahô.[12]

The document lists around a hundred persons. Most have specifically Hebrew names such as Hoshea, Nathan, or Yahô-containing theophoric personal names such as Zephaniah and Zebadiah. The end of the list, however, contains a surprise. As expected, such a list would be completed with a sum: "so and so much shekel/silver for Yahô." This list ends quite unexpectedly:

126	In it: for Yahô:	126 Shekel
127	For Eshembethel:	70 Shekel
128	For Anathbethel:	120 Shekel Silver.[13]

This note implies that two deities, Eshembethel and Anathbethel, were connected to the temple of Yahô in Elephantine. Bezalel Porten has tried to explain this fact by assuming that Eshembethel and Anathbethel were worshiped by "non-Jews."[14] But such an assumption does not explain why the deities then appear in a list for the temple of Yahô. In addition, these deities are mentioned elsewhere in the documents from Elephantine.[15]

---

9. E.g.: Gen 31; Judg 17–18; 1 Sam 15.
10. See Karel van der Toorn, "The Nature of the Biblical Teraphim in the Light of the Cuneiform Evidence," *CBQ* 52 (1990): 203–22; Oswald Loretz, "Die Teraphim als 'Ahnen-Götter-Figur(in)en' im Lichte der Texte aus Nuzi, Emar und Ugarit," *UF* 24 (1992): 133–78; Theodore J. Lewis, "Theraphim," in *DDD*, 844–50; Ziony Zevit, *The Religions of Ancient Israel: A Synthesis of Parallactic Approaches* (London: Continuum, 2003), 255–56; Gerstenberger, *Theologies*, 41–42.
11. *TADAE* C3.15.
12. *TADAE* C3.15:1.
13. *TADAE* C3.15 vii:126–28; see, e.g., Urs Winter, *Frau und Göttin: exegetische und ikonographische Studien zum weiblichen Gottesbild im Alten Israel und in dessen Umwelt*, OBO 53 (Fribourg: Academic Press; Göttingen: Vandenhoeck & Ruprecht, 1983), 496–97.
14. Bezalel Porten, *Archives from Elephantine: The Life of an Ancient Jewish Colony* (Berkeley: University of California Press, 1968), 163n41.
15. Anat-Yahô in the oath text: *TADAE* B7.3. See Porten, *Archives*, 109nn154–56; Winter, *Frau und Göttin*, 497–98. Ḥerembethel in another oath-text: *TADAE* B7.2. See also Winter, *Frau und Göttin*, 498. The god Eshembethel is not mentioned elsewhere in documents from Elephantine.

The archaeology of Israel/Palestine has revealed many important artifacts these last decades. I will mention two groups of finds in this connection:

1. The abundance of so-called pillar-figurines[16] and
2. The uncovering of Paleo-Hebrew inscriptions at Kuntillet ʿAjrud and Khirbet el-Qom containing the phrase "I bless you by Yahweh and his Asherah."[17]

Blessing is a feature of religion at the level of family life. I interpret both these finds as indications that, in the religious symbol system at the family level, a deity Asherah played an important role. At this level she is not so much the transcendent "Queen of Heaven" as she is a protecting *dea nutrix* that could be invoked in times of danger and despair, especially in the process of giving birth. The breasts so manifestly present in many pillar figurines should not be construed as an erotic symbol but as the heavenly milk that mother earth has given to the poor and the needy.

All this evidence provokes a question. How did the ancient Israelites/Judeans cope with the apparent contradiction between belief system and reality? I will argue that three different models can be detected.

Intolerant Monotheism

Traces of intolerant monotheism can be easily found in the HB. There are various texts that refer to a monotheistic belief system, such as the oneness creed in Deut 6:4 or the texts in the second part of Isaiah. In Isa 40 and onward, YHWH receives praise as the only deity worthy of the Israelites' reverence. A striking text is the following:

The name assumedly occurs three times in the Palmyra section of P. Amh. 63 (Karel van der Toorn, ed., *Papyrus Amherst 63*, Alter Orient und Altes Testament 448 [Münster: Ugarit-Verlag, 2018]), xvi 1, 14–15: *'šbtylG*. See also Karel van der Toorn, "Eshem-Bethel and Herem-Bethel: New Evidence from Amherst Papyrus 63," *ZAW* 128 (2016): 668–80.

16. See mainly Thomas A. Holland, "A Typological and Archaeological Study of Human and Animal Representations in the Plastic Art of Palestine during the Iron Age" (DPhil, Oxford University, 1975); see also Raz Kletter, "Between Archaeology and Theology: The Pillar Figurines from Judah and the Asherah," in *Studies in the Archaeology of the Iron Age in Israel and Jordan*, ed. Amihai Mazar, JSOTSup 331 (Sheffield: Sheffield Academic, 2001), 197–216.

17. The inscriptions can be found in Johannes Renz, *Text und Kommentar*, vol. 1. of *Die althebräischen Inschriften*, Handbuch der althebräischen Epigraphik 2.1 (Darmstadt: Wissenschaftliche Buchgesellschaft, 1995), 47–64, 202–11; see also Karl Jaroš, *Inschriften des Heiligen Landes aus vier Jahrtausenden* (Mainz: Zabern, 2001), CD-ROM, nos. 93, 112. There is an abundance of secondary literature on these inscriptions.

> Thus says the LORD, the King of Israel
>   and his Redeemer, the LORD of hosts:
> "I am the first and I am the last;
>   besides me there is no god.
> Who is like me? Let him proclaim it.
>   Let him declare and set it before me,
> since I appointed an ancient people.
>   Let them declare what is to come, and what will happen.
> Fear not, nor be afraid;
>   have I not told you from of old and declared it?
> And you are my witnesses!
>   Is there a God besides me?
> There is no Rock;
>   I know not any." (Isa 44:6–8)

The "other gods" are set aside as having been manufactured by humankind. Veneration of them is hence misleading, as in a passage from the book of Jeremiah:

> A tree from the forest is cut down
>   and worked with an axe by the hands of a craftsman.
> They decorate it with silver and gold;
>   they fasten it with hammer and nails
>   so that it cannot move.
> Their idols are like scarecrows in a cucumber field,
>   and they cannot speak;
> they have to be carried,
>   for they cannot walk.
> Do not be afraid of them,
>   for they cannot do evil,
>   neither is it in them to do good. (Jer 10:3–5)

Jeremiah 44 presents an interesting example of intolerant monotheism. When the text emerged and by whom it was written will not detain us here.[18] The text relates the adventures of a group of Judeans who sought refuge in Egypt after the fall of Jerusalem in 587 BCE. The text focuses on their confrontation with the prophet Jeremiah. The starting point is a Jeremianic prophecy of doom that

---

18. For an introduction to the scholarly discussion, see William L. Holladay, *Jeremiah 2: A Commentary on the Book of the Prophet Jeremiah Chapters 26–52*, Hermeneia (Minneapolis: Fortress, 1989), 280–87.

consists of two parts: The first part (vv. 2–10) contains a retrospective view on the recent events that both Jeremiah and the group of Judeans went through. The second part of the prophecy (vv. 11–15) foresees the doom they will encounter in Egypt. After this first prophecy, the word is given to the Judeans who relate their view on the immediate past (vv. 15–19). The unit closes with a repetition of the prophecy of doom in even more bitter words (vv. 20–30).

In this confrontation, the veneration of the "Queen of Heaven" is a bone of contention. The identity of this goddess is not completely clear. Most probably she can be equated with Asherah. This identification is supported by the fact that the HB sometimes indicates YHWH by the epithet "King of Heaven."[19] By analogy, some could have referred to Asherah, as consort of the main deity, as "Queen of Heaven."[20]

Of interest here are the two retrospectives of Jeremiah and of the Judeans. They relate roughly the same events, but each from a different perspective. The events are the siege and capture of Jerusalem by the armies of the Babylonian king Nebuchadnezzar II and the finding of refuge in Egypt. These events brought about the end of the autonomous kingdom of Judah and the worship of YHWH in the temple allegedly built by Solomon. Jeremiah relates and interprets these events from a prophetic perspective. He can be construed as offering a characteristic representative of exclusive monotheism. Within the parameters of his belief system, the sack of Jerusalem should not be seen as the outcome of interplay between political, military, and economic forces. To Jeremiah, the catastrophe of 587 BCE spells out the wrath of YHWH, provoked by the guilt of the people of Judah. Jeremiah, as witnessed by the biblical book bearing his name, condemned the inhabitants of Judah and Jerusalem for worshiping "other gods" and for neglecting prophetic warnings. Strangely enough, after finding refuge in the Egyptian exile, the Judeans continued their "evil ways." As if they meant no harm, they went on venerating "other deities" in a way that provoked Jeremiah's prophecy of doom: even in Egypt they cannot escape the punishing wrath of YHWH.

This prophecy catalyzes a reaction from the Judeans who had fled to Egypt. They have a different evaluation of the recent events. In their plea, they develop the following argument:

> The word which you have spoken to us in the name of YHWH—
> we are not listening to you,

---

19. See, e.g., Lowell K. Handy, *Among the Hosts of Heaven: The Syrian-Phoenician Pantheon as Bureaucracy* (Winona Lake, IN: Eisenbrauns, 1994); Jan A. Wagenaar, "King," in *DDD*, 483–86.

20. See Cornelis Houtman, "Queen of Heaven," in *DDD*, 678–80; Judith Hadley, "The Queen of Heaven: Who is She?," in *Prophets and Daniel: A Feminist Companion to the Bible*, ed. Athalya Brenner (Sheffield: Sheffield Academic, 2001), 30–51.

instead we shall do every word that comes forth from our mouth,
    to offer sacrifices to the Queen of Heaven
and to offer her drink offerings, just as we and our fathers,
our kings and our officials did,
in the cities of Judah and the streets of Jerusalem;
and we ate enough bread,
and we were well off, and evil we did not see.
But since we stopped offering sacrifices to the Queen of Heaven
[and offering drink offerings to her],
we have lacked everything,
and by sword and by famine we have been consumed. (Jer 44:16–18)[21]

They have a different view as to the cause of the destruction of Jerusalem. To them the catastrophe is not the outcome of their continued veneration of "other deities" but results from a breach in what they construe as legitimate religion. They communicate the fact that from times of old they have worshiped the Queen of Heaven. At some point they stopped this veneration. Most probably this should be interpreted as a reference to the cult reformation under King Josiah. 2 Kings 22–23 narrate how this king of Judah reacted to the discovery of a law-book in the temple of Jerusalem. After finding this book of law—which most probably contained the kernel of what is now the book of Deuteronomy—Shaphan the royal secretary reads it aloud to the king. Josiah then takes drastic measures: the worship of YHWH must be concentrated in the temple of Jerusalem. All other sanctuaries throughout the land are declared illegitimate. Next, the cult is purified of strange and foreign elements. It is plausible that, in that process, the veneration of Asherah and/or the Queen of Heaven was banned. The Judeans whom Jeremiah confronts in Egypt understand the ruination of Jerusalem and their exile to Egypt as the consequence of this cult reformation. Their abandonment of the worship of the Queen of Heaven has caused the disfavor of this goddess. Ending their offerings to this deity has, in their perception, ended her protection, patronage, and blessing of the people of Judah, with catastrophic results. To regain the blessing of the Queen of Heaven, they start to appease her by bringing offerings.

Both Jeremiah and the Judeans appeal to history as an argument for their case. These Judeans interpret recent events from a different perspective than Jeremiah. Both apply their belief system when constructing history. Who is right? That is an unanswerable question. Many readers of the HB are inclined to side with Jeremiah. The Judeans produce a consistent view. Nevertheless,

---

21. See Holladay, *Jeremiah 2*, 279; Keith Bodner, *After the Invasion: A Reading of Jeremiah 40–44* (Oxford: Oxford University Press, 2015), 127–47.

many readers of Jer 44 will not accept their view. This denial of their view arises because many readers think that the belief system of Jeremiah is more in accordance with what they themselves believe to be appropriate and legitimate. In fact two choices are involved: first, Jeremiah's choice, and then later, the Jewish and the Christian traditions, which assent to his choice. Finally, I would like to remark that the example of Jer 44 has again shown that belief in YHWH was not a static state, but a dynamic process. Time and again, the historical dynamics and development of faith are detectable. The ultimately unknowable that many call God has undergone various and tentative definitions.

Many more examples could have been quoted to support the existence of the YHWH-alone movement.[22] All these texts have a clear message: the earth in its entirety is summoned to venerate YHWH. This belief system can be classified as exclusive monotheism, since it presents the veneration of one deity, YHWH, as the only possibility for all human beings. Although other deities might have received veneration from some people, these deities are seen as powerless entities. It needs no argument that the position of intolerant monotheism could be abused for religiously motivated violence.

Conditional Acceptance

Within the HB itself, a second model is identifiable; I would label it as conditional acceptance. Important parts of the HB imply a belief system that can be classified as monolatry, mono-Yahwism, or inclusive monotheism. "Monolatry" means recognizing the existence and value of other gods but discouraging their veneration by the members of the community. The concept of mono-Yahwism presupposes the possibility that the veneration of YHWH differed from region to region in ancient Israel. Rainer Albertz has called this phenomenon "religionsinterner pluralismus" (religion-internal pluralism).[23] The archaeological discovery of the "YHWH and his Asherah" inscriptions has increased the plausibility of this model.

The idea of "monolatry" requires further clarification. The Ten Commandments open in both biblical versions with the exhortation not to venerate other deities (Exod 20; Deut 5). These words acknowledge the existence and possibility of worshipping other deities but preclude this practice for Israelites.

---

22. The term was coined by Bernhard Lang in *Monotheism and the Prophetic Minority: An Essay in Biblical History and Sociology*, Social World of Biblical Antiquity 1 (Sheffield: Almond, 1983).

23. Rainer Albertz, *Religionsgeschichte Israels in alttestamentlicher Zeit*, Grundisse zum Alten Testament 8/1–2 (Göttingen: Vandenhoeck & Ruprecht, 1992), 41–43; Rainer Albertz and Rüdiger Schmitt, *Family and Household Religion in Ancient Israel and the Levant* (Winona Lake, IN: Eisenbrauns, 2012), 46–56.

Monolatry supposes that, among the abundance of deities, only one God should be venerated. An interesting example in this connection is Judg 11:24:

Will you not possess what Chemosh your god gives you to possess?

In this report on the exploits of Jephthah, one passage mentions that the various ANE deities each had their own territory. Chemosh is presented as the god of the land of Moab. This text ascribes acts of salvation to Chemosh that are comparable to those YHWH had done for Israel. The idea of territorial limitation of the deity also underlies the following text:

When the most High divided to the nations their inheritance, when he separated the sons of Adam, he set the bounds of the people according to the number of the sons of God.[24]

This line from the Song of Moses refers to the concept that each of the sons of God had an inherited territory within which they should be venerated. The same idea is present in 2 Kgs 5. When the greed of Gehazi confronts Naaman after his healing, the Aramean military leader responds:

If not, please let there be given to your servant two mule loads of earth, for from now on your servant will not offer burnt offering or sacrifice to any god but YHWH. In this matter may YHWH pardon your servant: when my master goes into the house of Rimmon to worship there, leaning on my arm, and I bow myself in the house of Rimmon, when I bow myself in the house of Rimmon, YHWH pardon your servant in this matter.

Naaman's wish to take some of the soil of Israel home to Damascus reflects the belief that there is a clear connection between land and deity. By bringing some earth from Israel to his home, he symbolically carries the presence of the God of Israel beyond the border.

The condition limiting the acceptance of deities other than YHWH can be phrased as follows: to each country its own god, and for each deity their own community—*cuius regio eius religio*.[25] As long as the official cult was not polluted by the veneration of the gods of the nations, ancient Israel could live with

---

24. Deut 32:8; with the Septuagint and the Qumran documents, I prefer the reading "sons of God" over the Masoretic Text's "children of Israel," which can be seen as an adaptation to the monotheistic creed.

25. Summarizing the religious peace between Catholics and Protestants in Germany at the Council of Augsburg (1555 CE); see Axel Gotthard, *Der Augsburger Religionsfrieden*, Reformationsgeschichtliche Studien und Texte 148 (Münster: Aschendorff, 2004).

their existence. It stands to reason that this model has a diplomatic implication and consolidates peaceful relations between nations.

Lending Deities

The third model is not present in the HB, with the exception of the book of Ruth. In her passionate declaration that she will not return to Moab without Naomi, she expresses an intriguing belief system. Her adoption of the deities of her mother-in-law sounds like an example of lending a divinity. Outside the HB, this model is attested at Elephantine and in the text of Papyrus Amherst 63.

As I have argued in full elsewhere, two Aramaic documents from fifth-century-BCE Elephantine witness to this principle.[26] The first case is to be found in the heading of an unfinished letter written by Yarhu to his brother Haggai:

1. To my brother Haggai, your brother
2. Yarḥu. Peace to my brother
3. from Bel and Nabu, Shamash and Nergal.[27]

The brothers, Yarḥu and Haggai, were of Yehudite origin; yet this communication invokes Babylonian deities. This claim contains two assumptions that some scholarship has questioned: First, were the siblings Yehudite? And second, were the deities Babylonian? The personal name Haggai is known from the HB and should be construed as a hypocoristic form of the name "YHWH is my feast."[28] The name occurs on a few dozen Hebrew seals[29] and on a recently published Hebrew ostracon from the seventh century BCE.[30] Inscriptions from Elephantine and Syene refer to about ten individuals with the name Haggai.[31] It is quite clear that the personal name *yrḥw* refers to the West Semitic moon god *yrḥ*,

---

26. Bob Becking, "Exchange, Replacement, or Acceptance? Two Examples of Lending Deities among Ethnic Groups in Elephantine," in *Jewish Cultural Encounters in the Ancient Mediterranean and Near Eastern World*, ed. Mladen Popovic, Myles Schoonover, and Marijn Vandenberghe, Supplements to the Journal for the Study of Judaism 178 (Leiden: Brill, 2017), 30–43.

27. *TADAE* D7.30 :1–3; see Hélène Lozachmeur, *La collection Clermont-Ganneau: Ostraca, épigraphes sur jarre, étiquettes de bois*, Mémoires présentés à de l'Académie des inscriptions et belles-lettres 35, 2 vols. (Paris: De Boccard 2006), no. 277.

28. Hag 1–2; Ezra 5:1; 6:14.

29. For a list, see *Dictionary of Classical Hebrew*, ed. David J. A. Clines, 9 vols. (Sheffield: Sheffield Phoenix, 1993–2014), 3:159–160.

30. André Lemaire and Ada Yardeni, "New Hebrew Ostraca from the Shephalah," in *Biblical Hebrew in Its Northwest Semitic Setting: Typological and Historical Perspectives*, ed. Steven E. Fassberg and Avi Hurvitz, Publication of the Institute for Advanced Studies, Hebrew University of Jerusalem 1 (Jerusalem: Magnes, 2006), 215–17; ostr. 12.2.

31. See already André Dupont-Sommer, "'Bêl et Nabû, Šamaš et Nergal' sur un ostracon araméen inédit d'Éléphantine," *Revue de l'histoire des religions* 128 (1944): 28–39, at 31.

whose name occurs as a theophoric element in Ugaritic, Phoenician, and West Semitic personal names.[32] I would, however, refer to the fact that Gen 10:26 and 1 Chr 1:26 list the name *yeraḥ* among the decedents of Eber as an indication that Yarḥu could easily have been a Yehudite.[33]

The letterhead under consideration is not unique for Elephantine in containing the names of other deities. Various letters from the archives of Elephantine—both for inner-group and for intra-group communications—include salutations that bless the recipient by various deities. In the letter of a certain Giddel to his master Michayah, Yahô and Khnum appear in parallel:

I send you peace and wellbeing. I bless you by Yahô and Khnum.[34]

This formula gives the impression that both deities were of equal importance. In addition, several letters have been found that are written by people with Yahô-containing names, but which also bless the recipient by a plurality of deities:

May all deities seek your well-being at all times.[35]

The collective language of "deities" in these letter formulae is probably not meaningful for the question of the complexity of the Yehudite pantheon in Elephantine. The supporting documents are too general and too formal.[36] The formula is also attested in non-Yehudite letters:

May a[l]l deities seek after the welfare of my brothers at all times.[37]

This piece of evidence suggests that the phrase under consideration was part of the standard letter matrix of the scribes in Elephantine. The letter by Yarḥu to

---

32. See, e.g., Frauke Gröndahl, *Die Personennamen der Texte aus Ugarit*, Studia Pohl 1 (Rome: Biblical Institute, 1967), 145; Frank L. Benz, *Personal Names in the Phoenician and Punic Inscriptions*, Studia Pohl 8 (Rome: Biblical Institute Press, 1978), 326.

33. See also Dupont-Sommer, "'Bêl et Nabû,'" 31–32.

34. *TADAE* D7.21.

35. E.g., *TADAE* A3.7, A4.2, A4.4, and D1.13. See Porten, *Archives*, 158–60; Dirk Schwiderski, *Handbuch des nordwestsemitischen Briefformulars: ein Beitrag zur Echtheitsfrage der aramäischen Briefe des Esrabuches*, Beihefte zur Zeitschrift für altorientalische und biblische Rechtsgeschichte 295 (Berlin: de Gruyter, 2000), 130–37.

36. See also Herbert Niehr, *Der höchste Gott: alttestamentlicher JHWH-Glaube im Kontext syrisch-kanaänischer Religion des 1. Jahrtausends v. Chr.*, BZAW 190 (Berlin: de Gruyter, 1990), 48.

37. E.g., *TADAE* A3.10:1 (Spentadata—probably a Persian name—to "his brothers" Ḥori and Peṭemachis—both Egyptian; see Bezalel Porten, "The Aramaic Boat Papyrus (P. Ber. 23000): New Collation," *Or* 57 [1988]: 76–78) and *TADAE* A5.3 (Paḥim—probably West Semitic or Arabic—to Mithravahisht, a Persian). In general, see Bezalel Porten, "The Address Formulae in Aramaic Letters: A New Collation of Cowley 17," *RB* 90 (1983): 396–415.

his brother Haggai is unique in the sense that four deities of Babylonian origin are mentioned.

The deities invoked in the letterhead are Babylonian in origin.[38] They occur often as a pair in texts from the Persian period onward.[39] All these texts were written within a multi-ethnic context, a fact implying that the four Babylonian deities mentioned do not refer to specific deities, but to the divine realm as such. All in all, the letterhead in question can be understood as evidence for an open society in which it was acceptable to use the names of deities originating in other religious traditions in order to refer to the divine realm in general.

The second example from Elephantine of the phenomenon of lending deities occurs in two documents that describe the sale of a house and an oath in connection to that sale. The two legal documents refer to a quarrel about a piece of land between Dargamana, a Khwarezmian, and the Yehudite Mahseiah son of Jedaniah. Both men were wealthy, though they belonged to different ethnic backgrounds. Since we are informed only by two documents, it is difficult to reconstruct their quarrel in detail. What is clear is a conflict between two house owners whose properties in the more well-to-do neighborhood of Elephantine adjoined one another. The ownership of Dargamana, however, seems to be disputed. The case is brought to a court presided over by Damidata, a Persian judge. This first document presents a withdrawal of his legal claim by Dargamana.[40] The Khwarezmian, who had earlier claimed ownership to a certain house with land, attests that he is now convinced of Mahseiah's legal ownership. The turning point in the legal procedure had not been the presentation of a legal

---

38. See the relevant entries in *DDD*.

39. E.g., Cyrus Cylinder, ll. 20–22 and 30–35; Amélie Kuhrt, *The Persian Empire: A Corpus of Sources from the Achaemenid Period* (London: Routledge, 2007), 70–74; see now Irving L. Finkel, ed., *The Cyrus Cylinder: The King of Persia's Proclamation from Ancient Babylon* (London: Tauris, 2013), with a new translation in the appendix. See also a legal document from 515 BCE: BM 27797 (see Ran Zadok, "The Geography of the Borsippa Region," in *Essays on Ancient Israel in its Near Eastern Context: A Tribute to Nadav Na'aman*, ed. Yaira Amit, Ehud ben Zvi, Israel Finkelstein, and Oded Lipschits [Winona Lake, IN: Eisenbrauns, 2006], 389–453, at 407); an early Hellenistic funerary stele found in Daskyleion in Northwestern Anatolia (see André Dupont-Sommer, "Une inscription araméenne inédite d'époque perse trouvée à Daskyléion (Turquie)," *Comptes rendus de l'Académie des inscriptions et belles-lettres* 110 [1966]: 44–57, and F. M. Cross, "An Aramaic Inscription from Daskyleion," *BASOR* 184 [1966]: 7–10); late calendrical texts from Hellenistic Uruk containing the description for clothing ceremonies (*lubuštu*) of Bel, Nabu, and others (see George A. Reisner, *Sumerisch-babylonische Hymnen nach Thontafeln griechischer Zeit* [Berlin: W. Spemann, 1896], nos. 8 and 56); a spell in a Mandaic text (see Matthew Morgenstern, "Mandaic Magic Bowls in the Moussaieff Collection: A Preliminary Survey," in *New Inscriptions and Seals Relating to the Biblical World*, ed. Meir Lubetski, ABS 19 [Atlanta: Society of Biblical Literature, 2012], 157–70).

40. *TADAE* B2.2; see Alejandro F. Botta, *The Aramaic and Egyptian Legal Traditions at Elephantine: An Egyptological Approach*, Library of Second Temple Studies 64 (London: T & T Clark, 2009), 124–26; Collin Cornell, "The Forgotten Female Figurines of Elephantine," *Journal of Ancient Near Eastern Religions* 18 (2018): 111–32, at 123–24.

document of sorts by Mahseiah, but an oath that the Yehudite swore. The court had forced Mahseiah to take an oath:

You swore to me by Yahô, and satisfied my heart about that land.[41]

Thereupon Dargamana cancels his prior claims. Some five years later, Mahseiah bequests this plot of land and the building upon it to his daughter Mibtaiah. In the cadastral boundaries in the document of that bequest, it states that "above it [= the land of Mahseiah/Mibtaiah] the house of Dargamana the son of Xvarshaina adjoins."[42] Most probably Dargamana had become owner of an adjacent plot. Two aspects of this text deserve discussion.

To swear an oath is a performative act. Swearing by a deity is a precarious and daring speech-act.[43] The practice of swearing an oath was well-known in the ANE, including Pharaonic Egypt.[44] The oath-taker indirectly invokes the deity as an observing witness to the case. Ancient Egyptians, Persians, Israelites, and Khwarezmians respected the divine realm as a powerful reality. This implies that the contents of Mahseiah's oath were understood as truth. The oath goes beyond a mere declaration; it signifies that Mahseiah's statements could never be a lie. In case these words turned out not to be true, the court and the disputants expected the deity to punish the liar.[45] It should be noted that swearing by the deity of another group within Elephantine was not uncommon.[46] On a legal document of withdrawal from goods, the Yehudite woman Mibtaiah—a daughter of Mahseiah—satisfied the heart of her opponent, the Egyptian Peu, by swearing an oath by Sati. The goddess Sati, an alternative spelling of the divine name Satet, was the deification of the flooding of the Nile. She was also venerated as the protective deity of southern Egypt.[47] The act of swearing by the deity of the other party should not be construed as an act of conversion to the religion of the other, but rather as a peaceful acceptance of the religious values of the other and the power of the divine being that she or he venerated.

As a result of the swearing of the oath, Dargamana states that his heart is satisfied. The expression here is used in an active construction: *y-ṭ-b ha+lbb*+suff.:

---

41. *TADAE* B2.2:11–12.
42. *TADAE* B2.3:5–6.
43. Karel van der Toorn, "Ḥerem-Bethel and Elephantine Oath Procedure," *ZAW* 98 (1986): 282–85; van der Toorn, "Anat-Yahu, Some Other Deities, and the Jews of Elephantine," *Numen* 39 (1992): 80–101.
44. John A. Wilson, "The Oath in Ancient Egypt," *JNES* 7 (1948): 129–56; Blane Conklin, *Oath Formulas in Biblical Hebrew*, Linguistic Studies in Ancient West Semitic 5 (Winona Lake, IN: Eisenbrauns, 2011).
45. Conklin, *Oath Formulas*.
46. See already Hedwig Anneler, *Zur Geschichte der Juden von Elephantine* (Bern: Drechsel, 1912), 39.
47. *TADAE* B2.8.

"to make good/content the heart of X."[48] The oath of Mahseiah has set the uncertainties of Dargamana at rest, so that he is satisfied as well as contented. The expression—cognates of which occur in Aramaic, Akkadian, and Demotic texts—indicates remuneration, especially in texts that describe the transfer of goods. In the text under consideration, the phrase refers to the fact that the claimant is content and that there is no longer a bone of contention between him and Mahseiah.

It is my assumption that, in the texts mentioned, the oath is taken in front of the deity—or deities—of the more important partner in the quarrel. If this is correct, then Mahseiah possessed higher social standing than Dargamana. The text does not imply that Dargamana converted to Judaism—or to its predecessor. The text confirms the acceptance of a deity of someone else as an observing witness to a human agreement. As such, it represents a form of religious acceptance that was without problems and limited by no conditions.

My final example for this model is derived from an enigmatic text: Papyrus Amherst 63. This papyrus was found in an unknown place in Egypt. The Demotic text can be dated to the last part of the fourth century BCE. The contents evince a syncretistic form of religion from an earlier age.[49] The text consists of five sections. The first three sections can be connected to ethnic groups: Babylonians (cols. i–v), Syrians (cols. vi–xi), and Israelites (col. xii).[50] I would prefer to label the third section as Israelite and not as Samarian, as Karel van der Toorn suggests.[51] The fourth section (cols. xiv–xvii) is situated in a *ḥlt's's* | *tm'r*, ("fortress of palms"), to be identified with either Palmyra,[52] Tayma,[53] or Jericho.[54] This fourth section clearly witnesses to the peaceful living together of

---

48. See Yochanan Muffs, *Studies in the Aramaic Legal Papyri from Elephantine*, Handbuch der Orientalistik 66 (Leiden: Brill, 2003), 27–194; Botta, *Aramaic and Egyptian Legal Traditions*, 125.

49. See Raik Heckl, "Inside the Canon and Out: The Relationship Between Psalm 20 and Papyrus Amherst 63," *Semitica* 56 (2014): 359–79; van der Toorn, *Papyrus Amherst 63*.

50. The absence of the delimitor *sp.C* at the end of col. xi might be an indication that col. xii 1–11, a mockery by the victors over a destructed city, could be the final part of the Syrian section, and hence should not be treated as a reflection on the conquest of Samaria by the Assyrians. On the delimitor *sp.C*, probably *s'k* | *p'r'š'H* (סך פרשא; "end of section"), see Sven P. Vleeming and Jan W. Wesselius, "Betel the Saviour," *Jaarbericht van het Vooraziatisch-Egyptisch Gezelschap (Genootschap) Ex Oriente Lux* 28 (1983): 110–40, at 136; van der Toorn, *Papyrus Amherst 63*, 6.

51. Van der Toorn, *Papyrus Amherst 63*.

52. P. Amh. 63, xvi 7; van der Toorn, *Papyrus Amherst 63*, 18–37.

53. This oasis was part of the area controlled by the Qedarites and was a centre for Arabian trade routes. The neo-Babylonian king Nabonidus stayed in the oasis for many years; see Paul-Alain Beaulieu, *The Reign of Nabonidus, King of Babylon (556–539 BC)*, Yale Near Eastern Researches 10 (New Haven: Yale University Press, 1989). In the late classical period, a group of Jews lived in Tayma; see Gordon D. Newby, *A History of the Jews of Arabia: From Ancient Times to Their Eclipse under Islam*, Studies in Comparative Religion (Columbia: University of South Carolina Press, 1988).

54. In the HB, Jericho is referred to as *'îr hattəmārîm* "city of palms" (Deut 34:3; Judg 1:16; 3:13; 2 Chr 28:15).

the ethnic groups mentioned. The section has an obviously syncretistic subtext. The final, fifth section (cols. xviii–xxiii) is a kind of appendix, and it contains the "tale of two brothers," a narrative on the fate of the Neo-Assyrian king Ashurbanipal and his brother Shamas-shumu-ukin.[55] Since the Aramaic of Papyrus Amherst 63 does not contain Persianisms or Persian loanwords—as for instance the majority of the Elephantine documents and the Aramaic sections in the biblical books of Ezra and Daniel—and since the text does not refer to Egypt,[56] it can safely be assumed that the text stems from a period between the end of the reign of Ashurbanipal[57] and the Persian conquest of the ANE.[58] The text was not, however, recovered in the "fortress of palms," but somewhere in Egypt. The provocative question of how this text ended up in the Land of the Nile will not be discussed here.

One may assume that the text of Papyrus Amherst functioned as a unifying catalyst for the various ethnic groups living in the "fortress of palms." The text indicates that the deities of these groups were seen as on par and all as manifestations of the divinity named *mry* (מר), "Lord," the Aramaic noun for a divine being comparable to *ba'al* or *'ādôn*, and attested throughout the text.

The unconditional acceptance of deities from ethnic groups with whom people lived together in a community also lies behind a blessing in the Syrian section of Papyrus Amherst 63:

All the gods will bless you.
The Lord will bless you from Rash
   The Lady will bless you from Siryon
Baal will bless you from Zaphon
   Pidraya will bless you from the Orontes
Bel with bless you from Babylon
   Belet will bless you from Esağil
Nabû will bless you from Barsippa
   Nanay will bless you from the sanctuary

---

55. First edition by Richard C. Steiner and Charles F. Nims, "Ashurbanipal and Shamash-shum-ukin: *A Tale of Two Brothers* from the Aramaic Text in Demotic Script," *RB* 92 (1985): 60–81.

56. With the exception of P. Amh. 63, xx 4 where in a list of tribute, mention is made of "wonderful linen from Egypt."

57. Since the Tale of Two Brothers in P. Amh. 63 is obviously dependant on the description of the deeds and doings of Ashurbanipal in his Royal Inscriptions, a date in the seventh century of this fifth section can be assumed. See Ingo Kottsieper, "Die literarische Aufnahme assyrischer Begebenheiten in frühen aramäischen Texten," in *La circulation des biens, des personnes et des idées dans le Proche-Orient ancien: Actes de la XXXVIIIe Rencontre Assyriologique Internationale (Paris, 8–10 juillet 1991)*, ed. Francis Joannès and Dominique Charpin (Paris: Editions Recherche sur les Civilisations, 1992), 283–89; van der Toorn, *Papyrus Amherst 63*, 37.

58. See also van der Toorn, *Papyrus Amherst 63*, 37–39.

> Will bless you throne-of-Yahô
> and Asherah from the south.[59]

The penitent invokes a plethora of divine couples for blessing. The text gives the impression that these gods from all corners of the world, venerated by the various ethnic groups at the "fortress of the palms," are on par and interchangeable. The impression emerges that these deities were seen as expressions of a shared divine realm and could be loaned between the different ethnic groups.

The model of lending deities is an expression of a liberal open-mindedness toward the other. It is clear that this model was connected to a situation in which various ethnic lived together in a peaceful harmony—or were forced to do so.

Conclusion

This contribution is neither a sermon nor a political pamphlet, but a description of the various ways in which Israelites found a way to bridge the gap between the monotheistic creed and the realities of religious pluriformity confronting them in the era before the coming of Alexander the Great. I will not utter a preference for one of the three models. Such a preference should not be the choice of an individual made in the safe serenity of a study room, but a way in which religious communities all over the world have to negotiate their religious identity in a pluriform and global cultural landscape.

---

59. P. Amh. 63 viii 1–7; see van der Toorn, *Papyrus Amherst 63*, 125–27.

CHAPTER 4

Who Is Like You Among the Gods? Some Observations on Configuring YHWH in the Old Testament

J. Andrew Dearman

YHWH (יהוה), THE GOD OF ISRAEL, portrayed in the Old Testament or Tanak as the supreme deity of all creation, has responsibilities and characteristics that are typically distributed among various deities in the ancient Near East. His identity, therefore, like that of the supreme deity Marduk in the Enuma Elish, is constructed through a "convergence" of some characteristics common to other ANE deities and a "differentiation" from them in other aspects of his persona.[1]

Convergence and differentiation, or related dynamics in the portrayal of a deity, are constituent elements in most taxonomies of religion, and they are thus helpful in considering the identity of an ANE deity in its cultural matrix. Understanding that cultural matrix, in turn, is necessary for theological analysis and the work of translating and assessing an ancient identity in a new context. "Convergence" can mean anything from the cults of distinct deities merely sharing terminology and practices to the complete assimilation and absorption of one deity by another. "Differentiation" in portrayal can range from barely perceptible differences all the way to complete uniqueness in conception and practices. An enduring religious movement typically displays both continuity with its cultural setting and tensions that define its particular identity within that setting.[2] In the matter of YHWH's identity, the dynamics of convergence variously underscore continuity with aspects of the larger ANE culture, as seen in text, artifact, and cult. Differentiation vis-à-vis other ANE deities represents part of a particularizing process on Israel's part as it portrayed its national deity as singular among the gods.

---

1. This use of the terms "convergence" and "differentiation" comes from Mark S. Smith, *The Early History of God: Yahweh and the Other Deities in Ancient Israel* (Grand Rapids: Eerdmans, 2002) and *The Origins of Biblical Monotheism: Israel's Polytheistic Background and the Ugaritic Texts* (New York: Oxford University Press, 2001). See also Smith, *God in Translation: Deities in Cross-Cultural Discourse in the Biblical World* (Grand Rapids: Eerdmans, 2008), where he discusses "translatability" and "non-translatability" in the representation of ANE deities. For additional perspectives, see the collected essays in *The Origins of Yahwism*, ed. Jürgen van Oorschot and Markus Witte, BZAW 484 (Berlin: de Gruyter, 2017).

2. Rodney Stark, "Why Religious Movements Succeed or Fail: A Revised General Model," *Journal of Contemporary Religion* 11 (1996): 133–46.

In what follows, I want to look first at the most commonly used terminology for deity in the OT/Tanak from the perspectives of convergence and differentiation. The texts show clear patterns of each in broad measure. Part 1 of the present essay looks briefly at some basic terminology, arranged in three categories. Part 2 looks at these same dynamics at work in samples from the "master"/"lordship" semantic field (*'ādôn*; *ba'al*) used of YHWH.[3] This latter topic also allows a brief look at the most common epithets for YHWH, and thus another perspective on basic terminology for deity in the OT.

We might think of such an approach as a type of canonical analysis for theological assessment, concentrating as it does on the OT rather than on extrabiblical textual or artifactual data, or even on the prehistory of the biblical texts, but it is also a basic look at terminology for deity in an ANE collection of texts. To adapt the proverbial metaphor of seeing a forest or trees, we first want to look briefly at some broad patterns of an ancient, vibrant forest, seen from a bird's-eye, as it were, instead of concentrating on the variety of its trees at ground level.

Part 1: Basic Terms for God in the OT/Tanak

YHWH as an 'elōhîm

I. YHWH is (the) God. In the OT, YHWH is designated as a "god"/"deity" (*'ēl*; *'elōhîm*; *'elôah*). As is well-known, these terms are semantically related and common West Semitic terms for deity in Hebrew morphology. In several aspects of their use in the OT, they are interchangeable. Such common terminology applied to YHWH, while helpful in seeing broad patterns of convergence, does not itself assume much by way of particular characteristics. As with the common English noun "god," these terms are still context-specific and require additional data to portray YHWH as a divine king, creator, judge, warrior, and so on.

YHWH is one deity among several called *'ēl* in the ANE. In the OT, the noun can be used in direct address ("God") or serve as an appellative in reference to a deity, YHWH or otherwise. And, as in other ANE texts, it occurs with epithets.[4] Interpreters have discussed not only the representation of various ANE *'ēl*

---

3. A foundational study of the terms for God in the OT is that of T. N. D. Mettinger, *In Search of God: The Meaning and Message of the Everlasting Names* (Minneapolis: Augsburg Fortress, 1988). See more recently Friedhelm Hartenstein, "Die Geschichte des JHWHs im Spiegel seiner Namen," in *Gott nennen: Gottes Namen und Gott als Name*, ed. Ingolf U. Dalferth and Phillip Stoellger, Religion in Philosophy and Theology 35 (Tübingen: Mohr Siebeck, 2008), 73–95.

4. See Gen 14:18–24, where YHWH is identified with "God most high [*'ēl 'elyôn*], creator of heaven and earth." The latter's expanded name contains epithets for deities used in various ANE texts. See Patrick D. Miller Jr., "El, The Creator of Earth," *BASOR* 230 (1980): 43–46.

traditions in the OT, but also whether one can discern indications of *'ēl* worship in early Israel separate from, or prior to, the worship of YHWH.[5] However we sort out this aspect of Israel's religious history diachronically, we must also take into account the basic lexical data for *'ēl* in the OT, where the noun is overwhelmingly an appellative with reference to deity/divinity, with Israel's God as the primary referent.[6] YHWH is the *'ēl* among the gods.

YHWH is *'elōhîm*. The noun is the most common term for "god" in the OT, where it occurs some twenty-six hundred times. It is morphologically plural but can take either a singular or plural referent.[7] Its usage ranges from direct address as a virtual name ("God") to an abstract adjective ("divine"). Approximately 90 percent of occurrences in the Masoretic Text are for a singular referent, Israel's God. Although it is the most frequently used term for "deity" in the OT, one could imagine the OT collection without it, where either *'ēl* or its plural (*'ēlîm*) occurs in its stead.

The use of a morphologically plural term for a singular referent that is a deity is an ANE literary convention, where it is used to flatter an Amarna-era pharaoh or refer to a Phoenician deity. Interpreters have considered this manner of marking a singular referent as an honorific expression, a plural of majesty, an expression of a superlative nature, or most plausibly in the case of the OT, as an abstraction indicating the essence of deity. However we sort out the motives of the biblical tradents in their uses of the term,[8] we note that the *frequency* of its employment in the OT is a distinguishing characteristic of the collection in its ANE setting and a mark of differentiation in the use of generic vocabulary for deity.

II. YHWH, the name of the God of Israel, occurs some sixty-eight hundred times in the Masoretic Text. It is thus the primary identity marker for Israel's God, and

---

5. Note, for example, the name of the altar in Gen 33:20, *'ēl 'elōhê yiśrā'ēl*, which can be translated "El, the God of Israel" or as "God, the God of Israel."

6. The term is used some 236 times in the singular and seven times in the plural. Its essential appellative function is clear from its employment with the definite article, and its construct and plural forms. See further Rolf Rendtorff, "El als israelitische Gottesbezeichnung," *ZAW* 106 (1994): 4–21.

7. See for example, 1 Kgs 11:33, where *'elōhîm* is used thrice, with three different singular deities as referents, one of whom is a goddess. Classical Hebrew does not have a specific term for goddess. On the term, see further Joel S. Burnett, *A Reassessment of Biblical Elohim*, SBLDS 183 (Atlanta: Society of Biblical Literature, 2001), 1–78.

8. There are numerous issues here that cannot be pursued. It is commonly recognized, for example, that the compilers of the Psalter included a collection of psalms (42–83) characterized by the use of Elohim for Israel's God. See Frank-Lothar Hossfeld, "The Elohistic Psalter, Formation and Purpose," in *The Psalter as Witness: Theology, Poetry, and Genre*, ed. W. Dennis Tucker Jr. and W. H. Bellinger Jr. (Waco: Baylor University Press, 2017) 117–32; and Joel S. Burnett, "The Elohistic Psalter, History and Theology," in Tucker and Bellinger, *Psalter as Witness*, 134–51.

the OT/Tanak is rightly described as a Yahwistic collection, even if the name is absent from some of its documents. A personal name may convey meaning in and of itself—or at least that may be the intention of its giver—but its central role is to mark its referent, such that the "name" evokes an identity otherwise constructed through encounter and testimony. Various traditions in the OT associate the significance of YHWH's name with the rescue of Israel from Egyptian slavery, including a play on the name with the verb "to be."[9]

Having a personal name to mark an identity is typical of ANE deities. In YHWH's case, his name also differentiates him vis-à-vis other deities. Although YHWH shares epithets and characteristics with them, no other ANE deity shares his name. And while YHWH may be venerated by other peoples, act in their historical affairs, and claim them eschatologically as his own, he is not named in the OT as the current deity of another people. The OT contains no theogony[10] for YHWH, and while he is associated with more than one earthly locale, he is not limited by terrestrial geography.

The brief, inadequate summary above concerns the differentiating role of the divine name YHWH in the OT collection. We might ask about convergence with respect to YHWH's name from a history of religions approach. Is there data to show pre-Israelite YHWHs whose identities contribute to the OT portrayal? With regard to the name itself, interpreters have explored both verb and noun options for its etymology[11] and suggested, among other theories, that it originated as an epithet of Canaanite El or as the name of a storm deity from northwestern Arabia. YHWH's martial march from the southland, as depicted in some OT poetic texts (e.g., Judg 5:4–5 and Hab 3:3–7), could be an example of a convergence whereby a YHWH venerated south of Palestine has been absorbed into the YHWH venerated in Israel and Judah.

In spite of intriguing possibilities, the data does not provide much to go on with regard to pre-Israelite manifestations of YHWH's name and veneration.[12]

---

9. Exod 3:1–15; cf. 6:2–8. These texts, furthermore, emphasize that YHWH is to be identified as the deity ('*elōhîm*; '*ēl*) who appeared previously to Israel's ancestors.

10. Correspondingly, YHWH is not included in any extrabiblical pantheon.

11. See Austin Surls, *Making Sense of the Divine Name in Exodus: From Etymology to Literary Onomastics*, Bulletin for Biblical Research, Supplement Series 17 (Winona Lake, IN: Eisenbrauns, 2017), 42–115, who surveys the question of etymology in both biblical and extrabiblical contexts, concluding that the name YHWH is "etymologically opaque" (66, 115). Similarly, Andrea D. Saner, *"Too Much to Grasp": Exodus 3:13–15 and the Reality of God*, Journal for Theological Interpretation Supplements 11 (Winona Lake, IN: Eisenbrauns, 2015), 13–31, proposes that the play on the name YHWH with the verb "to be" (*h-y-h*) in Exod 3:13–15 conceals elements about YHWH's identity, even as he is revealed as the God who is with and for Israel.

12. For a survey of texts and theories regarding YHWH outside of ancient Israel, see Lester L. Grabbe, "'Many Nations Will be Joined to Yhwh in that Day': The Question of Yhwh Outside of Judah," in *Religious Diversity in Ancient Israel and Judah*, ed. Francesca Stavrakopoulou and John Barton (New York: Bloomsbury, 2010), 175–89.

A discovery tomorrow could reshape the whole discussion of YHWH's name and the extent of its use, but after decades of research, we are faced with a historical phenomenon that is also a broad pattern in the OT: Israel's God has a name that differentiates him from other ANE deities.

III. YHWH is the only sufficient deity. Affirming YHWH's sufficiency is one way to summarize a broad pattern in the OT: advocacy of monolatry. Israel should have no other *'elōhîm* beside YHWH (Exod 20:3; Deut 5:7), which covers anything from benign neglect of YHWH to hostile rejection. Such a profile differentiates the OT from much of the ANE tradition, with its various permutations of polytheism. Monolatry of this kind is not, however, unknown, and some of Israel's neighbors (e.g., Ammon and Moab) may represent forms of it in their state cult.

YHWH's sufficiency with respect to other deities is maintained more particularly against rival deities known collectively as "the baals" (Judg 2:11; Hos 2:19[17]), employing a common Semitic noun with the basic meanings of "owner," "master," or derivatively, "husband." As with other appellatives and epithets, the term could function essentially as the name of a deity and was widely used in the Levant as a divine referent for gods and goddesses. In the category of forbidden deities, the baals are the most frequently opposed deities in the OT. How is, or is not, YHWH a baal? In order to explore that question, we need not sort out definitively such matters as how many baals[13] were YHWH's rivals, nor why for a time[14] there was such intense opposition to the baals among the OT tradents.

Evidence for invoking YHWH as "Baal" is explicit in the eighth century, such as in the prophecy of Hosea 2:18[16], where the practice is opposed.[15] In this instance, differentiation is not simply distinction but includes opposition to a popular means of invoking deity when applied to YHWH. YHWH may share some of the characteristics of the baals, but not the common epithet itself.[16]

---

13. There are several candidates (e.g. Hadad, Melqart, Baal Shamayim) for consideration. The question is complicated by the possibility that one cosmic rival, albeit in various regional manifestations, is the object of polemic in the OT and that the plural term "baals" is little more than a cipher for other deities. YHWH's rival is more frequently referred to in the singular (e.g.: 1 Kgs 18:16–46; Hos 2:10[8]; Jer 2:8).

14. The Deuteronomistic History presents the ninth century, with the Omride dynasty's intertwining with the Phoenician city states, as a crisis point. Polemic against the "baals" is part of Hosea and Jeremiah's opposition to the worship of other deities. There are several possible reasons for the opposition to Baalism in preexilic Israel and Judah on the part of the biblical tradents. One of them is plausibly a reverse convergence of YHWH with Baal, whereby YHWH was absorbed into the rising popularity of Baal. The argument from theodicy is an explicit reason. The books of 1–2 Kings, Hosea, and Jeremiah blame the fall of Israel and Judah, at least in part, on the worship of deities other than YHWH.

15. The prophet proposes that YHWH can be called *'îšî* ("my husband"), but "no longer my baal." See further discussion below.

16. For all the opposition to the name and worship of Baal, YHWH has many of the same characteristics. See W. S. Boshoff, "Yahweh as God of Nature: Elements of the Concept of God in

The practice of invoking YHWH as Baal, however, is implicit elsewhere in the OT, and not always opposed. Saul's family had male members named Ishbaal and Meribbaal, and David had a son named Beeliada.[17] These theophoric names plausibly represent a cultural convergence of religious practice in portraying YHWH as a divine baal, just as the name Adonijah, another son of David, explicitly represents YHWH as a divine *'ādôn* (below). Neither Saul nor David are portrayed as worshipping a "foreign" deity invoked as "Baal." A report of YHWH's victory over the Philistines in 2 Sam 5:20 notes that the place of battle is named Baal Perazim, because there YHWH "broke through" (*p-r-ṣ*) David's enemies. This etiological comment is most naturally taken as a reference to YHWH as the baal (master) who defeated the enemies of Israel and David.

Convergence and Differentiation in the Primary Terminology for Deity

The three broad patterns (contours) sketched above all pertain to the foundational terminology for deity in the OT, spread through the collection. As *'ēl* (and *'elôah*), including several epithets, YHWH is rendered in common terminology for deity. This represents convergence on a broad scale and is evidence for continuity/commonality in the broader West Semitic culture. Similarly, the designation of YHWH as an *'elōhîm* further confirms a common ANE recognition as divinity, while at the same time distinctively undergirding divine status as honored and exalted.

So much of YHWH's identity in the OT is marked by attention (and even devotion) to his name. Textually speaking, the most distinctive characteristic of Israel's God is the personal name YHWH, given the frequency of usage in the OT and its nonappearance in ANE pantheons. This is differentiation at a fundamental level, even with the convergence of many attributes from the ANE world. In emic perspective, "most distinctive" applied to YHWH can also be a value judgment, but in etic perspective, it indicates a fundamental identity marker. The Ammonite deity Milkom, similarly, has a distinctive name not shared among the deities of its closest Iron Age neighbors, a name that apparently distinguishes him as the patron deity of the Ammonite clans, a deity who may or may not be identified with a high god El, also worshipped in Ammon.

---

the Book of Hosea," *Journal of Northwest Semitic Languages* 18 (1992): 13–24, and more broadly, James S. Anderson, *Monotheism and Yahweh's Appropriation of Baal*, LHBOTS 617 (New York: Bloomsbury, 2015).

17. Ishbaal (1 Chr 8:33; "man of baal") is Ish-bosheth ("man of shame") in 2 Sam 2:8. Meribaal (1 Chr 8:34; perhaps "baal advocates") is Mephibosheth ("from the mouth of shame") in 2 Sam 4:4. The names in the Samuel narrative are examples of dysphemism, opposing the divine element *ba'al* in the personal names. Beeliada in 1 Chr 14:7 ("baal knows") is Eliada in 1 Chr 3:8 and 2 Sam 5:16. The Chronicler, writing at a later age when the rivalry between YHWH and Baal had subsided, preserves the correct names. Note also the name Bealiah in 1 Chr 12:6[5], probably "YHWH is my master."

Those tradents who opposed invoking YHWH as baal rejected a common epithet for deity. While this phenomenon is another example of differentiation in defining YHWH vis-à-vis other deities, it also represents an Israelite cultural tension, since others considered YHWH as Israel's divine master. For reasons persuasive to the biblical writers, YHWH was to be distinguished from one or more of the popular Iron Age baals not just by exclusive worship, but also by rejection of a commonly used epithet. Convergence with other attributes of Baal, nevertheless, is evident in portraying YHWH.

To return to the proverbial forest metaphor: convergences and differentiations in the basic terminology for deity in the OT outline a West Semitic forest, a matrix with some distinctive subspecies of regional flora prominently displayed, including the ways they are named, and also lacking some otherwise common plants.

Part 2: YHWH as Lord

YHWH as 'ādôn and ba'al

The portrayal of YHWH as Lord employs some of the most frequently used epithets for him in the OT. They show additional patterns of convergence and differentiation in common terminology broadly distributed in the collection.

I. YHWH is *'ādôn*. Signifying sovereignty/authority in relationships, the term is used for both humans and deities in the Levant. Although OT tradents are keen to distinguish YHWH from his baalistic rivals, there is repetitive use of this similar epithet to mark his cosmic authority.[18] One can only speculate on the reason(s) why there is no polemic against invoking YHWH as *'ādôn*, but a plausible one is that no Levantine deity so invoked was a serious rival to YHWH in Israel. The name of David's son Adonijah affirms YHWH's sovereignty as cosmic Lord.[19] Additionally, addressing YHWH as Adonay (e.g.: Gen 15:2; Ps 8:2) follows a pattern noted earlier of using plural nouns to mark him. As the Deuteronomist puts it (Deut 10:17): "YHWH is God ['*elōhê*] of Gods and Lord ['*ădōnê*] of Lords."[20]

---

18. See Josh 3:11. The noun *'ādôn* is used of YHWH some four hundred times in the OT, making it the most common epithet for him. It indicates someone in authority as a lord or master, including royal status. YHWH is also portrayed as cosmic king (e.g., Isa 6:5).

19. 2 Sam 3:4. The name can be translated "YHWH is my Lord." Cf. Bealiah in 1 Chr 12:6, on which see n. 17 above.

20. There is also the practice of substituting *'ādônay* for the name YHWH, which developed over time. The Masoretic Text will use the name Adonay as a common liturgical substitution for

A form of *'ādôn* is joined several times with formulations of the name "YHWH (of) Hosts."[21] That compact name is difficult syntactically and linguistically, with a variety of theories of its origin. It is, nevertheless, enmeshed in the root metaphor of YHWH as cosmic ruler. Our concern is to put the name in the context of the broad patterns we have identified. Possibly the noun "hosts" (*ṣəbā'ôt*) functions like the plural nouns previously noted, projecting an abstract/honorific identity for YHWH. Morphologically the noun is similar to abstract feminine plurals when used of deity such as "God of Knowledge" (1 Sam 2:3) and "YHWH, God of Vindication" (Ps 94:1). As an abstract plural, "hosts" would preserve something of the mystery regarding its referent(s). It reinforces claims of YHWH's cosmic power and authority over any and all forces, whether they be the divine council, the heavenly bodies, or the earthly armies of Israel, all of which have been suggested as the original referent of the "hosts."

II. YHWH as Israel's and Judah's husband (*ba'al*).[22] The marital metaphor of "husband" is not used of Phoenician deities otherwise invoked as Baal, where one might expect to find it. Moreover, there is no extant evidence of this metaphor for deity in ANE texts, and it is plausibly an inner-Israelite development. In any case, it is a mark of distinctiveness in YHWH's portrayal. The relative infrequency of identifying YHWH explicitly as a "husband," using the lemma *ba'al*, is belied by the broader employment of the marriage and household metaphors for relating YHWH and people in the OT.[23]

Consider Deutero-Isaiah's portrayal of YHWH as Jerusalem's "husband" in Isa 54:5: "Your husband [*bō'alayik*] is your maker [*'ōśayik*], YHWH of Hosts is his name." The plural participles are further examples of honorific rhetoric employed when portraying YHWH. They are used in the context of a prophetic address to Jerusalem (54:1–8), with the city metaphorically portrayed as a barren

---

YHWH. Early Greek translations often substituted the term *kyrios* (Lord) for YHWH. On the term and its application to God, see Martin Rösel, *Adonaj: Warum Gott 'Herr' genannt wird*, FAT 29 (Tübingen: Mohr Siebeck, 2000).

21. The name "YHWH (of) Hosts" occurs some 285 times in the OT, with occasional variation in longer forms such as "YHWH, God of [the] Hosts" (2 Sam 5:10; Amos 6:14) and "YHWH *'elōhîm* of Hosts" (Ps 59:6; 80:5). Cf. "God (*'elōhîm*) of Hosts" in Ps 80:8, 15. Some examples with *'ādôn* include: Ps 69:7[6]; Isa 1:24; Jer 2:19; Amos 3:13. See further T. N. D. Mettinger, "YHWH SABAOTH—The Heavenly King on the Cherubim Throne," in *Reports from a Scholar's Life: Select Papers on the Hebrew Bible*, ed. Andrew Knapp (Winona Lake, IN: Eisenbrauns, 2015), 62–91.

22. As noted above, the noun *ba'al* can refer to a husband (Gen 20:3; Exod 21:3). The verb *ba'al* can refer to act of marriage (Deut 21:13). In Hos 2:18[16], YHWH is Israel's *'îš*, which in context means "husband."

23. On the importance of the household for understanding ANE cultures, see J. David Schloen. *The House of the Father as Fact and Symbol: Patrimonialism in Ugarit and the Ancient Near East*, Studies in the Archaeology and History of the Levant 2 (Winona Lake, IN: Eisenbrauns, 2001).

widow, whose restoration as YHWH's spouse represents the repopulation of Judah and Jerusalem. This passage, in turn, is but one of several in which Jerusalem is directly addressed, personified, and portrayed in Isa 40–66. Her land is also metaphorically "married" (*bəʿûlâ*) to YHWH (Isa 62:4–5), indicating the fruitfulness to come in restoration from the Babylonian exile as a part of YHWH's rejoicing over his "bride." YHWH's restorative work is thus portrayed as engendering fertility, a role widely recognized in the ANE, where the gods are concerned with the vitality of people, city, and land.

ANE cities were broadly personified as female, so that Jerusalem's portrayal is an aspect of cultural convergence. In the OT, Jerusalem/Zion has the roles of queen/princess, mother, wife, daughter, widow, and prostitute,[24] representing variously people and land in their connection to YHWH. And in doing so, she is the most frequently portrayed female figure in the OT. The analogy of a marriage between YHWH and Jerusalem plausibly derives from the root metaphor of Israel and Judah as YHWH's patrimony, since the household is a common denominator of the roles of YHWH as husband and father, with Jerusalem as mother, daughter, wife, and widow, and Israel/Judah as son or daughter.

III. YHWH as covenant partner (*baʿal*). The marital metaphor is also entwined in portrayals of a covenant (*bərît*) YHWH established with Israel and Judah. The metaphor is but one of several ways to depict the Sinai/Horeb covenant, itself also a distinctively Israelite construal of relationships between deities and people in an ANE setting.

Several prophetic books reflect this formulation in the context of a covenant between YHWH and people.[25] As part of its opposition to the worship of other gods, the book of Jeremiah contains polemic against baal deities (e.g.: 2:8, 23; 7:9; 19:5), who collectively threaten Judah's relationship with YHWH. As the people's "husband" in 3:1–5, YHWH is the victim of Israel's and Judah's metaphorical adultery in their religious dalliances with other deities (3:6–18).[26] YHWH seeks the return of the wayward people, describing himself in first-person speech as the one who had been their "master" or "husband," using the same verb (*baʿal*) in 3:14, and promising to restore the people and land in a new

---

24. Samaria joins Jerusalem in some of these roles (see Mic 1:3–7; Ezek 23:1–49). On the metaphorical roles of Jerusalem, see Mark J. Boda, Carol J. Dempsey, and LeAnn Snow Flesher, ed., *Daughter Zion: Her Portrait, Her Response*, Ancient Israel and Its Literature 13 (Atlanta: Society of Biblical Literature, 2012).

25. R. Abma, *Bonds of Love: Methodic Studies of Prophetic Texts with Marriage Imagery (Isaiah 50:1–3 and 54:1–10, Hosea 1–3, Jeremiah 2–3)*, Studia Semitica Neerlandica 40 (Assen: Gorcum, 1999).

26. Jeremiah 3:1–5 assumes the case law in Deut 25:5–10. Israel and Judah are depicted as "sisters" in Jer 3:7–8.

faithful relationship.[27] Similar sentiments are expressed in 31:31–34, again cast in first-person speech and using the verb, in which YHWH decries Israel's and Judah's breaking of the covenant that he made with their ancestors in bringing them out of Egyptian slavery and confirming them as his people, deeds that are described as "acting as their husband" (v. 32). Included in the promise of a new covenant is the reaffirmation of what is often described as the covenant formula, "I will be their God and they will be my people" (31:33b), an affirmation that is similar to a marriage declaration.

The marital metaphor for covenant is used also in prophetic texts where the lemma *ba'al* is not employed with it. Hosea probably has the earliest formulation of it in the OT. The prophet's family becomes the literary vehicle to present Israel as a wayward spouse and as rebellious children (Hos 1–3; 11:1–11), with YHWH as wounded husband and father. The land engages in faithless activity (1:2) and the house of Israel breaks covenant with YHWH (8:1). Ezekiel preserves a form of the two-sisters allegory in chapter 23, complementing that in Jer 3, where Samaria and Jerusalem represent respectively Israel and Judah in their adultery against YHWH. In Ezek 16, Jerusalem is a metaphorical foundling whom YHWH subsequently engaged in marriage, thereby establishing his "covenant" (*bərît*) with her (v. 8).

YHWH *as Lord of His Household and the Cosmos*

The vocabulary for YHWH's lordship surveyed above is rooted in the central institutions of the Levant. His singularity in these roles is formulated contextually, yet with distinguishing traits that are particular to the Israelite matrix and that are either not reflected in the ANE or are distinctively formulated. It is thus similar to the broader pattern seen in the previously examined common terms for deity. To return again to the forest metaphor in light of this semantic field: Some of its flora, while indigenous to the region, bears distinctive fruit in its environment.

Conclusion

These (cursory) examinations of terminology for deity in the OT/Tanak are good mechanisms for insight into the broader portrayal of YHWH within it. This is chiefly because such terminology is widespread through the relevant texts and

---

27. Note the juxtaposition of father and husband imagery in Jer 3:19–20. This is perhaps evidence for the primacy of the household metaphor in depicting relations between YHWH and people, where both parties can be depicted in multiple household characters.

because patterns of convergence and differentiation that produced the terminology have counterparts elsewhere in the collection. There is theological method at work in these patterns that can be relevant for modern appropriation, since religious communities today, like those behind the OT, seek to define themselves in their own context through what they inherit and in response to their sense of the divine and its unique claim upon them. The metaphorical forest of the OT/Tanak contains a vibrancy in it, in which its ANE flora can take root in a new context. The Abrahamic religions are primary evidence for this vibrancy, and there is every reason to assume its continuance.

CHAPTER 5

Why Should the Look-Alikes Be a Problem?

Robert Goldenberg

THE PREMISE OF THIS COLLECTION is that similarities between ancient Israel's deity and those of Israel's neighbors and contemporaries constitute a theological problem, and it will be useful to consider the premises and assumptions that are implied in this view of the situation. There are two salient dimensions to this question. One is hermeneutical, arising from some of the claims made by YHWH's prophets on his behalf, and the other reflects the national character of Israel's covenant with its God. I shall examine each of these in turn.

I.

The Hermeneutical Dimension. The look-alikes become a problem because certain scriptural passages go beyond asserting YHWH's greatness or power; they acclaim his uniqueness. If Isaiah[1] had been satisfied to deny that any other god can match the strength of YHWH, the problem of the look-alikes would not have arisen; it would have been enough to say that those other so-called deities just could not match YHWH's power.[2] But Isaiah seems to deny that there is any god other than YHWH at all,[3] and that denial is found in the collection of holy Scripture, with the result that many of the readers of Scripture have believed him. Once it has become clear, however, that Israel's neighbors worshiped national gods who seem very like YHWH in numerous respects, such readers no longer know what to make of Isaiah's proud boast.

---

1. The "Isaiah" intended here is actually the unidentified author of the second part of the book bearing that name. This prophet is often designated by a hyphenated name such as "Deutero-Isaiah" or the like, but for purposes of convenience, I shall usually refer to the author of any biblical passage by the name of the book in which that passage appears. I do not propose here to enter into the literary history of the scriptural canon or its parts.
2. After all, YHWH's superior power is a major theme of the exodus story: the gods of Egypt are real; they just can't compete.
3. See, most famously, Isa 44:6.

Other biblical writers only seem to provide a solution to the problem. Various passages in Psalms simply dismiss the claims of those other nations as either perverse or deluded, but this dismissal cannot by itself provide a way to read Isaiah. It becomes necessary to know how Isaiah could have said what he did, and for many of the readers under discussion, this knowledge must preserve the straightforward truth of his words. Such readers need a method of reading Scripture that both acknowledges the apparent recognition of the "look-alikes" in certain books and also affirms the denial of this recognition in others. In other words, one needs a method that aims to understand any given passage in Scripture in the light of others or in the light of overarching principles that can embrace the totality of the collection. Such a method is at the heart of the rabbinic tradition of midrash, to which I shall return below.

It is also possible to wonder how Isaiah himself wished to be understood. I see the Bible as having been composed by the people to whom the various books are attributed or by other people like them. I recognize the possibility that the human authors of Scripture wrote in the aftermath of some kind of contact with divinity, though I do not mean here to explore the various major conceptions of that contact,[4] but I cannot see them as mere secretaries or amanuenses. I therefore cannot help being aware that those authors were subject to some of the same temptations that all authors must confront, and such temptations can lead speakers or writers to say things that they do not quite mean. Was Isaiah exaggerating for rhetorical purposes or out of momentary fervor? Did he speak those words in the context of a particular confrontation with the gods of Babylon?[5] When a besotted suitor tells his beloved, "You're the only one in the world," this is not to be taken as a metaphysical assertion. Is it possible that something like this was going on in Isa 44:6? When Isaiah reported YHWH's claim to be the only real deity, there were several things he might have understood himself to be saying, and only a few of those possibilities turn the "look-alikes" into a theological problem.

II.

The National Dimension. The biblical writers[6] spoke from within the framework of Israel's national covenant with YHWH. Israel's God might indeed have been a universal God, creator of heaven and earth, but his covenant with Israel was

---

4. For two Jewish views, see Neil Gillman, *Sacred Fragments: Recovering Theology for the Modern Jew* (Philadelphia: Jewish Publication Society, 1990), 1–34, and Abraham J. Heschel, *God in Search of Man: A Philosophy of Judaism* (New York: Farrar, Strauss, and Giroux, 1955), 167–278.

5. See 1 Kgs 18 (Elijah at Mount Carmel). Such confrontations may have been a regular feature of the prophets' experience.

6. I mean, of course, the contributors to the Hebrew Scriptures, the so-called Old Testament.

not a universal covenant, and theological assertions within the context of that covenant did not have to be universal either. For the authors of Scripture, this meant the look-alikes were the concern of other peoples and need not have been their problem. Examples of this attitude in Scripture itself are not hard to find. Psalm 96:5 (=1 Chr 16:26), having identified the look-alikes as belonging to "the nations," simply dismisses them as fraudulent "godlets." Micah more politely concedes (4:5) that other nations may well worship other deities; he just adds that this has nothing to do with him. Deut 4:19–20 explicitly authorizes the nations to worship the heavenly bodies, but insists that this authorization does not extend to Israel.

Even when uttering apparently global claims on YHWH's behalf, the biblical writers may not have intended that those claims be understood globally. The world in Isaiah's time was not yet familiar with the notion of universal religion, the notion that a religious truth ought to be true everywhere and at all times.[7] Even leaving aside the possibility mentioned above that Isaiah was carried away by his own rhetorical enthusiasm, we can also ask whom he was addressing when he asserted the uniqueness of his God. Was he even trying to get the attention of foreign nations?[8] Would they have understood him if he was?

III.

The Protestant tradition, which understandably dominates both this volume and the American discussion overall, is committed to finding its *regula fidei* in the canonical scriptures. This creates the possibility that any biblical passage that does not seem straightforwardly true can turn into a stumbling block, a problem that requires a solution. Coming from a different tradition, and keeping both the previous topics in mind, I would like to suggest that the tradition of rabbinic midrash offers a method to address such situations. Convinced that

---

7. In the time of Deutero-Isaiah, "the concept of abstract monotheism, in the sense of the existence of one God and one only, would ... have been impossible for him" (Claus Westermann, *Isaiah 40–66*, trans. D. M. G. Stalker, OTL [London: SCM, 1969], 140).

8. Several prophets addressed particular foreign nations, but it remains possible (I think likely) that this was a rhetorical device; the actual intended audience was still the prophet's own community. See, e.g., Isa 23, Jer 46–50, Ezek 25, Zeph 2, and Nah 3. Rabbinic literature reports numerous incidents of what might be called religious dialogue: conversation between a rabbi and a gentile interlocutor that concerned fundamental theological issues. It is noteworthy, however, that all such conversations are described as having been initiated by the outsider. Then, once challenged, one needed to have a response, but nowhere do we find a rabbi eager to engage in such an exchange, and nowhere does the rabbinic participant in the dialogue fail to overcome his challenger. There can be little doubt that all these stories were designed for circulation within the rabbinic community, where they might serve a number of useful ends. See Robert Goldenberg, *The Nations that Know Thee Not* (New York: New York University Press, 1998), 88.

some biblical texts were not meant to be read straightforwardly, the authors of classical rabbinic midrash declined in principle to be constrained by the straightforward meaning of Scripture.[9] Forced to choose between a straightforward reading that produced a religiously unacceptable result and one that departed from the straight meaning of the text but led to an outcome they might willingly affirm, the authors of midrash often chose the latter.[10]

Some examples of midrash may prove helpful. In a typical expression of his monotheistic confidence, Isaiah has YHWH say "You are my witnesses and I am God" (Isa 43:12). Here is a straightforward assertion of YHWH's divinity, if not quite of his uniqueness, but an oft-quoted midrash does not take it that way: "When you are my witnesses I am God, and when you are not my witnesses I am not God" (Sipre 2.346).[11] It is not clear what the rabbinic author meant to say here, but surely he was not guided by the straightforward meaning of Isaiah's claim.

The same disregard for the straightforward meaning of Scripture can be found in nontheological contexts as well. The separation of meat and dairy foodstuffs that is a striking feature of the Jewish dietary laws is grounded, as is widely known, on the triple repetition of the ban "Do not cook a kid in its mother's milk" (Exod 23:19; 34:26; Deut 14:21). It is unlikely that Scripture really meant to ground a basic legal category on an apparent cultic detail, and scholars continue to seek the sources of both the detail and the basic category, but the point for now is that the tradition simply used these verses in a fashion that left their straightforward meaning far behind.

And sometimes, of course, the straightforward meaning can be very unclear. In a famous case, Lev 23:16 ordains that, seven weeks following "the day after the Sabbath," another rite be performed. This instruction immediately follows mention of the week-long Festival of Unleavened Bread, but the text does not say which Sabbath is meant or even whether "Sabbath" here means what it would mean today; in the preceding verse, the word clearly means "week." The ancient results were as might have been predicted: some Jewish groups[12]

---

9. Barry Wimpfheimer has written: "Even a work as profoundly canonical as the Bible has been transformed in modernity by the way its content no longer possesses the unequivocal authority it once did" (*The Talmud: A Biography*, Lives of Great Religious Books [Princeton: Princeton University Press, 2018], 162). The authors of midrash carried out just such a transformation long before modernity had dawned.

10. See Robert Goldenberg, "The Problem of False Prophecy: Talmudic Interpretations of Jeremiah 28 and 1 Kings 22," in *The Biblical Mosaic: Changing Perspectives*, ed. Robert Polzin and Eugene Rothman, Society of Biblical Literature Semeia Studies (Philadelphia: Fortress; Chico, CA: Scholars, 1982), 87–103.

11. Many variants add "so to speak" to soften the harshness of this denial.

12. Apparently the Sadducees, also known as Boethusians (see Hag 2:4, also Menah. 65ab, Sanh. 60b), surely the sectaries at Qumran. See also 1 Enoch 72:32 and Jubilees 6:38. A "sectarian" 364-day calendar was apparently in wide use among dissident groups; a full introduction to the Qumran calendar can be found at Sacha Stern, "Qumran Calendars and Sectarianism," in *Oxford*

thought the count should start on the intermediate Sabbath of the feast, while the rabbinic tradition, along with Philo and Josephus, interpreted "Sabbath" as not meaning the familiar Sabbath at all,[13] but rather the first day of the festival; on that day, labor was indeed forbidden as though on the Sabbath, even though it might fall on any day of the week. The result was that, in the late Second Temple period, different Jewish groups followed competing calendars, a situation that was surely uncomfortable and that sometimes led to violence.[14]

Certain biblical passages actually invite nonstraightforward interpretation.[15] The talking animals in Gen 3 and Num 22 are widely (though not universally) understood as representing something other than real talking animals. The lavish imagery in the later apocalyptic books is widely (though not universally) understood as not meant to depict ordinary reality. The question that any interpretive tradition must face, therefore, is when to remain within a straightforward reading of a perplexing text and when to move outside it.[16] That question bears directly on Isaiah's assertion of YHWH's uniqueness.

One last example. Jeremiah, speaking in God's voice, throws a double accusation at the prophet's contemporaries: "They deserted me and did not keep my instruction" (Jer 16:11). An oft-quoted midrashic inversion reads as follows: "Would they had abandoned me but kept my instruction" (Lamentations Rabbah, proem 2; translation mine). Such disregard for the clear meaning of Scripture demands attention.

This choice was grounded in the central rabbinic teaching that the "Written Torah" was never the exhaustive revelation of God's word, indeed that Scripture could not properly be understood on its own but had to be read through and in connection with the oral teachings that constituted the rest of that revelation.[17]

Handbook of the Dead Sea Scrolls, ed. Timothy H. Lim and John J. Collins (Oxford: Oxford University Press, 2010), 232–253.

13. See Josephus, *Jewish Antiquities* 3.250; Philo, *On the Special Laws* 2.162.

14. See the Qumran commentary in 1QpHab 11:2–8 (on Hab 2:15).

15. It should be noted that, in a kind of counterpoint to the examples just given, the Talmud also will use the expression "if this had not been written it would have been impossible to say" to introduce a theological conception based on the literal meaning of Scripture. Examples can be found in the appendix to this chapter.

16. The medieval philosopher Maimonides took for granted that any scripture with a philosophically unacceptable meaning had to be interpreted nonliterally: since God is incorporeal, all references to parts of God's body (eye, hand, ear, finger, etc.) had to be read as metaphors (*Foundations of the Torah* 1.8–9).

17. "If one has learned Scripture and Mishnah but has not served the Sages: R. Eleazar says, 'Such a person is an ignoramus.' R. Samuel b. Nahmani says, 'Such a person is a boor.' R. Yannai says, 'Such a person is a heretic.' R. Aha b. R. Jacob says, 'Such a person is a Magus'" (b. Sotah 22a; translation mine). To "serve the Sages" meant to become integrated into the rabbinic thought world with its double Torah: written and oral. Anyone who failed to undergo this integration lacked all religious legitimacy. Textual knowledge by itself, even of "Scripture and Mishnah," did not qualify. The contrast with the principle *sola scriptura* could not be more striking.

This claim, of course, had to be accepted on faith, just as the more basic identification of Scripture as the "Word of God" must be accepted on faith. But "faith" here does not mean—or does not mean only—willed acceptance of unprovable assertions as correct; it means acceptance of the intellectual and behavioral norms of the community to which one has committed one's adherence. The "faith" is ultimately in that community, which is the matrix of one's link to the divine and the source of Scripture as the word of God.[18]

IV.

In light of the foregoing, it should come as no surprise that I do not see, and have never seen, the "look-alikes" of YHWH as a problem in need of solution. These other deities had their place outside the specifically national covenant of Israel to which I consider myself an heir, and so they have nothing to do with me. The question is only why Isaiah should have spoken in such a way as to give a different impression, and even here it is possible to suggest an answer.

It is well-known that Israel's prophets for centuries pleaded with their people to abandon what seemed to be a constant readiness to worship the gods of their neighbors. Facing this widespread stubbornness, the prophets' rhetoric became increasingly angry, and even frantic.[19] One can easily imagine that the prophets' appeals grew more and more intemperate as the generations wore on.[20] Eventually they started saying things that conveyed the depth of their horror at "idolatry" and its likely consequences, but the literal meaning of their words could not always withstand scrutiny.[21]

At this point, several theological or hermeneutical questions coalesce. To whom were the prophets' words addressed? Was the audience expected to understand these words literally, or were they expected to recognize and make allowance for rhetorical excess? If the latter, what were the prophets' words, shorn of excess, meant to convey? Working backward, my tentative answer to the problem of the look-alikes emerges from my equally tentative answers to these questions.

---

18. Comparison of this notion of "faith" with that underlying Heb 11:1 would constitute a worthwhile project, but this is not the place for it.

19. The prophets' desperation is one of the main themes of Abraham J. Heschel's classic work *The Prophets* (New York: Harper and Row, 1962).

20. The prophets were a minority faction in Israelite society throughout the period, up until the point that Ezra and Nehemiah, loyal supporters of prophetic monotheism, managed with royal support to take over the leadership of the emerging community in Judea.

21. An early example is Hosea's analogy between idolatry and adultery. I have long wondered at his persistent loyalty to his marriage even as he fulminated against his wife in exceedingly violent language. This suggests to me that his language went far beyond his actual intentions.

The prophets spoke in two different modes.[22] The mode of furious threat was designed to frighten hearers away from the constant temptation of personal and social corruption (this does not bear directly on the question of look-alikes), and from the equally constant temptation to placate as many divine forces as possible (this does so bear). Both these temptations were hard to resist, and the second in particular seemed to make a lot of sense, as refusal to worship all these deities seemed counterintuitive or even dangerously irrational.[23] The other mode in which the prophets spoke, that of comfort and encouragement, represented their method of keeping the violence intrinsic to the mode of threat from becoming inescapable. The goal, after all, was to induce a change in the hearers' behavior, not simply to announce an inescapable fate, and this meant that deciphering the literal meaning of their words was not always the best way to grasp their actual message.

The story of the prophet Jonah hints at how this might have worked. After some resistance, Jonah travels to the great city of Nineveh and announces that the city is to be destroyed in forty days. He says nothing about the possibility of avoiding this fate or why the decree was issued in the first place, but the people correctly understand that Jonah is speaking in the prophetic mode of threat and adopt a regimen of drastic penitence, and the decree is averted. Jonah, for his part, is displeased: he delivered his prophecy as instructed and now the prophecy has failed to come true. Jonah understood the theology of prophecy with less discernment than the wicked people of Nineveh.[24]

If we allow for the possibility that the prophets' monotheistic rhetoric included an element of dramatic exaggeration, then the problem of the look-alikes disappears. Isaiah and the others were desperately trying to prevent the disaster that would eventually engulf Israel if wholesale violation of the national covenant persisted. To do so, they depicted the other deities—the "idols" whom their fellow Israelites could not bear to insult or to ignore—in the most unappealing terms they could muster: weak and unreliable, unable to protect the people from YHWH's wrath once that wrath burst forth, and hardly worthy of being called gods at all, as though they do not even exist.

Still, this relentless denigration acknowledged the look-alikes' existence, their presence in the cosmos. How could this be if YHWH himself asserted

---

22. Of course, not every prophet used the two "modes" equally. I am speaking at the moment of the prophetic movement overall.

23. See in particular Jer 44. This is the only chapter in Scripture where the prophets' "idolatrous" antagonists have an opportunity to explain how the world appears to them and why the prophets' radically different view is dangerous and makes no sense.

24. Jeremiah also faced the problem of prophecies that were not supposed to come true; see especially Jer 28.

(or certain prophets claimed) that no other deity existed at all?[25] On the construction being offered here, it must be repeated that it was the prophet who was speaking, not the God in whose name he spoke. He was serving that God, but with words of his own choosing.

In the end, not only the substance of the prophets' message but also the language in which that message was delivered shaped Jewish and later Christian monotheism. The problem of the look-alikes that this volume addresses arises not from the substance of the prophets' monotheism, but from their language. The look-alikes could have been incorporated into a monotheistic scheme[26] without threatening YHWH's supremacy, but this would have required acknowledging at least their existence, and the prophets' rhetoric made this harder and harder. The solution to "the problem of the look-alikes" is to adopt any of the solutions that can be found in other biblical contexts[27] and reduce the "gods of the nations" to their proper size and place in YHWH's world.

Appendix. In the body of this chapter, I presented rabbinic midrash as a set of techniques for resolving ambiguities in the biblical text or for avoiding implications that the rabbinic authors were not willing to affirm. All such techniques displayed a willingness to set the literal meaning of Scripture aside—even when that meaning was apparently quite clear—in favor of a different interpretation that yielded a preferred outcome. The purpose of this appendix is to present a few cases that move, so to speak, in the opposite direction, that rely precisely on the literal meaning of Scripture in order to say something that otherwise would appear unacceptable for one reason or another.

> "And the Lord passed before him and cried out . . ." [Exod 34:6]. Said R. Yohanan: Were this not written it would be impossible to say: This teaches that the Blessed Holy One wrapped himself like a prayer leader and showed Moses the order of prayer and said to him, "Whenever Israel sin have them act before me according to this order and I shall forgive them." (b. Rosh Hashanah 17b)

---

25. It was not unheard of that participants in openly polytheistic cultures might in times of stress address a certain deity as the only real god in existence. See Morton Smith, "The Common Theology of the Ancient Near East," *JBL* 71 (1952): 135–47; see also Adrianus van Selms, "Temporary Henotheism," in *Symbolae Biblicae et Mesopotamicae F. M. T. de Liagre Böhl dedicatae*, ed. M. A. Beek, A. A. Kampman, C. Nijland, and J. Rijckmanns, Studia Francisci Scholten Memoriae Dicata 4 (Leiden: Brill, 1972), 341–48.

26. The look-alikes could have been turned into angels or YHWH's subordinates (Daniel) or could have been acknowledged even as they were being sentenced to death (Ps 82), and surely these were not the only two possibilities.

27. Midrash reads all of Scripture intertextually: any passage might shed light on any other.

This teaching (an affirmation that repentant prayer can lead to divine forgiveness) cannot really be dependent on the literal sense of the passage in Exodus: surely the narrative does not *literally* mean that God taught Israel to pray in precisely this manner. But the rhetoric serves to anchor a striking image in Scripture and, thereby, to protect it from the charge of inventing an unacceptable image of the Creator.

> R. Huna said in the name of Bar Kappara: If the matter were not written it would have been impossible to say: "At the beginning God created [the heavens]." From where did they and the earth come from? From "formless void." (Genesis Rabbah 1:5; on Gen 1:1; translation mine)

That the world which God declared to be "very good" should have been created from disreputable raw materials was not something to be spoken out loud; it was only with the permission of a biblical passage taken literally that the idea might be put forth.

> R. Judah said: Were the Scripture not written down it would be impossible to say. "Where did Moses die?" In the portion of Reuben, as it is written "Moses went up from the Plains of Moab to Mount Nebo" [Deut 34:1], and Nebo was in the portion of Reuben, as it is written "And the children of Reuben built . . . and Nebo, etc" [Num 32:37–38].[28] And where was Moses buried? In the portion of Gad. . . . Now from the portion of Reuben to the portion of Gad is four miles; who brought him over those four miles? Moses was carried in the wings of God's presence (*shekhina*), while the ministering angels recited "He carried out the Lord's righteousness and his judgments for Israel" [Deut 33:21]. (b. Sotah 13b)

These examples suffice to show that early rabbis' attitude toward the literal meaning of Scripture could vary according to their need. This is not meant cynically, nor is it the point that they could be arbitrary in their interpretations. Rather, they display a flexible recognition that not all revealed passages can or should be read according to the same methods or canons. The key to my understanding of the Creator's "look-alikes" lies in this realization.

---

28. Omissions in printed text.

PART 2

Chemosh as a Case Study

PART 2 OF THE VOLUME provides a sustained case study of one divine doppelgänger: the Moabite god named Chemosh. The first chapter of the section, by Collin Cornell, segues from the broader and introductory considerations of part 1. It opens by describing several biblical texts that create the conditions for the theological problem of YHWH's ancient look-alikes in the first place: texts that praise YHWH's incomparability and texts that mock other gods as the work of human hands. Next the chapter discusses three constructive approaches to this theological problem. A few scholars argue that other gods resemble YHWH because they are demonic counterfeits; others propose that, exactly in their similarity to YHWH, these other gods are true manifestations of divinity. This chapter submits another, paradoxical way forward: it radicalizes the Bible's own rhetoric against idols so that it includes even the god YHWH—while also confessing that, by God's own decision, this one individual human artifact, the god YHWH, corresponds to the divine self. The god Chemosh serves as a point of reference throughout.

The next chapter of part 2 inspects the similarity of YHWH and Chemosh more closely. Josey Bridges Snyder first argues for the special significance of Chemosh, and of Moabite religion more broadly. Relative to other ancient gods and the artifacts that attest them (like texts from Ugarit), Chemosh presents a compelling look-alike to YHWH, and from a time and place nearby to Israel. Snyder takes Moabite names preserved on stamp seals as her main data set, and she sets about answering the question of Chemosh's similarity to YHWH in one regard: whether Chemosh is, like YHWH, a "bachelor god," the sole recipient of his people's worship. She reflects in her conclusion on the theological ramifications of this line of inquiry.

M. Patrick Graham's chapter subjects the "look-alike" status of YHWH and Chemosh to a searching textual appraisal. After reviewing the main contents of the Mesha Inscription—the primary text depicting Chemosh—Graham proposes Moral Foundations Theory (MFT) as his analytic tool. Six moral foundations thus organize his theological comparison of the Mesha Inscription with Hebrew Scripture. In the end, Graham's procedure isolates several differences between the two look-alike gods: Chemosh emerges as "unidimensional," war-like, and immediate, where YHWH shows a richer profile including such features such as justice, faithfulness, and compassion. Besides yielding a fresh interpretation of the Mesha Inscription, Graham's chapter offers key data to reframe and sophisticate accounts of the theological problem of YHWH's divine doppelgängers.

Brent A. Strawn's chapter treats Chemosh as one among a number of ancient look-alikes to YHWH. Strawn criticizes two common responses to this theological problem. On one hand, many scholars reduce YHWH to being just "one of the ancient Near Eastern gang"—utterly continuous with other gods. On the other, some scholars insist that YHWH is unique and utterly dissimilar. Strawn splits the difference and provides a theological rationale for both the continuities and discontinuities of YHWH's profile relative to other gods like Chemosh. Strawn acknowledges continuities as evidence of prevenient divine grace at work in the cultures antecedent to Israel, and he locates discontinuities within the scriptural canon. YHWH shows a richer "interior life" and a more complex character than his would-be look-alikes because of the far deeper reservoir of experiences with him that the holy writings of Israel transmit and also, in turn, generate. Strawn's chapter renders a wide-ranging and theologically engaged resource for working through God's relation to the gods.

Jon Levenson's chapter begins by considering the tenacity of age-old, negative Christian stereotypes of Judaism, even in historical-critical scholarship. Levenson identifies the cause: the New Testament. But Levenson also challenges Jewish critics who argue that there is no parallel in Hebrew Scripture to the New Testament's anti-Judaism. Hebrew Scripture developed over a far longer time than the New Testament, and therefore softened somewhat in its judgments, but it, too, emerged in contexts of religious competition. As such, it demonizes its rivals, the Canaanites, and their practices. This polemic continues to resurface even in works of critical history, in spite of the fact that critical scholarship has demonstrated massive continuity between YHWH and the gods of Canaan; Levenson cites Chemosh as so similar an example to YHWH as to destabilize the whole framing of Israelite religion vis-à-vis "paganism." For working out an approach to the problem of YHWH's ancient look-alikes, Levenson's chapter showcases a striking comparison laden with theological implications. Keel's chapter in part I of the volume took inspiration from it.

CHAPTER 6

Theological Approaches to the Problem of God's Ancient Look-Alikes

Collin Cornell

> God has become "a" god in order to be known to humanity.
>
> K.H. Miskotte

I FIRST READ THE MESHA INSCRIPTION in seminary. The occasion was a small, informal seminar on West Semitic texts. The effect was, in a word, theological vertigo.

The Mesha Inscription gives a first-person account of a king's reign: "I am Mesha son of Chemoshyat, king of Moab." This king, the speaker, tells how he built a high place for his god named Chemosh to commemorate the god's saving power. The text then details several episodes describing that salvation. These stories show that Chemosh is capable of anger against his own country, resulting in their subjugation to foreign rule. Chemosh also issues military commands to his client king; he receives ritual slaughter, or *ḥerem*; and he gloats over captured cultic paraphernalia belonging to other gods, in this case, YHWH. "I took from there," says Mesha, "the vessels of YHWH and I dragged them before Chemosh" (ll. 17–18).

In all these regards, Chemosh looks exactly like the biblical god named YHWH. YHWH, too, has kings who build high places in his honor. His anger against his own country is notorious, and their subjugation to foreign rule forms a major biblical theme. YHWH commands kings in battle and humiliates the cultic paraphernalia of other gods: after the Philistines drag the ark of YHWH in front of their god Dagon's statue, YHWH decapitates it during the night (1 Sam 5). Reading the Mesha Inscription was, then, like seeing a photo negative: all the same components but just with colors reversed—or rather, with names interchanged. "If the name of Jehovah were substituted for Chemosh," wrote one

---

Author's Note: I thank M. Justin Walker for his exacting comments on an earlier draft of the present work. I am also grateful to Mirjam Elbers and David W. Congdon for their encouragement about the piece.

early scholar, "[the inscription] would read like a chapter from the book of Kings."[1]

The similarities between Chemosh and YHWH caused me theological vertigo: an uneasy sense of going off balance; of theological coordinates gone blurry. But why? On the face of it, there should be no surprise: one text from the ancient southern Levant—the Mesha Inscription—resembles another and far more famous textual survivor from that time and place—Hebrew Scripture—and their gods mirror each other. Indeed, the Mesha Inscription presents only one instance (though a rather acute one) of a far broader phenomenon: the ancient world was full of gods, and the biblical God is like them in manifold ways (and vice versa). Numerous examples of "divine parallelism" could be cited, and have been.[2] The source of my vertigo thus requires some explanation.

The Problem

The situation that gave rise to my disorientation is not unique to me.[3] It is one shared by generations of theological students, Jewish and Christian, and its roots are deep and complex. I can evoke its several aspects only in broad brushstrokes before considering three possible constructive approaches to it.

The first and most enormous fact that informs "the problem of God's ancient look-alikes" is also, paradoxically, the one that most often goes unspoken in scholarly discussions of the issue.[4] This concerns the Christian Old Testament—or the Tanak, for Jews—and its purported relationship to the living God. Jews and Christians hold a common body of literature as their basic religious norm and resource, each in their own distinctive ways and with a bewildering complement of sectarian inflections. But they do more than that: the mainstream of each tradition frames the importance of this text corpus as more than just inspirational. This book does more than, say, jumpstart insights into the human condition. Rather—and once more, with all due caveats to denominational

---

1. David Ginsburg is quoted in Archibald H. Sayce, *The Higher Criticism and the Verdict of the Monuments* (London: SPCK, 1894), 374.

2. See, perhaps most famously, Morton Smith, "The Common Theology of the Ancient Near East," *JBL* 71 (1952): 135–47.

3. Matthew J. Schlimm uses the words "anxiety," "distress," and "crisis" to describe his own undergraduate encounter with ANE texts ("Wrestling with Marduk: Old Testament Parallels and Prevenient Grace," *Wesleyan Theological Journal* 48 [2013]: 181–92, at 181). Brent A. Strawn speaks of students "find[ing] such parallels off-putting and discouraging" (Steve Delamarter, Javier Alanís, Russell Haitch, Mark Vitalis Hoffman, Arun W. Jones, and Brent A. Strawn, "Technology, Pedagogy, and Transformation in Theological Education: Five Case Studies," *Teaching Theology and Religion* 10 (2007): 64–79, at 67). See also Patrick D. Miller, Jr: "It is hard enough to relate to Yahweh, but if Yahweh looks a lot like Marduk, that makes it even tougher" ("God and the Gods," in present volume, 15).

4. "Look-alikes" is Miller's word ("God and the Gods," 15).

flexion—these communities believe that this book subsists in a special relationship to God. It reflects and gives access to a true divine counterpart.[5]

The point is, Hebrew Scripture is treasured because it sustains these religious communities in their engagement with a deity whom they perceive as *present*, or capable of becoming *present*, and not only or mostly absent, dead, or otiose.[6] This much cannot be said of the texts recovered from the ancient Near East. Such texts are not and never were a basic norm and resource for a religious community, and no present-day institution treats them as a means of accessing spiritual agency or presence. They are historical detritus, discovered and deciphered under a regime wholly different from that of spiritual love and devotion.

All this usually goes without saying, but it forms the context within which Jewish and Christian readers operate, and the context that encircles the following, more specific observations. Besides the general expectation that these readers bring with them that the Bible somehow enables contact with a divine counterpart, their vision of that counterpart oftentimes bears the imprint of biblical rhetoric in at least two further ways.[7] First, Hebrew Scripture praises YHWH for his *incomparability*. This praise can take the form of a negative declaration, as in Ps 86: "There is none like you among the gods, O Lord!" (v. 8).[8] But it can also assume a positive form, as it does in the Song of the Sea, an iconic biblical "high point" of celebrating YHWH's saving power, and one lodged deep in the shared memory of Judaism and Christianity. Moses and Miriam sing: "Who is like you, O YHWH, among the gods? Who is like you, majestic in holiness, awesome in splendor, doing wonders?" (Exod 15:11). The answer to the rhetorical question is, of course, no one: *no one is like YHWH*.

Expressions like this are not measured and doctrinal: they are impassioned, doxological, and at times persuasive.[9] Nonetheless, biblical praise of YHWH as

---

5. Dennis Olson speaks of "the reality of an external, out-there-in-the-world, living God who continues to speak through the use of the Bible in the church's life and ministry" ("Zigzagging through Deep Waters: A Guide to Brevard Childs's Canonical Exegesis of Scripture," *Word and World* 29 [2009]: 348–56, at 350). In context, he is describing one of Brevard S. Childs's key theological assumptions—but church (and synagogue) would seem largely to share it.

6. See also Miller's comment: "What I am talking about is finally not just Yahweh and the gods, an interesting analysis of an Iron Age deity. It is God and the gods. Whatever we say about Yahweh as an El figure or in conflict with Baal is conversation about the God we know and worship in Jesus Christ" ("God and the Gods," 29).

7. To be sure, the whole massive weight of "monotheism," including the rather more Hellenistic and philosophical parts of that inheritance, presses on Jewish and Christian interpreters and shapes expectations about YHWH. But the concern of the present section is to indicate the specifically biblical threads that make YHWH's ancient look-alikes theologically problematic.

8. For this and similar expressions, see C. J. Labuschagne, *The Incomparability of Yahweh in the Old Testament*, Pretoria Oriental Series 5 (Leiden: Brill, 1966).

9. Davida H. Charney, *Persuading God: Rhetorical Studies of First-Person Psalms*, Hebrew Bible Monographs 73 (Sheffield: Sheffield Phoenix, 2015).

incomparable contributes to the backdrop of expectations that Jewish and Christian readers have about their deity. (Ironically enough, praising gods for their incomparability was a widespread practice in the ancient world, and it thrived in contexts where many gods were worshipped.)[10]

A second kind of biblical rhetoric that shapes expectations about YHWH is so-called "anti-idol polemic"—and its even more radical extension. Several biblical passages clustered in the prophets savagely mock the makers of cult images (idols) for seeking divine help from the objects they construct.[11] As products of human manufacture, idols can never exceed their makers' own limitations: "People are mortal, and what they make with lawless hands is dead" (Wis 15:17a). In fact, idols fall far short of even human capacity: according to these texts, they are as inert as firewood (Isa 44:15, 19; Wis 13:10–19). A few passages directly identify cult statuary as the "work of human hands" (Ps 115:4 // 135:15; cf. Jer 10:3).

But in one biblical story, this same phrase receives a critical theological extension. The Chronicler writes of the envoys of Sennacherib the Assyrian king that they "spoke of the God of Jerusalem as if he were like the gods of the peoples of the earth, *which are the work of human hands*" (2 Chr 32:19; cf. the parallels in 2 Kgs 19:18 and Isa 37:19; cf. also Deut 4:28). In other words, the Chronicler here describes other gods not merely as inferior to YHWH, but as altogether human creations: as projections, to use a modern word. This sort of negative claim about other gods dovetails with biblical forms of rhetoric in which YHWH asserts his solitude on the divine plane (e.g., Isa 45:5a: "I am YHWH, and there is no other; besides me there is no god").[12] The cumulative impression that these texts leave is this: *YHWH is not a human invention—but other gods are.*

No doubt many other biblical texts help to make the experience of reading ancient inscriptions fraught for Jewish and Christian interpreters. In the case of the god of the Mesha Inscription, Chemosh, one thinks of the epithet given him in Kings: "the abomination of the Moabites" (1 Kgs 11:7[5], 33; 2 Kgs 23:13). Taken together, however, these threads coalesce into a set of theological expectations that induce vertigo when they are exposed to one or more of YHWH's divine look-alikes. Instead of a horrific abomination, one encounters a deity that looks very much like YHWH, the divine counterpart known and loved by one's religious tradition. The cry of praise that *no one is like YHWH* must falter; many are like him.

---

10. Labuschange, *Incomparability*, 31–63.

11. Ryan P. Bonfiglio lists these passages as representative: "Jeremiah 10:1–16, Deutero-Isaiah (Isa 40:18–20; 41:6–7; 44:9–20), certain psalms (Pss 115:4–9; 135:15–18), and, though in a less developed manner, several texts in the minor prophets (Hos 8:4–6; 13:2–3; Mic 5:12–13 [Heb 11–12]; Hab 2:18–19)" ("Art, Agency, and Anti-Idol Polemic," forthcoming in *Hebrew Bible and Ancient Israel*).

12. Claims that Second Isaiah (and especially texts deploying the so-called "exclusivity formulae" (as in: Isa 43:10; 44:6; 45:5–6; 46:9) represents the zenith and parade example of "monotheism" in the Bible may, however, be overstated; see Saul M. Olyan, "Is Isaiah 40–55 Really Monotheistic?," *Journal of Ancient Near Eastern Religions* 12 (2012): 190–201.

Perhaps most ominously, the biblical judgment made about other gods—that they are human inventions—threatens to redound back onto YHWH as well. If he is so similar to human projections, what is to say he is not one of them? And as such, not *present* or *potentially present*, but rather very much absent, dead, and otiose?

Three Approaches

Since the discovery and expropriation of ANE texts and artifacts in the nineteenth century and onward, theological scholars have developed a number of approaches to the problem of "YHWH and the gods." These approaches share a few features in common: they seek to honor the Jewish and Christian traditions' sense of engaging with a true divine counterpart, and they draw inspiration from the Bible itself for their negotiation of YHWH and his peers. The latter is, of course, a complicated and recursive exercise: the problem of YHWH's "ancient look-alikes" is one that the Bible creates, and so the Bible must also, in some form or fashion, aid in relieving it. Descriptions of each approach given below consequently include some evaluation of its scriptural ingredients. Each approach also makes room for similarities between the biblical God and his ancient congeners, though to varying degrees.[13]

The first approach is the least well-known and the most outré, at least as scholars are considered. In response to the dilemma of confessing to YHWH that "there is none like [him]" and then finding numerous gods that are quite like him, this approach points to *demonic trickery*. That is, Chemosh resembles YHWH because Chemosh is a counterfeit: the design of hostile spiritual powers to approximate YHWH's divine profile. Or perhaps Chemosh is not just the creation of hostile powers, but rather *is* just such a power himself, directly. Regardless, his similarity to YHWH is that of predatory imitation.

Jeffrey Niehaus is one recent exponent of this strategy. In his book on *Ancient Near Eastern Themes in Biblical Theology*, he writes: "Demonic inspiration of false religion ... produces the sort of parallels we have discussed."[14] In the same summary chapter, Niehaus presses yet further, specifying that "fallen angels" misled "the ancients" through their "theological counterfeit[ing]."[15]

---

13. Several essays relevant to the topic acknowledge similarity so minimally that they are not useful for this paper: Edward L. Greenstein, "The God of Israel and the Gods of Canaan: How Different Were They?," in *Proceedings of the World Congress of Jewish Studies*, ed. Ron Margolin (Jerusalem: World Union of Jewish Studies), 47*–58*; Nahum M. Sarna, "Paganism and Biblical Judaism," in *Studies in Biblical Interpretation* (Philadelphia: Jewish Publication Society, 2000), 13–28.

14. Jeffrey J. Niehaus, *Ancient Near Eastern Themes in Biblical Theology* (Grand Rapids: Kregel, 2008), 179.

15. Ibid., 181. See also the critical reception of Niehaus's point about demonic causation by William Edgar in a review of this book in *Themelios* 35, no. 2 (2010): 238–44.

Niehaus cites two New Testament verses in support of this interpretation.[16] In 1 Cor 10, the apostle Paul urges his audience to "flee from the worship of idols [*eidōlolatrias*]" (v. 14)—a nonce word, apparently, but one that hearkens back to Old Greek translations of the Hebrew terminology in anti-idol polemic.[17] But the apostle then enriches the concept of idols as purely human creations with some superhuman density: "What do I imply then? That food sacrificed to idols is anything, or that an idol is anything? No, I imply that what pagans sacrifice (*daimoniois*) and not to God" (vv. 19–20a). First Timothy 4:1 depicts the demonic in an even more active aspect, not as receiving human devotion but as promoting deceitful teaching.

This approach honors certain facets of the scriptural witness. Above all, it allows for continued, full-throated celebration of YHWH as nonpareil: *daimonioi* are, after all, not equal to the true God, and so basically unlike. It also protects the sense of horror and revulsion with which various tracts of Hebrew Scripture regard "other gods": Chemosh considered as a demon would still count, presumably, as an "abomination." It picks up on the seductive dimension of other gods: Israelites succumb to their worship through wiles and chicanery. Exodus 34:16 warns that Canaanite women, once married, would "make thy sons go a whoring [*z-n-h* in *hiphil*] after their gods" (KJV), thereby linking womanly charms with the allure of other gods. Or again, Num 25:18 speaks of *niklêhem*, "their tricks" by which the Midianites "tricked" (*n-k-l*) Israel into prostrating before the god Baal of Peor.

Where this interpretation may run aground is simply in its relatively slim representation within the whole biblical canon. In most of the Hebrew Bible (pace Paul), it does not seem that any malignant spiritual power lurks behind idols; as noted, the goal of anti-idol polemic is to mock idolatry as a solely human production. And nor are the gods of the nations generally portrayed as malevolent fraudsters. In texts that give "other gods" some ontological weight, they are mostly shown "minding their own business": taking care of their own

---

16. See Niehaus, *Ancient Near Eastern Themes*, 179: "Passages such as Deuteronomy 32:16–19; 1 Corinthians 10:20; and 1 Timothy 4:1 tell us clearly enough that demonic powers and intelligences are behind false religion, and even behind false theology in the church." Second Corinthians 11:14 says that Satan himself "masquerades" as an angel of light. This perspective also counts a patristic witness: Origen writes that "we do not consider Jupiter and Sabaoth [i.e., YHWH] to be the same, nor Jupiter to be at all divine, but that some demon, unfriendly to men and to the true God, rejoices under this title" (*Against Celsus* 5.46; in *The Ante-Nicene Fathers*, ed. Alexander Roberts, James Donaldson, and A. Cleveland Coxe, 10 vols. [Grand Rapids: Eerdmans, 1956], 4:564).

17. Friedrich Büchsel, "εἴδωλον," in *Theologische Wörterbuch zum Neuen Testament*, ed. Gerhard Kittel and Gerhard Friedrich, 5 vols. (Stuttgart: Kohlhammer, 1932–1979), 2:377 (=*Theological Dictionary of the New Testament*, ed. Gerhard Kittel and Gerhard Friedrich, trans. Geoffrey W. Bromiley, 10 vols. [Grand Rapids: Eerdmans, 1964–1976], 2:375–80). Compare Büchsel's list here of occurrences of *eidōlon* in the Septuagint with the anti-idol polemic texts listed in note 11 above.

national constituency very much as YHWH does Israel. Judges 11 is an example of this. In this passage, Jephthah beseeches the king of the Ammonites: "Should you not possess what your god Chemosh gives you to possess? And should we not be the ones to possess everything that the LORD our God has conquered for our benefit?" (v. 24). Jephthah's argument depends on the homology between "your god" and "our god." Other passages evince a comparably benign view of other gods.[18] Wiles and chicanery, when they appear, apply more to the human worshippers of other gods than to the activity of gods themselves.

The second approach is the best represented among the theological scholars who discuss the relation of YHWH to "other gods."[19] It appeals, in short, to a "ray of truth" explanation for the "divine parallelism" between YHWH and other ancient gods.[20] Patrick Miller represents one of the most thoughtful spokesmen for this point of view. In his seminal essay "God and the Gods," he expands and elaborates a point made earlier by Hermann Gunkel, who wrote: "The seed of divine revelation has not been strewn only on Jewish soil."[21] In other words, Israel's scriptures have no monopoly on divine truth or the profile of deity. Perhaps these writings constitute an especially successful divine planting, which has grown up into "the greatest among herbs" (Matt 13:32; KJV), but "Jewish soil" remains, as it were, only one seed plant among other spiritual seed plants—apparently of the same divine varietal.

The implications of this latter claim become clearer in Miller's treatment of theological history. With an eye toward the work of systematic theologians Gordon Kaufman and Wolfhart Pannenberg, Miller addresses all of human history as "the locus of God's presence and activity and thus of God's self-disclosure."[22] Similarities between gods at the observable, phenomenological level attest to their common origin: the one divine being, in the process of making itself known, causes history, including religious history, to "ripple" and "echo" (so to speak). Chemosh looks like YHWH because they are both in some way

---

18. In Deut 32:8, for example, "the Most High apportioned the nations, when he divided humankind, he fixed the boundaries of the peoples, according to the number of the gods" (NRSV). See Yair Hoffman, "The Concept of Other Gods in Deuteronomistic Literature," in *Politics and Theopolitics in the Bible and Postbiblical Literature*, ed. Henning Graf Reventlow, Yair Hoffman, and Benjamin Uffenheimer, JSOTSup 171 (Sheffield: JSOT Press, 1994), 66–84; Hans J. Lundager Jensen, "Yahweh and the Other Gods: Acceptance, Rejection, and Cognitive Care," in *Interreligious Relations: Biblical Perspectives*, ed. Hallvard Hagelia and Markus Zehnder, T&T Clark Biblical Studies (London: Bloomsbury T&T Clark, 2017), 12–30, at 18–21.

19. Miller, "God and the Gods"; Schlimm, "Wrestling with Marduk."

20. This is an influential phrase from *Nostra Aetate*, the Roman Catholic Church's Declaration on the Relation of the Church to non-Christian Religions from the Second Vatican Council.

21. Miller, "God and the Gods," 10, citing Werner Klatt, *Hermann Gunkel: zu seiner Theologie der Religionsgeschichte und zur Entstehung der formgeschichtlichen Methode*, FRLANT 100 (Göttingen: Vandenhoeck & Ruprecht, 1969), 75.

22. Miller, "God and the Gods," 31.

extrusions of divinity. Maybe—one hopes—the biblical portraiture of YHWH hews closer to divine reality than does the Mesha Inscription's Chemosh, but they are both truth-bearing relative to the divine, and in view of this shared status, Chemosh deserves at least some of the respect and love accorded to YHWH by Jews and Christians. As Gunkel puts it in regard to the Assyrian god Marduk, "the theologian will do well to handle even the Marduk myth with piety; one honors his parents not by thinking less of his ancestors"—and if ancestors, so also with divine "siblings."[23] Other gods, on this telling, assume a sort of "deuterocanonical" rank.[24]

This approach gains some biblical traction through passages that show YHWH acting in the life of other peoples besides Israel. Amos 9:7 is an example much-loved among Christian Bible scholars. In this verse, YHWH deflates Israel's sense of specialness by putting "exodus in the plural,"[25] by claiming responsibility for relocating other peoples: "Did I not bring Israel up from the land of Egypt, and the Philistines from Caphtor and the Arameans from Kir?" (cf. Deut 2:16–25). Brent Strawn extrapolates from this verse: "All branches of human history, in one way or another, experience the power of the Exodus God."[26]

But this kind of statement bypasses the fact that these peoples would not have recognized YHWH's exodus action *as YHWH's*. They had their own gods, as other biblical texts indicate. The Philistines worshipped Dagon, whose statue YHWH topples during the night (1 Sam 5).[27] The Arameans worshipped Rimmon, as Naaman the cleansed leper regretfully acknowledges to Elisha in 2 Kgs 5:15–19. Is Amos then engaging in a form of willful theological misattribution? Was YHWH going incognito, acting beneficently for Philistines and Arameans under the assumed names of Dagon or Rimmon?

This would seem to go further than Amos intends: it makes of his particular, deflationary rhetorical strategy a global claim about YHWH's operation in the personae of other gods. It also reverses the direction of the theological

---

23. In my own work, I have called Chemosh a "brother" to YHWH, even "twin-like" (Collin Cornell, "What happened to Kemosh?," *ZAW* 128 [2016]: 284–99).

24. This is the direction of Schlimm's remarks: "To what degree is God's revelation present in these other works? Obviously, some works are more revelatory than others. However, can we be more specific and tease out the extent to which we can expect divine revelation outside the Bible? If ancient Near Eastern texts are true when they parallel the Bible, are they (sometimes) also true when they do not parallel scripture?" ("Wrestling with Marduk," 187n22).

25. Walter Brueggemann, "'Exodus' in the Plural (Amos 9:7)," in *Many Voices, One God: Being Faithful in a Pluralistic World*, ed. Walter Brueggemann and George W. Stroup (Louisville, KY: Westminster John Knox, 1998), 7–26.

26. Brent A. Strawn, "What Is Cush Doing in Amos 9:7? The Poetics of Exodus in the Plural," *VT* 63 (2013): 99–123, at 123.

27. So also Judg 16:23 (NIV): "Now the rulers of the Philistines assembled to offer a great sacrifice to Dagon their god and to celebrate, saying, 'Our god has delivered Samson, our enemy, into our hands.'"

misattribution that *is* explicit in Hebrew Scripture. In Hosea 2, for example, YHWH expresses rage that Israel did not recognize that it was *he* and not "her lovers" who gifted Israel with agricultural plenty (v. 8). He pledges to "remove the names of the Baals from [Israel's] mouth" (v. 17). In other words, accurate theological attribution is very important for this passage; getting the name right matters.

This consideration illustrates a critical weakness of the "ray of truth" approach. Such thinking hinges on a certain separability between divinity per se and the god named YHWH. Divinity per se can act under the "guise" of Chemosh, or Marduk, or other gods. The name YHWH is then only one title for divinity, maybe the most privileged or the fullest of truth, but certainly not *the* Name of God in any exclusive or delimiting sense. And yet this is exactly the function of the Tetragrammaton throughout Hebrew Scripture: it specifies and delimits in explicit contrast to other divine claimants. The awed response of the people to the fire falling on Elijah's altar exemplifies the point: "YHWH—*he* is God!" (1 Kgs 18:39); *this* one, under this name, and not that other, named god.[28] As a proper name, the Tetragrammaton distinguishes.[29] Although Christians have sometimes grown forgetful of the biblical God's proper-namedness, it remains theologically primordial: excepting Esther, Song of Songs, and Ecclesiastes, all of Hebrew Scripture uses it.[30] Walther Zimmerli identifies it as "the center of OT speech about God."[31] The second, "ray of truth" approach would seem to diminish, if not to deny, this pervasive biblical testimony. Where God repeatedly declares, "I am YHWH," this approach replies, "but you are also in some sense these other gods." Where Exod 23:13 exhorts not even to let the names of other deities be heard on one's lips, this approach reserves for them, as Gunkel says, some measure of piety.

It is also unclear how this approach could give weight to biblical rhetoric about YHWH's incomparability, or how it would accommodate "other gods" as human products. If other gods, even rivals to YHWH, can be understood as

---

28. This refrain also occurs in: Deut 4:35, 39; Ps 100:3. See Hellmut Rosin, *The Lord is God: The Translation of the Divine Name Names and the Missionary Calling of the Church* (Amsterdam: Netherlands Bible Society, 1956), whose work inspired both K. H. Miskotte and Kendall Soulen, two champions of "name theology."

29. See Kornelis Heiko (K. H.) Miskotte, *Bijbels ABC*, 8th ed. (Utrecht: Kok, 2016), 29: "The name *distinguishes* God *from other beings, gods and demons*. The Bible does not reckon with a general concept of God, only later to add specific names, images, and qualities. The text speaks first and foremost about God as *one god* among other gods." All translations are adapted from the forthcoming English translation of this book by Eleonora Hof and Collin Cornell for Lexington/Fortress.

30. Greek Esther does use *kyrios*.

31. Walther Zimmerli, "Erwägungen zur Gestalt einer alttestamentlichen Theologie," *Theologische Literaturzeitung* 98 (1973): 81–98, at 84 (trans. from Gerhard Hasel's trusty *Old Testament Theology: Basic Issues in the Current Debate* [Grand Rapids: Eerdmans, 1975)], 68n184).

emanations of the same single, more all-encompassing divinity, YHWH is not matchless. God, the one behind and above all names, may be matchless, but YHWH is precisely that: matchable, one of those comparable names, one manifestation among others. The Jewish and Christian intellectual traditions have at times affirmed descriptions of this kind about the absoluteness and anonymity of a divine One. But such thinking bears (at most) an indirect relationship with biblical celebrations of YHWH's incomparability.[32] By the same token, if Chemosh or Marduk are, as some prophetic texts allege, exclusively the result of human craftsmanship, this is difficult to reconcile with their ostensive status as "rays of truth."

The third and final approach to the problem of YHWH and the gods takes departure from the Bible's anti-idol polemic. In fact, it radicalizes yet further the radical extension of idol parody that 2 Chr 32:19 effects. This verse pictures Assyrian messengers treating YHWH "as if he were like the gods of the peoples of the earth, which are the work of human hands." In context, this statement functions as a setup: like Goliath's taunting of the armies of the living God, it is an act of blasphemous defiance placed on the lips of Israel's enemy and preceding the LORD's self-vindication. The profound mistakenness of the Assyrians to classify YHWH as a human projection would soon be proven: the LORD saved Hezekiah and "he was exalted in the sight of all nations from that time onward" (2 Chr 32:23).

Despite this rousing refutation, the blasphemy and theological mistake of the Chronicler's Assyrians was only just beginning its long career. The conviction that many or most—even all—ideas about God amount to "the work of human hands" would exert a massive influence on Christian apophaticism and mysticism. Arguably, a similar notion experienced a resurgence at the hands of the modern "masters of suspicion," who interpreted the Jewish and Christian God as, at base, a human contrivance: a narcotizing weapon in class warfare, a surrogate fantasy father, vengeful mental malware, a collective totem, and so on.

Some thinkers from within Christianity and Judaism made common cause: Karl Barth's *Epistle to the Romans* (first edition, 1918; second edition, 1922) is oftentimes described as "iconoclastic," and Franz Rosenzweig's masterwork *Star of Redemption* (1921) places idolatry at the center of its theological consideration. These theologians in effect charge their own religious traditions with worshipping and serving the product of human religiosity, even and especially

---

32. Interestingly, even during the era of ambient Neoplatonism, a theologian like Origen could still warn Christians not even to speak the names of other gods, lest they thereby inadvertently work a miracle (see Robert M. van den Berg, "Does it Matter to Call God Zeus? Origen *Contra Celsum* 1.24–25 Against the Greek Intellectuals on Divine Names," in *The Revelation of the Name YHWH to Moses: Perspectives from Judaism, the Pagan Graeco-Roman World, and Early Christianity*, ed. George H. van Kooten, Themes in Biblical Narrative 9 [Leiden: Brill, 2006], 169–83).

when it is called "God." They radicalize the Bible's anti-idol polemic. As such, they embrace anthropogenic explanations for god proposed by secular theorists. Garrett Green writes of Karl Barth that his "phenomenology of religion shows him to be in general agreement with the dominant tendency in sociology of religion since Durkheim that interprets religion as a structural aspect of human societies."[33] Gods—including the biblical god—are the precipitate of human, societal forces.

This line of thinking offers a robust answer to the question of YHWH's ancient look-alikes. Chemosh and YHWH resemble one another because they are both patron gods of the southern Levant, and therefore generated by many of the same societal needs and conditions.[34] This approach has the advantage of simplicity. It faces the phenomena of similarity and renders a squarely historical account of it. It would seem, however, to create an insuperable drawback: it results in a YHWH who is as dead, absent, and otiose as all the other ancient deities long since consigned to the "graveyard of the gods."[35] Not only would this result fly in the face of the Bible's bedrock confidence in YHWH's livingness; it would belie the basic sensibility of Jews and Christians that their communities relate to a *true divine counterpart*.

But more may be said: for Barth and his accomplices, the reducibility of deities into human society is not the whole story, or at least not necessarily the whole story. It is a sufficient story.[36] One may, nevertheless, also believe another reality: one can confess, in the words of Barth's friend and disciple, the Dutch theologian K. H. Miskotte, that "God has become 'a' god in order to be known to humanity."[37] By a miracle, that is, God has appointed a particular human construct that we identify as a "god" to reveal the divine self. No inherent qualities of such a thing commend it to this service; it is and remains a

---

33. Garrett Green, "Introduction: Barth as Theorist of Religion," in Karl Barth, *On Religion: The Revelation of God as the Sublimation of Religion*, trans. Garrett Green (London: T&T Clark, 2006), 1–29.

34. Of course, things must have gone otherwise with YHWH, since he survived and thrived where Chemosh faded (on which, see Cornell, "What happened to Kemosh?").

35. See the first line of H. L. Mencken's essay "Memorial Service": "Where is the graveyard of dead gods?" (*A Mencken Chrestomathy: His Own Selection of His Choicest Writings* [New York: Vintage, 1982], 95–98).

36. On the non-necessity of God as an explanation for the world, see, e.g., Dietrich Bonhoeffer: "God as a working hypothesis in morals, politics, or science, has been surmounted and abolished; and the same thing has happened in philosophy and religion. . . . For the sake of intellectual honesty, that working hypothesis should be dropped, or as far as possible, eliminated" (Letter to Eberhard Bethge of July 16, 1944, in *Letters and Papers from Prison, New Greatly Enlarged Edition*, ed. Eberhard Bethge, trans. Reginald Fuller [New York: Touchstone, 1971], 360). See also Eberhard Jüngel, *God as the Mystery of the World: On the Foundation of the Theology of the Crucified One in the Dispute Between Theism and Atheism*, trans. Darrell Guder (Grand Rapids: Eerdmans, 1983), 22, 23.

37. Miskotte, *Bijbels ABC*, 30.

wholly human artifact alongside other, similar artifacts like Chemosh. Yet it now, impossibly and paradoxically, attests to God—*is* God. And it is not as though the LORD "adopted" such a vessel as an occasional, disposable act. God made a human token, "the work of human hands," to be a true replica of God's own self, because God is, by God's own decision, eternally *en route* toward humankind.[38]

There is a christological analogy here, or rather, as Miskotte would have it, a christological episode exemplifying the entire, longstanding divine project.[39] Miskotte retrieves an old dogmatic label for this enterprise: *assumptio carnis*, "assumption of flesh."[40] According to Miskotte, God has truly taken on humanity, and both testaments of the Christian Bible witness to this selfsame event.[41] In Hebrew Scripture, YHWH sanctified and indwelt what is completely and exhaustively human—but not just by inhabiting the tabernacle and temple. Throughout the pages of the Bible, God interacts as humanoid god among humans; all the features of God's working are shaped to human scale. The only "plus" of the New Testament relative to Hebrew Scripture is its specification of the event of God's humanization to one life: that of Jesus Christ.[42] As Miskotte says:

> Anybody who simply cannot "put up" with the incarnation will also not know what to do with YHWH, who speaks and hears, who wounds and heals, who comes down and visits us, who walks in the garden and confuses the language of the tower builders, who accompanies his people in pillars of fire and cloud, who sits enthroned on the cherubim and precisely as such is the God of heaven and earth.[43]

---

38. See K. H. Miskotte, *When the Gods Are Silent*, trans. John W. Doberstein (New York: Harper & Row, 1967), 131: "Just as in the Nativity, so here in these anthropomorphic concepts—no not these concepts, but facts—the whole Godhead is hidden.... God's 'being-one-with' and God's 'being-with' human life are revealed simultaneously in the theophany. And this not as if something happened to God that is alien to him; it is inherent in his° nature to be allied with [humankind], to be intelligible to [humankind], to have communion with [humankind], indeed, to be a man among men." See also Eberhard Jüngel, "The Relationship between 'Economic' and 'Immanent' Trinity," *Theology Digest* 24 (1976): 179–84.

39. Compare the christological analogy deployed by, e.g., Miller, "God and the Gods," 30–31.

40. Miskotte, *When the Gods Are Silent*, 131.

41. See ibid., 128 : "[The one] hears from the witness of the time of remembrance will not wonder at the witness of the time of expectation—or rather [they] will stand before it in utmost wonder, but in such a way that both will equally arouse [their] wonder. [They] will marvel at both as signs that the Lord God has truly taken on human nature. This is not a dogma but a fact of salvation." See also the recent work by Sören Petershans, *Offenbarung des Namens und versöhntes Leben: eine Untersuchung zur Gotteslehre bei Kornelis Heiko Miskotte*, Arbeiten zur Systematischen Theologie 11 (Leipzig: Evangelische Verlagsanstalt, 2016), esp. 186.

42. Miskotte, *When the Gods Are Silent*, 163–64.

43. Ibid., 128.

In sum: out of love, God has freely chosen to be God-with-us, which is to say, human. This much is uncontroversial for Christian theology. Miskotte's innovation is to say that this humanity of God somehow also includes God's appearance as one god among other, comparable gods, considered as the work of human hands. By radicalizing the Bible's anti-idol polemic and acknowledging that YHWH is a human construct, this approach invites sociological explanations of religion to run their course; it does not deny or downplay these avenues of research. At the same time, it lays hold of divine election as the factor binding the true and living God to this particular human production. In its character as God's *free decision*, this link relativizes the theological significance of any observable or historical qualities pertaining to the biblical God. YHWH does not need to "qualify" as unique or powerful or compelling in a way that is traceable by historians: just as YHWH set his love on Israel, "the smallest of nations" (Deut 7:7), so too, and by analogy, God freely self-identified as YHWH, the patron deity of two minor Iron Age kingdoms.[44]

Because it is *God's* free decision to become a god among gods, the equation of YHWH and God ("YHWH—*he* is God!") is sealed with the tensile strength of God's own volition. It is thus *not* like the association of divinity and YHWH in the "ray of truth" approach, which does not embrace the fullness of God's coincidence with this one, specific god, instead imagining a divine being that YHWH only partially concretizes–and which other gods partially concretize also! This third theological way of addressing YHWH's ancient look-alikes also improves on the "ray of truth" approach in that it can full-heartedly praise YHWH's incomparability. It does not divert that praise solely to an all-transcending One who connects only tenuously back to the biblical God. Rather, like Israel, it wonders at the singularity of God's act *of drawing near*—in Deuteronomy, by exodus and fire: "Has any people ever heard the voice of a god speaking out of a fire? . . . Or has any god ever attempted to go and take a nation for himself from the midst of another nation?" (4:33–34a)—but also, on this line of thinking, by taking on human form, and even by accepting a human artifact as true divine self-disclosure.

Conclusion

In the end, then, there may be no easy relief for the theological vertigo I experienced back in seminary: it *is* disorienting to praise YHWH as peerless while looking at his ancient divine peers; it *is* dizzying to experience YHWH as a true

---

44. After all, and remembering the christological focus of Miskotte's work: "He hath no form nor comeliness. . . . There is no beauty that we should desire him" (Isa 53:2; KJV).

divine counterpart at the same time that one explains him as the result of human and societal forces. What Miskotte and his theological colleagues provide is a lens for holding these truths together, or perhaps better, a reframing of that vertigo as a fitting response to the *skandalon* ("scandal") of God's willfully humble self-presentation to the world (1 Cor 1:23). "God is for us," Miskotte writes, "smaller"[45]—smaller than whatever grand attributes we would naturally ascribe to divinity, and which would save God from appearing so much like Chemosh, the forgotten god of a bygone nation.

---

45. Miskotte, *Bijbels ABC*, 48.

CHAPTER 7

Chemosh Looks Like YHWH, but That's Okay

Josey Bridges Snyder

Growing up in the church, I was taught from a young age that there is only one God. I was aware that other peoples in the Bible worshipped other gods, but I knew them only as "fake" and "bad." They did not warrant any attention because they were not real. To the extent that we did discuss the gods of other peoples in the Bible, we contrasted them to the one true God. There was no room for acknowledging similarity between, say, the ("little g") god of Moab and the ("big G") God of Israel. One was fake and one was real. End of story.

I am still a person of faith grounded in my belief in one, true God. However, I no longer feel that beliefs about other deities in the ancient world are irrelevant to my faith. Beliefs about the God of Israel did not emerge in a void. The ancient world was full of ideas about the gods and how they interacted with the human and natural world, and the Israelites were clearly familiar with these other peoples and their deities.

Whether the earliest Israelites themselves worshipped one god or many—a question debated among scholars of the ancient world—we know that they lived in a world where the existence of multiple deities was assumed.[1] Moreover, examination of these other gods and the beliefs and practices associated with them reveals many similarities with the beliefs and practices of the earliest Israelites.

That such similarities exist is not surprising. The Israelites received categories and frameworks for understanding and expressing belief in the divine from the surrounding culture. Thus, even if we hold that Israel had a unique

---

1. Clearly, the dominant perspective preserved in the Bible is that there is only one God (e.g., Isa 45:5), or at the very least, only one God that matters. However, it is likely that this theology developed later, and that earlier Israelites believed in the existence of (and perhaps even worshipped) other deities. Certainly there are places in Scripture where the existence of other deities is simply assumed (e.g., Exod 12:12), even if those deities are presented as powerless in the face of the all-powerful YHWH.

experience with the one true God, they spoke about their experience of God using words, concepts, and images that were familiar to them.

This fact is the basis for much comparative research about the God of Israel and other ancient deities. But should this research, and the evidence it has unearthed, be cause for alarm to modern-day people of faith? In other words, are these "other deities" and their similarities with YHWH a problem? And to the extent that the answer is "yes," how ought modern-day people of faith think about the evidence emerging from the ancient world and what it means for religious practice today?

In this essay, I will consider these questions within the context of my own research on Moab and the Moabite national deity, Chemosh.[2] To do so, I'll start out by offering an overview of why I find Moab to be a useful point of comparison with Israel. Then, I will review the evidence available for studying Moabite religion, with particular attention to the question of whether Moabites worshipped any deities other than Chemosh. Finally, I will speak as a person of faith and offer my own view on the extent to which Chemosh presents a theological problem as an "ancient look-alike."

Why Moab?

For some time, scholars have gravitated toward the wealth of data from Ugarit (a Canaanite city-state in northern Syria that was destroyed around 1200 BCE) to provide a framework for how ancient Israelites might have thought about God, and with good reason.[3] The Ugaritic language shares many similarities with Hebrew, and many known deity names from Ugarit show up in the Bible. Moreover, we have a lot of evidence from Ugarit, giving scholars a deeper knowledge of their religion than we have for many other ancient peoples.

In Ugarit, the people venerated multiple deities who existed in a pantheon, ruled by the supreme deity El and his consort Athirat, both of whom have made their imprint in Hebrew Scripture. In addition to being the name of a specific deity, "El" is a common noun for "god" in Semitic languages like Hebrew, and it is found all over Hebrew Scripture as another name or title for Israel's God, YHWH. Scholars have also found evidence of Athirat in the Bible, by suggesting a connection with Asherah, a goddess associated with Baal in Scripture (Judg 3:7) whose name is highly similar to the Ugaritic Athirat.

2. Josey Bridges Snyder, "Did Kemosh Have a Consort (or Any Other Friends)? Re-assessing the Moabite Pantheon," *UF* 42 (2010): 645–75.
3. The first Ugaritic tablets were discovered in 1928. Once they were identified and deciphered (early 1930s), their import for biblical scholars was clear and Ugarit became a focus of comparative study with ancient Israel.

Yet even the presence of the goddess Asherah in Scripture is not completely clear. A form of the word *'ăšērâ* appears in Hebrew Scripture forty times, but in almost every case, it clearly refers to a wooden cult object, not the name of a goddess. Again and again, the Israelites are commanded to "cut down" these "asherahs" (e.g., Exod 34:13 and Deut 7:5) and to rid their worship of these and other foreign objects and practices (Deut 12:3).

Yet the very frequency of these prohibitions has caused some to suggest that the use of "asherahs" must have been somewhat prevalent in ancient Israel. Why would there be a specific injunction against "planting an *'ăšērâ* beside the altar of the LORD (Deut 16:21) unless there were people doing just that? Even more compelling are two extrabiblical inscriptions that refer to YHWH and "his asherah."[4] Clearly some associated this wooden cult object with the worship of YHWH, even if the Bible did not approve.

But does the use of the sacred pole *'ăšērâ* mean that ancient Israelites also worshipped the goddess by that name? Does the model from Ugarit whereby the supreme deity is paired with a consort mean that ancient Israelites also imagined a wife for their god, YHWH?

Direct evidence for ancient Israelite goddess worship is tenuous. Most who argue for it do so on the assumption that ancient Israelite religion would have looked, more or less, like the religion of their neighbors. In other words, if all ancient Canaanite peoples worshipped goddesses as consorts alongside their supreme deities, then surely ancient Israelites did as well. But did all ancient Canaanite peoples imagine that their deities were married?

Scholars who answer these questions in the affirmative tend to rely heavily on the comparative evidence from Ugarit to establish a Canaanite pattern of pairing supreme deities with consorts. But is Ugarit—a society removed in space and time from ancient Israel—the best model for understanding the culture and worldview of ancient Israelites? In my work, I have questioned the over-reliance on Ugarit and instead offered an alternative: Moab. In particular, I asked whether Moab, a neighbor closer in time and place to Israel than Ugarit, provided an example of a Canaanite people who worshipped a single God.[5]

---

4. The inscriptions, found at Khirbet el-Qom and Kuntillet ʿAjrud, are quite similar. One recognizes YHWH for the act of saving "by his *'ăšērâ*," and the other recognizes YHWH for the act of blessing "by his *'ăšērâ*." These inscriptions clearly associate the *'ăšērâ* with YHWH, but they do not clearly identify any goddess as YHWH's consort. In particular, scholars have noticed that the 3ms suffix "his" would not likely apply to a proper name, meaning this reference is most likely to a cult object and not a deity. For a recent interpretation of these inscriptions, see Joel M. LeMon and Brent A. Strawn, "Once More, Yhwh and Company at Kuntillet ʿAjrud," *Maarav* 20 (2013): 83–114 and plates VI–VII (appeared 2015).

5. In taking this position, I follow the work of Othmar Keel and Christoph Uehlinger, who have criticized other scholars for being too drawn to the textual data from places like Ugarit and instead insist that research should begin with whatever evidence is available for the period and location in

We know that Moabites worshipped Chemosh, but it is less clear whether Chemosh (like El) had a wife or consort and pantheon. If Moabites worshipped a single deity apart from any consort or pantheon, then this would provide an alternative model to that provided by Ugarit. Moreover, such an alternative model would challenge those who presume an Israelite polytheism on the basis of comparative data.

The Biblical Portrayal of Moab and Its God(s)

The Moabites are frequent players in Hebrew Scripture and are usually depicted in negative ways. Genesis narrates their origin story, describing them as the ill-conceived child of Lot and his eldest daughter (Gen 19:37). Numbers depicts them as a rival neighbor threatened by Israel's emergence in the land (Num 22–24) and as a dangerous influence, easily luring Israelites into faithlessness (Num 25:1–5). As a result, God commands Israel to exclude all Moabites from their assembly, even to the tenth generation (Deut 23:3–4; cf. Neh 13:1–2). Even more, Israel is prohibited from promoting the welfare or prosperity of Moab (Deut 23:6), a sharp contrast with the many biblical mandates to care for foreigners and other outsiders (e.g., Lev 19:33–34 and Deut 10:19).

Indeed, Moab becomes a bit of a favorite rival, with many biblical stories clearly intended to poke fun at them. One can easily imagine Israelites sitting around a campfire laughing at the Moabite King Balak, whose many attempts to get Balaam to curse Israel were thwarted—once even by a talking donkey (Num 22:22–35)! Moreover, the story of Ehud and King Eglon is full of satire—and even potty humor (Judg 3:24–25)—offering plenty of laughs for Israelites to remember how their left-handed hero defeated the Moabite king (Judg 3).

And yet, the Bible also offers plenty of countervoices against this "Moabites are awful" tradition. In the book of Ruth, an Israelite family finds refuge in Moab during a time of famine (1:1). Then, Ruth the Moabite is welcomed into Israel. She demonstrates great loyalty and is shown favor by an Israelite landowner (2:8–9) who eventually takes her as his wife (4:13), ensuring her security and that of her mother-in-law, Naomi. Her great-grandson, David, then becomes king of Israel. Even more, during his rise to power, when David has conflict in Israel, he reaches out to the Moabite king, who offers refuge and protection to David's mother and father (i.e., Ruth's grandson; see 1 Sam 22:3–4). Talk about

---

question. For the religion of ancient Israel, this leads Keel and Uehlinger to focus on iconographic data and, in particular, stamp seals, which often contain text (most notably, the name of the owner of the stamp) and images. See Othmar Keel and Christoph Uehlinger, *Gods, Goddesses, and Images of God in Ancient Israel*, trans. Thomas H. Trapp (Minneapolis: Fortress, 1998).

a counternarrative! David is only three generations removed from Moab, and yet he becomes king of Israel (cf. Deut 23:6).

Biblical data about Moabite religion are similarly fraught with challenges. The clearest and most frequent biblical message about Moabite religion is that Moabites worshipped Chemosh (Num 21:29; 1 Kgs 11:7, 33; 2 Kgs 23:13; Jer 48:7, 13, 46), though there is one errant reference that associates Chemosh with the Ammonites (Judg 11:24). However, there is also some evidence Moabites may have worshipped other deities. In particular, Num 25 tells a story where Moabites venerate Baal of Peor, and Judg 10:6 mentions the "gods of Moab," which makes it sound like the Moabites worshiped more than one god.

Yet, it is unclear if either of these references mean the Moabites actually worshipped multiple deities. First, Baal of Peor could be an epithet—"the lord of Peor"—that actually refers to Chemosh, or any deity. Moreover, the plural reference to Moabite "gods" in Judg 10:6 occurs in a list that includes the gods of Aram, the gods of Sidon, the gods of the Ammonites, and the gods of the Philistines—so it is possible that the plural reference to Moabite deities reflects patterned language, rather than a detailed knowledge of a Moabite pantheon.

Other references to Moabite god(s) are even more difficult to interpret, primarily due to the literary difficulty that the Hebrew *'elōhîm*—while technically plural in form—can be used to refer either to multiple deities ("gods") or to a single deity ("God"). This problem is illustrated most clearly in Ruth 1:15–16:

> And she said, "Look, your sister-in-law has returned to her mother and to her *'elōhîm*. Return after your sister-in-law." But Ruth said, "Do not press me to abandon you, to turn back from following you. For where you go, I will go. Where you stay, I will stay. Your people will be my people. Your *'elōhîm* will be my *'elōhîm*."

The same Hebrew word *'elōhîm* occurs three times in this passage (with different suffixes—first "her," then "your," and finally "my"). Yet, many English translations choose to translate the first as "gods" and the latter two as "God"—based on the assumption that Orpah worshipped multiple deities whereas Naomi (and by extension Ruth) worshipped only one.[6] Grammatically, there is no difference

---

6. See, e.g., CEB, ESV, KJV, New International Version, New Jewish Publication Society *Tanakh*, New Living Translation, and NRSV. In part, this tradition may originate with the Septuagint, the second-century-BCE translation of the HB into Greek. Greek lacks the grammatical anomaly where the plural "gods" can also be used as a name for "God." In that translation, the translators similarly chose the plural for Orpah's "god" and the singular form for Naomi's. Since early Christians accepted the Septuagint as Scripture, this translation has been highly influential in Christian translations and interpretations.

to justify this distinction, leading other translators to choose the singular for both Orpah's "god" and Naomi's.[7]

Even if biblical data concerning Moabite god(s) were clear, it would be difficult to determine how precisely it depicts Moabite religion. On the one hand, Israelites clearly interacted with Moabites and, as such, must have known something about them. On the other hand, biblical writings about Moab and Moabites are much more interested in using them to demonstrate the superiority of Israel's God than in preserving Moabite culture and traditions. Moreover, many—if not all—of these texts were written later, well after contact with actual Moabites would have ceased.

Thus, in my research, I took the biblical data about Moabite religion as a starting point, but instead of using it to answer a question, I used it to pose a question: did the Moabites worship multiple deities? And, in particular, did the Moabite deity Chemosh have a consort (wife) or a pantheon? The answer to this question matters because it provides a possible counterexample to the frequent scholarly narrative about ancient Near Eastern religion, where every people group had a national deity, and every god existed in a network of gods and goddesses who competed with one another for power and prestige.

Other Evidence for Multiple Moabite Deities?

Evidence outside of the Bible for multiple Moabite deities is scarce, but not nonexistent. Those who claim Moabites worshipped a goddess alongside Chemosh tend to do so on the basis of one or more of the following (not convincing) pieces of evidence: a reference in the Mesha Inscription to Ashtar-Chemosh; the depiction of a male and female deity on the Balua stele; the existence of both male and female figurines of Moabite provenance; and the presence of star and moon iconography on Moabite stamp seals. Each of these data constitutes valuable evidence for the study of Moabite religion, but—as I argue in my prior work—none offer sufficient evidence for a consort to Chemosh.

The possible connection between Ashtar in the Mesha Inscription and the goddess Astarte or even Ishtar is intriguing, but in the end, there is simply not enough evidence to make that leap. On its own, Ashtar is the name of a male god, not a goddess. Moreover, in context, it is clear that Ashtar-Chemosh is used as an alternative name for Chemosh, and not as a reference to any other deity (male or female). Here is the relevant quote:

---

7. See, e.g., the original Jewish Publication Society *Tanakh* (1917), American Standard Version, Complete Jewish Bible, New American Bible, New English Translation, and Young's Literal Translation. Note that, in these latter examples, the translators still distinguish between Orpah's "god" and Naomi's "God" (lower- versus upper-case).

Chemosh said to me, "Go seize Nebo from Israel." So I went at night and fought against it from the break of dawn until noon. I seized it and killed all of them: 7000 men, boys, women, girls, and concubines—because to Ashtar-Chemosh I devoted it. And I took from there the vessels of YHWH and I dragged them before Chemosh.[8]

It would not make sense for Mesha to devote the city to a deity other than the one who commanded him to conquer it, especially when the Mesha Inscription never refers to a deity other than Chemosh. If anything, the name Ashtar-Chemosh might reflect the assimilation of characteristics of a deity Ashtar into the deity Chemosh. Moreover, if assimilation did happen, that could be evidence that Moabites did not venerate another deity, preferring to apply all divine characteristics to one god in lieu of worshipping multiple gods side-by-side.

Similar problems exist with the other data named above. While the Baluʻa stele does clearly present a male and female deity flanking a human figure, it is not at all clear that the image comes from Moab. In fact, the stele may predate the emergence of Moab, and the human figure may actually be a Shashu king rather than a Moabite.[9] Similarly problematic, the male and female figurines—which can be identified as Moabite with confidence—may not represent deities. They could, instead, be votive images of the worshipper, a sort of proxy that would worship the deity in the worshipper's absence.[10] In that case, the female figurine would not be a goddess at all, but rather a female worshipper of any deity.

The most compelling evidence from this list is actually the sun and moon iconography on Moabite stamp seals. Sun and moon images are known to represent deities in the ancient world, and their frequent use on Moabite stamp seals could reflect Moabite veneration of deities like Sin and Ishtar, a god and goddess identified with these symbols in other Mesopotamian contexts.[11] Yet this evidence would be much stronger if it were accompanied by any other indication that Moabites worshipped Sin and Ishtar, or any other god–goddess pair.

---

8. Mesha Inscription, ll. 14–18. For more on the interpretation of Ashtar-Chemosh in its literary context, see Josey Bridges Snyder and Brent A. Strawn, "Reading (in) Moabite Patterns: 'Parallelism' in the Mesha Inscription and Its Implications for Understanding Three Cruxes ('*štr kmš*, line 17; *ḥ/ryt*, line 12; and *'r'l dwdh*, line 12)" (forthcoming).

9. For the suggestion that the king is Shashu, not Moabite, see W. A. Ward and M. F. Martin, "That Baluʻa Stele: A New Transcription with Palaeological and Historical Notes," *ADAJ* 8–9 (1964): 5–29, at 17.

10. See P. M. Michèle Daviau, "New Light on Iron Age Religious Iconography: The Evidence from Moab," *Studies in the History and Archaeology of Jordan* 7 (1999): 317–26, at 324.

11. For a scholar who draws this connection with Moabite stamp-seal iconography, see Paul J. Ray, "Kemosh and Moabite Religion," *Near East Archaeological Society Bulletin* 48 (2003): 17–31, at 20.

To investigate whether this evidence existed, I turned to an often-overlooked source: personal names inscribed on stamp seals. Stamp seals were small, often coin-shape pieces of clay that were used to identify the owner. For example, a stamp seal might be pressed into a clay jar that had not yet dried, thus leaving an impression that would mark the jar as belonging to the owner of the seal. These seals often included imagery—like the sun and moon iconography—and, in many cases, the name of the owner of the seal.

Ancient Semitic personal names frequently included mention of deities, much like the modern names "Christina" and "Christopher" include the deity name "Christ." This phenomenon is even stronger with ancient Semitic names, which often form sentences. For example, the Hebrew name "Elijah" means "YHWH is my God" and the name "Joshua" means "YHWH saves." So, at least in theory, it is possible to learn something about a people's religion by studying the names they choose for their children.

One further advantage of studying stamp seals is that they give us access to the names of real Moabite people, not just literary characters, whose names may be invented by the author, or kings, whose names are more likely to reflect state-sponsored religion than actual "religion on the ground." Thus, studying the names on stamp seals provides small windows into the lives and values of real Moabite people, who may or may not follow state-sponsored religious practice with full devotion and accuracy.

So what do Moabite personal names tell us about the religious values of Moabites? First, as expected, Moabite personal names confirm that Chemosh is the dominant deity. Of the names I surveyed, twelve included the deity name "Chemosh" as a part of the personal name, including Chemosh versions of the two Hebrew names mentioned above: Chemoshel (Chemosh is god) and Chemoshua (Chemosh saves). These names confirm what we already know: Moabites worshipped Chemosh.

But did Moabites worship any other deities? Six of the names I surveyed might indicate "yes." One name could refer to El (Amarel, "El speaks"), one could refer to Baal (Baalnatan, "Baal gives"), two could refer to Melek, or perhaps Malk (Mlky'zr,[12] "May Melek help," and Padmelek, "Melek redeems"), one could refer to Horon (Ebedhoron, "Servant of Horon"), and one could refer to Rahban (Ebedrahban, "Servant of Rahban"). However, four of these suffer from the same difficulty as biblical references to "El." Namely, the deity name in question (El, Baal, and Melek) are synonymous with common nouns ("god," "lord," and

---

12. None of these names actually has vowels on the stamp seals. In the names where I include vocalization, I am offering a best guess based on knowledge of how Semitic languages work. In this case, at least two very different options exist, and so I played it safe and left the name consonantal. *'Ebed* was probably pronounced *abd in an earlier form of Hebrew (cf. its suffixed forms like *'abdekā*, "your servant").

"king," respectively). As such, any of these names could be epithets referring to a human king or another deity, including Chemosh. The Moabite personal name Chemoshel ("Chemosh is god") offers further evidence for this possibility, since, in this name, 'ēl clearly means "god" and not the supreme god El from Ugarit.

Given these difficulties, I found the names Ebedhoron and Ebedrahban to hold the strongest evidence for Moabite worship of a deity other than Chemosh, with Horon being the most likely candidate for Moabite veneration. While there could be some ambiguity over whether *hrn* refers to the deity Horon or the place Hauron (Ezek 47:16, 18), the appellation *'ebed* (or perhaps **abd*) or "servant of" confirms that this personal name has the deity in mind. Horon is a Northwest Semitic deity who pops up in multiple places, including Mari, Ugarit, and Phoenicia.[13] Moreover, the name "Horon" also appears in the name of a place mentioned in the Mesha Inscription as a place that King Mesha "restored" to Moab (l. 31). A place-name may not be strong evidence for concurrent veneration of a deity, but given how small the Moabite corpus is, the presence of the same deity name in both a personal name and a place name cannot be ignored.

The significance of the personal name Ebedrahban is less clear, if only because we have no idea who Rahban is. The structure of the name, with "servant of" as the appellation, makes it appear that Rahban must refer to a deity. However, Rahban does not occur in any other names on West Semitic stamp seals, and instead is only found in pre-Islamic Arabian sources, and may be an epithet for the goddess Timna—in which case it is probably an Arabian name reflecting worship in Arabia.

This possibility raises an important caveat to the study of personal names: people travel. Just because a name appears on a stamp seal found in Moab does not necessarily mean that the name reflects religious practice in Moab. In order for evidence from personal names to be convincing, there needs to be a pattern—like the pattern of Moabite personal names that include reference to Chemosh. When it comes to other deities, that pattern simply does not exist.

However, there is one other pattern that emerges from the study of Moabite personal names: names that include a kinship term like "father," "brother," or "uncle" in the place where a deity name would otherwise appear. In my study of Moabite personal names, I identified six, two that mentioned father and four that mention brother. Even more, two of these names are directly parallel to Moabite personal names mentioning Chemosh. Abaz ("the father is strong") parallels Chemoshaz ("Chemosh is strong"), and Aḥyiḥi ("May the brother live") parallels Chemoshyiḥi ("May Chemosh live"). These names demonstrate a reverence for ancestors that parallels reverence for Chemosh, and they could be evidence for ancestor worship in Moab.

---

13. See Udo Rüterswörden, "Horon," in *DDD*, 426.

However, that possibility—that worship of Chemosh might have existed alongside of some form of ancestor veneration—is not the same thing as the Moabites venerating a pantheon of deities. Moreover, there is still no convincing evidence that Moabites worshipped a goddess alongside Chemosh. On those points, the current evidence points to Moabite veneration of a single national deity who did not have a wife or a pantheon.

Conclusion

So, what should all of this mean to a modern-day person of faith? First, and perhaps most importantly, people of faith should not be afraid of the data. No matter the direction the evidence points, the evidence itself need not become a stumbling block. Faith in God cannot be challenged or changed by any evidence or data one might unearth. Simply put, no data could ever prove or disprove God's identity or existence. That is why belief in God is called faith. As a scholar and a person of faith, I find great comfort in this fact. Yes, it is possible that the data will challenge things we believe about history or the Bible. It may even challenge things we believe about God or ourselves. But the data has no power to change God, to make God any less real, or to make us any less beloved by God.

Second, God gave us brains, and it is okay to use them. Faith will always be belief in things we cannot know, but it does not require turning a blind eye to things that can be known.[14] Nor does it require forcing the evidence to fit any particular viewpoint in order to "prove" a certain perspective. Studying the Bible can and should change what we believe about who God is. The more we learn, the more our faith grows and matures. Sometimes that growth is uncomfortable, and sometimes it takes us places we did not expect, but God does not abandon us along the journey.

In this essay, I have reviewed the evidence available for Moabite religion, with particular attention to answering the question of whether the Moabites worshipped any deities other than Chemosh. The evidence I found was conclusive on only one point: Moabites definitely worshipped Chemosh. As for other deities—the picture is much less clear. Still, I found that fact—the inconclusive

---

14. For other scholars who seek to articulate how their faith interacts with their practice of biblical scholarship, see Marc Zvi Brettler, Peter Enns, and Daniel J. Harrington, *The Bible and the Believer: How to Read the Bible Critically and Religiously* (Oxford: Oxford University Press, 2012). Other works by Peter Enns may also be useful, especially to Protestant Christians wrestling with how to maintain faith when evidence challenges things we thought we were supposed to believe. See, most recently, Peter Enns, *How the Bible Actually Works: In Which I Explain How an Ancient, Ambiguous, and Diverse Book Leads Us to Wisdom Rather than Answers—And Why That's Great News* (San Francisco: Harper Collins, 2019).

nature of the evidence—to be very interesting. It means we cannot assume that Moabites worshipped multiple gods or that Chemosh was part of a pantheon. It means that the Moabites might provide an ANE example of a people who worshipped a "bachelor god"—and that, in turn, might provide corroborating evidence that ancient Israel too could have been a single-deity people.

Yet I would caution modern-day people of faith from finding either "good" or "bad" news in this conclusion. Certainly, the possibility that Moabites worshipped only one god could be comforting to a Christian who is not keen on suggestions that YHWH had a wife. However, even if new evidence emerged tomorrow that proved that not only did Chemosh have a wife, but YHWH did too, this would not need to pose a challenge to people of faith today. It would simply paint a different picture of our past.

We can believe that ancient Israelites had real experiences with the real God without capturing that God completely within their imaginings or writings—just as people of faith today can have real experiences with the real God without comprehending the fullness of who and how God is in the world. So too, we can believe that Scripture is fully divine and fully of God without capturing the fullness of who God is.

When we accept that our faith is in a living God who meets us in history but is not fully contained or defined by that history, it frees us to study the history with an open mind and genuine curiosity. In this way, the ancient look-alikes need not pose a problem to people of faith at all. In fact, rather than a problem, I might call it an opportunity. If other ancient peoples believed similar things about their deities, then we have even more opportunity to study and learn about the world the Israelites inhabited and how that world shaped their depictions of God. This, in turn, gives us more opportunity to come to understand our own story and the myriad ways God has entered into it to seek us.

CHAPTER 8

YHWH and Chemosh: An Investigation of Look-Alike Gods Using the Moral Foundations Theory

M. Patrick Graham

Introduction

The Mesha Inscription

The Mesha Inscription first came to the attention of Europeans in August 1868, when Arab bedouin showed the monument to F. A. Klein, a German missionary serving the Church Missionary Society. This set off a race by representatives of England, Germany, and France to secure the stone for their nations, and eventually, the monument was severely damaged by the bedouin so that what remained was an incomplete artifact. Nevertheless, the French scholar Charles Clermont-Ganneau was able to outbid the English and secure fragments of the stone as well as an earlier impression of it so that he could publish a translation and analysis of the monument and place the reconstructed monument in the Louvre Museum. The entire affair was controversial and generated much public interest in the Bible and archaeology generally.[1] After more than a century of subsequent archaeological exploration, the Mesha Inscription still "remains the longest Iron Age inscription ever recovered east or west of the Jordan, the major evidence for the Moabite language, and a unique epigraphic source of stories about military campaigns in this region."[2]

God's Ancient Look-Alikes as a Theological Problem

The task of this paper is not to advance the scholarly investigation of the various gods and their cults from antiquity but to focus on the theological issues

---

1. For an account of the discovery and early interpretation of the Mesha Inscription, see my article "The Discovery and Reconstruction of the Mesha' Inscription," in *Studies in the Mesha Inscription and Moab*, ed. J. Andrew Dearman, ABS 2 (Atlanta: Scholars Press, 1989), 41–92.
2. Simon B. Parker, *Stories in Scripture and Inscriptions: Comparative Studies on Narratives in Northwest Semitic Inscriptions and the Hebrew Bible* (Oxford: Oxford University Press, 1997), 44.

posed for contemporary audiences because of the similarities between Israel's God and Moab's Chemosh. Stated succinctly, although the Hebrew Bible made exclusive and extravagant claims for Israel's God—creator of the world, ruler over the forces of nature and human affairs, and superior to all deities—scholars have found that some of what Israel claimed for YHWH had also been claimed for Chemosh and by Israel's neighbors for their gods. Therefore, as a relative late-comer to the ancient Near East, would it not make better sense to conclude that ancient Israel simply imitated the religious beliefs and practices of her neighbors?[3]

Limitations

Any attempt to address the foregoing question will confront serious methodological and other difficulties. For example, archaeological investigation and interpretation of ancient texts remains incomplete and continues to revise historical reconstructions. In addition, while texts from Egypt and Mesopotamia are plentiful, those from Moab are not, especially in comparison with the religious texts of the HB: the primary text surviving from Moab is an incomplete, thirty-four-line royal inscription. Therefore, we recognize from the outset that the effort of this paper is of necessity a comparison of texts that differ in genre and other respects. In addition, the HB was produced by many persons over centuries, resulting in a complex that continues to generate scholarly and religious controversy. Finally, as it stands now, the HB is thoroughly theological, and it is impossible for most contemporary readers not to read its components as theological documents.[4] The Mesha Inscription, however, may derive from a single authorial hand, created at one point in time, and suffered nothing at the hands of later editors or copyists.[5] It is an incomplete memorial or building inscription intended for public display, and while it has religious elements, it was not a theological document.[6] As noted earlier, no Israelite monumental text of similar size or significance has yet to be discovered in Palestine.

---

3. See Mark S. Smith, *The Origins of Biblical Monotheism: Israel's Polytheistic Background and the Ugaritic Texts* (Oxford: Oxford University Press, 2001), 149–66; Patrick D. Miller, *The Religion of Ancient Israel*, Library of Ancient Israel (Louisville, KY: Westminster John Knox, 2000), 12–13, 24–29, 31–43; Gerald L. Mattingly, "Moabite Religion and the Meshaʿ Inscription," in Dearman, *Studies*, 211–38.
4. See Parker, *Stories*, 6–8.
5. Parker sees two editions for the Mesha Inscription (*Stories*, 53–54).
6. Klaas A. D. Smelik, "King Mesha's Inscription," in *Converting the Past: Studies in Ancient Israelite and Moabite Historiography*, OtSt 28 (Leiden: Brill, 1992), 59–92; Smelik, "Moabite Inscriptions," in *The Context of Scripture*, ed. William W. Hallo, 3 vols. (Leiden: Brill, 2003), 2:137; Joel F. Drinkard, "The Literary Genre of the Meshaʿ Inscription," in Dearman, *Studies*, 131–54.

The Path Forward

In the pages that follow we will move through three steps of presentation. First, we will offer a brief summary of the Mesha Inscription, note the similarities between what it says about Chemosh and what the HB says about YHWH, and identify the qualities of the deity Chemosh that resemble what the HB has to say about Israel's God. Next, we will introduce the Moral Foundations Theory (hereafter, MFT) and use it as a hermeneutical lens for comparing the Mesha Inscription with the HB. Finally, we will end with theological reflections for contemporary audiences interested in look-alike deities.

The Mesha Inscription, the Hebrew Bible, and Look-Alike Gods

The Mesha Inscription has been dated to the mid-ninth century BCE and celebrates the military and public works achievements of the Moabite King Mesha, with particular focus on his successes against Israel and the Omride dynasty (cf. 2 Kgs 1–3) in the area of the northern plateau in Transjordan. Correlations with texts from the HB about this region and period continue to be difficult.[7]

The inscription[8] may be divided into four parts:

1. Introduction (ll. 1–4a);
2. Reports of how Mesha drove Israel from regions of Moab (ll. 4b–21a);
3. Mesha's building projects (ll. 21b–31a);
4. A fragmentary part continues, perhaps similar to the building projects listed in no. 3 above (ll. 31b–34).[9]

The language and certain social, political, and military practices in Iron Age Israel resonate well with those in ancient Moab, as one would expect, and the HB itself notes the affinity of the peoples of Israel and Judah with their neighbors, roundly condemning along the way Israelite adoption of the practices of their neighbors and the intermarriage of Israelites with their neighbors. A comparison of the Mesha Inscription and the HB shows similarities in

---

7. For the historical setting of the Mesha Inscription, see Andrew Dearman, "Historical Reconstruction and the Mesha Inscription," in Dearman, *Studies*, 155–210, and Eveline J. Van der Steen and Klaas A. D. Smelik, "King Mesha and the Tribe of Dibon," *Journal for the Study of the Old Testament* 32 (2007): 139–62, at 154.

8. K. C. Hanson's translation of the Mesha Inscription is available online at kchanson.com/ANCDOCS/westsem/mesha.html; for the most recent and authoritative translation, though, see Smelik, "Moabite Inscriptions," 2:137–38, from which all quotations in this essay will be taken.

9. Parker, *Stories*, 44.

historiography, descriptions of royal building and military projects, and resettlement of populations in conquered lands. As for similarities between Chemosh of Moab and YHWH of Israel, the following roster is offered.

1. Chemosh and YHWH were portrayed as male deities (l. 4).[10]
2. Kings and others bore theophoric names honoring deities (l. 1).[11]
3. Kings built shrines for their gods (ll. 3, 4, 9).
4. Deities punished their peoples (l. 5).
5. Deities communicated with kings (ll. 14–18).
6. Deities directed their kings to attack enemies (ll. 14–18, 32).
7. Deities defeated foreign armies (ll. 4, 9, 19, 33).
8. Deities received those slaughtered by their rulers as offerings/tribute (ll. 11–13, 16–18).
9. Deities received cult objects of the defeated as offerings/tribute (ll. 11–13, 16–18).

A Moral Foundations Theory Reading of the Mesha Inscription

When comparing two distinct phenomena, the temptation is always toward reduction—to count things in each to see which is greater or to list things for quick and easy comparison. Results are typically superficial. More substantive and useful comparisons require some sort of qualitative approach. What follows in the current project is the use of the Moral Foundations Theory (MFT), one of the more recent theories of social psychology or moral psychology.[12]

Jonathan Haidt and fellow researchers assert that certain moral foundations have undergirded human thinking since the beginning and extend across the globe. While all people do not always use the full roster of moral foundations,[13] they do select from these to varying degrees, and their selections reveal much about their values. The six moral foundations comprising the current list are articulated in terms of pairs:

---

10. Although the HB's anthropomorphism typically portrays God as male but not as a *sexual* male, the HB also uses female images for God (Smith, *Origins*, 86–93).
11. Mesha's father was Chemosh-yat/Chemosh-yatti, and the HB preserves many names with Yah(weh) in them (e.g., Isa*iah*, Jos*iah*).
12. Jonathan Haidt, *The Righteous Mind: Why Good People Are Divided by Politics and Religion* (New York: Pantheon, 2012), xii. To take the "Moral Foundations Questionnaire," see moralfoundations.org/questionnaires.
13. Haidt and his colleagues express openness to other researchers making the case for additional foundations at moralfoundations.org/. The following list and quotes directly describing the individual pairings in the list are taken from this main page of their site.

1. Care/harm
2. Fairness/cheating
3. Loyalty/betrayal
4. Authority/subversion
5. Sanctity/degradation
6. Liberty/oppression

Although the MFT is still undergoing critique and refinement, scholars in a variety of fields have begun to experiment with it to see what light it might shed on the issues and texts with which they deal. It is in this spirit that we use it to explore two different Iron Age cultures in the Levant discussing matters of two closely intertwined areas, politics and religion. Assuming that the MFT is essentially correct, our aim is to see which moral foundations Moab and Israel favored and how they were used. Haidt's brief descriptions of the moral foundations (taken verbatim from moralfoundations.org) provide the template for analysis, and we will examine the Mesha Inscription in terms of each, offering comparisons with the HB and the broad sweep of its convictions about YHWH and the people of Israel along the way.[14]

Moral Foundation 1: Care/Harm

"Care/harm: This foundation is related to our long evolution as mammals with attachment systems and an ability to feel (and dislike) the pain of others. It underlies virtues of kindness, gentleness, and nurturance."

An important measure of a king's success in the ANE was his ability to secure his people against foreign attack and otherwise nurture their prosperity and wellbeing.[15] In the Mesha Inscription this finds expression in Mesha's actions to:

- end the oppression of Israel and others (ll. 4, 7, 11, 14–16, 19–21, 32–34),
- fortify and rebuild Moab's cities, install reservoirs and ditches for water, and build roads (ll. 9–10, 13–14, 21–30),
- and exterminate resident populations sympathetic to Israel (ll. 11–12, 15–17) and replace them with peoples loyal to him (ll. 13–14).

---

14. Miller, *Religion of Ancient Israel*, 48–62.
15. See Mark W. Hamilton, "Prosperity and Kingship in Psalms and Inscriptions," in *Literature as Politics, Politics as Literature: Essays on the Ancient Near East in Honor of Peter Machinist*, ed. David S. Vanderhooft and Abraham Winitzer (Winona Lake, IN: Eisenbrauns, 2013), 185–205 (195–96 on the Mesha Inscription).

The harm that Mesha did to his enemies through battle and enslavement was justified, since he acted to benefit his own subjects and often to restore historic Moabite rule over territories taken from him.

Since this is certainly one of the most important moral foundations in the Mesha Inscription, one might argue that its assertion is one of the chief aims of the monument: to elevate Mesha publicly as an exemplary ruler. There is also a strong religious justification for Mesha's attacks on his neighbors: Chemosh commanded Mesha to undertake these actions (ll. 4–5, 9, 14, 19, 32). In fact, the only role that Chemosh plays in the Mesha Inscription is a military one: Chemosh was angry with Moab and so gave her over to Israel, and he commanded Mesha to attack his neighbors.

As any reader of the HB can attest, Israel's leaders from Moses to the kings of Israel and Judah are portrayed in ways similar to the Mesha Inscription's presentation of Mesha. From Deuteronomy through 2 Kings, Israel defeats foreign nations (Josh 12), exterminates populations in Canaan (Deut 20:16–18), and often was at war with her neighbors (1 Sam 14; 2 Kgs 6; 8; 16). Many of these actions were undertaken at the command of YHWH—who is even called "a warrior" (Exod 15:3)—and when Israel or her rulers proved unfaithful to God, YHWH's anger burned against them, and the nation lost battles, territory, and even political independence (Josh 7; 2 Kgs 17; 21).[16] When David gathers materials to build the temple in Jerusalem, though, he praises God for making this possible (1 Chr 29:14–19), and God grants "rest" for kings to enjoy peace and build (2 Chr 14:6–7). Finally, God's aim is to bless all nations (Gen 12:3; Isa 2:1–4).

Moral Foundation 2: Fairness/Cheating

"Fairness/cheating: This foundation is related to the evolutionary process of reciprocal altruism. It generates ideas of justice, rights, and autonomy. [Note: In our original conception, Fairness included concerns about equality, which are more strongly endorsed by political liberals. However, as we reformulated the theory in 2011 based on new data, we emphasize proportionality, which is endorsed by everyone, but is more strongly endorsed by conservatives.]"

Mesha's claim of building a high place for Chemosh in gratitude for his deliverance and military success (ll. 3–4) presents him as fair in his dealings with the god and suggests their relationship was reciprocal. Mesha's infliction of harm on Gad (ll. 10–14a), his extermination of hostile populations (ll. 11, 16–17), his conscription of Israelite captives for his building projects (ll. 25–26), and his efforts generally to recovery cities and lands once part of his family's kingdom

---

16. All biblical texts are quoted from the CEB (2011).

(ll. 7–9) were fair, since he was only restoring what had been unfairly seized by others and taking retribution on the guilty.

On the positive side, Mesha's military actions benefitted his own subjects, rewarding them for their support, and the king showed his gratitude for Chemosh's protection by acknowledging his help publicly in the Mesha Inscription, building a high place for Chemosh in Karchoh/Qarhoh, enhancing Chemosh's worship with the plunder of foreign cultic centers, and slaughtering enemy populations in his honor. In this rough justice, Mesha behaved fairly to benefit his supporters and punish his enemies.

Therefore, using the idea of reciprocity as the guide for this moral foundation, the Mesha Inscription shows its application in both its negative and positive components, and by presenting Mesha's military adventures as it does, the monument offers an *apologia* for the king: all his actions were just and fair, since he undertook them as retribution and to redress the wrongs done to Moab by oppressive foreigners.

Once more, the Mesha Inscription presents a historical narrative that resonates well with that of the HB. On the other hand, as the product of religious leaders, the HB is typically more critical of the rule of the nation's kings, and when one behaves badly, the reader is alerted to the punishment that surely must follow—if not from a human hand, then from the divine (see, e.g., 2 Chr 24:17–26). In spite of all the foregoing and the recognition that the Mesha Inscription is concerned more with Mesha than Chemosh, it is essential to note that, at least in two respects, the HB differs strikingly from the Mesha Inscription. First, the HB goes to great lengths to show that Israel's God is righteous, just, and merciful and that humans routinely fall below the divine standard (Eccl 7:20), even the most righteous of the kings (see 2 Sam 11–12). In addition, God exemplifies grace by continually forgiving a wayward people and blessing them, even when they disregarded the divine faithfulness (1 Kgs 8:22–61; 2 Chr 30:6–9). Therefore, God violates the principle of reciprocity time and again, and the reason or justification for this is hidden in the mystery of God's grace and sovereignty (Exod 33:19).

Moral Foundation 3: Loyalty/Betrayal

"Loyalty/betrayal: This foundation is related to our long history as tribal creatures able to form shifting coalitions. It underlies virtues of patriotism and self-sacrifice for the group. It is active anytime people feel that it's 'one for all, and all for one.' "[17]

---

17. See especially Kevin Simler and Robin Hanson, *The Elephant in the Brain: Hidden Motives in Everyday Life* (New York: Oxford University Press, 2018), 261–81.

This foundation finds expression in interhuman relationships in the Mesha Inscription, as well as in Mesha's dealings with Chemosh. Though the Gadites had lived in Ataroth "from ancient times" (l. 10; cf. Num 32:3), Mesha took the city, exterminated the population as a sacrifice for Chemosh, brought its altar hearth back and set it before Chemosh at Kerioth/Qiryat, and replaced the Gadite population in Ataroth with Sharonites and Maharatites (ll. 11–13). As with the Gadites, Mesha's loyalty to Chemosh is also illustrated in this obedience and in his devoting the population of Nebo to Ashtar-Chemosh and the vessels of YHWH to Chemosh, and so this conquest illustrates the introductory summary (l. 4), showing both the enmity of Mesha toward Israel and the military success that Chemosh granted him, thus noting the reciprocity of their relationship.

The HB is usually much more explicit than the Mesha Inscription about motives and why God acts in certain ways, and due to the strong impulse in the HB to encourage Israel's faithfulness to God, this moral foundation plays a more dominant role in the HB than it does in the Mesha Inscription. An important way this is expressed is in terms of God's covenant with Israel and the faithfulness and loyalty that God expects from her.[18] For example, the structure of the book of Deuteronomy has been analyzed in terms of the ANE suzerainty treaties, which bound vassals to their suzerain or overlord,[19] and an influential Old Testament theology used covenant as its theme and organizing principle.[20] Key elements in Israel's loyalty to YHWH are: exclusive devotion to God (the first of the Ten Commandments prohibits idolatry; Deut 5:6–21), love for God completely (the Shema; Deut 6:4–5), and obedience ("what the LORD requires from you: to do justice, embrace faithful love, and walk humbly with your God"; Mic 6:8b). In addition, there are important inflection points in the HB signaled by the people's renewal of their covenant with God (e.g., Josh 24; 2 Kgs 23; Neh 9).

Moral Foundation 4: Authority/Subversion

"Authority/subversion: This foundation was shaped by our long primate history of hierarchical social interactions. It underlies virtues of leadership and followership, including deference to legitimate authority and respect for traditions."

The introduction to the Mesha Inscription (ll. 1–4a) not only provides historical details regarding King Mesha and his achievements but also not-so-subtly asserts his authority and legitimacy based on his royal lineage. As son of the prior king, he was not a rebel or usurper but the legitimate king, ruling from the

---

18. Miller, *Religion of Ancient Israel*, 4–6.
19. See Dennis J. McCarthy, *Old Testament Covenant: A Survey of Current Opinions*, Growing Points in Theology (Richmond, VA: John Knox, 1972).
20. Walther Eichrodt, *Theology of the Old Testament*, trans. J. A. Baker, OTL, 2 vols. (Philadelphia: Westminster, 1961).

capital city of his land. These lines affirm Mesha's royal authority within the political and social traditions of the ANE world.[21]

Since Chemosh reigned supreme over Moab, he granted military victory and sovereignty to whom he chose and was able to drive out Israel (ll. 4–9a), and so burnish the reputation of Mesha as a pious king who submitted to the authority and rule of Chemosh and in turn enjoyed the deity's favor (it may have been Mesha's father—rather than Mesha himself—who had angered Chemosh). Nevertheless, Mesha's obedience to the command of Chemosh to take Nebo (ll. 14–18) and Horonaim/Hawronen (ll. 32–33) shows both his respect for his god's authority and his ability to lead those over whom he had authority. Devoting the population of Nebo to Ashtar-Chemosh and the vessels of YHWH to Chemosh also served to acknowledge the authority of Chemosh. Similarly, although lines 18b–21a do not explicitly claim that Chemosh commanded Mesha to attack Jahaz/Yahas (an Israelite outpost in the subjugation of Moab), the section does report that Chemosh drove Israel's king from the city and so illustrates Mesha's service to Chemosh. Finally, Mesha's own subjects (Dibon and the "hundreds in the towns which I have added to the land") submitted to his authority (ll. 28–29).

This moral foundation is one of the most important in the HB, where YHWH is assigned many honorific titles attesting the authority of God over all Israel as her only lord (see Exod 20:3–6).[22] In addition, the installation of Saul as Israel's first king is seen as subversion and a rejection of YHWH as king (1 Sam 8; cf. Deut 17:14–20 and 33:5).[23] In addition, when biblical texts assess the reigns of the kings of Israel and Judah, this is typically done in terms of their obedience to God, occurring in the summary statements about their reigns, as well as in the details of each (e.g.: 2 Chr 12:14; 14:2; 2 Kgs 21:2–3). King David provides a concise summary of what was expected of the faithful king in his final instructions to his son Solomon: "Guard what is owed to the LORD your God, walking in his ways and observing his laws, his commands, his judgments, and his testimonies, just as it is written in the Instruction from Moses. In this way you will succeed in whatever you do and wherever you go" (1 Kgs 2:3). Finally, the people are expected to obey their leaders, and the rebellious are usually punished severely (Exod 15–17; Num 14; 2 Sam 12:7–14; 2 Chr 23; 25:3–4). Therefore, both the Mesha Inscription and the HB assign great importance to the moral foundation of authority, although the latter assigns greater authority to deity and highlights the potential for kings to subvert obedience to God.

---

21. See Keith W. Whitelam, "King and Kingship," *Anchor Bible Dictionary* [*ABD*], ed. D. N. Freedman, 6 vols. (New York: Doubleday, 1992), 4:40–48.

22. Martin Rose, "Names of God in the OT," *ABD* 4:1001–11.

23. This idea that a people's god or chief god was "king" and that the human king ruled as deity's representative is found in many ANE cultures (Whitelam, "King and Kingship," 43).

Moral Foundation 5: Sanctity/Degradation

"Sanctity/degradation: This foundation was shaped by the psychology of disgust and contamination. It underlies religious notions of striving to live in an elevated, less carnal, more noble way. It underlies the widespread idea that the body is a temple that can be desecrated by immoral activities and contaminants (an idea not unique to religious traditions)."[24]

This moral foundation is largely absent from the Mesha Inscription, perhaps due to the genre, function, and intent of the monument.[25] The one area where it might be found is in the concept of holy or divine war,[26] which emerges in the reports of Mesha's conquest of Ataroth and Nebo, where populations are exterminated in honor of Chemosh and cultic objects are devoted to the Moabite god (ll. 11–18a). In both cases, Mesha attacked a city successfully and slaughtered the population as an offering to Chemosh. In the case of Ataroth, this is a "sacrifice"(?),[27] and in the case of Nebo, the Hebrew form of the verb occurs in the HB in contexts of war and extermination of a population (sometimes as a sacrifice to God, such as in Deut 13:15–16 and Josh 11:12).[28] The HB also preserves a rich legal tradition regulating Israel's behavior in war (Deut 20; 21:10–14; 23:9–14), but YHWH's holiness would have excluded the use of cultic utensils from pagan shrines.[29]

On the other hand, while the motif of holiness may be found widely in ANE religions in religious-cultic settings,[30] it appears with distinctive wrinkles in the HB (see Exod 34:11–17; 2 Kgs 21:4–9), where God is the source of holiness ("the holy one of Israel"; 2 Kgs 19:22) and calls Israel to be holy (Lev 11:44). God's holiness is concentrated in the temple in Jerusalem and its sacrificial system (see Lev 1–7) but also extends throughout the land of Israel, and so it is important that God's commandments be observed throughout the land (Lev 18:1–5, 24–30):

---

24. "In the ethic of divinity, there is an order to the universe, and things (as well as people) should be treated with the reverence or disgust that they deserve.... As with the ethic of community, I had read about the ethic of divinity before going to India, and had understood it intellectually. But in India, and in the years after I returned, I felt it" (Haidt, *Righteous Mind*, 104–5).

25. See Smith, *Origins*, 93–97.

26. See Sa-Moon Kang, *Divine War in the Old Testament and in the Ancient Near East*, BZAW 177 (Berlin: de Gruyter, 1989), esp. 76–84.

27. This translation is still a matter of dispute. See Kent P. Jackson, "The Language of the Mesha Inscription," in Dearman, *Studies*, 111.

28. References to Moabite sacrifices occur in Num 22:40–23:30 and 25:1–5, and 2 Kgs 3:27 reports that Mesha sacrificed his firstborn son in his desperation to turn back an Israelite assault.

29. God commanded Israel to destroy pagan cults in Canaan (Exod 34:11–17), and kings were harshly condemned for bringing foreign cults into Jerusalem (2 Kgs 21:4–9).

30. Walter Kornfeld and Helmer Ringgren, "קדש," *Theological Dictionary of the Old Testament*, ed. G. Johannes Botterweck and Helmer Ringgren, trans. John T. Willis, Geoffrey W. Bromiley, and D. E. Green, 15 vols. (Grand Rapids: Eerdmans, 1974–2006), 12:524–26; Smith, *Origins*, 93–96.

the people were not only to eschew idolatry but also to honor parents, observe religious festivals that bound the community together, provide for the poor, and so on (Lev 19:3–37).[31]

Moral Foundation 6: Liberty/Opression

"Liberty/oppression: This foundation is about the feelings of reactance and resentment people feel toward those who dominate them and restrict their liberty. Its intuitions are often in tension with those of the authority foundation. The hatred of bullies and dominators motivates people to come together, in solidarity, to oppose or take down the oppressor."

Mesha's resentment of Israel emerges explicitly in the Mesha Inscription: "Omri was the king of Israel, and he oppressed Moab for many days, for Chemosh was angry with his land" (ll. 5–6; see also ll. 18–19). Such comments generate sympathy for Mesha as one resisting oppression and struggling for liberty, rather than as a predatory opportunist. Chemosh plays a critical role as the one who permitted foreign oppression but later brought liberation.

This moral foundation plays a critical role in the HB nationally with the exodus from Egypt and Israel's subsequent history (Neh 9), as well as within Israel, when the judicial system was articulated to protect the poor and other groups subject to exploitation and oppression (Mic 6:1–8).

Summary and Concluding Reflections

The similarities between the Mesha Inscription and the HB that began this essay have been confirmed by our MFT analysis: the religious practices of Moab were consonant in many respects with those of ancient Israel. Surely, this facilitated the ease with which Israelites adopted the worship of Chemosh and other foreign gods and initiated marriage and political relations with non-Yahwists in the Iron Age. The prevailing voice of the HB, though, harshly condemned these engagements with Israel's neighbors (Neh 13:23–27; 2 Kgs 16; Isa 7).[32] Although all six moral foundations appear in the Mesha Inscription and the HB, loyalty/betrayal and sanctity/degradation are more important in the HB, and there are striking differences in the ways that the MI and HB employ the foundations.

---

31. Miller, *Religion of Ancient Israel*, 14–15, 131–61.
32. An analysis of idol figurines from the seventh century BCE indicates that Israel and her neighbors were using the same cult objects in the sanctuaries they had established in their major urban centers (Ephraim Stern, "The Religious Revolution in Persian-Period Judah," in *Judah and the Judeans in the Persian Period*, ed. Oded Lipschits and Manfred Oeming [Winona Lake, IN: Eisenbrauns, 2006], 199–205).

Several important categories of difference between these two look-alike deities are clear.

First, the portrayal of Chemosh in the Mesha Inscription emerges as one-dimensional and superficial. Chemosh is primarily a god present in time of war, enabling either an aggressive Israel to oppress Moab or a resurgent Moab to drive out her enemies. There is no explanation given for Chemosh's anger or for his reversal. Nothing is said about the deity's character or the reason for his disposition toward Moab. He is a cipher and may have been viewed as arbitrary and been feared more than loved. His relationship with Moab was driven by the rational exchange of favors between god and devotee. While the HB presents YHWH as also capable of great violence, Israel's God is characterized by justice, faithfulness, and compassion. This God sought not just the respect of Israel but also her love, exclusive devotion, and understanding.

Second, the Mesha Inscription describes the relationship between Moab and Chemosh only in the most immediate terms: the reign of Mesha and perhaps his father. The HB, though, repeatedly directs the reader's attention to the past, when God made promises to earlier generations, delivered Israel from Egyptian slavery, and forgave transgressions. Current events appear only as a point in the stream that continues into God's future.

Third, while the Mesha Inscription has little to say about the ethical lives of nations, persons, and even Chemosh—except for its condemnation of Omri and Israel for oppressing Moab—the HB is rich with commentary about the morality of people and deity. It is only YHWH who is righteous and holy. The moral lives of nations and even exemplary individuals are frail, even tending to lurch aside into faithlessness. The HB shows little reticence in condemning even great kings for their missteps—worship of foreign gods, military alliances with other kings, and oppression of their own subjects. Yet, in the mystery of God's sovereignty and grace there is the desire to restore Israel in holiness and righteousness and even use them to bless all nations.

So, why did Moabites fail to pass along to succeeding generations their religious practices and convictions? Because military defeats destroyed their nation? Many of the same powers also destroyed Israel and Judah, and yet their documents and faith survived in forms that continued to capture the imagination and devotion of later generations that championed this God as not only the lord of ancient Israel and Judah but also universal sovereign. This is a final question worth pondering.

CHAPTER 9

YHWH, Chemosh, and the Rule of Faith

Brent A. Strawn

YHWH: From Chemosh to Marduk and Back Again

From its initial discovery, scholars have been fascinated with the presentation of Chemosh in the Mesha Inscription (*KAI* 181) because it so obviously and remarkably resembles the Old Testament's presentation of Israel's deity, YHWH. Chemosh, too, gets angry with his land and hands it over to be ruled by foreign powers (ll. 4b–5); Chemosh, too, appears to relent of such anger and thus restores the land (ll. 9, 33); Chemosh, too, grants military success and victory to his people, particularly the king (ll. 4b, 19), even giving the Moabites divine orders to engage in battle (ll. 14, 32); and Chemosh, too, receives acts of service and devotion from those people, especially his client king (ll. 3–4a, 8b–9, 11–13, 17–18, 33). Hence the question that motivates the present collection of essays in this book: how is it that YHWH and Chemosh look so much alike? Or, to put it more pointedly: what is the significance, especially the *theological* significance, of the fact that YHWH has look-alikes in the ancient world?

The plural form, *look-alikes*, is important, because the situation is not limited to Chemosh. While a nearby, next-door neighbor, Chemosh is rather small potatoes in the capacious ANE marketplace of divinity. He had a limited geographical range and, concomitantly, a limited shelf-life.[1] Comparisons between YHWH and Chemosh make sense given the localization of the two deities in the southern Levant, making them regional cousins of a sort, but YHWH's similarities to the leading lights or "big gods" of the ancient world's superpowers,

---

Author's Note: Thanks to Collin Cornell for his critique and assistance with earlier drafts. A version of this paper was first presented to a doctoral seminar at Emory University entitled "Theology of the Ancient Near East" (Fall 2017). I am grateful for the students who participated in that course and for the feedback I received at that time.

1. See H.-P. Müller, "Chemosh," in *DDD*, 186–89, for attestation of this god at Ebla (^d*Ka-mi/má-iš*) and elsewhere; see Collin Cornell, "What happened to Kemosh?," *ZAW* 128 (2016): 284–99, for Chemosh's later years and ultimate absorption into the Greek god Ares. On the one hand, that absorption certainly expanded Chemosh's range and "lifespan," but on the other, this extension was evidently due solely to the syncretism with Ares.

such as the great Babylonian god Marduk, are no less evident. So it is that, according to many scholars, the Babylonian creation epic, Enuma Elish, which stars Marduk, influenced the opening chapters of Genesis. In the Babylonian composition, we see a god conquering chaotic forces, creating and ordering the world, and so on in ways that are indeed recognizable—if not entirely or exclusively from Genesis, then certainly from the larger portrait of YHWH that emerges from the Hebrew Bible writ large. Furthermore, even if Gen 1 and 11 or other biblical compositions are deemed "countertexts" that are *opposed* in some fashion to Enuma Elish, they are still interacting with, and therefore dependent upon, if not actually deferential to, that great Babylonian epic.[2] Then, too, quite apart from the creation motifs in Enuma Elish, the integration of various gods into the persona of Marduk via this god's famous "fifty names" (tablets 6–7) is also downright YHWH-like in light of what some scholars have spoken of as the integrative, if not agglutinative, character of Yahwistic monotheism.[3] But, in light of the relative chronology of the texts at hand and the dominance of the Babylonian material at many crucial points in time, a more precise formulation would likely be that YHWH's "integration" is downright Marduk-like—*not* vice versa.[4]

If, for some reason, Enuma Elish strikes one as an unfair or otherwise inapt comparison,[5] there are others that commend themselves: *Ludlul bēl nēmeqi*, for example. Here one can find, in close concatenation, presentations of Marduk that are every bit as complex and bipolar, discomfiting and praiseworthy as one finds with YHWH:

2. See Eckart Frahm, *Babylonian and Assyrian Text Commentaries: Origins of Interpretation*, Guides to the Mesopotamian Textual Record 5 (Münster: Ugarit-Verlag, 2011), 345–68, esp. 364–68.

3. See, e.g., Othmar Keel, "Wie männliche ist der Gott Israels," *Diakonia* 24 (1993): 179–86; Keel, *Jerusalem and the One God: A Religious History*, ed. Brent A. Strawn (Minneapolis: Fortress, 2017); Patrick D. Miller, "The Absence of the Goddess in Israelite Religion," *Hebrew Annual Review* 10 (1986): 239–48; and Brent A. Strawn, "Whence Leonine Yahweh? Iconography and the History of Israelite Religion," in *Images and Prophecy in the Ancient Eastern Mediterranean*, ed. Martti Nissinen and Charles A. Carter, FRLANT 233 (Göttingen: Vandenhoeck & Ruprecht, 2009), 51–85.

4. See, e.g., W. G. Lambert, "A New Look at the Babylonian Background of Genesis," *Journal of Theological Studies* 16 (1965): 287–300, and Kenton L. Sparks, "*Enūma Elish* and Priestly Mimesis: Elite Emulation in Nascent Judaism," *JBL* 126 (2007): 625–48.

5. See A. Leo Oppenheim, *Ancient Mesopotamia: Portrait of a Dead Civilization*, rev. and ed. Erica Reiner (Chicago: University of Chicago Press, 1977), 174, 177–78, who famously downplayed the importance of mythological texts. See also Lambert, "A New Look," 291: "The *Epic of Creation* is not a norm of Babylonian or Sumerian cosmology. It is a sectarian and aberrant combination of mythological threads woven into an unparalleled compositum.... It happens to be the best preserved Babylonian document of its genre simply because it was at its height of popularity when the libraries were formed from which our knowledge of Babylonian mythology is mostly derived. The various traditions it draws upon are often perverted to such an extent that conclusions based on this text alone are suspect. It can only be used safely in the whole context of ancient Mesopotamian mythology." But see Frahm, *Babylonian and Assyrian Text Commentaries*, for a more recent and positive assessment of Enuma Elish's importance and influence.

> I will praise the lord of wisdom, judicious god,
> Enraged in the night, in the daylight calming,
> Marduk, the lord of wisdom, judicious god,
> Enraged in the night, in the daylight calming,
> Whose fury, like a storm blast, makes a wasteland,
> Whose breath is, like the dawn wind, pleasing.
> In his rage he's irresistible, a very deluge is his wrath,
> His is a pardoning mind, his a forgiving heart. (1.1–8)
>
> Whose soft palm saves a man about to die.
> When he is angry, many are the graves to be opened,
> When he pities, from the tomb he raises the fallen. (1.12–14)
>
> Terrible is his . . . punishment to the one *still not* absolved.
> He is moved to mercy, and suddenly *the god is like* a mother,
> Hastening to treat his loved one tenderly,
> And behind, like a cow with her calf, back and forth, round about he goes. (1.17–20)[6]

The similarities to YHWH's presentation, especially in the Psalms, are too obvious to need detailing.[7]

Once again, one need not see these ANE texts—and the Mesha Inscription, Enuma Elish, and *Ludlul bēl nēmeqi* are just three in a cast of hundreds, if not thousands—as existing in some direct, genetic relationship with the biblical materials for the problem of similarity to be manifest. Perhaps some instances in these or other examples are cases of rather straightforward derivation, but it seems likely that most instances are far more complicated than that—both chronologically and in terms of mechanism(s) of influence, transfer, and

---

6. The translation is from William L. Moran, "The Babylonian Job," in *The Most Magic Word: Essays on Babylonian and Biblical Literature*, ed. Ronald S. Hendel, Catholic Biblical Quarterly Monograph Series 35 (Washington, DC: Catholic Biblical Association, 2002), 182–200, at 199 (his emphases). Cf. Amar Annus and Alan Lenzi, *Ludlul bēl nēmeqi: The Standard Babylonian Poem of the Righteous Sufferer*, State Archives of Assyria Cuneiform Texts 7 (Helsinki: Neo-Assyrian Text Corpus Project, 2010), 31.

7. One should also note Marduk's re-creative, even resurrection power, as attributed to him in Enuma Elish 6.153: "The lord, who brought to life the dead gods by his pure incantation" (*be-lum šá ina šip-ti-šu el-le-ti ú-bal-li-ṭu ilāni^{meš} mi-tu-ti*; text and translation from W. G. Lambert, *Babylonian Creation Myths*, Mesopotamian Civilizations 16 [Winona Lake, IN: Eisenbrauns, 2013], 118–19). See also *Ludlul bēl nēmeqi* 4.33 ("Who but Marduk restores his dead to life? [*šá la ^{d}marduk man-nu mi-tu-ta-šú ú-bal-liṭ*]") and 4.35 ("Marduk can restore to life from the grave [^{d}*marduk ina gab-ri bul-lu-ṭa i-li-'i*]"; text and translation from W. G. Lambert, *Babylonian Wisdom Literature*, repr. ed. [Winona Lake, IN: Eisenbrauns, 1996], 58–59).

reception.⁸ Neither must one see the "hidden riches" of ANE material in the Bible⁹ as always or only polemical—whether in stridently apologetic mode or in something more sober than that. This is to reiterate the point that, even if the biblical materials are deemed "contrary" in some fashion, they are still subsequent to, and thus somehow deferential to, the antecedent source(s).

Whatever the precise case, the present issue remains: whether the texts are related or not—directly or otherwise, polemically or appreciatively—the fact is that YHWH still looks a whole lot like Chemosh and Marduk (and others, as well), and vice versa. And so, again: what is one to say about that?

Two Inadequate Responses to Divine (Dis)similarity

Two responses to that question are common but also too simplistic, and so, in the end, unhelpful.¹⁰

Response 1: Overly Similar

The first inadequate response is to posit YHWH as just one of the ANE "gang," no more and no less. In this perspective, YHWH looks like "Chemosh and Company" (and vice versa) simply because he is, like them, a deity from ancient southwestern Asia, and that's just the way things were back then and over there. Strong and extensive family resemblances between the various Semitic gods exist, therefore, because these deities are of a piece geographically and chronologically, at the very least, in the same way that Norse gods or Greek gods are of a piece and, as such, not of a piece with the other types or with the Semitic variety. We can, of course, parse the gang out more finely: YHWH is not just Semitic, he is southern Levantine and also strongly northwest Semitic. And so it is that he looks a whole lot like Ugaritic Ilu and Balu, but also like Moabite Chemosh and Edomite Qaus, and maybe Ammonite Milkom to boot. Insofar as YHWH controls the storm, he favors that specific branch of the divine family tree, which includes Balu but also others, especially as one moves further north into Hatti and eastward into Mesopotamia. Insofar as YHWH is sometimes said to come from desert climes, he reveals his relationship to other family members;

---

8. See, e.g., Lambert, "A New Look," 299, and his remarks throughout about certain shared elements between Enuma Elish and Genesis that might trace back to Amorite antecedents.

9. To evoke the title of Christopher B. Hays's helpful textbook on comparison: *Hidden Riches: A Sourcebook for the Comparative Study of the Hebrew Bible and Ancient Near East* (Louisville, KY: Westminster John Knox, 2014).

10. There are, of course, more than just the two that follow; see Paul F. Knitter, *Introducing Theologies of Religions* (Maryknoll, NY: Orbis, 2011).

as a god of the mountains, he favors still others. Maybe even YHWH's seriously depopulated pantheon—the fact that he often appears to be an austere bachelor mountain god[11]—is further evidence of his affinity to certain regional subgroups.[12]

Despite its large and impressive (though perhaps, in the end, unwieldy) *religionsgeschichtliche* apparatus, I deem this first response overly historicized—too enamored of history—and in ways that cannot be justified on the basis of the data presently available. (1) On the one hand, we typically lack knowledge of the specific ways or means by which these gods came to be so similar. Presumably it is via human interaction and interrelationship in some way at some point in the now unrecoverable past, on analogy with linguistic contact, perhaps, or even epidemiology.[13] But, as noted earlier, the data are rarely fully transparent on this front, such that one must constantly worry about overestimating interrelationships and/or dependencies within the comparative enterprise. "Parallelomania" is a real problem,[14] as are its various iterations: "Ugaritomania,"[15] for example, or the idea that Marduk is some sort of archetype for Christ.[16] Comparison, after all, is a *constructed* enterprise, and "development" is often something of a magic word.[17] At best, comparativists traffic in analogous structures, not homologous, let alone biological or genetic, ones; this is *history* after all! And so, to quote Jonathan Z. Smith, comparison is typically an act of exaggeration, even if that act is as disciplined as possible and one conducted in service of the truth.[18] Of course, in some ways, these latter caveats represent the best-case scenario; such a judgment cannot be made for every comparative endeavor, and certainly

---

11. I owe this formulation to David Petersen (in personal communication), who sometimes used it somewhat tongue-in-cheek in his classroom teaching.

12. See Josey Bridges Snyder, "Did Kemosh Have a Consort (or Any Other Friends)? Re-assessing the Moabite Pantheon," *UF* 42 (2010): 645–75.

13. For the former, I refer particularly to comparative historical linguistics. For the latter, I am thinking of certain approaches in the cognitive study of religion, for which see Pascal Boyer, *Religion Explained: The Evolutionary Origins of Religious Thought* (New York: Basic, 2002). With application to ancient Israelite religion, see Brett E. Maiden, "Cognitively Optimal and Costly Aspects of Ancient Israelite Religion" (PhD diss., Emory University, 2018).

14. Samuel Sandmel, "Parallelomania," *JBL* 81 (1962): 1–13.

15. For some discussion of the issues, see Brent A. Strawn, "*kwšrwt* in Psalm 68:7, Again: A (Small) Test Case in Relating Ugarit to the Hebrew Bible," *UF* 41 (2009): 631–48.

16. See Witold Paulus, *Marduk Urtyp Christi?*, Biblica et Orientalia 29 (Rome: Pontifical Biblical Institute, 1928).

17. Jonathan Z. Smith, "In Comparison a Magic Dwells," in *A Magic Still Dwells: Comparative Religion in the Postmodern Age*, ed. Kimberly C. Patton and Benjamin C. Ray (Berkeley: University of California, 2000), 23–44, at 26. (This essay originally appeared in Smith's *Imagining Religion: From Babylon to Jonestown* [Chicago: University of Chicago Press, 1982], 19–35.)

18. See Jonathan Z. Smith, *Drudgery Divine: On the Comparison of Early Christianities and the Religions of Late Antiquity* (Chicago: University of Chicago Press, 1990), 52: "a disciplined exaggeration in the service of knowledge."

not in equal measure. Hence (again), parallelomania is a real problem. But at the same time, despite the genuine difficulties posed by comparison, one must be equally cautious of "parallel-anoia."[19]

(2) And so, on the other hand, the data presently available must be reckoned with, and this includes the material from the OT, which, despite its distinction from texts recovered directly from the dirt and its more "traditioned" nature, still counts as evidence, and thus has to be taken into thorough consideration in any sort of discussion of YHWH.[20] To put the matter mildly, the profile of YHWH found in this corpus—quite apart from its particular problems or irregularities—outpaces every other ancient Semitic god we know, in quantity alone if not also in quality. There are similarities, to be sure, among YHWH, Chemosh, Marduk, and their other divine friends, but differences are also manifest—again in quantity alone, if not also quality. Simply put, we know a whole lot more about YHWH's "interior life"[21] than we do about Balu's. The differences between YHWH and the gods that are apparent at this juncture (and not only here) highlight the inadequacy of this first, overly-similar response (over-similarity), even as they also lead directly to the second unhelpful perspective.

Response 2: Overly Dissimilar

The second inadequate response to the problem of divine similarity is that YHWH is *not* one of the gang—definitively and decidedly. As already intimated, this sort of position is not (simply) one that deems a text like Gen 1 to be "counter" to Enuma Elish in some fashion; rather, this position would hold that Gen 1 is heavily, overtly, and unreservedly polemical against Enuma Elish—and this would be true not just for that text, but for (virtually) every text, and in both directions: from this perspective, almost every biblical text imaginable is thought to be polemically engaged with almost every ANE text imaginable. The OT is fundamentally and at its core "against its environment."[22]

---

19. See Howard Eilberg-Schwartz, "Beyond Parallel-anoia: Comparative Inquiry and Cultural Interpretation," in *The Savage in Judaism: An Anthropology of Israelite Religion and Ancient Judaism* (Bloomington: Indiana University Press, 1990), 87–102.

20. For the OT as a datum for religiohistorical analysis and the problems that obtain when it is underutilized, see Brent A. Strawn, "What Would (or Should) Old Testament Theology Look Like If Recent Reconstructions of Israelite Religion Were True?," in *Between Israelite Religion and Old Testament Theology: Essays on Archaeology, History, and Hermeneutics*, ed. Robert D. Miller II, Contributions to Biblical Exegesis and Theology 80 (Leuven: Peeters, 2016), 129–66.

21. I take this phrase from Walter Brueggemann, *Theology of the Old Testament: Testimony, Dispute, Advocacy* (Minneapolis: Fortress, 1997), e.g., 328 (YHWH's "rich, unsettled interior life"; cf. 387 on YHWH's "rich, alive, unsettled interior life"); he uses such phrasing in other works as well.

22. See, famously, G. Ernest Wright, *The Old Testament Against its Environment*, SBT 2 (London: SCM, 1957). From a Jewish perspective, see Yehezekel Kaufmann, *The Religion of Israel*, trans. Moshe Greenberg (Chicago: University of Chicago Press, 1960).

If the first response was overly historicized, this second one is overly apologetic—too confessional even, and to the extreme—but unnecessarily so, or perhaps better, in ways that are just too simple, especially theologically, if not also historically.[23] To take the *latter point* first, there is more than sufficient *historical* reason to deem a number of instances in the Bible as heavily and directly dependent on ANE antecedents in an appreciative, not solely contrarian way.[24] One simply has to admit this point, and let the comparative "team" put some points on the board, as it were. How could it be otherwise? Why *shouldn't* it be otherwise? Ancient Israel was, after all, part of the ancient world and located on a prime piece of real estate: an important crossroad between the superpowers to the south, north, east, and (later) west.

So, to take Ps 29 as an example, if Frank Moore Cross and those who have followed him are right, that psalm was originally one for a weather god who was *not* YHWH; for Cross, it was Balu.[25] Now, maybe Cross and company are wrong,[26] but assuming they are correct for the moment (even if only for sake of argument), Israelite reception of this "Baalistic" text need not be polemical in nature. The replacement of one god's name with another's is not polemic *per se*.[27] It is, instead, a matter of *reattribution* or *replacement*, *redaction* or *revision*. Polemic would seem to require more than that, and perhaps a lot more: it needs explicit and contrarian tone over against another subject, which, in this particular case, is another deity.[28] Barring that, Ps 29 looks more like a famous song that has been covered by another group on a different album from the

---

23. I place the following works (among others) in this camp: John D. Currid, *Against the Gods: The Polemical Theology of the Old Testament* (Wheaton, IL: Crossway, 2013); John N. Oswalt, *The Bible among the Myths: Unique Revelation or Just Ancient Literature?* (Grand Rapids: Zondervan, 2009); and Jeffrey J. Niehaus, *Ancient Near Eastern Themes in Biblical Theology* (Grand Rapids: Kregel, 2008).

24. So, among many others, see Lambert's sober-eyed analysis in "A New Look."

25. Frank Moore Cross, "Notes on a Canaanite Psalm in the Old Testament," *BASOR* 117 (1950): 19–21; Cross, *Canaanite Myth and Hebrew Epic: Essays in the History of the Religion of Israel* (Cambridge: Harvard University Press, 1973), 151–56. Cross is himself dependent on an earlier study by H. L. Ginsberg published in 1936 (see *Canaanite Myth*, 152n22).

26. See Rolf A. Jacobson, "Psalm 29: Ascribe to the Lord," in Nancy deClaissé-Walford, Rolf A. Jacobson, and Beth LaNeel Tanner, *The Book of Psalms*, New International Commentary on the Old Testament (Grand Rapids: Eerdmans, 2014), 281–88, esp. 281 and n. 2. Jacobson calls the question of how the psalm originated unsolvable and "rather uninteresting" (281).

27. Contra J. Clinton McCann, "The Book of Psalms," in *The New Interpreter's Bible*, ed. Leander E. Keck, 12 vols. (Nashville, TN: Abingdon, 1994–2004), 4:792: "Psalm 29 is fundamentally polemical, for it clearly attributes all power to Yahweh." But would the Elohistic psalter's presumed replacement of YHWH with Elohim be similarly construed as polemicizing—against YHWH?! "Persuasive" seems a far better term than "polemical"; see Jacobson, "Psalm 29," 281, who speaks of the psalm "borrowing" themes from the Canaanite environment and also "baptizing" them.

28. Contrast this, for instance, with the situation in Ps 68:5, on which see Bill T. Arnold and Brent A. Strawn, "$b^e y\bar{a}h$ $\check{s}^e m\hat{o}$ in Psalm 68,5: A Hebrew Gloss to an Ugaritic Epithet?," *ZAW* 115 (2003): 428–32.

original recording by the initial artists, rather than a protracted argument against the previous band that serves the primary if not sole function of making the new band look altogether better, completely unique, and entirely *sui generis*.[29]

The notion of covering songs, or of any selective reuse of one composition in another, musical or otherwise, leads to a consideration of the *former point*: the *theological simplemindedness* of this second inadequate response. Put simply: There are any number of reasons for one text borrowing a composition, trope, or idea from another, and an equal if not greater number of functions for such borrowing.[30] Overly apologetic approaches that have honed their polemical knives to the sharpest of surgical instruments are too beholden to a narrow range of reasons, and ultimately probably just one reason: borrowing (or, for present purposes, similarity) in this second response means nothing more than mindless derivation.[31] That, in turn—and somehow necessarily (though without adequate justification)—means that the biblical material is *not* better, unique, or *sui generis*, but altogether secondary, shared, or common, and that (again, somehow necessarily, but without sufficient argumentation) is deemed to spell bad news for the status of the biblical material. But the steps involved in this (non)argument are simply *non sequitur*, or at least *not necessarily* sequitur, and so the theological nervousness that apparently motivates this dissimilarity project, which becomes clear only in the endgame, is revealed to be entirely misplaced.

Splitting the Difference, or the Truth Is In Between

The two responses outlined above are inadequate: either YHWH is *too similar* to Chemosh and Co., ultimately disappearing in the common gene pool of Semitic southern Levantine "god-ness" without remainder; or YHWH is altogether *too different*, something akin to the arch-heretic Marcion's later (but decidedly non-Yahwistic) "alien god." The truth—as one would expect this side of Aristotle

---

29. See Brent A. Strawn, "On Covering (the Song of) Songs and the Importance of (Canonical) Context," in *Teaching the Bible: Practical Strategies for Classroom Instruction*, ed. Mark Roncace and Patrick Gray, Resources for Biblical Study 49 (Atlanta: Society of Biblical Literature, 2005), 216–18.

30. See Brent A. Strawn, "Ancient Near Eastern Parallels and Hip Hop Sampling," in Roncace and Gray, *Teaching the Bible*, 246–47; see also Steve Delamarter, Javier Alanís, Russell Haitch, Mark Vitalis Hoffman, Arun W. Jones, and Brent A. Strawn, "Technology, Pedagogy, and Transformation in Theological Education: Five Case Studies," *Teaching Theology and Religion* 10 (2007): 64–79, esp. 66–69.

31. The modern concept that is sometimes bandied about at this point is "plagiarism." Of course the ancient world knew no such concept of individual authorship, nor of copyright laws protecting the same.

or Ecclesiastes (see 7:16–18)—is somewhere in the middle; or, said differently, a better response is reached by trading on the best aspects of the inadequate ones while avoiding their worst. To quote Qoheleth: "It is good that you should take hold of the one, without letting go of the other, for the one who fears God shall succeed with both" (7:18; NRSV).

Aspect 1: Most Certainly Similar

We might begin by saying first that, while YHWH is *more* than just one of the gang, YHWH is nevertheless and most certainly a part of the gang, at least to some degree and to some extent. To what degree precisely and to what extent exactly will vary from scholar to scholar and will depend on the nature of the data (texts and/or artifacts) at hand, but the general point is (or should be) uncontroversial. As Patrick D. Miller rightly asserts, YHWH is the most distinctive aspect of Israelite religion.[32] But, with this point granted, it is important to note that the deity name YHWH appears to be attested outside and earlier than both the biblical material and Israelite epigraphic remains.[33] As if that wasn't galling enough (to the overly dissimilar crowd), no less a scholar than Cross argued that the name YHWH was nothing but a grammaticalized verbal form that originally referred to El![34]

Now, assuming that at least some (!) of the comparative work that has been conducted for the past few centuries (!) is at least partly (!) correct, YHWH is *not entirely dissimilar* to other deities, but instead *similar to some degree*. So, again, what is the significance of YHWH's similarity to these other "pagan" gods?

The answer is not simple and also not univocal, even among those scholars who think about this matter in ways that are not restricted solely to historical modes (though not entirely removed from the same). So, for example, in an important essay, Miller built on Hermann Gunkel's work to think about the entire "history of human humankind as the locus of revelation," such that, "in the movement of Israelite religion—and apparently history in general—the rule of the living God is revealed."[35] And so, "because the whole of human history is

---

32. Patrick D. Miller, *The Religion of Ancient Israel*, Library of Ancient Israel (Louisville, KY: Westminster John Knox, 2000), 1.

33. See ibid. See also, more recently: Thomas Römer, *The Invention of God*, trans. Raymond Geuss (Cambridge: Harvard University Press, 2015), 24–50; also Karel van der Toorn, "Yahweh," in *DDD*, 910–19.

34. Cross, *Canaanite Myth*, 60–75.

35. Patrick D. Miller, "God and the Gods: History of Religion as an Approach and Context for Bible and Theology," in *Israelite Religion and Biblical Theology: Collected Essays*, LHBOTS 267 (Sheffield, UK: Sheffield Academic Press, 2000), 365–96, at 370–71. This essay was first published in *Affirmation* 1 (1973): 37–62; it is republished in the present volume, 5–31, and all further citations will be to the page numbers in the present volume.

the sphere of revelation, the foreign, polytheistic myths of Mesopotamia also point, however incompletely to eternal truth."[36] To cite Gunkel directly: "The theologian would do well to treat even the Marduk myth with piety. One does not honor one's elders unless one gives thought to one's ancestors."[37] Miller's own approach, at least in this article, follows a history of religion approach, and so attends to matters of phenomenology, historical origins and development, comparisons of similarities and differences, and so forth. In his considered judgment:

> A preferable way of dealing with Israel's religion, historically and comparatively, is not to focus our concern primarily on the question of distinctiveness, but rather to describe the interplay of *continuity* and *discontinuity* that is always going on.... The effort to give attention to the interaction of those two factors is not only a more helpful way of describing the history of Israel's religion, but may be more useful and valid theologically than a singular focus on an ever-decreasing list of characteristics or elements peculiar to Israel.[38]

Although Miller's approach is a historical one, he is attentive to theological issues (he was a student of Frank Moore Cross and G. Ernest Wright), which include the significance of both similarity and difference and how similarity can particularly raise "disturbing questions about the absoluteness and revelatory character of Israel's faith."[39] As he puts it: "It is hard enough to relate to Yahweh, but if Yahweh looks a lot like Marduk [or Chemosh, we might add] that makes it even tougher, and what do we do with Tiamat and her look-alikes in the Old Testament? The norm for faith (Scripture) may seem less and less able to relate to our present existence."[40] So it is that Miller looks for the "theological character" of the history of religion and "its proper place in any theological system," and does so with the "conviction that it may be theological gain rather than embarrassment."[41] In the end, Miller appeals to an incarnational analogy so that, not unlike the divine-human savior of Christian faith, "the revelation of God in Israel's religion is manifest both in those complex ways by which it

---

36. Ibid., 10, citing W. Klatt, *Hermann Gunkel*, FRLANT 100 (Göttingen: Vandenhoeck & Ruprecht, 1969), 75.
37. Hermann Gunkel, *Creation and Chaos in the Primeval Era and the Eschaton: A Religio-Historical Study of Genesis 1 and Revelation 12*, trans. K. William Whitney Jr. (Grand Rapids: Eerdmans, 2006), 80.
38. Miller, "God and the Gods," 14; see also 29.
39. Ibid., 15.
40. Ibid.
41. Ibid.

shows its common ground with its religious world and in its equally complex differentiation from it."[42] Miller concludes on a personal note:

> Perhaps all I have been saying can be summed up as a reminder to myself that from a *religious* perspective the Canaanites were Israel's enemies. But they were also their kinfolk. Both aspects of that relationship must be kept in mind as we study the Old Testament and appropriate it for theological reflection and insight.[43]

Another, less historical, more explicitly confessional (in this case, Methodist) approach is found in an essay by Matthew Schlimm.[44] Drawing on the thought of John Wesley (1703–1791) and his notion of prevenient grace,[45] Schlimm argues that parallels between the OT and other ANE sources are traces of God's wider working in the world outside of and in addition to God's work in Israel. God's prevenient grace is "how people experience God before justification . . . God's loving activity toward a person that takes place prior to justification."[46] As Schlimm notes, "Wesley believed that this grace is available to all of humanity, a means by which God prevents the world from collapsing into evil and chaos."[47] Schlimm uses Wesley's notion "to wonder if maybe these ANE parallels were instances where God had revealed the divine self to those in other religions through this form of grace."[48] If so, these parallels "embody, or more precisely textualize, an important aspect of . . . prevenient grace."[49]

Schlimm's approach would see YHWH's look-alikes (or other instances of religious similarity) "less as utterly depraved forms of heathenism and more as forms of religion that reflect, however imperfectly, God's grace." One need not look at the bilingual Sumerian and Akkadian "Prayer to Every God,"[50] for example, and deem it only "a pathetic piece," nothing but "an indictment . . .

---

42. Ibid., 30.
43. Ibid., 31 (his emphasis).
44. Matthew Richard Schlimm, "Wrestling with Marduk: Old Testament Parallels and Prevenient Grace," *Wesleyan Theological Journal* 48 (2013): 181–92.
45. Wesley's own term was "preventing grace," not in the contemporary sense of restraining but in the (now obsolete) sense of going before: *preceding* grace. See ibid., 184–85, esp. n. 12.
46. Ibid., 185.
47. Ibid. See also 186n18, for Wesley's remark in his letter correspondence that "no man living is without some preventing grace," and 187n20 for his comment in a sermon that prevenient grace "is found in every human heart . . . not only in all Christians, but in all Mahometans, all Pagans, yea, the vilest of savages."
48. Ibid., 186.
49. Ibid., 186, citing Michael Lodahl, *God of Nature and of Grace: Reading the World in a Wesleyan Way* (Nashville: Abingdon, 2003), 38.
50. *ANET*, 391–92; Benjamin R. Foster, *Before the Muses: An Anthology of Akkadian Literature*, 3rd ed. (Bethesda, MD: CDL, 2005), 763–65.

on the religious systems of the world around ancient Israel."[51] To the contrary! There is hardly a line in this prayer that cannot be found, in one way or another, in the Bible, especially the Psalms.[52] Even more to the point, this prayer to no god in particular finds its New Testament equivalent in the book of Acts and the story of the altar in Athens "to an unknown god" (Acts 17:16–34). Paul's use of that *preexisting* bit of Athenian "extreme religiosity" (see v. 22b) to proclaim the God of Israel and a "man whom he has appointed ... by raising him from the dead" (v. 31) is well-known. At this point, there are several rather obvious connections between Wesley's *prevenient grace* and other systematic-theological notions like *natural theology* and *general revelation*.[53]

Still further, Schlimm's (Wesley's) approach is anticipated in material that is much earlier. One thinks, for instance, of Eusebius's *The Preparation for the Gospel*. An apologetic book that in many ways does not quite deliver on the promise of the title,[54] Eusebius's work nevertheless implies that something "went before" the Gospel, something that led up to it, perhaps even facilitated it in some fashion.[55] It is noteworthy, therefore, to observe that Eusebius devotes

---

51. Daniel I. Block, *The Gospel according to Moses: Theological and Ethical Reflections on the Book of Deuteronomy* (Eugene, OR: Cascade, 2012), 236.

52. See Charles Halton, "An Ershaḫunga to Any God," in *Reading Akkadian Prayers and Hymns: An Introduction*, ed. Alan Lenzi, Ancient Near East Monographs 3 (Atlanta: Society of Biblical Literature, 2011), 447–64. Block himself admits of a certain "enlightenment" in the prayer's "sense of sin" and "awareness of ultimate accountability before deity" (*Gospel according to Moses*, 236).

53. For a start on these topics, see Daniel L. Migliore, *Faith Seeking Understanding: An Introduction to Christian Theology*, 3rd ed. (Grand Rapids: Eerdmans, 2014), 30–34, 459. In the last century, Karl Barth famously argued against natural theology. For natural theology and the Bible, see James Barr, *Biblical Faith and Natural Theology: The Gifford Lectures for 1991 Delivered in the University of Edinburgh* (Oxford: Oxford University Press, 1993), esp. 21–38, for Paul on the Areopagus, and 81–101, on the OT. Schlimm, "Wrestling with Marduk," 187n22, appropriately asks: "If ancient Near Eastern texts are true when they parallel the Bible, are they (sometimes) also true when they do not parallel scripture?"

54. Or perhaps the preparation in question was simply with reference to Eusebius's subsequent volume *Proof of the Gospel*. For more on Eusebius and these books, see Andrew Louth, "Eusebius and the Birth of Church History," in *The Cambridge History of Early Christian Literature*, ed. Frances Young, Lewis Ayres, and Andrew Louth (Cambridge: Cambridge University Press, 2004), 266–74.

55. See Niehaus, *Ancient Near Eastern Themes*, who speaks several times of "common grace" at work in the ancient religions (e.g., 29: "God allowed concepts that are true of him and his ways to appear in the realm of common grace"), but then, in a footnote (29n52), contradicts himself blatantly and inexplicably by suddenly attributing such "revelation" to demons! The latter idea is where he seems to place the emphasis of his theological interpretation of parallels from that point on: "the activity of deceiving, demonic spirits (producing parallels between supposed acts of pagan gods and the acts of God as they appear in the Bible)" (177); "Demonic inspiration of false religion" (179); "theological counterfeit ... imposed upon the ancients by the misleading inspiration of fallen angels" (181). I myself am at a profound loss to know how, in theological perspective, grace—"common" or otherwise—could ever be termed "demonic." Niehaus also speaks of the OT's preservation of "true and accurate accounts of major events" that are also found in extrabiblical

a good bit of the opening material to the theology of the ancient Egyptians, Greeks, Romans, and Phoenicians (see, e.g., bks. 1–3), and that he also discusses Greek philosophy, even if he roots that, ultimately, in Moses and the Prophets (bks. 10–12).[56] Another ancient antecedent to prevenient grace or general revelation—this one within the Bible itself—may be found in the Noachic covenant of Gen 9:1–17, which Jon Levenson believes reflects "the inchoate insight that the non-Israelite can be in a relationship with God parallel to Israel's own."[57]

The above considerations can be taken as a partial response to YHWH's similarity to Chemosh, Marduk, and all the rest: God was at work in Christ, says Paul (Eph 1:20); and in Israel too, added Gerhard von Rad much, much later;[58] and before Israel, say both the Yahwistic and Priestly strands of the Pentateuch much, much earlier.[59] And perhaps God was even at work in other religions and their divine foci, says Deuteronomy, or so it would seem, in two verses that may be the ancient equivalent of an unguarded moment or unfiltered Tweet:

> Don't look to the skies, to the sun or the moon or the stars, all the heavenly bodies, and be led astray, worshipping and serving them. The LORD your

---

sources, but admits of them only "in distorted forms" (29). The purpose of God's "common grace," he goes on say, was "to make such ideas somewhat familiar to God's people so that, when he actually broke into the historical plane and acted, his acts would be recognizable *against* their cultural background. God's self-revelation was so dynamic and (in his holiness) so challenging ... that a background preparation for at least some aspects of that revelation was necessary for his people" (29–30; emphasis added). So, while Niehaus allows for "a shared theological structure of ideas" in the ANE, that structure "finds its complete and true form [only] in the Old and New Testaments" (30). He concludes:

> [God] is the one who, in his providential care for humanity, has allowed such theological parallels as we have explored to become manifest over many centuries in the ancient world so that truth would appear, even in darkened and polytheistic forms. Truth in such forms could have no saving power. But it did prepare a matrix of thought, a background of theological understanding, so that when God truly appeared and did such things as the pagans had claimed for their gods, ... his revelation would come to a people who had some theological preparation for it. In this way God was glorified even by the distortions of pagan religion, for even in their darkness the pagans had retained or obtained common grace reflections of his truth (181).

On the basis of remarks like these, I deem Niehaus to be conflicted on the point at hand and, for some reason, unable or unwilling to think through the matter in a more integrated way. Wesley's notion of prevenient grace strikes me as vastly superior and unencumbered by Niehaus's demons, both literal and figurative.

56. Louth, "Eusebius," 268.
57. See, e.g., Jon D. Levenson, "Is There a Counterpart in the Hebrew Bible to New Testament Anti-Semitism?," *Journal of Ecumenical Studies* 22 (1985): 242–60, at 252 (also in the present volume, 170).
58. See Gerhard von Rad, *God at Work in Israel*, trans. John H. Marks (Nashville, TN: Abingdon, 1980).
59. Namely, in Gen 1–11. I hope to return to this point in a later essay.

God has granted [*ḥālaq*] these things to all the nations who live under heaven. (Deut 4:19; CEB)

They [Israel] followed other gods, serving them and worshipping them—other gods that they hadn't experienced before and that the Lord hadn't designated [*lō' ḥālaq*] for them. (Deut 29:26; CEB)[60]

Aspect 2: Nevertheless Distinct

But there is also YHWH's distinctiveness to consider. So, while YHWH is part of the gang—at least some of the time, and maybe more frequently than that—there are still moments when he is *not* one of the gang, or at least not *only* that. This judgment is no less historical than were assertions about YHWH's similarity, since the same could be said for each and every ANE deity, at least to some degree.[61] Each one of these gods, that is, is unique in some fashion. Marduk is not Baal, and Hathor is not Isis, and Ishtar is not Nabu—well, until they sort of are. The gods retain individuality, except when they don't, which is what happens in certain relatively rare cases where they are collapsed into each other via a focus on just one high god in a move that is summodeistic, henotheistic, monolatrous, or monotheizing, if not fully monotheistic.[62] Or it can happen in moments of god mergers, where formerly if not formally distinct gods are equated and identified thereafter.[63]

YHWH seems to have not suffered from the god-merger phenomenon much, if at all. If there were such moments, they didn't last, and the traces that remain of any such thing are truly anomalous, quite far off the beaten track of the mainstream presentation of YHWH, and thus they are (rather minor) exceptions that proverbially prove the rule true.[64] The mergers that may have occurred appear

---

60. See further Patrick D. Miller, "God's Other Stories: On the Margins of Deuteronomic Theology," in *Realia Dei: Essays in Archaeology and Biblical Interpretation in Honor of Edward F. Campbell Jr. at His Retirement*, ed. P. H. Williams Jr. and T. Hiebert (Atlanta: Scholars Press, 1999), 185–94.

61. Of course the judgment is also a *theological* one, since it concerns the gods. For a thoughtful collection that recaptures the term "theology" for the study of ancient materials in fields that have sometimes avoided such language, see Esther Eidinow, Julia Kindt, and Robin Osborne, ed., *Theologies of Ancient Greek Religion*, Cambridge Classical Studies (Cambridge: Cambridge University Press, 2016).

62. For some discussion on the terminology, see Nathan MacDonald, *Deuteronomy and the Meaning of "Monotheism,"* FAT 2.1 (Tübingen: Mohr Siebeck, 2003), esp. 5–58.

63. See, e.g., Collin Cornell, "A Moratorium on God Mergers? The Case of El and Milkom in the Ammonite Onomasticon," *UF* 46 (2015): 49–99. Note also, to some degree, the issues raised by Mark S. Smith, *God in Translation: Deities in Cross-Cultural Discourse in the Biblical World* (Grand Rapids: Eerdmans, 2010).

64. I have in mind here (for example) the odd conjunctions of divine names, including forms of YHWH, that are occasionally found among the much later texts from Nag Hammadi. See James M.

to lie mostly *behind* the biblical material we now have and play to YHWH's strengths: if and when this sort of thing transpired, YHWH was the god who remained after incorporating and assimilating other gods and/or other divine profiles.⁶⁵ That YHWH endured is a major difference between him and so many other ancient gods.

Another major difference between YHWH and his ANE confreres is the biblical corpus, already mentioned above, which is large in size and scope. It is this corpus of sacred, authoritative literature—and one need not posit formal canonicity or an early date for canonical forms for the point to hold—that seems to have helped YHWH survive, since the other gods we know of seem to have lacked anything remotely comparable and went the way of the dodo bird as a result.⁶⁶

Text, Community, Faith: The *Regula Fidei* Meets YHWH but Not Chemosh

But where did this corpus of Yahwistic texts come from? Who preserved it and so forth? Obviously and most mundanely, it was originally the people of Israel and Judah, and then, belatedly, the early Jewish and Christian communities that descended from them and composed, preserved, and transmitted the religious literature that eventually came to be recognized as the canonical writings of the OT/HB. Religious literature, however, emerges from religious experience,⁶⁷ except in the most cynical and secular interpretations of religion. What that means is that it was *Israel's experience of the god YHWH* that led to the composition, preservation, and transmission of a massive amount of literature about

---

Robinson, ed., *The Nag Hammadi Library in English*, rev. ed. (San Francisco: HarperSanFrancisco, 1990); Bentley Layton, *The Gnostic Scriptures: A New Translation with Annotations and Introductions*, Anchor Bible Reference Library (New York: Doubleday, 1987), esp. 16. See also the Enlightenment equation of YHWH with Isis, and thus "biblical *deus* with *Natura*," which is discussed in J. M. F. Heath, *Paul's Visual Piety: The Metamorphosis of the Beholder* (Oxford: Oxford University Press, 2013), 254. For YHWH mergers in antiquity, see Cornell, "What happened to Kemosh?," esp. 296–97 (on YHWH and Zeus), though I regard his data to be slightly different (also postbiblical) and, more importantly, as not disconfirming the comments above regarding (1) the short-lived nature of all such YHWH mergers and (2) YHWH as the god who dominates or survives the encounter. Cornell's emphasis is squarely on the importance of religious literature: "Yhwh's translation could only go so far, because unlike his cognate Levantine deities, the worship of Yhwh had become recentered on an authoritative body of literature" (297).

65. See note 3 above, to which can be added Mark S. Smith, *The Early History of God: Yahweh and the Other Deities in Ancient Israel*, 2nd ed. (Grand Rapids: Eerdmans, 2002).

66. For the importance of YHWH's scripture, see Cornell, "What Happened to Kemosh?"

67. Mark S. Smith, "Recent Study of Israelite Religion in Light of the Ugaritic Texts," in *Ugarit at Seventy-Five*, ed. K. Lawson Younger (Winona Lake, IN: Eisenbrauns, 2007), 1–25, at 5: "Out of experience comes literature, and out of religious experience comes religious literature."

YHWH, which in turn helped to insure YHWH's survival and also served to separate him from his more plodding ANE peers. Since this is mostly a historical judgment based on sociohistorical factors and the existence of certain literary *realia*—one that could be taken in a thin way—I wish to thicken it up a bit with some theological considerations.

I do so by appealing to the notion of "the rule of faith" (*regula fidei*), a term used in the study of early Christianity for a statement of belief that existed in something of a symbiotic relationship with further development and practice of that belief. According to Robert Louis Wilken (speaking of Ireneaus, ca. 130–200 CE):

> In his day there were no creeds as such, but at baptism catechumens answered a set of questions that took the form of a simple statement of belief, or "rule of faith." "Do you believe in God the Father Almighty?" "Do you believe in Jesus Christ his only Son our Lord?" "Do you believe in the Holy Spirit?" The rule of faith had a trinitarian structure whose narrative identified God by the things recorded in the Scriptures: the creation of the world, the inspiration of the prophets, the coming of Christ in the flesh, and the outpouring of the Holy Spirit. The rule of faith, which, of course, was *drawn from* the Bible, *reverberated back on the Bible* as *a key to its interpretation*. Yet in practice it stood apart from the Scriptures as a confession of faith received from tradition and recited at Baptism during the liturgy of Easter. *An arc of understanding stretched from what the church practiced to what it read in the Scriptures.*[68]

---

68. Robert Louis Wilken, *The Spirit of Early Christian Thought* (New Haven: Yale University Press, 2003), 66 (emphases added). Cf. the definition of the *regula fidei* in *The Oxford Dictionary of the Christian Church*, ed. F. L. Cross and E. A. Livingstone, 3rd rev. ed. (Oxford: Oxford University Press, 2005), 1424:

> Outline statements of Christian belief which ... were designed to make clear the essential contents of the Christian faith, to serve as guides in the exegesis of Scripture, ... and to distinguish the orthodox tradition from traditions to which heretics appealed. Alternative names were the "rule of truth," the "law of faith" or the "norm (κανών) of truth." Unlike creeds, which came later, these formularies varied in wording, though it was claimed that they faithfully reflected NT teaching, and did not differ from one another in their essential content. This content was held to have descended unchanged from apostolic times, in contrast to the spurious traditions of the heretics, which were taken to be later developments and mutually incompatible.

For more on the rule of faith, see J. N. D. Kelly, *Early Christian Creeds*, 3rd ed. (London: Continuum, 2006), 62–99, esp. 76–88. See also Wolfram Kinzig, *Faith in Formulae: A Collection of Early Christian Creeds and Creed-related Texts*, 4 vols. (Oxford: Oxford University Press, 2017), esp. 1:165–267, for various creedal formulae and rules of faith from the second and third centuries. Kinzig includes thirty-seven different traditions (some with multiple texts) ranging from 1 Clement to the gnostic *Tripartite Tractate* from Nag Hammadi.

What one sees in the rule of faith, therefore, is something of a feedback loop, what Wilken calls a reverberation of sorts and an "arc of understanding." A community of faith, because of the faith that emerges from its experience of the divine (even if that experience, at its most direct, lies in the distant past, preserved in sacred literature), now engages in practices of faith whereby it re(de)fines both faith and practice through the course of time and in close conjunction with its central locus of revelation: in this case, its authoritative religious texts.[69]

This makes good enough sense in the grand scheme of things, regardless of ongoing uncertainties about the specifics of the *regula fidei* in early Christianity.[70] A crucial theological issue, quite apart from those important matters, is to somehow prevent an unhelpful and overly historicized "developmentalism." "Development" is, let it be underscored once more, something of a magic word—not only because it is hard to determine cause and effect in sciences outside the natural ones (and even there, it is not always easy), but also because development often connotes a kind of upward trajectory, a myth of progress. In such instances "developmentalism" is at root little more than a kind of dressed-up dispensationalism, the ramifications and outcomes of which I wish to strenuously avoid, not only because they so often reek of supersessionism, but also because they are inherently and conceptually unable to mark an end to the development in question, which is to say, they are unable to justify why the current, always-superior moment in time will not be surpassed by the next development, stage, or "dispensation." The whole thing smacks of arrogance, if nothing else, but also arbitrariness: one must simply draw a line in the sand *somewhere* when it comes to development, a line that, again, does not seem theoretically justifiable, even if in some cases it is theologically understandable.[71]

One way to avoid such developmental dispensationalism (or dispensational developmentalism) is to return to the arc of understanding or reverberating

---

69. On the relationship to prior tradition, see Kelly, *Early Christian Creeds*, 29: "The second-century conviction that the 'rule of faith' believed and taught in the Catholic Church had been inherited from the Apostles contains more than a germ of truth. Not only was the content of that rule, in all essentials, foreshadowed by the 'pattern of teaching' accepted in the apostolic Church, but its characteristic lineaments and outline found their prototypes in the confessions and credal summaries contained in the New Testament documents." See also 2: "The rule of faith must not be confused with the creed, but ... the relationship between them was close."

70. One might compare, in a very different and modern context, the theory–praxis feedback loop argued by David A. Schön in *The Reflective Practitioner: How Professionals Think in Action* (New York: Basic, 1983) and *Educating the Reflective Practitioner: Toward a New Design for Teaching and Learning in the Professions* (San Francisco: Jossey-Bass, 1987).

71. So, e.g., Brevard S. Childs, *Biblical Theology of the Old and New Testaments: Theological Reflection on the Christian Bible* (Minneapolis: Fortress, 1992), 381: "We are neither prophets nor Apostles." As Childs's oeuvre shows, the notion of canon is very much a line in the sand, not entirely without arbitrariness, though the theological convictions and traditions involved would at least serve to limit that somewhat.

feedback loop that marks the unfolding and functioning of the rule of faith. On the one hand, the trajectories of that unfolding and that functioning are thoroughly *time-bound*, which is to say that these are *in time*, even if they are moving *through time* and changing and developing as part of that linear, temporal movement. On the other hand, the fact that both the faith and the practice of faith are constantly being renegotiated in conversation with the texts of faith and their practice lends the entire project a timeless quality: a sort of repetition, as it were, that can stand outside of time and feel simultaneous, like an instance of the eternal now.[72]

I would argue that the dynamic that seems clear enough in the *regula fidei*, even if still somewhat fuzzy, was operative long before the second-century church fathers. This same feedback loop, dynamic "arc of understanding," and reverberation between faith, practice, and authoritative locus (underwritten by the experience of faith and of its practice) is evident, for example, in 1–2 Maccabees, though of course not only there. Still, this example is useful, since it demonstrates that the kind of *regula fidei* dynamic I am suggesting actually was operational in later stages of Second Temple Judaism.

Mark McEntire has offered a narrative-theological reading of 1–2 Maccabees in which he stresses what he calls "the elusiveness of the divine character."[73] McEntire identifies this attenuation vis-à-vis other texts, especially biblical ones wherein God is more prominent or active (e.g., 1 Macc 2:23–26 vs. Num 25:10–13).[74] But if there are differences from prior biblical accounts, there are also points of significant continuity.[75] Alongside these—or better, intermixed with them, incorporating both—are moments of synthesis, development, and even transformation. So, for example, while there is no explicit mention of God "throughout the purifying campaign of Mattathias," there is nevertheless mention of being dedicated to the law (e.g., 1 Macc 2:21, 26–27, 42, 48, 50, 58,

---

72. For the timelessness of repetition and its manifestation in biblical literature, see Brent A. Strawn, "Keep/Observe/Do—Carefully—Today! The Rhetoric of Repetition in Deuteronomy," in *A God So Near: Essays on Old Testament Theology in Honor of Patrick D. Miller*, ed. Brent A. Strawn and Nancy R. Bowen (Winona Lake, IN: Eisenbrauns, 2003), 215–40, and Strawn, "Slaves and Rebels: Inscription, Identity, and Time in the Rhetoric of Deuteronomy," in Sepher Torat Mosheh: *Studies in the Composition and Interpretation of Deuteronomy*, ed. Daniel I. Block and Richard M. Schultz (Peabody, MA: Hendrickson, 2017), 161–91. My thinking in both of these essays was profoundly shaped, respectively, by Bruce F. Kawin, *Telling It Again and Again: Repetition in Literature and Film* (Boulder: University Press of Colorado, 1989), and Jon D. Levenson, "The Eighth Principle of Judaism and the Literary Simultaneity of Scripture," in *The Hebrew Bible, the Old Testament, and Historical Criticism: Jews and Christians in Biblical Studies* (Louisville, KY: Westminster John Knox, 1993), 62–81.

73. Mark McEntire, *An Apocryphal God: Beyond Divine Maturity* (Minneapolis: Fortress, 2015), 129.

74. Ibid.

75. Ibid., 156.

64, 67–68).[76] McEntire would see God's retreating as a factor at odds with the law predominating, but such opposition is not necessary. In McEntire's own words: "The divine actions the story mentions are all in the past, the making of covenants and giving of the law, and the response of present Jews produces a paradox that causes even the zealous Mattathias to rethink and reinterpret adherence to the torah."[77]

When seen via the lens of the rule of faith, such rethinking and reinterpreting is no paradox at all, but part and parcel of the kind of reverberating arc of understanding that the *regula fidei* encapsulates. This is not to say that the nonmention of God's direct activity, or even of the word "God" (*ho Theos*), in 1 Maccabees is not an important consideration—which it most certainly is.[78] It is only to say that what one sees in 1 Maccabees is not simply or only some sort of withdrawal of the divine subject (so McEntire), but instead, the ongoing feedback loop between prior tradition and present practice, and so on and so on and so on.[79] To use the words of 1 Macc 2:48, in this sort of way, Mattathias and his colleagues "rescued the law out of the hands of the Gentiles and kings" (NRSV). Other examples of the same sort of dynamic in 1–2 Maccabees (and elsewhere) could easily be adduced.[80]

Moreover, a rule-of-faith kind of understanding nicely explains things that McEntire otherwise finds "surprising," like Judas's mention of the deliverance of Jerusalem from Sennacherib in 2 Macc 8:19.[81] Even the comment that Judas and company distribute the spoils of war "to those who had been tortured and to the widows and orphans" (2 Macc 8:28) becomes intriguing in this light. The widow–orphan combination is common in the HB, which consistently enjoins their care upon Israel. But, now, in the Maccabean period, a new group requires assistance, the tortured, and indeed, these individuals can be mentioned first

76. Ibid., 130.
77. Ibid.
78. See W. O. E. Oesterley, "1 Maccabees," in *The Apocrypha and Pseudepigrapha of the Old Testament*, ed. R. H. Charles, 2 vols. (Oxford: Clarendon, 1913), 1:60–61. Contrast 2 Maccabees on this point, and compare the Masoretic Text of Esther and Song of Songs. Unlike these latter two compositions, 1 Maccabees has far more references to religious topics such as the law (*ho nomos*, presumably the Torah). McEntire notes this distinction between 1 Maccabees and the Masoretic Text of Esther and states that even the difference between 1 and 2 Maccabees "is subtle" (*An Apocryphal God*, 139–40). McEntire wonders if the differences between 1 and 2 Maccabees have to do with their respective audiences: the former living in the homeland and the latter among the diaspora (ibid., 157; for more on 2 Maccabees, see ibid., 141–54).
79. See Oesterley, "1 Maccabees," 60, who attributes the religious characteristics of the book partly to "the writer's sober and matter-of-fact way of looking at things, and partly ... [to] the somewhat altered religious outlook of the age as compared with earlier times." See also Jonathan A. Goldstein, *1 Maccabees: A New Translation with Introduction and Commentary*, Anchor Bible 41 (Garden City, NY: Doubleday, 1976), 13.
80. E.g.: 1 Macc 2:39–42; 3:46–57; 4:24, 30; 12:15; 2 Macc 5:11–20. See McEntire, *Apocryphal God*, 131–33, 138, 155.
81. See ibid., 150.

in the sequence of those who deserve financial help. This kind of "plus" to the traditional dyad of widow and orphan and the practice of their care represents a kind of *thinking with the tradition in light of new circumstances*: continuity amidst necessary growth and change.[82] By way of contrast, the situation I am describing for 1–2 Maccabees could be compared with what one finds in the Jewish colony at Elephantine. When the temple of YHW was destroyed there, that community sought assistance from the leadership in Jerusalem (*TADAE* A4.5 and A4.7–8; cf. *TADAE* A 4.9), but as far as the extant texts reveal, there is little evidence of the same kind of reflection and integration of tradition at Elephantine as one finds in 1–2 Maccabees.[83] Perhaps this is one of the reasons why the Jewish community at Elephantine ultimately disappeared, whereas the Maccabees left a considerable legacy within early Judaism. Whatever the case, what one can see in the case of the Maccabees is an instance of resistance that is based not only on inscripturation[84] but also on a tradition-and-praxis feedback loop similar to the rule of faith. And so, as McEntire rightly notes, comparing 1 and 2 Maccabees reveals the struggle to find the right kind of theological language for new and changed circumstances.[85] But these texts also demonstrate the struggle over how to best live out that theological language, and then (subsequently) to talk about it, and then (thereafter) to live it, and so on *ad infinitum*.

I would suggest that this kind of *regula fidei* dynamic—not just large amounts of sacred literature alone, therefore, but the "arc of understanding" between that religious literature and ongoing religious practice and experience[86]—is what ultimately separated YHWH from the rest of the gods who evidently specialized, instead, in the religion of static triumphalism.[87] This type of dynamic shows

---

82. See ibid., 154: "Divine favor is no straightforward concept but must be shaped around very difficult events."

83. This may simply be due to the nature of the texts that have survived. An exception, furthermore, may be found in the Passover Letter (*TADAE* A4.1); see Bezalel Porten, *Archives from Elephantine: The Life of an Ancient Jewish Military Colony* (Berkeley: University of California Press, 1968), 279–82.

84. So, rightly, Cornell, "What happened to Kemosh?," 297.

85. McEntire, *Apocryphal God*, 238.

86. Of course these two are related and precisely so in the *regula fidei*, if not also in Scripture itself. For the connections between the rule of faith and Scripture, see note 69 above. For the dynamic within Scripture, see R. W. L. Moberly's description of a community's engagement with canonical texts: "Initial reduction and then ingenious variegation is the pattern" (*The Bible in a Disenchanted Age: The Enduring Possibility of Christian Faith* [Grand Rapids: Baker Academic, 2018], 81). See also J. A. Sanders, "Adaptable for Life: The Nature and Function of Canon," in *Magnalia Dei: The Mighty Acts of God: Essays on the Bible and Archaeology in Memory of G. Ernest Wright*, ed. Frank Moore Cross, Werner E. Lemke, and Patrick D. Miller Jr. (Garden City, NY: Doubleday, 1976), 531–60.

87. I take the last phrase from Walter Brueggemann, *The Prophetic Imagination, 40th Anniversary Edition*, foreword by Davis Hankins (Minneapolis: Fortress, 2018), 6–8, who uses it of Egypt under Pharaoh according to Exodus. See also ibid., 28–37, for static religion *within* Israel itself. Stasis is a perennial problem, but one that the *regula fidei* actually serves to counter.

how YHWH can act so similarly to Chemosh and others in the warp and woof of human history, which is entirely as expected in the time-bound aspect of the dynamic; but it also shows how, in the end, YHWH can be so profoundly different in the ongoing, timeless aspect of the dynamic. And so it is that YHWH can be both quite like an austere bachelor mountain god but also "maker of heaven and earth" (Pss 115:15; 121:2; 124:8; 134:3; 146:6) and "of all that is, seen and unseen" (Nicene Creed), present not only back *then* in the Iron Age Levant or only *there* in the biblical texts, but also present *hic et nunc* because of and via the texts, the community, and the faith—and the intersection of all of the above (*regula fidei et vita!*). And, so, it is not surprising that, in one such belated instance of this faith, according to its creeds, YHWH is affirmed not only as maker of heaven and earth, of things seen and unseen, but also as father of the Lord Jesus Christ.

CHAPTER 10

Is There a Counterpart in the Hebrew Bible to New Testament Anti-Semitism?

Jon D. Levenson

Preface (2019)

Looking back on my essay "Is There a Counterpart in the Hebrew Bible to New Testament Anti-Semitism?" after thirty-five years, I experience considerable ambivalence. On the one hand, I continue to believe strongly in its central claim: the unfairness and severity of the treatment of other religious, cultural, or ethnic groups in some sources in the Hebrew Bible parallel to a worrisome degree the treatment of the Jews in much New Testament literature and should thus occasion more discomfort among Jewish traditionalists than was the case when the essay was published (and is the case today). On the other hand, I am also struck by a lack of nuance and careful distinction in the way I handled some of the material. For example, although anti-Judaism and anti-Semitism are related and usually coincide, I could have offered a better conceptual differentiation of them and described each in a more historically precise and careful manner. To give another example, on the subject of the genocide various biblical sources (most prominently, Deuteronomy) decree against the Canaanite nations, I would, if possible, now discuss what I termed "the puristic theology" that motivates it at more length and with substantial sympathy, informed by the sophisticated theology of R. W. L. Moberly's approach to the subject and the thinking in my latest book, *The Love of God: Divine Gift, Human Gratitude, and Mutual Faithfulness in Judaism*. Similarly, had I the opportunity, I would today qualify my claim that "the Hebrew Bible and rabbinic literature regard all pagan religion as idolatry," noting some exceptions and countermovements to that grand generalization. Finally, if I were redoing the essay (and also able substantially to expand it), I would mention both the honorable Christian efforts to deal with the legacy of supersessionism and the philo-Semitism that has become especially prominent in

---

Author's Note (1985): For Mary Lefkowitz on her 50th birthday—Judges 4:9. Thanks are owed to Professors Robert Cohn and Arthur Droge for their careful reading of this article and their sage counsel. Any errors that remain are the author's sole responsibility.

various churches in recent decades. But I would also address the virulent resurfacing of the broad outlines of the older theology in both the Christian and the secular left in our time, especially evident in their treatment of the State of Israel.

I reiterate, however, that, although I have my regrets, I continue to believe that this essay from 1985 is, on the whole, valid and important, and I hope those who read it will make the same judgment.

—JDL

I.

The most effective impediment to ecumenical dialogue is the persistence of stereotypical views of the potential partner. These stereotypes derive from the religious traditions themselves; they present the other community in a fashion that minimizes its appeal, even its humanity, and thus neutralizes the competition the other community might offer or the threat that it might present to one's own self-understanding. Where the community confronted is the parent or immediate antecedent of one's own, then the urge to present it stereotypically and reductionistically is much more irresistible, for, if the older religion had been adequate, then the suspicion arises that the younger need never have appeared. This is not a suspicion which members of the newer community are likely to be willing to entertain; it strikes at their very existence.

The presentation of Judaism by Christian scholars is a case in point. In 1921, the great Christian Judaicist George Foot Moore published an extensive study entitled "Christian Writers on Judaism." Its opening sentence states his conclusion succinctly: "Christian interest in Jewish literature has always been apologetic or polemic rather than historical."[1] Lest his reader think that the emergence of historical criticism in modern times has destroyed, at least among its practitioners, the old confessional posture, Moore pointed out that "The title of Bousset's first work, *Jesu Predigt in ihrem Gegensatz zum Judentum*, is the programme of the younger school."[2] In other words, instead of using the ancient argument that Jewish sources actually sustain the Christian claim, the newer approach presented Judaism as the foil for Christianity, and the rabbis as the foil for Jesus, who is assumed to have been their superior. The assumption that Judaism should have yielded to Christianity (and that the Jews are therefore obsolete) remained unshaken.

In 1977, the Pauline scholar E. P. Sanders lamented the fact that in the half century since the appearance of Moore's article and of his *magnum opus* on

---

1. George Foot Moore, "Christian Writers on Judaism," *HTR* (1921): 197–254, at 197.
2. Ibid. 253.

Tannaitic Judaism,³ the old stereotypes continued to flourish, even among scholars who had read Moore and listed him in their bibliographies.⁴ An example is the most influential New Testament scholar of the century, Rudolf Bultmann. The Judaism Bultmann described is most unattractive. Its God is no longer vital to the present moment; it values ritual above ethics; it mandates an absurd amount of observances, which can only be a burden; the obedience it produces is "formal rather than radical"; it afflicts its practitioner with a "morbid sense of guilt"; and its legalism promotes self-righteousness.⁵ On the one hand, Bultmann, unlike other scholars who came into their own during the Third Reich, cannot be convicted of anti-Semitism. He was an outspoken opponent of efforts to marry the church to the doctrine of Aryan supremacy.⁶ On the other hand, his description of Judaism raises the question of how a member of the species Homo sapiens could ever be attracted to such a degraded and unhappy way of life and even give his own life rather than abandon it. At the least, his work implies the presence of something like a mass psychosis among Jewry. That implication is the nexus between anti-Judaism, which is a theological judgment, and anti-Semitism, which is an ethnic prejudice, one which, in the case of the Third Reich, produced a remarkably successful attempt at genocide. The distinction between anti-Judaism and anti-Semitism is real, but so is the historical connection between them.

The source of the persistently negative presentation of Judaism among so many New Testament scholars is the anti-Judaism of the New Testament itself.⁷ Paul's judgment upon the Jews and Judaism, for example, is an integral part of his christocentric eschatology. As Rosemary Ruether puts it: "His 'two aeons' are not two historical eras, but an antithesis between the historical and the eschatological 'worlds.' Judaism belongs, by nature, to the historical world of fallen,

---

3. George Foot Moore, *Judaism in the First Centuries of the Christian Era*, 3 vols. (Cambridge: Harvard University, 1927–1930). Of course, the study of Tannaitic Judaism has progressed greatly since the issuance of Moore's study, particularly on the issue of ritual, which Moore's work does not properly stress. Still, his argument that the New Testament images fail to do justice to the Judaism of the time remains unshaken.

4. E. P. Sanders, *Paul and Palestinian Judaism* (Philadelphia: Fortress, 1977), 33–59.

5. Sanders, *Paul and Palestinian Judaism*, 44–45. See also Charlotte Klein, *Anti-Judaism in Christian Theology*, trans. Edward Quinn (London: SPCK, 1978), 27–28; 56–57.

6. See Rolf Rendtorff, "The Jewish Bible and Its Anti-Jewish Interpretation," *Christian Jewish Relations* 16 (1983): 1–20, at 6–7.

7. Of the burgeoning bibliography on Christian anti-Semitism, note especially the following: James Parkes, *The Conflict of the Church and the Synagogue* (New York: World; Philadelphia: Jewish Publication Society, 1961); León Poliakov, *The History of Anti–Semitism*, 3 vols. (London: Elek, 1966); A. Roy Eckardt, *Elder and Younger Brothers* (New York: Charles Scribner's Sons, 1967; note his bibliography on 179–84); Alan T. Davies, *Anti-Semitism and the Christian Mind* (New York: Herder and Herder, 196); Rosemary Radford Ruether, *Faith and Fratricide* (New York: Seabury, 1974); Alan T. Davies, ed., *Antisemitism and the Foundation of Christianity* (New York: Paulist, 1979); and Samuel Sandmel, *Anti-Semitism in the New Testament?* (Philadelphia: Fortress, 1978).

finite, Adamic man."[8] Paul is thus able to contrast the "new covenant," a thing of the spirit, with the old one, which is confined to writing. Here, Torah is at best a foil for Christ: "The letter kills, but the spirit gives life" (2 Cor 3:4–6). In fact, obedience to the Torah is, in Paul's mind, equivalent to being under a curse; he contrasts it with faith, through which the baptized gentile lays a valid claim upon the status of Abraham's lineage (Gal 3:5–14). Thus, the true Jew is not such by descent or by observance of *mitsvot* (commandments from God), but by the heart, by the spirit (Rom 2:25–29). Therefore, Israel "according to the flesh," the Jews, are not Israel at all. In fact, since the coming of Christ, they have been in a state of blindness and disobedience to God. It is their offense which makes possible the inclusion of gentiles in the "new Israel," whose inevitable vindication will be signified by its eschatological absorption of the Jews, then to be forgiven (Rom 11:11–32). Thus, even when Paul asserts the meaningfulness of Jewish existence, he does so only within a theological framework in which the Jews play a negative role. He is not anti-Semitic, but he is profoundly anti-Judaic.[9]

The Gospels continue and even intensify the bias. Matthew, for example, asserts that, even when the Jews perform an act of philanthropy or prayer, it is only an illusion. They are hypocrites and act only for show (Matt 6:1–18)! But the harshest anti-Judaism in the New Testament appears in John.[10] Time and again, this Gospel insists that the Jews do not know God.[11] In fact, their denial of "the son" is a denial of "'the father" (John 5:23). Moreover—and here we are surely entitled to speak of anti-Semitism alongside anti-Judaism—John's Jesus demonizes the Jews. "Your father is the devil," he tells them (John 8:44), "and you willingly carry out his desires." Thus began the persistent view of the Jews as not merely odious but even diabolical, paragons of perfidy, duplicity, and obscenity.[12] The persistence to this day of that view in Christendom, where alone it has thrived, is owed in no small measure to one clause in the Gospel of Matthew: "His blood be upon us, and on our children" (Matt 27:25). This could be taken as a confession of the Jews to the charge of deicide and, thus,

---

8. Ruether, *Faith and Fratricide*, 103.

9. On the mistake of imagining that Rom 9–11 can serve as the basis for any authentic Jewish–Christian dialogue, see ibid., 105–7.

10. See Eldon Jay Epp, "Anti-Semitism and the Popularity of the Fourth Gospel in Christianity," *Central Conference of American Rabbis Journal* 22 (1975): 35–57. Epp's conclusion is "that the Fourth Gospel, more than any other book in the canonical body of Christian writings, is responsible for the frequent anti-Semitic expressions by Christians during the past eighteen or nineteen centuries" (35). See also Janis E. Leibig, "John and 'the Jews': Theological Antisemitism in the Fourth Gospel," *Journal of Ecumenical Studies* 20 (1983): 209–34.

11. E.g.: John 5:19–47; 7:28; 8:19, 47; 15:18–25; 16:1–3.

12. On this image, see Joshua Trachtenberg, *The Devil and The Jews: The Medieval Conception of the Jew and Its Relation to Modern Antisemitism* (New York: Harper and Row; Philadelphia: Jewish Publication Society, 1966).

as a justification of endless Christian persecution of them. They condemned themselves.

The various New Testament documents should not be homogenized. They differ in date, locale, setting, and theology. Still, one generalization does hold: The Jews who have not become Christians and Judaism that adheres to the Torah and not to Jesus are always presented negatively in the New Testament. Only the idiom and the degree vary. The cause of the negative presentation undoubtedly lies in controversy between the older and the younger communities. Most of the documents of the New Testament originated in a context of polemic. They are marked by much rhetorical hyperbole, anger, and even hate. Where the opponent is their own parent religion, Judaism, these factors are naturally even more pronounced, since in many instances the writers are attacking their former selves—or their former selves as they would like to remember them. The church, by defining these documents as Scripture, has, in a sense, frozen that moment of bitter separation and ensured its preservation for the last two millennia, if not for all eternity.

There is a tragicomic irony here, that a tradition which sets such great store on love and reconciliation should have canonized literature deriving, in part, from a situation of hatred and strife. However, read against their historical context, the New Testament documents exemplify a truism of human nature: We are rarely generous with our competitors, especially when the competitors have *prima facie* first claim upon a status to which we aspire. If we are to replace them, we had better show that they deserve to be replaced, and, if we dare not boast that we are better than they, then let us at least portray them as worse than we.

II.

The connection of Christian anti-Semitism with the aspiration of the church to inherit the claims and promises of the Jews has been drawn most forcefully in Rosemary Ruether's classic study, *Faith and Fratricide*. Ruether argued that the denigration of the Jews followed from Christianity's supersessionism, its claim to be the new and eternally valid "Israel." This doctrine was supported by its "christological midrash," the exegetical maneuvers by which the church deprived the Jews of their Bible and reapplied the desired passages to itself. Her argument has the advantage of showing that anti-Semitism is not extraneous to the church's self-conception—how could anything so enormous, so intense, and so persistent have been extraneous?—but inheres in the very process by which the Christian community first sought to establish its identity. I would add that the need for a foil is especially pressing in Christianity: The church's claim that Jesus was a perfect person (and, later, that he was God) would seem more credible if the imperfections of those whom he encountered in his lifetime, especially those who were unimpressed with him, were conspicuous and glaring. Against such a background, he could appear as "the light that shines in the dark" (John 1:5). Their uncommon badness makes the faith in his uncommon goodness seem more sensible. This aspect of Christology is a motivation also in the persistent denigration of Judaism among New Testament scholars.

Recently, Hyam Maccoby has challenged Ruether's identification of supersessionism as the root of Christian anti-Semitism. Instead, he argues that the hatred of the Jews follows from the inner dynamics of the Christ-myth itself. Under the influence of gnostic doctrines, Maccoby claims, Christianity developed the idea that humankind has been condemned "to hell by an angry Father-god."[13] The only hope was "the killing of its best and most innocent man to avert the anger" of God. Jesus is thus the scapegoat who provides redemption from a cruel, despotic, and misanthropic deity:

> The Jews in the scheme are thus the earthly agents of the cosmic powers of evil. They are the deicides who by their wickedness unwittingly save mankind, but who are thus doubly damned, both because the death of Christ is not efficacious for *them* and because they have crowned a long career of sin with the greatest of all sins.[14]

Maccoby's theory has the advantage of better accounting for the phenomenal ferocity, ubiquity, and durability of Jew-hatred in Christendom. These are less likely to be only the aftereffects of a bitter controversy in the first century; they are more likely to follow from the ongoing spiritual experience of participation in Christ. For example, Paul's battle with those to his theological left should not divert us from the affinities of his own theology with Gnosticism. One of the greatest puzzles to Jews is how something seen universally in the Hebrew Bible as good, life-giving, and a sign of freedom and love—the commandments of the Torah—could have become, in the apostle's mind, a form of slavery, curse, and death, a regime from which one must seek redemption (e.g., Gal 4). Does the loving and redeeming God of the Exodus condemn God's own people to slavery? Obviously, to one who answers in the affirmative, as Paul did, God's inner nature is not altogether loving and redeeming; another redeemer, the Christ, must come to lift the slavery God imposed. It is hard to avoid the conclusion that, with all due regard for Paul's intentions and his ambivalences (e.g., Rom 7:12), his basic drama is one which has somewhat demonized the God of Israel.

---

13. Hyam Maccoby, "Theologian of the Holocaust," *Commentary* 74 (1982): 33–37, at 36. Maccoby promised a fuller development of these themes in *The Sacred Executioner: Human Sacrifice and the Legacy of Guilt* (New York: Thames & Hudson, 1982).

14. Maccoby, "Theologian of the Holocaust," 36.

From here, it is a stone's throw to the Johannine demonization of the servants of that diabolical deity, the Jews, and to the notion that they worship the devil rather than God (see Rev 2:9; 3:9).[15]

The chief difficulty with Maccoby's theory is its generality. It accounts for certain important and currently downplayed features of Pauline and Johannine theology, but it applies less well, if at all, to other New Testament documents and to the greater Christian Bible. After all, the last does include the Hebrew Bible, although redefined as only an "Old Testament." The Christian canon does testify to the benevolent and philanthropic God of creation, Exodus, and even Sinai. How to integrate this God with Paul's and John's is a great problem. I think it fair to say that to many Jews it appears insurmountable and that Christian anti-Semitism seems to be only the flashpoint of an ambivalence deep in the very heart of Christianity. Still, it would be an error to attribute only one spiritual experience to all Christians, or even all Christian anti-Semites, and to assume that all Christology reduces to one cosmic drama, understood in first-century terms.

Maccoby contrasts the apocalyptic-gnostic dualism of Christianity, which accounts for its tendency to demonize, with the more humane attitude of the Hebrew Bible:

> In contrast to this, the Hebrew Bible is remarkable in that it contains no palpable villains, only fallible, understandable human beings. But the Hebrew Bible contains no devil either, nor the dualism that underlies the marking out of a people as representatives of cosmic evil.[16]

This would imply that, although Judaism and its Bible may not be exemplars of enlightenment and toleration, as many liberal expositors of Judaism would have it, still they offer nothing comparable to Christian anti-Semitism. If so, then the hermeneutical challenge confronting the Christian seeking to rid the church of theological anti-Semitism has no parallel in Judaism. It is to an examination of this issue of a Jewish parallel to Christian anti-Semitism that we now turn.

III.

The religion of Israel never claimed to be the fulfillment of any earlier religion. Israel's traditions (and, eventually, its Scriptures) never based themselves upon anyone else's. Judaism knows no "Old Testament"; it does not suffer from the problematic of a bifurcated Bible, as Christianity does. Consequently, the Jews

---

15. The demonization of the Jew(s) survived the canonical period and came to fevered pitch in the sermons of John Chrysostom. See Ruether, *Faith and Fratricide*, 170–81.
16. Hyam Maccoby, in an untitled response, *Commentary* 75 (1983): 18.

are not afflicted with the problems of the "younger brother" eager to assert his equality or superiority to an "older brother" whose existence and birthright he cannot altogether negate. Nonetheless, it would be a mistake to conclude that nothing reminiscent of Christian supersessionism is to be found in the Hebrew Bible. For, if Israel did not seek to appropriate anyone else's religion and its promise for itself, it did seek to justify its appropriation of the lands of the Canaanites, which it redefined as the promised land of Israel. That process of self-justification on the part of a threatened newcomer does indeed present us with parallels to some of the foundations of Christian Jew-hatred.[17] There are others.

One of the main justifications for the Israelite conquest offered in the Torah is the moral turpitude of the Canaanite nations. "It is not on account of your merit and your rectitude that you are about to take possession of their land," Moses tells Israel (Deut 9:5), "but it is on account of the wickedness of these peoples that YHWH your God is dispossessing them before you." At times, this wickedness of the Canaanites is seen to lie in their religion, with its emphasis upon magic (e.g., Deut 18:9–12), but at other times, the mortal sin was held to be sexual in character—again, in part, because of cultic associations (e.g., Lev 18). In fact, Israelite tradition presents a highly unflattering picture of Canaan's eponymous ancestor, who was cursed with slavery to his brothers (including Israel's ancestor Shem) because of his own or his father's sexual misdeed (Gen 9:20–27). In Lev 18, Israel is warned not to indulge in the perversions of the Canaanites, lest the land "vomit out" the newcomer as it did its former tenant (v. 28). In fact, Lev 18:24–30 is a good, if inexact, parallel to Rom 11. In each case, it is the offense of the predecessors which justifies their supplantation. They have become a standing warning to the newcomers of what can happen should they, too, stumble (cf. Rom 11:21–22). Similarly, in Num 33, Moses, speaking an oracle from his God, warns Israel that if they fail to disinherit any of the former inhabitants, those who remain will prove to be "hooks in your eyes and thorns in your sides, and they shall harass you in the land in which you dwell, so that I will do to you what I had planned to do to them" (33:55–56).[18] Deuteronomic tradition is especially insistent that there is only one way to meet the danger of apostasy to Canaanite religion: the decimation of the Canaanite cults and, to call it what it is, the *genocide* of the Canaanites themselves (e.g., Deut 7:1–5, 23–26).

As one might surmise from the eventual elevation of the Pentateuch above all other Scripture, the period of the Exodus and the wandering in the wilderness

---

17. The blunt term "Jew-hatred" is, in some contexts, preferable to the genteel euphemism "anti-Semitism." It is not Semites that most "anti-Semites" despise; many speak Semitic languages themselves (e.g., the Mufti of Jerusalem, who carried on a flirtation with the Nazi regime in Germany).

18. In the election campaign in Israel in 1981, the author heard radio advertisements for a tiny (and ultimately unsuccessful) right-wing party, in which this verse was quoted, obviously to serve as a proof text in support of the deportation of Palestinian Arabs.

fulfilled the function of a classical statement in ancient Israel; many institutions were derived, if somewhat fancifully, from legends about that period. A particularly gruesome instance is the commandment to annihilate the Amalekites, a group on the southern fringe of Canaan, which was not included in the seven Canaanite nations. Deut 25:17–19 derives the commandment to commit genocide against the Amalekites from the fact that Amalek "fell upon you on the way, and cut down all the stragglers in your rear, when you were weary and exhausted; he showed no fear of God" (v. 18). Israel's mandate to eradicate Amalek is, in fact, only the human side of a larger struggle, in which YHWH swears by the divine throne to be "at war with Amalek in every generation" (Exod 17:14–16). These traditions about Amalek cause one to question Maccoby's confidence in asserting that "the Hebrew Bible [never marks out] a people as representatives of cosmic evil." In fact, nothing less than the deposition of Israel's first king, Saul, was attributed to his sparing some Amalekite booty and the life of their king, Agag, whom an indignant prophet, Samuel, then hacks to pieces (1 Sam 15)!

These passages in Exodus, Deuteronomy, and Samuel might be attributed to nothing more than old tribal feuds—Israel and Amalek as the Hatfields and the McCoys of ancient Palestine. However, in the book of Esther, even the Persian prime minister, Haman, fiercest of anti-Semites (until modern times), is assigned descent from Agag (Esth 3:1). No wonder that, at the order of his Jewish successor, Mordecai (whose lineage suggests that of Saul),[19] the Jews executed the ten sons of Haman, "but touched not the booty" (Esth 8:9–9:10). At this point, the Amalekites have become archetypes of murderous evil. Later, in rabbinic midrash, this thrust becomes even more explicit. For example, a statement in the name of Rabbi Eliezer (flourished ca. 80–120 CE), using 2 Sam 1:13–16 as a proof text, stipulates that "if anyone from any of the nations of the world comes to convert [to Judaism], they [the Jews] must accept him, but from the House of Amalek, they are not to accept him."[20]

But the last stage in the demonization of the Amalekites appears in a midrash on Deut 25:19, related in the name of the Amora, Rabbi Aḥa ben Ḥanina (third century CE):

So long as the progeny of Amalek are in the world, "the name" is not complete, and the throne is not complete. When the progeny of Amalek have disappeared, "the name" is complete, and the throne is complete.[21]

19. See Esth 2:5 and 1 Sam 9:1–2.
20. Mek. Amalek 2. For an English translation, see Jacob Z. Lauterbach, ed. and trans., *Mekilta de-Rabbi Ishmael*, 3 vols. (Philadelphia: Jewish Publication Society, 1933), 2:160–61. A very handy collection of rabbinic statements about Amalek appears in the Pesiqta of Rab Kahana, Parshat Zachor. See William G. Braude and Israel J. Kapstein, trans. *Pěsiḳta dě-Rab Kahăna* (Philadelphia: Jewish Publication Society, 1975), 37–56.
21. Tanh. Ki Teitzei 10 (translation mine).

Here, Amalek has assumed the character of an "anti-Christ."[22] So long as he lives, "the name," which means the ineffable four-letter name of God (YHWH), is incomplete, as is God's very throne.[23] Thus, if the Hebrew Bible does not yet know "cosmic evil" and the dualism that goes with it, as Maccoby asserts, then rabbinic tradition does know a touch of it. And since the rabbis were closer in time to the New Testament than the Hebrew Bible was, the New Testament demonization of the Jews is more justly compared with midrash than with the latter. But even if the inquiry is to be restricted—unfairly—to the Hebrew Bible, Maccoby's statement above that "it contains no palpable villains, only fallible, understandable human beings" is too optimistic.

We have seen that Jewish tradition does include some materials comparable to both foundations of Christian anti-Semitism which we explored, supersessionism and demonization. The parallels are not perfect, but neither are they unreal. Like the Jews in some New Testament and much patristic literature, the Canaanites in the Hebrew Bible are, without exception, wicked in the worst of ways. It is their wickedness, *inter alia*, which justifies their loss of the land to Israel and which condemns them eternally in the sight of God, who has graciously and mysteriously (Deut 7:6–8) chosen Israel to supplant them. It is, to be sure, doubtful whether the campaign of genocide mandated in the Torah and narrated in the book of Joshua ever took place. Many scholars are today persuaded that Israel assumed the land not through a genocidal *Blitzkrieg*, but through a social revolution in which disaffected Canaanite peasants redefined themselves as Israelites.[24] In fact, most of the language of genocide and of decimation of the Canaanite cult is written under the influence of Deuteronomy, which may not predate the seventh century BCE, i.e., a half millennium after the putative conquest under Joshua. In that case, the *Blitzkrieg* may be only a later idealization, motivated by the puristic theology of Deuteronomic circles, but it is not a pleasant ideal to contemplate.

One of the great assets of the Jews is that the period of the Hebrew Bible lasted so much longer than the period of the New Testament, perhaps a thousand years longer. This allowed perspectives to develop, as well as distance from the heat of polemic, which, in turn, led to the softening of old judgments (although, as the rabbinic materials have shown us, the development should not be seen

---

22. The term is from Jakob J. Petuchowski, "Thinking in Our Ancestors' Categories," *Judaism* 32 (1983): 196–204, at 199–200.

23. Rabbi Aḥa ben Ḥanina's midrash is derived from the fact that the word for throne (*kēs*) and the word for "Lord" (*Yāh*) in Exod 17:16 are not the usual and fuller forms, *kissē'* and YHWH, respectively.

24. E.g., George E. Mendenhall, *The Tenth Generation* (Baltimore: Johns Hopkins University Press, 1973), especially chs. 1, 5, and 7; and Norman Gottwald, *The Tribes of Yahweh* (Maryknoll, NY: Orbis, 1979).

as linear and progressive). One thinks, for example, of the hatred of Edomites. Edom, or Esau, was—as Genesis would have it—literally the older brother of Israel (Jacob). On the other hand, there is much material, most of it centered on the destruction of the First Temple in 587 BCE, which presents the Edomites as the epitome of perfidy and treachery,[25] a tradition undoubtedly related to the genealogy of Amalek as Esau's grandson (Gen 36:12). Here the venom is searing, yet Deut 23:8 commands, in a mere six words, "You shall not abhor an Edomite, for he is your brother." Or one thinks of the prohibition upon the admission of Ammonites and Moabites into the cult, even to the tenth generation, "because they did not meet you with bread and water on your way out of Egypt and hired Balaam ben Beor from Pethor in Aram-Namaraim to curse you" (23:5). But the book of Ruth offers a case of a Moabite's acceptance in Israel. Ruth is anything but cruel and unfeeling. She is a paragon of good faith (*ḥesed*), and, Moabite or not, she becomes an ancestor of David and thus of the messiah (Ruth 4:18–22). In short, the old stereotypes are not uprooted, but new perspectives quietly juxtapose themselves. The canonical result is a nuanced and textured statement which is far from the Christian dualism and demonization of which Maccoby speaks.

In the rabbinic period, we see a further softening of some of the old stereotypes. For example, the Talmud relates that Rabbi Joshua (flourished ca. 80–120 CE) authorized the admittance of an Ammonite proselyte, in spite of Deut 23:4–7, on the grounds that Sennacherib, the Assyrian conqueror, had "mixed up all the nations ... and anyone who separates is assumed to have separated from the larger group" (b. Berakhot 28a). This ruling effectively abolished the old national distinctions and made it impossible to apply the scriptural stereotypes to any contemporary individual. If it is defensible to generalize from the ruling, then we can conclude that even if the Ammonite, Moabite, Canaanite, and other peoples had continued to exist, and even if the Jews had been in a position of political power, nothing like the history of Christian anti-Semitism would have developed in rabbinic Judaism. This is true not only because rabbinic judicial procedures would have forbidden it but also because the rabbis showed a deep sensitivity to the human dimension, which is only dimly adumbrated in their Scripture. They even went so far as to say that "descendants of Haman studied Torah in [the rabbinic community of] Bnei Braq" (b. Gittin 57b; b. Sanhedrin 96b). This statement must be considered alongside the midrash quoted earlier which saw Amalek (whom they considered an ancestor of Haman) as a kind of antichrist. One should avoid the mistake of assuming that the dualism and demonization of that midrash played the same important role as those elements play in some New Testament documents. They did not; however, the two-sidedness of rabbinic thinking on these issues demonstrates the tenacity of

---

25. E.g.: Amos 1:11; Ps 137:7; Lam 4:21–22; and Obadiah.

the grip of the unhappy legacy even on the minds of those who, at times, find it distasteful. Midrash alone seems inadequate as an antidote.

IV.

In its totality, the New Testament is undecided on the issue of whether the outsider can have a proper relationship with God. On the one hand, the Gospel of John takes a position of extreme exclusivism, which is the ancestor of the doctrine *extra ecclesiam nulla salus* ("There is no salvation outside the church"). "I am the way, the truth, and the life," Jesus tells Thomas in John 14:6. "No one comes to the Father except through me." This exclusivism is closely related to the Johannine insistence that the Jews do not know God. Against it, however, one can cite the broader view of Matt 25:31–46 ("Whatever you did for the least of these ... you did for me"). The attitude of the Hebrew Bible and of rabbinic literature is closer to the Matthean position. Genesis presents humanity as primordially monotheistic and even YHWHistic (e.g., Gen 4:26), and, throughout the Hebrew Bible, gentiles are judged by whether they practiced "the fear of God," a term which seems to mean simply ethics and human decency (e.g., Gen 20). Ultimately, the inchoate insight that the non-Israelite can be in a relationship with God parallel to Israel's own finds concrete formulation in the priestly idea of the covenant with Noah (Gen 9: 1–17). The latter plays a more important role in rabbinic thought.

The idea that gentiles can, without conversion, stand in a proper relationship with God or, in rabbinic parlance, "have a share in the world-to-come," must not be interpreted to mean that Judaism regards all religions as valid paths to the true God. On the contrary, biblical and rabbinic sources are unanimous in their contempt for idolatry and their insistence that it can only arouse God's punitive wrath. In fact, the rabbis counted the prohibition of idolatry as one of the seven commandments incumbent upon Noahides, that is, all persons (b. Sanhedrin 56a). Neither Jew nor gentile may worship an idol.

A serious complication arises from the fact that the Hebrew Bible and rabbinic literature regard all pagan religion as idolatry.[26] This follows naturally from

---

26. See Saul Lieberman, "Rabbinic Polemics against Idolatry," in his *Hellenism in Jewish Palestine: Studies in the Literary Transmission, Beliefs and Manners of Palestine in the I Century B.C.E.–IV Century C.E.*, Texts and Studies of the Jewish Theological Seminary of America 18 (New York: Jewish Theological Seminary, 1962), 115–27. The question later arose as to whether Christianity and Islam were to be considered forms of idolatry. The tendency of rabbinic authorities over the centuries increasingly was to answer in the negative, although the doctrine of the Trinity and the presence of iconography in the church complicated the issue in a way not paralleled in Islam. See Jacob Katz, *Exclusivism and Tolerance: Studies in Jewish–Gentile Relations in Medieval and Modern Times*, Scripta Judaica 3 (New York: Schocken, 1962), 196.

the biblical identification of the god with his or her icon. The great Israeli biblical scholar, Yehezkel Kaufmann (1889–1963), overstated his case when he claimed that, in the Hebrew Bible, "the sole argument advanced against pagan religion is that it is a fetishistic worship of 'wood and stone.'"[27] But that argument is surely at the heart of Israelite anti-paganism. Because the Hebrew Bible does not recognize any dimension to the deities other than their material manifestation, Kaufmann was right that, "had we only the Bible, we should know nothing of the real nature of the 'gods of the nations' ... [for] image worship is conceived to be nothing but fetishism."[28] This total identification of the god with the icon is the source of some of the most powerful prophetic polemic. Second Isaiah, for example, conjures up the ludicrous picture of a man who plants a tree, raises it, and cuts it down, using part of it for fuel for heat, part for fuel for baking, and part for making an icon, to which he prostrates himself, saying, "Save me, for you are my god!" (Isa 44:14–20). The sarcasm is sharp and effective, but is it fair?

It is surely true that iconography played a major role in ancient religion (other than that mandated in the Hebrew Bible). It is probably also true that the icon was considered an incarnation, so to speak, of the deity, a participating manifestation and not merely a conventional symbol. But what is not true is the assumption that underlies Second Isaiah's and all other Israelite polemic on this subject: The god was not thought to be limited to the material in the icon. He or she had a mythology, in which the god played a role, a story. The god had a character and the power to act, even to act upon the material world. It is thus unlikely that any of Second Isaiah's Babylonian neighbors would have recognized their religion in his parody of it; whether he intended to do so or not, he preached to the converted. H. W. F. Saggs points out that the Babylonian god Marduk

> was a spiritual being, creator of heaven and earth, and so transcendent that it was impossible to see or to comprehend him. He was indeed so vast that he filled the universe, so that the Babylonian in his prayer to the god could say: "The underworld is your basin, the sky of Anu your censer." Of another Babylonian god it was said: "He wears the heavens on his head like a turban; he is shod with the underworld as with sandals."[29]

In short, Second Isaiah paints a highly polemical and grossly unfair portrait of paganism. Saggs points out that his implication "that a tree-trunk might pass immediately from sculptor to worshipper" is one that he probably knew

---

27. Yehezkel Kaufmann, *The Religion of Israel: From Its Beginnings to the Babylonian Exile*, trans. Moshe Greenberg (New York: Schocken, 1960), 13.

28. Ibid., 9.

29. H. W. F. Saggs, *The Encounter with the Divine in Mesopotamia and Israel*, Jordan Lectures in Comparative Religion Series 12 (London: Athlone, 1978), 15.

to be false.³⁰ Against the assumption that the god was coterminous with the manifestation, he quotes a lament addressed to the Mesopotamian deity Dumuzi (Tammuz):

> You who are not the cream were poured out with the cream,
> You who are not the milk were drunk with the milk.³¹

The translator, Thorkild Jacobsen, cites this text in support of his point "that Dumuzi is the divine *power* in and behind milk and may not simply be identified with milk as concrete matter."³²

I have argued elsewhere that the cause of this reductionistic misrepresentation of pagan religion is the desire to neutralize the threat it poses to YHWHistic purism.³³ Gods who are spiritual, creative, loyal to their worshippers, intent on punishing wickedness and rewarding goodness, insistent upon the establishment of justice and equity and upon the prevention of the victimization of the weak—these gods stand too close to YHWH to allow the unqualified choice for him and against them which the covenantal monotheism of ancient Israel requires. In contrast, a piece of inert matter shaped by human hands into a cult object poses no threat; it is only ridiculous. A prime objective of interreligious polemics is to make the competitor look exactly so—ridiculous. It is here that the parallel with the misrepresentation of Judaism in the New Testament confronts us: a religion centered on a Torah given in love and able to increase love, on a Torah through which the Holy Spirit still speaks, on a Torah which holds out the possibility of reconciliation through repentance by the grace of God but without an innocent victim or other intermediation, on a Torah open to Jew and gentile alike, if only the latter will choose it—this is a religion too close to early Christianity not to threaten it. But a religion of externals only, of hypocrisy, of the letter and the flesh without the spirit, of ritual without ethics, of one bloodline only, of spiritual blindness, deviltry, and misanthropy is no threat. Anyone in command of his or her senses will reject it at once, without entertaining the notion that it might be combined with the true way. This is *not* to assert the phenomenological identity of YHWH and the other ancient Near Eastern gods, nor is it to assert the identity of the characteristic spiritual experiences of Judaism with those of Christianity. In each case, essential differences exist. Rather,

30. Ibid., 191n38.
31. Ibid, 90.
32. Thorkild Jacobsen, *Toward the Image of Tammuz and Other Essays*, ed. William L. Moran (Cambridge: Harvard University, 1970), 337n16.
33. Jon D. Levenson, "Yehezkel Kaufmann and Mythology," *Conservative Judaism* 36 (1982): 36–43.

my point is that the material in the Hebrew Bible which touches on non-Israelite religion, like the material in the New Testament which touches on Judaism, is born in the white heat of polemic. In both cases, the sarcastic, reductionistic literature of polemic has come to be regarded as sacred Scripture. In the case of the church, awareness of the continued existence of the Jews has sparked, in some elite quarters, a painful reassessment of the Scriptures and the damage that the stereotype in them can do. In the case of Judaism, the absence of paganism in the societies in which Jews have lived since rabbinic times has made such a reassessment academic. Whether Jews have the right to feel relieved because of this is something I leave to the reader to decide.

V.

One should not anticipate that those religious traditionalists who reject biblical criticism or remain unaware of it will cease to transmit the old, inaccurate stereotypes. On the contrary, their lack of involvement in the explosion in knowledge of the biblical world insures that, among them at least, the old biases will have clear sailing. Some Christians will, thus, continue to render the charges of deicide against the Jews and to describe Judaism in the classroom, in the pulpit, and on the air in grossly unfair ways. Some Jews (and Christians) will continue to tell the ancient (but post-biblical) story of Abraham's shattering his father's idols, without a hint of suspicion that they, in the process, may be doing a profound injustice to Mesopotamian religion. In many ways, interfaith understanding is the child of historical criticism. Those of us who advocate the former must not forget that it is less likely to flower in the absence of the latter.

What is more surprising is the tenacity of the traditional distortions among biblical critics. We have already discussed E. P. Sanders's pungent remarks about the inability of so many New Testament scholars to recognize the import of George Foot Moore's work, even a half century after it became available. An analogous situation exists among both Christian and Jewish scholars of the Hebrew Bible. To be sure, the argument is not identical to the biblical position, which equates paganism with fetishism, the deity with the icon. Rather, the dominant tendency in biblical scholarship, especially theological scholarship, is one that equates the gods variously with natural processes or with primordial world-ordering events, but denies them access to the realm of history, the realm in which Israel's uniqueness is supposed to have become manifest. For example, Walther Eichrodt wrote in his massive and influential *Theology of the Old Testament* that "it never occurred to [the other religions of "the ancient East"] to identify the nerve of the historical process as the purposeful activity of God.... Their view of the divine activity was too firmly imprisoned in the thought-forms of their Nature mythology."[34]

This idea that the pagan gods were, like Vergil's Polydorus or Dante's Pier delle Vigne, "imprisoned" in nature is usually combined with a distinction between cyclical time (paganism) and linear time (Israel), as in this statement from Sigmund Mowinckel: "All the ancient religions and civilizations, even those of Greece, conceived of the course of history as a circle, corresponding to the annual cycle of the life of nature. The Old Testament conceives of history as a straight line, pointing to a goal."[35] G. Ernest Wright developed this theme into a classic statement which well served the goals of Protestant neo-Orthodoxy, especially in the Calvinistic mode through which it dominated the Biblical Theology Movement in the United States.[36] Wright went so far as to argue that "pagan religions have no sense of history," for the attention of "polytheistic man ... is upon the yearly cycle," "upon nature, which is the kingdom of the gods, and his existence moves with the natural rhythm."[37]

Wright's student, Paul D. Hanson, drew out the social implication:

> For the Babylonian or the Canaanite, the decisive divine acts were primordial in character, and their annual reenactment attested to the fact that new creative or redemptive acts were not to be anticipated, but only the repetition of the old. Thus the pragmatic side of the polarity ... was emphasized to the exclusion of the visionary side. The cult existed to sanctify and uphold social structures which were subservient to the monarchy.[38]

It is this implication which is the nexus between the old Biblical Theology Movement, a phenomenon essentially of the 1940s and 1950s, and some newer approaches with affinities to Liberation Theology. Just as the pagan's god is imprisoned in nature, so is the pagan supposed to be imprisoned in an oppressive status quo which his or her mythic consciousness cannot transcend. Israel,

---

34. Walther Eichrodt, *Theology of the Old Testament*, trans. J. A. Baker, OTL, 2 vols. (Philadelphia: Westminster, 1961), 1:41. The original German publication was in 1933.

35. Sigmund Mowinckel, *He That Cometh*, trans. G. W. Anderson (Oxford: Oxford University, 1956), 551, quoted in Bertil Albrektson, *History and the Gods: An Essay on the Idea of Historical Events as Divine Manifestations in the Ancient Near East and in Israel*, Coniectanea Biblica: Old Testament Series 1 (Lund: Gleerup, 1967), 93–94. Mowinckel's statement does not take account of the fact that the most explicit meditation upon the nature of time in the Hebrew Bible expresses a concept of cyclicality (Qoh 1:4–9). Nonetheless, Qohelet is clearly in the minority.

36. On the larger intellectual context in which those contrasts were developed, see Brevard S. Childs, *Biblical Theology in Crisis* (Philadelphia: Westminster, 1970), especially 39–50.

37. G. Ernest Wright, *God Who Acts: Biblical Theology as Recital*, SBT 8 (London: SCM, 1952), 24.

38. Paul D. Hanson, *Dynamic Transcendence: The Correlation of Confessional Heritage and Contemporary Experience in a Biblical Mode of Divine Activity* (Philadelphia: Fortress, 1978), 61.

by contrast, with its openness to divine acts in history, exemplifies a redemptive dynamic which produces justice through social change in the direction of a kind of Rawlsian egalitarianism.[39]

Recently, this same contrast has been invoked in explanation of yet another facet of Israelite culture: the importance of prose fiction in the Hebrew Bible. Robert Alter attributed this to "the vigorous movement of biblical writing away from the stable closure of the mythological world and toward the indeterminacy, the shifting causal concatenations, the ambiguities of a fiction made to resemble the uncertainties of life in history."[40] What is striking in the examples is that, however diverse the various scholars may be in focus, method, and commitment, they all build upon the same analogy: paganism is to history as the rest of the ancient world is to Israel. Needless to say, most scholars of the Hebrew Bible identify with Israel rather than with the pagans. Their interest in the latter is usually restricted to an effort to develop a foil against which to highlight the strength of the biblical worldview—a Richard III for their Henry Tudors. Here again, the parallel with Judaism as it tends to appear in New Testament scholarship is patent. In fact, the title of Wright's first major book, *The Old Testament Against Its Environment*,[41] recalls the title of Bousset's first work, *Jesu Predigt in ihrem Gegensatz zum Judentum*. The key word is "against."

The great irony in the history of this school of thought is that it came to dominate only after the material that undermines it had been discovered. For example, the discovery of the Moabite Stone in 1868 and its ready availability throughout our century should have given second thoughts to those who thought that belief in divine control of history was unique to Israel.[42] In that inscription, Mesha, king of Moab in the latter half of the ninth century BCE (the age of Elijah in Israel), attributes his defeats to the anger of his god, Chemosh, and his triumphs to the latter's favor. In both idiom and theology, it is highly reminiscent of the Deuteronomic conception of holy war (*ḥerem*) and of the prophetic interpretation of history in general. Chemosh is very obviously not imprisoned in nature: he is not the personification of any natural element, nor does he uphold the status quo. Nothing is said about him that could not have been said about YHWH. At the very least, the Moabite Stone suggests that Israel's worldview had its most immediate roots in the new tribal kingdoms of Iron Age Palestine. It raises the interesting question of whether Moabite religion was "pagan" at all, in the sense in which the scholars discussed employ that term.

39. See the works referred to in notes 24 and 38 above.
40. Robert Alter, *The Art of Biblical Narrative* (Philadelphia: Jewish Publication Society; New York: Basic, 1981), 27. See the author's review of Alter in *Biblical Archaeologist* 46 (1983): 124–25. Alter's use of the terms "away from" and "toward" does provide a nuance missing in most other discussions from the same perspective.
41. G. Ernest Wright, *The Old Testament Against Its Environment*, SBT 2 (London: SCM, 1950).
42. The text can be found in *ANET*, 320–21.

In 1967, considerations like these brought about an ominous defection from the ranks of the biblical scholars who believed that divine action in history was a distinguishing mark of Israel. In that year, Bertil Albrektson, a Swedish scholar who earlier, in a study of the book of Lamentations, had endorsed the consensus, published a detailed study entitled *History and the Gods*.[43] In it, he examined numerous texts, mostly from Mesopotamia and Anatolia, which confirm the suspicion that the conventional antithesis rests on sand. Albrektson pointed, for example, to "The Curse of Agade," a Sumerian text probably first published early in the second millennium BCE.[44] This long poem tells of the arrogance of Naram-Sin, King of Akkad in the twenty-third century BCE, who, when his request for a divine oracle had been refused, mustered his army and proceeded to devastate and plunder a sacred shrine. The sight of this enraged Enlil, whose task it was to enforce the decrees of the divine council. In punishment for Naram-Sin's sacrilege, Enlil summoned a semibarbarian tribe, the Gutians, who, in turn, devastated cities and left famine and death in their wake. The gods pronounced a curse on the capital Agade: it would no longer be habitable. In fact, when the Gutians were at last deposed, other cities dominated Sumer, and the precise location of Agade remains unknown to this day.

To a biblical scholar, the story has a familiar ring. It suggests the events that led to the destruction of the shrine at Shiloh (eleventh century BCE) or to the fall of Jerusalem and the First Temple in 587 BCE; it also recalls the fall of the Second Temple to the Romans in 70 CE. The theology of "The Curse of Agade" approaches Israel's prophetic theology: Both correlate political events with decisions reached in the heavenly council, and both attribute historical change to the moral character of human agents, especially kings. In both cases, the gods are active, historical, political, somewhat mysterious, and not altogether beyond reproach (e.g., Jer 12:14), yet attuned to the moral dynamics of the human heart.[45] Albrektson argued that this historical theology was hardly exceptional in the ancient Near East. He pointed with approval to Jacobsen's evaluation which deserves to be quoted here in full:

> Yet in the case of Israel the new beginnings were not in all respects new; Israel came into being in a millennium when the concept of a moral universe had been achieved and when men could enter into a covenant of social justice with God as acting in History and under this covenant live

---

43. See note 35, above.
44. For the text, see *ANET*, 646–51.
45. See Jacob J. Finkelstein, "Bible and Babel: A Comparative Study of the Hebrew and Babylonian Religious Spirit," *Commentary* 26 (1958): 431–44, esp. 432: "There were indeed many Babylonian compositions that for moral and spiritual elevation could hold their own with some of the noblest passages in the Bible."

collectively and individually in moral responsibility. And one need only leaf through the books of the Old Testament to see—and see in detail—how major themes and modes of approach directly continue Mesopotamian themes and approaches, but with a freshness and with a deeper humility. Israel is heir—and a worthy heir—to preceding millennia.[46]

It would be just as wrong to deny the elements of apparent discontinuity between Israel and its environment as it has been to deny the overall continuity. One can point out, as one of Albrektson's generally appreciative reviewers did, that "the Mesopotamian gods ... were very much part of the physical universe" and that "all were born of divine parents."[47] Or, one can suggest, as Saggs did, that the tendency of Israel to speak of God "by a negative—not by what God is but by what he is not" is "a marked divergence."[48] And one can point to the generality, the unboundedness, of some prophetic oracles in Israel, as an element without parallel from its environment (so far)[49]—and so on. My point is not that the discontinuities do not exist, but rather that, from the biblical texts themselves, one usually comes away with the impression that this was all there was. It is this notion of radical discontinuity which is continued in most discussions of biblical theology. It is as though the hot, reductionistic polemic which attended Israel's emergence into self-consciousness had attained the status of sacred doctrine—and such is precisely what happened. The surprising point is that so much of critical scholarship, never known for its reverence for inherited doctrine, transmits, nonetheless, the false picture. The decade after *History*

---

46. Jacobsen, *Toward the Image of Tammuz*, 46. The passage was originally published in Jacobsen, "Ancient Mesopotamian Religion: The Central Concerns," *Proceedings of the American Philosophical Society* 107 (1963): 473–84, at 484. For a history of Mesopotamian religion, see Thorkild Jacobsen, *The Treasures of Darkness: A History of Mesopotamian Religion* (New Haven: Yale University Press, 1976). On Israel's debt to its "pagan" antecedents, see E. A. Speiser, "The Biblical Idea of History in Its Common Near Eastern Setting," in *The Jewish Expression*, ed. Judah Goldin (New Haven: Yale University Press, 1976), 1–17; Lynn Clapham, "Mythopoeic Antecedents of the Biblical World-View and Their Transformation in Early Israelite Thought," in *Magnalia Dei: The Mighty Acts of God: Essays on the Bible and Archaeology in Memory of G. Ernest Wright*, ed. Frank Moore Cross (Garden City, NY: Doubleday, 1976), 108–19; and Saggs, *Encounter with the Divine*. On the continuities between Canaanite religion and YHWHism, see Frank Moore Cross, *Canaanite Myth and Hebrew Epic: Essays in the History of the Religion of Israel* (Cambridge: Harvard University Press, 1973), 3–194; and Gösta W. Ahlström, *Aspects of Syncretism in Israelite Religion*, trans. Eric J. Sharpe, Horae Soederblominae 5 (Lund: Gleerup, 1963). The Bible's fierce polemic against Baal masks the continuities between Baal and YHWH. More revealing still is the absence of polemic anywhere in the Bible against another Canaanite high god, El. In fact, many of El's characteristics have been assumed by YHWH, who is actually identified with El (e.g., Isa 43:12 and 45:22)! A similar identification of YHWH and Baal probably also took place, although its exponents' position never became, or ceased to be, "normative" (e.g., Hos 2:18).
47. W. G. Lambert, "History and the Gods: A Review Article," *Or* 39 (1970): 171.
48. Saggs, *Encounter with the Divine*, 92.
49. Ibid., 150–51.

and the Gods appeared saw remarkably little cognizance of its import. Finally, in 1976, J. J. M. Roberts, taking Hanson as his prime example, again protested the continuation of the old stereotype,[50] which yet endures. Alter's qualified endorsement of the old scholarly stereotype shows no awareness of Albrektson or Roberts, even though it came five years after the latter's protest.

The parallel between the situations in the study of the two testaments of the Christian Bible is striking: Roberts is to Albrektson as Sanders is to Moore. In each case, a later authority protests the continuation of an unflattering and largely inaccurate stereotype which is suggested by the scriptural documents themselves but was refuted by earlier pieces of scholarship. In each case, at least one aspect of the motivation for misrepresentation is the same, the need for a foil: if a certain element in a given culture is esteemed, then it must have been unique in its time, an unanticipated advance. In the hands of modern historians, the unstated implication is clear: That which is discontinuous must be due to divine interruption of the natural order of things. Much of this ostensibly critical scholarship is really only apologetic: It constructs naturalistic arguments in support of the old supernaturalistic dichotomies.

It remains to be seen whether Christianity and Judaism can hold fast to what they have traditionally esteemed without continuing the ancient and pernicious stereotypes or falling into relativism. The nearly two decades since the Six-Day War have not encouraged Jews to believe that the churches generally have truly decided to relate to them fairly and honestly. However, lest the discouragement produce more contempt than understanding, Jews would do well to consider that the factors which impede the banishment of Christian stereotypes are not quite without their counterparts in Judaism.

---

50. J. J. M. Roberts, "Myth *Versus* History: Relaying the Comparative Foundations," *CBQ* 38 (1976): 1–13. It must not be overlooked that the cultural contrast in question is not essential to Hanson's important and influential theory of the origins of apocalyptic eschatology. Roberts targeted what was something of an obiter dictum in Hanson's essay, "Jewish Apocalyptic against Its Near Eastern Environment," *RB* 78 (1971): 31–58. Note also that Hanson retreated somewhat from the bold contrast in a later work, *The Diversity of Scripture: A Theological Interpretation*, Overtures to Biblical Theology 11 (Philadelphia: Fortress, 1982), 19. As Roberts acknowledges ("Myth *Versus* History," 2n5), Hanson's rethinking of these issues predates the publication of Roberts's critique. Unfortunately, such openness to new ideas is not universal among scholars, as the study of both the Hebrew Bible and the New Testament shows. See also Roberts's study of "Divine Freedom and Cultic Manipulation in Israel and Mesopotamia," in *Unity and Diversity: Essays in the History, Literature, and Religion of the Ancient Near East*, ed. Hans Goedicke and J. J. M. Roberts, Johns Hopkins Near Eastern Studies (Baltimore: Johns Hopkins University Press, 1971), 181–87. It also should be mentioned that, just as it is possible to doubt the interpretation of the pagan worldview as totally mythical, so is it increasingly doubted that history was really all that central to Israel's worldview. See James Barr, "Story and History in Biblical Theology," *Journal of Religion* 56 (1976): 1–17.

PART 3

Other Case Studies

PART 3 OF THE VOLUME turns in closing to three distinct case studies, three chapters pursuing three of YHWH's divine doppelgängers: fate, the Divine Wet Nurse, and the imagery of bulls and horses. Stephen B. Chapman's chapter analyzes fate, or, as biblical Hebrew terms it, *miqreh*. Chapman proposes that, with reference to fate, biblical traditions share much in common with their ancient Near Eastern contexts. Both affirm the basic divinity of fate and the relative fixity of human destinies. In Israel, however, YHWH's profile underwent expansion to include aspects of fate, such that even chance events of life somehow operate within the divine sovereignty. This theological adaptation impacted the very form, or poetics, of biblical literature. Chapman attends to one poetic feature called "literary simultaneity": narrated moments when human life in all its mundane and helter-skelter unfolding, usually so opaque to God's will, coincides with divine providence. To those wrestling with the problem of God's ancient look-alikes, Chapman furnishes an entry rich with literary insight and theological subtlety.

Christopher B. Hays's chapter examines the history and legacy of one theological motif, the *dea nutrix* or Divine Wet Nurse. This image of the feminine divine was widespread in the ANE, and some biblical texts, notably from the Priestly materials of the Pentateuch, play on it positively. It also appears even more directly in postbiblical traditions, both Christian and Jewish. Because, however, Hebrew Scripture promotes the worship of one God and mostly imagines that God as masculine, biblical writings often avoid or replace the concept of divine breastfeeding. Hays reflects on the spiritual cost of this loss, and he urges Christian churches to repent of patriarchy and misogyny by reclaiming the femininity of God. In effect, Hays observes that one ancient look-alike to the biblical God is the maternal goddess, and he mobilizes that parallel to constructive theological purpose. Like Othmar Keel's chapter, Hays's is reclamatory and provocative.

The final chapter of the volume, by Michèle Daviau, investigates the iconographic traditions of the Iron Age Transjordanian kingdoms of Ammon, Edom, and Moab—the next-door neighbors of ancient Israel and Judah—as represented in plastic art and distributed across the social and cultic landscape. Daviau's primary focus is on zoomorphic images of bulls and horses as attribute animals of gods and goddesses. The depiction of deities with these animals and the concentration of such images at Transjordanian sites point to broadly shared religious beliefs throughout the region. This shared religious outlook includes Israel and Judah, whose iconography Daviau considers in closing. Her contribution thus rounds out the profile of YHWH's ancient look-alikes to include its pictorial dimensions, a necessary complement to an otherwise textual discussion.

CHAPTER 11

Miqreh and YHWH: Fate, Chance, Simultaneity, and Providence

Stephen B. Chapman

IS FATE A LOOK-ALIKE FOR YHWH? Notions of fate and coincidence rest uneasily within the belief structures of monotheism. The idea of fate seems to leave too little for God to do—or if fate is equated with divine agency, too much. Can there then still be free will for human beings? To what extent does God ordain or even preordain the events of daily life and human history? The possibility of coincidence likewise poses challenging questions about divine sovereignty and a divinely given order of creation. Is there room in a monotheistic worldview for chance or luck or accidents?

The persistence of these questions in present-day theological discussions should temper any expectation of completely resolving them. The goal of this essay is instead to refract such concerns through the lens of ancient Israel's theology as it is represented in the Hebrew Bible, in the hope that Israel's premodern wrestling with recognizably similar questions may illuminate the present as well as the past. For the ancient world, fate itself was a divine force or even a deity, so the question of fate in ancient Israel is also the question of ancient Israelite God-belief and monotheism.

Israel's Monotheism in the Context of the Ancient Near East

The last century of biblical scholarship has witnessed a dramatic reversal in how ancient Israelite monotheism is regarded.[1] Whereas YHWH-belief had once

Author's Note: I am grateful to Brent A. Strawn and Lauren F. Winner for reading earlier drafts of this essay and offering helpful comments on it

1. The terms "monolatry," "henotheism," and "summodeism" have sometimes been used instead of "monotheism" to designate a belief system in which YHWH was the primary but not exclusive deity for Israel. On the methodological difficulties of using a modern category like monotheism as a descriptor of (or criterion for) ancient religious convictions, see Gregor Ahn, "Monotheismus und Polytheismus als religionswissenschaftliche Kategorien?," in *Der eine Gott und die Götter: Polytheismus und Monotheismus im antiken Israel,* ed. Manfred Oeming and Konrad Schmid, Abhandlungen zur Theologie des Alten und Neuen Testaments 82 (Zurich: Theologischer Verlag,

been characterized as monotheistic (or at least monotheistically inclined) and attributed to Israel from the outset of its history,[2] it is now, especially in its exclusive form, usually considered a gradual achievement rather than a primordial inheritance.[3] Both inner-biblical clues and extra-biblical (particularly

---

2003), 1–10; Michael S. Heiser, "Monotheism, Polytheism, Monolatry, or Henotheism? Toward an Assessment of Divine Plurality in the Hebrew Bible," *Bulletin for Biblical Research* 18 (2008): 1–30; Jens-André P. Herbener, "On the Term 'Monotheism,'" *Numen* 60 (2013): 616–48; Nathan MacDonald, "The Origin of 'Monotheism,'" in *Early Jewish and Christian Monotheism*, ed. Loren T. Stuckenbruck and Wendy E. S. North, Journal for the Study of the New Testament Supplement Series 263 (New York: T & T Clark, 2004), 204–15; Beate Pongratz-Leisten, "A New Agenda for the Study of the Rise of Monotheism," in *Reconsidering the Concept of Revolutionary Monotheism*, ed. Beate Pongratz-Leisten (Winona Lake, IN: Eisenbrauns, 2011), 1–40; Mark S. Smith, *God in Translation: Deities in Cross-Cultural Discourse in the Biblical World*, FAT 57 (Tübingen: Mohr Siebeck, 2008), 163–69. The term "monotheism" was apparently first employed in the work of seventeenth-century Cambridge Platonist Henry More, *An Explanation of the Grand Mystery of Godliness* (London: W. Morden, 1660).

2. E.g., William F. Albright, *From the Stone Age to Christianity: Monotheism and the Historical Process* (Garden City, NY: Doubleday, 1957), 12, dated the birth of monotheism to 1350–1250 BCE, with the slightly earlier "solar monotheism" of Akhenaten as its immediate predecessor. In Albright's historical reconstruction, the monotheism of Moses played a highly prominent role; see, e.g., *From the Stone Age to Christianity*, 271–72 and 400–401: "Mosaism is a living tradition... which did not change in fundamentals from the time of Moses until the time of Christ; Moses was as much a monotheist as was Hillel." An original monotheism was also posited by Yehezkel Kaufmann, *The Religion of Israel from Its Beginnings to the Babylonian Exile*, trans. and ed. Moshe Greenberg (New York: Schocken, 1972).

3. The scholarly literature on this topic is vast, but for more recent studies see Rainer Albertz, "'Jahwe allein!' Israels Weg zum Monotheismus und dessen theologische Bedeutung," in *Geschichte und Theologie: Studien zur Exegese des Alten Testaments und zur Religiongeschichte Israels*, ed. Ingo Kottsieper and Jakob Wöhrle, BZAW 326 (Berlin: de Gruyter, 2003), 359–82; James S. Anderson, "El, Yahweh, and Elohim: The Evolution of God in Israel and its Theological Implications," *Expository Times* 128 (2017): 261–67; Ronald E. Clements, "Monotheism and the God of Many Names," in *The God of Israel*, ed. Robert P. Gordon (Cambridge: Cambridge University Press, 2007), 47–59; Robert K. Gnuse, *No Other Gods: Emergent Monotheism in Israel*, JSOTSup 241 (Sheffield: Sheffield Academic, 1997); Reinhard G. Kratz and Hermann Spieckermann, eds., *Götterbilder, Gottesbilder, Weltbilder: Polytheismus und Monotheismus in der Welt der Antike*, 2 vols., FAT 2.17/18 (Tübingen: Mohr Siebeck, 2006); André Lemaire, *The Birth of Monotheism: The Rise and Disappearance of Yahwism* (Washington, DC: Biblical Archaeology Society, 2007); Christoph Levin, "Integrativer Monotheismus im Alten Testament," *Zeitschrift für Theologie und Kirche* 109 (2012): 153–75; Nathan MacDonald, *Deuteronomy and the Meaning of "Monotheism,"* FAT 2.1 (Tübingen: Mohr Siebeck, 2012); Herbert Niehr, *Der höchste Gott: alttestamentlicher JHWH-Glaube im Kontext syrisch-kanaanäischer Religion des 1. Jahrhunderts v. Chr.*, BZAW 190 (Berlin: de Gruyter, 1990); Niehr, "The Rise of YHWH in Judahite and Israelite Religion: Methodological and Religio-Historical Aspects," in *The Triumph of Elohim: From Yahwisms to Judaisms*, ed. Diana Vikander Edelman (Grand Rapids: Eerdmans, 1995), 45–72; Thomas Römer, *The Invention of God* (Cambridge: Harvard University Press, 2015); Römer, "Le Problème du monothéisme biblique," *RB* 124 (2017): 12–25; Konrad Schmid, "Differenzierungen und Konzeptualisierungen der Einheit Gottes in der Religions- und Literaturgeschichte Israels: methodische, religionsgeschichtliche und exegetische Aspekte zur neueren Diskussion um den sogennanten 'Monotheismus' im antiken Israel," in Oeming and Schmid, *Der eine Gott und die Götter*, 11–38.

archaeological) evidence have led to this sea change.⁴ That Israel's ancient God-belief did eventually take an exclusive form or was ever adequately described as "monotheism" is also contested,⁵ though not as successfully, since a more exclusive type of God-belief does appear to be reflected in Greco-Roman as well as Jewish sources of the later Second Temple period.⁶ Yet the precise character of that God-belief is very much debated, and the historical process by which it developed within Israel remains unclear and controversial.⁷

Mark Smith has mounted a detailed and persuasive argument for regarding the development of Israel's monotheism as involving "complex processes of convergence and differentiation" between YHWH and other ANE deities.⁸ In other words, YHWH became YHWH by a lengthy cultural exchange in which YHWH-believers attributed to this deity some of the characteristics of other deities

---

4. See especially Bob Becking, Meindert Dijkstra, Marjo C. A. Korpel, and Karel J. H. Vriezen, eds., *Only One God? Monotheism in Ancient Israel and the Veneration of the Goddess Asherah* (New York: Continuum, 2001); Izak Cornelius, *The Many Faces of the Goddess: The Iconography of the Syro-Palestinian Goddesses Anat, Astarte, Qedeshet, and Asherah c. 1500–1000 BCE*, OBO 204 (Fribourg: Academic Press; Göttingen: Vandenhoeck & Ruprecht, 2004); John Day, *Yahweh and the Gods and Goddesses of Canaan*, JSOTSup 265 (Sheffield: Sheffield Academic, 2000); William G. Dever, *Did God Have a Wife? Archaeology and Folk Religion in Ancient Israel* (Grand Rapids: Eerdmans, 2005); Othmar Keel and Christoph Uehlinger, *Gods, Goddesses, and Images of God in Ancient Israel*, trans. Thomas H. Trapp (Minneapolis: Fortress, 1996); Christopher A. Rollston, "The Rise of Monotheism in Ancient Israel: Biblical and Epigraphic Evidence," *Stone-Campbell Journal* 6 (2003): 95–115; Francesca Stavrakopoulou and John Barton, eds., *Religious Diversity in Ancient Israel and Judah* (New York: T & T Clark, 2010); Ephraim Stern, "From Many Gods to the One God: The Archaeological Evidence," in *One God—One Cult—One Nation: Archaeological and Biblical Perspectives*, ed. Reinhard G. Kratz and Hermann Spieckermann, BZAW 405 (Berlin: de Gruyter, 2010), 395–403; Ziony Zevit, *The Religions of Ancient Israel: A Synthesis of Parallactic Approaches* (New York: Continuum, 2001).

5. Some scholars, such as Paula Fredriksen, "Mandatory Retirement: Ideas in the Study of Christian Origins Whose Time has Come to Go," *Sciences religieuses* 35 (2006): 231–46, and Peter Hayman, "Monotheism—A Misused Word in Jewish Studies?," *Journal of Jewish Studies* 42 (1991): 1–13, have rejected the term "monotheism" altogether as an appropriate descriptor for ancient Judaism and early Christianity.

6. Yehoshua Amir, "Der jüdische Eingott-glaube als Stein des Anstoßes in der hellenistisch-römischen Welt," *Jahrbuch für biblische Theologie* 2 (1987): 58–75; Lester L. Grabbe, *Judaic Religion in the Second Temple Period: Belief and Practice from the Exile to Yavneh* (London: Routledge, 2000), 210–31; Larry W. Hurtado, "First-Century Jewish Monotheism," *Journal for the Study of the New Testament* 71 (1998): 3–26. For a more nuanced account, however, see Smith, *God in Translation*, 275–322.

7. Nili Fox, "Concepts of God in Israel and the Question of Monotheism," in *Text, Artifact, and Image: Revealing Ancient Israelite Religion*, ed. Gary Beckman and Theodore J. Lewis, Brown Judaic Studies 346 (Providence, RI: Brown Judaic Studies, 2006); Larry W. Hurtado, "'Ancient Jewish Monotheism' in the Hellenistic and Roman Periods," *Journal of Ancient Judaism* 4 (2013): 379–400; Ernst Axel Knauf, "Ist die Erste Bibel monotheistisch?," in Oeming and Schmid, *Der eine Gott und die Götter*, 39–48; Benjamin D. Sommer, "Monotheism," in *The Hebrew Bible: A Critical Companion*, ed. John Barton (Princeton: Princeton University Press, 2016), 239–70.

8. Mark S. Smith, *The Early History of God: Yahweh and the Other Deities in Ancient Israel* (San Francisco: Harper & Row, 1990), 161.

present in the polytheistic landscape of early Israel, simultaneously learning to draw emerging lines of distinction between YHWH and his divine colleagues.

According to Smith, divine conflation is already found in the oldest traditions in the HB, in which "imagery regularly applied to El, Baal, and Asherah in Northwest-Semitic literature was attributed to Yahweh at a relatively early point in Israel's religious history."[9] On one level, such an idea should occasion no surprise. Identities always have a history, and identity formation—divine as well as human—is a process of adopting existential possibilities glimpsed in others and distinguishing one's self from them over time. Yet the developmental aspect of God-belief raises concerns about the extent to which there may be a perduring core or identifiable essence lodged somewhere within all the historical give and take. Was there something about YHWH that early Israelites considered distinctive or unique, and if so, what was it?[10] It remains suggestive that no convincing trace of YHWH-belief on the part of non-Israelites has been discovered outside the land of Israel.[11] YHWH seems to have been viewed as the national god of Israel and Judah already within early traditions represented in the HB (e.g., Deut 32:8–9), even if YHWH may have shared that honor for a certain amount of time with other deities, popularly or perhaps officially.[12]

Greater awareness of Israel's persistent polytheism has led to new questions about the degree of monotheism that can be attributed to preexilic Israel, even as it has suggested that monotheism itself may be better conceived not as the oppositional term of a conceptual binary (in relation to polytheism), but as a range of possibilities, or even a mode of discourse. Smith summarizes the new perspective pointedly: "Within the Bible, monotheism is not a separate 'stage' of religion in ancient Israel, as it is customarily regarded. It was in fact a kind of ancient rhetoric reinforcing Israel's exclusive relationship with its deity."[13] Relatively late texts

---

9. Smith, *Early History*, 22.

10. See further Mark S. Smith, "YHWH's Original Character: Questions about an Unknown God," in *The Origins of Yahwism*, ed. Jürgen van Oorschot and Markus Witte, BZAW 484 (Berlin: de Gruyter, 2017), 23–43.

11. And not for lack of trying. For a review of the evidence and the discussion, see Lester L. Grabbe, "'Many Nations will be Joined to Yhwh in That Day': The Question of Yhwh Outside Judah," in Stavrakopoulou and Barton, *Religious Diversity*, 175–87. Yet Jörg Jeremias, "Three Theses on the Early History of Israel," in van Oorschot and Witte, *Origins of Yahwism*, 145–56, also notes that there are not any attested place-names with theophoric YHWH elements in ancient Syria-Palestine either, although there are a number with "El." This oddity reinforces the often-held view that YHWH originally came to Canaan from somewhere else, perhaps through migration; see Smith, "YHWH's Original Character," 25–28, and J. David Schloen, "Caravans, Kenites, and *Casus belli*: Enmity and Alliance in the Song of Deborah," *CBQ* 55 (1993): 18–38.

12. Jeremias, "Three Theses," 145, cites the reference to El as "the God of Israel" in Gen 33:20. As has been observed many times, even the first commandment ("you shall have no other gods before me") implies the existence of other gods. Cf. 1 Cor 8:4–6!

13. Mark S. Smith, *The Origins of Biblical Monotheism: Israel's Polytheistic Background and the Ugaritic Texts* (New York: Oxford University Press, 2001), 9.

such as Jer 44 and Ezek 8 demonstrate that the worship of other deities continued into the exilic period. Indeed, it appears likely that the catastrophe of exile encouraged Israel's monotheizing process through its intepretation as a consequence of insufficient YHWH-devotion.[14] But, to the extent that a group of YHWH-devotees or even a "YHWH-alone party" is envisioned during the era of the First Temple, what was it about?[15] What was it for? What did it think it was doing?

These questions are all the more challenging within a historical reconstruction in which YHWH-ism is not necessarily identical with monotheism (as it has traditionally been understood). The presumed characteristics of monotheism were once routinely ascribed to YHWH-belief, such as an active disbelief in other deities, an antagonism to superstition and magic, a higher standard of ethics, and a sense for history rather than myth.[16] But critical biblical scholarship chipped away at such distinctives throughout the twentieth century and into the early years of the twenty-first,[17] with the result that early Israel looks less and less monotheistic, and the place and function of YHWH within a more polytheistic worldview is increasingly challenging to identify.

The Divine Aspect of Fate

Smith has also helpfully described the notion of the sacred within the ANE world. "Divinity" was attributed not only to deities but also to other cosmic forces and phenomena such as the sun, stars, demons, fate/destiny (Akkadian *šīmtu*), and even larger-than-life superheroes from the distant past (e.g., Gilgamesh and Enkidu). Broadly speaking, the category of divinity might be viewed as demarcating by negation—that is, by referring not so much to a recognizable essence or core, but to the nonhuman or more-than-human.[18]

---

14. James A. Sanders, *The Monotheizing Process: Its Origins and Development* (Eugene, OR: Cascade, 2014), esp. 28–46.

15. The idea of a First Temple "Yahweh-alone party" was initially theorized in Morton Smith, *Palestinian Parties and Politics that Shaped the Old Testament* (London: SCM, 1987).

16. All four of these claims feature prominently in the influential presentation of G. Ernest Wright, *The Old Testament Against Its Environment*, SBT 2 (London: SCM, 1950).

17. A number of stimulating studies have revealed the robust practice of ancient Jewish magic, e.g.: Gideon Bohak, *Ancient Jewish Magic: A History* (New York: Cambridge University Press, 2008); Peter Schäfer, "Magic and Religion in Ancient Judaism," in *Envisioning Magic: A Princeton Seminar and Symposium*, ed. Peter Schäfer and Hans G. Kippenberg, Studies in the History of Religions 75 (Leiden: Brill, 1997), 19–44; Michael D. Swartz, *The Mechanics of Providence: The Workings of Ancient Jewish Magic and Mysticism*, Texte und Studien zum antiken Judentum 172 (Tübingen: Mohr Siebeck, 2018). So too, Bertil Albrektson, *History and the Gods: An Essay on the Idea of Historical Events as Divine Manifestations in the Ancient Near East and in Israel*, Coniectanea Biblica: Old Testament Series 1 (Lund: Gleerup, 1967), amply illustrates how a sense of history as a sphere of divine action was evident in other ANE cultures as well as in Israel.

18. Smith, *Origins of Biblical Monotheism*, 6: "In general, to be divine is not to be human."

What is particularly interesting about the notion of destiny or fate is that it was understood to affect deities as well as humans. Drawing on the distinctive approach of Yehezkel Kaufmann, Benjamin Sommer stresses how deities other than YHWH were conceived as being created or born from something that preceded them, and how they remain "subject to matter and to forces stronger than themselves."[19] He continues:

> In Mesopotamian religion, there exists a realm of power independent of, and greater than, the realm of divinity. It is for this reason that in some Mesopotamian texts, humans attempt to ward off evil without turning in any significant way to the gods.... The role of the gods, when they are mentioned in texts of this kind, is merely to aid the humans in accessing those powers, which transcend even the gods' realms but are better understood by the gods than by humans.[20]

One of the most powerful of these forces is fate, which the gods themselves cannot merely overturn or negate.[21] Indeed, the contrast between polytheism and monotheism may finally be less about the number of deities within a particular worldview and more about the relationship between deity and the divine forces of nature and fate. Monotheism thus entails what Peter Machinist has termed "a restructuring of the comic order."[22]

In a polytheistic worldview, deities are not all-powerful or unconditionally immortal. They are subject to nature and fate. The divine forces of nature and fate are themselves typically imagined as old, primordial (e.g., pre-Olympian) gods that already existed prior to the currently reigning pantheon.[23] "Monotheism" is then not so much about reducing divine actors to a single deity, but rather repositioning deity to hold an authority beyond nature and fate. The determining aspect of monotheism in this account can be expressed as "transcendence":

---

19. Sommer, "Monotheism," 258–59.
20. Ibid., 259. However, I would also consider this metarealm "divine."
21. See Walter F. Otto, *The Homeric Gods*, trans. Moses Hadas (New York: Thames and Hudson, 1979), 263–64 (as cited in Sommer, "Monotheism," 260): "Sometimes it is said that the gods 'can do all things,' but a glance at the stories of the gods shows that this is not to be taken literally. Their one-ness with nature would of itself contradict their ability to do all things.... There is a fixed limit to their power, a basic 'so far and no farther.'"
22. Peter Machinist, "How Gods Die, Biblically and Otherwise: A Problem of Cosmic Restructuring," in Pongratz-Leisten, *Reconsidering*, 189–240, at 235.
23. Examples in the HB may include *gād* ("luck/fortune") and *'āšēr* ("happiness/fortune"?), terms that were also the names of two Israelite tribes. It has long been suspected that *gād* and *mənî* ("destiny"?) in Isa 65:11 refer to deities of fate/chance. See further Peter Machinist, "Fate, *miqreh*, and Reason: Some Reflections on Qohelet and Biblical Thought," in *Solving Riddles and Untying Knots: Biblical, Epigraphic, and Semitic Studies in Honor of Jonas C. Greenfield*, ed. Ziony Zevit, Seymour Gitin, and Michael Sokoloff (Winona Lake, IN: Eisenbrauns, 1995), 159–75, at 163.

Because this approach sees the core of monotheism in the transcendence of one deity over all other beings, whether earthly or heavenly, we may also refer to it as the monotheism of transcendence (rather than a monotheism of enumeration).[24]

Such an approach to monotheism centers on a quality of deity rather than a quantity and suggests that the relationship between deity and fate is a crucial consideration for understanding God-belief in the ancient world.

Yet Smith explicitly rejects the idea of "an independent order having mastery over deities" in Ugaritic or Mesopotamian mythologies. He further asserts, citing the work of Jack Lawson,[25] that Akkadian *šīmtu* is better understood as "determined course" than as "fate" and that such a designated course of events was not inflexible, but subject to change.[26] Smith is right to suspect that a deterministic interpretation of ancient polytheism as "a vast, dark, and uncomfortable world" might be inappropriately apologetic.[27] However, his reference to Lawson's study moves too quickly past the qualified support that Lawson's work provides to interpreters like Kaufmann and Sommer.[28]

While it is indeed the case that Lawson rejects "as foreign to Mesopotamian religion" the idea of "an absolute and singular divine will, which is the cause of all being and which orders all existence," he nevertheless acknowledges that:

> The problem of free will versus predetermination stands at the very heart of this inquiry into the meaning of *šīmtu*. It is impossible to understand

---

24. Benjamin D. Sommer, "Yehezkel Kaufmann and Recent Scholarship: Toward a Richer Discourse of Monotheism," in *Yehezkel Kaufmann and the Reinvention of Jewish Biblical Scholarship*, ed. Job Y. Jindo, Benjamin D. Sommer, and Thomas Staubli, OBO 283 (Fribourg: Academic Press; Göttingen: Vandenhoeck & Ruprecht, 2017), 204–39, at 206–7, with responses following by Adrian Schenker (240–42) and Othmar Keel (243–49). See further Adrian Schenker, "Le monothéisme israélite: un dieu qui transcende le monde et les dieux," *Biblica* 78 (1997): 436–48, also cited by Sommer, "Yehezkel Kaufmann and Recent Scholarship."

25. Jack N. Lawson, *The Concept of Fate in Ancient Mesopotamia of the First Millennium: Toward an Understanding of* Šīmtu, Orientalia Biblica et Christiana 7 (Wiesbaden: Harrassowitz, 1994).

26. Smith, *Origins of Biblical Monotheism*, 12.

27. The quotation is from Wright, *Old Testament*, 78. Wright later tips his hand by musing: "So perfectly clear is the Old Testament on this point that it seems strange to me its resources together with those of the New Testament are not more vigorously used by the modern Church to combat our modern superstitions which ultimately go back to the same pagan environment as that of Israel" (87–88). See also A. Leo Oppenheim, *Ancient Mesopotamia: Portrait of a Dead Civilization*, rev. ed. (Chicago: University of Chicago Press, 1977), 203–4, on how "every organized religion of ancient Near Eastern extraction" today offers space neither for "the caprices of luck nor for the rigidity of destiny, and moreover, no possibility of provoking or changing events by magic means." He then proceeds to detail how ANE culture was different in holding to a "deterministic concept of life."

28. For additional criticism of Smith on this point, see Sommer, "Yehezkel Kaufmann," 233–34.

this aspect of the problem of *šīmtu* for the ancient Mesopotamians without examining the role the gods played in human life and affairs. Enlil, Marduk, and Ishtar (among others) are referred to as gods who determine human fate. However, the gods themselves are apparently subject to fate or determination if only in the form of "necessity"; for, as can be seen in *Enuma Elish* and *Atrahasis*: they gestate, give birth, die; they eat, drink, suffer illness, etc. Furthermore, inasmuch as an absolute and singular divine will, which is the cause of all being and which orders all existence, is foreign to Mesopotamian religion, it would appear that the gods are themselves subject to some form of fate or determination.[29]

Lawson thus upholds the idea that the gods are subject to fate, just not completely.

Like Kaufmann, Lawson views fate as having a prior authority over divinities, even as he explores how acquiring possession of the mythic *ṭuppi šīmāti* ("tablet of destinies") may bestow upon one god a limited power over other deities and a degree of flexibility over against fate. Lawson adds:

The real source of power in the cosmos comes from the primal, meta-divine realm. The gods and their individual offices may give form and direction to this power but they are not the final masters over the cosmos or even their own fate.[30]

The point can also be expressed by saying that, while the gods are subject to fate, they exercise a degree of agency.[31] On the human plane—the "downstairs" level to the gods' "upstairs" habitat—the fixed character of destiny was that much stronger and the degree of agency even smaller, to judge from omen texts and the logic of divination.[32] The only exception seems to lie in the notion of prayer.[33] For mortals, prayer could sometimes alter destiny.

---

29. Lawson, *Concept*, 2.
30. Ibid., 39.
31. Ibid., 38.
32. Ibid., 81: "Nothing—as far as human life was concerned—was left to chance.... For divination to be taken seriously there had to be the underlying assumption that the lives and actions of individuals had planned consequences. Only when these were discovered could the individual then have a modicum of 'freedom' to make alternate decisions." Elsewhere Lawson describes human fate as fixed and determined but not inevitable (71). For further support, he cites W. G. Lambert, "Destiny and Divine Intervention in Babylon and Israel," in *The Witness of Tradition: Papers Read at the Joint British-Dutch Old Testament Conference Held at Woudschoten, 1970*, ed. M. A. Beek et al., OtSt 17 (Leiden: Brill, 1972), 65–72.
33. Lawson, *Concept*, 71: "This would seem to be what we find in Akkadian prayers and hymns: the god's word is fixed and firm, one's personal fate is decreed by the god or gods, yet prayer can still make a difference."

In the end, Lawson sees ANE deities as working "within the realm and operation of *šīmtu*," but he also views the relationship between these two sets of forces as somewhat porous, noting that, "although some documents seem to suggest that the gods have prepared the fate of mortals, others would seem to indicate that whilst the gods are privy to the designs of fate—and can communicate them to mortals—they are not responsible for its decisions."[34] So Lawson does argue against a mechanistic view of omens and (divine) causality. Yet he excludes the possibility of genuine chance or free will on the part of human beings from the ANE worldview altogether:

> There is no free-will in the way we in our modern Western society conceive of it—the freedom to determine one's own destiny. The only sort of free decisions one could make, according to our findings, would be those of choosing to avail oneself of divination, and, having once chosen to do that, availing oneself of a ritual to avoid an unpleasant fate.[35]

While *šīmtu* (like Greek *moira*[36]) may therefore also be translated, perhaps less prejudicially, as "destiny" or "course" or "portion" or "share" rather than "fate,"[37] the accent apparently needs to remain on its qualities of predetermination and inflexibility, even if that inflexibility is finally less than absolute.

Chance and (Mis)Fortune in the Hebrew Bible

In contrast to treatments differentiating the worldview of the rest of the ANE from that of Israel with regard to fate, I would like to explore their common ground. Indeed, these worldviews should not be conceived as entirely separate from one another. I want to suggest that, just as YHWH's identity grew over time by incorporating features of other deities and being distinguished from them, there was a similar movement of convergence and divergence between the notion of fate/chance and YHWH. This movement is easier to envision when it is understood that both fate/chance and YHWH were recognized as divine.

The most significant Hebrew term usually translated "chance" or "fortune" is *miqreh*, from the Semitic root *q-r-h*, "to happen, encounter, meet."[38] A chance

---

34. Ibid., 86. On the way that Mesopotamian deities sometimes determined fate and other times were determined by it, see Machinist, "Fate," 164n15.
35. Lawson, *Concept*, 100.
36. See further William Chase Greene, *Moira: Fate, Good, and Evil in Greek Thought* (Cambridge: Harvard University Press, 1944).
37. See further *CAD* 17, s.v. *šīmtu*.
38. On this term, see Helmer Ringgren's treatment of *q-r-h* in *Theological Dictionary of the Old Testament*, ed. G. Johannes Botterweck and Helmer Ringgren, trans. John T. Willis, Geoffrey W.

event (*miqreh*) is one that happens "to someone not through their own will or actions and without any known instigator."[39] The term's use as an apparent euphemism for a nocturnal seminal emission (Deut 23:11: "a happening of the night") underscores a lack of conscious control and seems to designate a cause beyond individual human agency (i.e., an "accident").

A classic instance is found in 1 Sam 6, at the conclusion of the Ark Narrative (1 Sam 4–6). The ark is captured by the Philistines but then causes chaos in the cities of Ashdod, Gath, and Ekron when it is taken in turn to each one (1 Sam 5). In response to a request from the Philistine people to send the ark back to Israel, their priests and diviners recommend doing so but propose adding an indemnity to pacify YHWH further: five gold tumors and five gold mice (1 Sam 6:4). These gold figures, it should be noted, are representations of the plagues that have broken out among the Philistines since the ark has been among them. The priests' idea is that, if "weight/honor" (*kābôd*) is added to YHWH, he may "*lighten* [*q-l-l* in *hiphil*] his hand on you and your gods and your land" (1 Sam 6:5; my emphasis),[40] which reflects a compensatory understanding of ritual as a means of maintaining a stable balance or order. YHWH is suspected by the Philistines to be the active agent in this scenario, and their priests believe that he may be encouraged in a particular direction by an appropriate ritual means.

The priests also introduce what Deborah Bennett has termed a "randomizer."[41] Artificial mechanisms of chance were used in antiquity, just as they are today, to seek divine guidance, to make decisions, and to play. The best-known example from the Bible is that of the sacred lots used to ascertain YHWH's will.[42] Many cultures have manipulated dice or bones or sticks or coins as a means

---

Bromiley, and D. E. Green, 15 vols. (Grand Rapids: Eerdmans, 1974–2006), 13:159–62. For a discussion of other terms in the HB with nuances of fate, chance, or luck, see Machinist, "Fate," 161–65. YHWH is also confessed to have an *'ēṣâ* or *maḥăšābâ* ("plan") for the world (Isa 55:8–9; Jer 18:11), which is written in a heavenly book (Ps 69:29; cf. Exod 32:32–33; Isa 4:3; Dan 10:21). See further S. M. Paul, "Heavenly Tablets and the Book of Life," in *Divrei Shalom: Collected Studies of Shalom M. Paul on the Bible and the Ancient Near East 1967–2005*, CHANE 23 (Leiden: Brill, 2005), 59–70; Lynn R. LiDonnici and Andrea Lieber, eds., *Heavenly Tablets: Interpretation, Identity and Tradition in Ancient Judaism*, Supplements to the Journal for the Study of Judaism 119 (Leiden: Brill, 2007). Nevertheless, events and divinatory acts may reveal to humans at discrete moments what has already been determined by the divine will.

39. For this definition of *miqreh*, see *The Hebrew and Aramaic Lexicon of the Old Testament*, ed. Ludwig Koehler, Walter Baumgartner, and Johann J. Stamm, trans. and ed. Mervyn E. J. Richardson, Study Edition (Leiden: Brill, 1994–2000), 1:629.

40. Biblical translations are my own unless otherwise indicated.

41. Deborah J. Bennett, *Randomness* (Cambridge: Harvard University Press, 1998), 8.

42. See Cornelis Van Dam, *The Urim and Thummim: A Means of Revelation in Ancient Israel* (Winona Lake, IN: Eisenbrauns, 1997). See also Frederick H. Cryer, *Divination in Ancient Israel and its Near Eastern Environment: A Socio-Historical Investigation*, JSOTSup 142 (Sheffield: JSOT Press, 1994); Esther J. Hamori, *Women's Divination in Biblical Literature: Prophecy, Necromancy, and Other Arts of Knowledge* (New Haven: Yale University Press, 2015).

of reaching a decision. According to Bennett, there are three main reasons for employing randomizers: (1) to ensure fairness; (2) to prevent dissension; and (3) to acquire divine direction. The basic idea is to establish a level playing field so that "no amount of intelligence, skill, strength, knowledge, or experience can give one player an advantage."[43] From this perspective, chance is an "equalizing force" and an important means of maintaining communal cohesion.

However, the priests' randomizer consists of a procedure that is not neutral, but leans in favor of the Philistines. Two cows heavy with milk are taken from their calves and hitched to the wagon carrying the ark. The Philistines are directed not to steer the wagon and let the cows take their own course. If the ark goes toward Israel—which would be contrary to the strong natural inclination of the cows to be with their calves—then YHWH will be confirmed as the powerful deity behind the Philistines' misfortunes (1 Sam 6:9). If the wagon does not go toward Israel, then all that happened previously to the Philistines will have been "chance" (*miqreh*) instead. It is notable that this way of viewing the situation is expressed in the narrative by Philistines rather than Israelites. Nevertheless, it is fully possible that the idea of a contest between YHWH and chance does not reflect an Israelite perspective *or* a Philistine one, but a Philistine perspective as imagined by an Israelite.

Still, what is striking about the outcome of this contest is not so much that the ark travels toward Israel, revealing YHWH's hand at work, but that YHWH works in and through the constraints of the randomizer as it has been established. The biblical denouement reads rather laconically: "The cows went straight ahead along the road in the direction of Beth-shemesh, on a single path, lowing as they went, and did not turn aside to the right or the left" (1 Sam 6:12). Here divine action transpires in a quite modest manner that might be interpreted by contemporary observers as every bit as much a "chance" outcome as any other—no big miracle, no visible intervention by God. Moreover, when the cows and the golden objects are presented to YHWH in Beth-Shemesh, it appears to fix things for the Philistines, just as their priests had forecast (1 Sam 6:16). The surprise ending to the story comes when YHWH strikes down seventy men in Beth-Shemesh because the descendants of Jeconiah did not rejoice at the ark's arrival (1 Sam 6:19). While it is at one level an example of poetic justice (people are rejected from the community because they did not welcome the ark to it), the lack of context and proportion in this divine action ironically conveys a capriciousness not unlike chance. In this regard, YHWH is presented by the passage as superior to the Philistines' conception of chance but not entirely different from it.

---

43. Bennett, *Randomness*, 12.

This ironic interpretation is more persuasive than the view that 1 Sam 6 simply intends to exalt YHWH by denigrating chance as a pagan idea,[44] especially since chance also appears later in 1 Samuel as a way of describing an action that seems to be chance and yet represents YHWH at work—or, it might just as well be said, is YHWH at work but also looks like chance. This time, the notion is placed in Saul's mouth when he interprets David's absence from a cultic meal with the words "it is an accident (*miqreh*); he must be unclean, he is not clean" (1 Sam 20:26).[45] However, the preceding narrative has established that David and Jonathan, invoking YHWH's support and blessing, have planned David's absence as a test of Saul's anger (1 Sam 20:5–16). Just how hostile to David has Saul become? On the one hand, it is tempting to see Saul's recourse to the idea of "chance" as another indication of Saul's failure to gain a proper theological perspective on his life and reign.[46] Here, as with the Philistines in 1 Sam 6, what is identified by Saul as "chance" is understood to be a lack of perception with regard to YHWH and his ways.

But here too YHWH is shown to operate in a fashion that is not altogether different from the ways of chance. There is first the matter of the suppertime test: why can David and Jonathan not just ask YHWH whether Saul is dangerous? Why construct an elaborate randomizer based on what might or might not happen at the meal? Then there is the follow-up procedure introduced by Jonathan to contact David and inform him that the coast is clear once the meal is over: Jonathan will shoot three arrows in a field and employ coded phrases when he calls out for his servant to retrieve them (1 Sam 20:17–22). Not only was this type of activity with arrows a standard form of divination in the ancient world (belomancy),[47] it is "theologized" in this biblical narrative as indicative of YHWH's will (v. 22: "Then leave, for *YHWH* has sent you away"; my emphasis). Once more YHWH is depicted as similar to chance while simultaneously being differentiated from it.

Robert Hubbard has observed the same complexity in a reference to *miqreh* within the book of Ruth. The biblical text notes how Ruth "happened" upon the property of Boaz in the process of gleaning (Ruth 2:3). Of special interest in this

---

44. For such a reading, see David Penchansky, *Twilight of the Gods: Polytheism in the Hebrew Bible* (Louisville, KY: Westminster John Knox, 2005), 13–22.

45. Compare the NRSV: "Something has befallen him; he is not clean, surely he is not clean." Penchansky, *Twilight*, 16–17, interprets *miqreh* here as referring to a nocturnal emission, which is a possible but not necessary inference.

46. See further Stephen B. Chapman, *1 Samuel as Christian Scripture: A Theological Commentary* (Grand Rapids: Eerdmans, 2016).

47. See further Bill T. Arnold, "Necromancy and Cleromancy in 1 and 2 Samuel," *CBQ* 66 (2004): 199–213; Samuel Iwry, "New Evidence for Belomancy in Ancient Palestine and Phoenicia," *Journal of the American Oriental Society* 81 (1961): 27–32; Ann Jeffers, "Magic and Divination in Ancient Israel," *Religion Compass* 1 (2007): 628–42.

case is that the biblical narrator, rather than pagans or a mad king, is attributing the event to chance.[48] Furthermore, the noun "chance" appears here, for the only time in the HB, with a pronominal suffix: "her chance." The verse could thus be translated: "And her happening happened, she entered a part of the field belonging to Boaz." Not only is this peculiar syntax suggestive of a conception of chance as something like a personal destiny; it also aligns YHWH with chance, even as it insists that chance is merely apparent and not the whole story. Hubbard intriguingly suggests that YHWH "often lurks in contexts where *qrh* occurs" in the rest of the canon as well.[49]

The purpose of this conjunction between YHWH and chance, in Hubbard's view, is to offer testimony to YHWH's providential guidance, and yet at the same time to acknowledge its often hidden nature. Hubbard points out that explicit theological affirmations bracket the book of Ruth (1:6; 4:13), but also that "no miracles or wonders punctuate the narrative space between those signposts."[50] Characters throughout the narrative refer to God, who therefore seems present and personal but otherwise keeps to the background. The narrator even appears to avoid mentioning God on several occasions when it could have been possible to do so, such as the reference to "chance" in Ruth 2:3. Still, the book nevertheless strongly conveys the idea that YHWH is at work behind the scenes. Why then the understatement and indirection? Hubbard identifies its purpose as inviting reflection on the hidden quality of divine action:

> In this theological perspective, Yahweh does not guide human affairs through intermittent miracles followed by long periods of apparent retreat. Rather, his activity is hidden behind the actions of human agents, yet he is presumed to be the implicit, immanent cause of events. Hence, he is the cause of even the smallest "accidental" details of life. In sum, one theological foundation on which the book of Ruth firmly rests is belief in God's hidden but continuous all-causality.[51]

So chance may be described as only apparent in this kind of theological perspective: God remains very much in control in spite of any suggestion to the contrary. But on another level, chance is actually professed to be the way that God sometimes works. Chance can also function as a divine look-alike for YHWH.

---

48. Robert L. Hubbard Jr., *The Book of Ruth*, New International Commentary on the Old Testament (Grand Rapids: Eerdmans, 1988), 69.
49. Hubbard, *Book of Ruth*, 141. He cites as examples: Gen 42:28; Exod 1:10; Num 11:23; Deut 31:29; Josh 11:20; Isa 41:2; 51:17, 20; Jer 13:24-7; 44:22-3; Job 4:14; Esth 4:14 and Dan 10:14.
50. Hubbard, *Book of Ruth*, 69.
51. Ibid., 70.

Hubbard notes that *miqreh* can be employed for both "fortune" and "misfortune,"[52] which offers a vantage point for understanding one of the HB's most profound and challenging theological claims: God may also work through misfortune. This theme is particularly prominent in the Joseph narrative and elsewhere in the book of Genesis. Thus Joseph can tell his brothers: "At last you see that you did not send me, God did, and he has placed me as a father to Pharaoh, as lord of all his house, and ruler over all the land of Egypt" (Gen 45:8). And again: "While you intended harm for me, God intended it for good, in order to bring about this day, to bring life to many people" (Gen 50:20). To style this perspective "deterministic" would be to the miss the point. The thrust of this aspect of the biblical tradition is not that God determines every outcome in advance or that everything that happens is for the best. The point is rather that God is continuously, redemptively working to bring goodness out of misfortune and calamity (cf. Rom 8:28).

Even where the term *miqreh* is absent, the same idea may be present, sometimes with verbal forms of *q-r-h*, as Hubbard suggested, and sometimes without them. Simultaneity of action is often featured as well. Verbal simultaneity is in fact one of the standard literary devices used in biblical poetics to convey divine providence in its veiled or hidden form. To return to 1 Samuel, an especially interesting example is found in chapter 9. Ostensibly the most banal of stories—Saul has been sent to go find his father's lost donkeys—the entire episode, in all its apparently coincidental particulars, is revealed midstream to have been foreordained by God. As Samuel is finally identified to the reader as the man of God residing in the remote little village in which Saul and his servant have accidently arrived (1 Sam 9:14), a parenthetical flashback provides the information that God had in fact *sent* Saul to Samuel so that Samuel could anoint him king of Israel. Moreover, God had informed Samuel of this eventuality *on the day before* Saul's arrival (1 Sam 9:15): "At this time tomorrow I will send [*š-l-ḥ*] you a man from the land of Benjamin, so that you may anoint him before my people Israel, and he may rescue my people from the hand of the Philistines, for I have taken note of my people because their cry has come to me" (1 Sam 9:16). The belated presentation of this information ensures that the reader's perspective at the beginning of the chapter is similar to Saul's but then shifts dramatically when an ironic disjunction is introduced between what the reader belatedly perceives and what Saul still does not understand.

Nor is this all. When Saul does finally confer with Samuel, Samuel tells him that his father's donkeys have *already* been located (1 Sam 9:20). Food has *already* been reserved for Saul (1 Sam 9:23–24). Noteworthy is not just the high view of providential action contained within this chapter, but also the combination of that

---

52. Ibid., 141. The same term may be used for both; context determines the sense.

high view with what might be called a low observer perspective. Another way to put it would be to say that the providential dimension of the chapter lies at the level of the story while its ironic aspect exists at the level of its discourse.[53]

With such a literary strategy, what the chapter evidently means to thematize is not simply a high view of providence but also the contrast between how providence works and how it appears when it does. The chapter's theological purpose is no doubt to provide reassurance to the implied reader that God is in control despite how things seem, but this reassurance is not given in such a way as to sweep aside as misinformed or ignorant the admittedly real difficulty of spotting God in action. Religious faith, the chapter is saying, can embrace the epistemological deficits of human experience. Indeed, those deficits are themselves marks of true faith and genuine faith experience. This insight will be pressed even further in the wisdom literature of the HB (whether to the breaking point or past the breaking point is debated[54]), and so more references to *miqreh* cluster in Ecclesiastes than in any other biblical book.[55] Ecclesiastes is thus not the first biblical book to recognize the tension between the objective and subjective aspects of divine providence,[56] but it might be the first one to pull them apart by questioning the objective reality of providence from the subjective perspective of its human participants.[57]

In biblical narrative, simultaneity of action is employed precisely to stage the tensive interaction between these objective and subjective perspectives. Ferdinand Deist has called attention to how 1 Sam 9 confronts the reader as a seeming digression after the grand political events of 1 Sam 8 and how the most minute details of the story take on a deeper meaning after the revelation of verses 15–16.[58] What the reader then understands is that:

> It was Yahweh who organised/used the disappearance of the donkeys. It was he who let Saul take with him the *particular* servant who had

---

53. For this narratological distinction, see Seymour Chatman, *Story and Discourse: Narrative Structure in Fiction and Film* (Ithaca: Cornell University Press, 1978).

54. It should be noted that the category of "wisdom literature" is itself undergoing renewed questioning. See Will Kynes, *An Obituary for "Wisdom Literature": The Birth, Death, and Reintegration of a Biblical Corpus* (New York: Oxford University Press, 2019); Mark R. Sneed, ed., *Was There a Wisdom Tradition? New Prospects in Israelite Wisdom Studies*, Ancient Israel and Its Literature 23 (Atlanta: Society of Biblical Literature, 2015).

55. The term *miqreh* appears seven times in Ecclesiastes (Eccl 2:14–15; 3:19 [3x]; 9:2–3). For a close examination, see Machinist, "Fate, 165–75."

56. See ibid.," 174.

57. The crucial point in Ecclesiastes is not that fate/chance exists, but that the "same fate" (*miqreh 'eḥād*) awaits all creatures regardless of their actions, namely death. This is the emphasis creating the greatest degree of tension with Israel's traditional God-belief, since it casts doubt on divine justice.

58. Ferdinand Deist, "Coincidence as a Motif of Intervention in 1 Samuel 9," *Old Testament Essays* 6 (1993): 7–32.

knowledge of the seer, who made the servant take with him a few shekels, and who arranged the route they would follow to be such that Saul would give up hope *exactly* at the village where Samuel would coincidentally be on that *particular* day; he made sure that they would approach the city *just* as the maiden went out to fetch water, that Samuel had been warned *just in time* of the approaching future "leader" of Israel, that Saul and the servant reached the city at *the very moment* when Samuel set out for the place of offering, and who whispered to Samuel: "This is the man I told you about."[59]

A key marker of the chapter's motif of timely coincidence is found in the comment of the village girls (1 Sam 9:12) that Saul and his servant need to "hurry" (*m-h-r* in *piel*): "As soon as you enter [*kəbōʾăkem*] the town, you will find him" (1 Sam 9:13). "So they went up to the town: *they were coming into the town just as, behold, Samuel was coming out to meet them* [*liqrōʾtām*], to offer sacrifices at the outdoor altar" (1 Sam 9:14; my italics). As Deist observes, the reason to hurry in this situation is not the mundane circumstances at hand. What creates the sense of urgency is not anything to do with the timing of the sacrifice, but the necessity for events to unfold in the manner in which God has planned them.[60] Depicting the entrance of Saul and his servant into the town as happening at the same exact moment as Samuel's exit underscores the providential timing of their actions.

Such literary simultaneity is a common feature of biblical poetics.[61] Its frequency should not obscure its nature as a theological confession about God's hidden way within the world. In style as well as content, the biblical literature invokes a God who is relentlessly present but whose actions are characteristically disguised, with the result that the arena of human experience is full of beckoning coincidences: "Truly you are a God who hides yourself, O God of Israel, the Savior" (Isa 45:15).

Conclusion

I have argued that the conception of fate/destiny in the ANE was more deterministic than some contemporary scholars envision. However, rather than

59. Ibid., 14 (his emphases).
60. Ibid.: "Yahweh's secret plan is coming to a close and everything should now happen at the right time."
61. Shemaryahu Talmon, "The Presentation of Synchroneity and Simultaneity in the Biblical Narrative," in *Studies in Hebrew Narrative Art throughout the Ages*, ed. J. Heinemann, Scripta Hierosolymitana 27 (Jerusalem: Magnes, 1978), 9–26.

making the usual apologetic move of framing Israel's commitment to free will against the "dark" deterministic world of magic and divination in the ANE, I have advanced a more similar, more providential understanding for the biblical tradition. Indeed, I strongly suspect that the entirety of the ancient world thought somewhat differently about human agency, cosmic order, and divine action than we as moderns do today, after a fashion that we find uncomfortable to contemplate—with appreciably less room for human self-determination and free choice.

Yet a fuller recognition of chance as a divine look-alike for YHWH in ancient Israel serves to highlight the strong account of providence evident throughout the biblical witnesses. The HB is drenched in a providential understanding of God's activity within the world. At the same time, it offers what might be termed a realistic understanding of how divine providence works. Sometimes there are indeed miracles: God is not restricted by the world's standard operating system.[62] However, God often chooses to act more locally, more incrementally, and more indirectly, working *through* human agents, social institutions, inherited customs, and ordinary circumstances.[63] This hidden quality of YHWH's work had the effect of compelling an interpretation of current events on the part of YHWH's Israelite worshipers, a pressure that is now actually preserved even in the literary style of biblical poetics. The Bible is written so as to pose the character of God's action as a question to its readers. Even a random arrow may kill a disguised king and thereby fulfill God's sure prophetic word (1 Kgs 22:34, 38; cf. 21:19).[64] So too, God's express will may occur in the form of an accident.

In this respect, the divine characteristics of fate/chance at home in the ANE have apparently been monotheized, but YHWH's divine profile has been expanded at the same time to include aspects of fate/chance. The conceptuality and discourse of fate/chance gave Israelite adherents of YHWH a means of understanding and describing this deity in a manner that extended his divine silhouette. In the effort of the biblical writers to confess the fullness of God's nature and activity, retaining a role for fate/chance proved essential. For them, this too is what God is like.

---

62. R. W. L. Moberly, "Miracles in the Hebrew Bible," in *The Cambridge Companion to Miracles*, ed. Graham H. Twelftree (Cambridge: Cambridge University Press, 2011), 57–74. Moberly makes the interesting point that some portions of the HB (e.g., the Moses narratives and the Elijah-Elisha stories) tend to view divine action in a more miraculous fashion, while others (e.g., the traditions about David and Jeremiah) appear to prefer a providential perspective (62–63).

63. See Terence E. Fretheim, "Issues of Agency in Exodus," in *The Book of Exodus: Composition, Reception, and Interpretation*, ed. Thomas B. Dozeman, Craig A. Evans, and Joel N. Lohr, VTSup 164 (Leiden: Brill, 2014), 591–609.

64. See further R. W. L. Moberly, "Does God Lie to His Prophets? The Story of Micaiah ben Imlah as a Test Case," *HTR* 96 (2003): 1–23.

For contemporary interpretation of the Bible, awareness of this more complex perspective on divine action should destabilize superficial generalizations about portions of the canon in which God is present and portions in which God is absent.[65] There are indeed differences to be observed between places where God's action is overt and places where God's action is less obvious, but that is not the same thing as divine presence and absence.[66] One of the most remarkable things about the Bible is how it can offer such a robust account of divine providence by sometimes hardly mentioning God at all. The continuation of this faith perspective is evident in Judaism, which has traditionally combined a firm sense of God's providence with an appreciation for the human experience of tragedy, fate, chance, luck, and wry humor.[67] The rabbis codified this mysterious fusion in the formula: "Everything is foreseen, and free will is given, and with goodness the world is judged" (m. Avot 3:15; translation mine).

The same seemingly paradoxical combination of divine providence and human freedom persisted within Christianity.[68] At least two main trajectories can be charted.[69] One, likely the more familiar of the two, emphasizes divine sovereignty and predestination, and runs from Augustine (*City of God* 5.1), to the Westminster Assembly, to Mary Baker Eddy:

---

65. E.g.: Richard Elliott Friedman, *The Disappearance of God: A Divine Mystery* (Boston: Little, Brown, 1995); Jack Miles, *God: A Biography* (New York: Knopf, 1995). See also Deist, "Coincidence," 8: "It certainly is tempting to describe the various degrees of divine involvement in the Old Testament narratives in terms of points on a devolutionary scale (i.e., from myth to sacred to secular story), and date texts accordingly."

66. For recent discussion of this topic, see Joel S. Burnett, *Where is God? Divine Absence in the Hebrew Bible* (Minneapolis: Fortress, 2010); Amelia Devin Freedman, *God as an Absent Character in Biblical Hebrew Narrative*, Studies in Biblical Literature 82 (New York: Lang, 2005); Brittany N. Melton, *Where is God in the Megilloth? A Dialogue on the Ambiguity of Divine Presence and Absence*, OtSt 73 (Leiden: Brill, 2018); Nathan MacDonald and Izaak J. de Hulster, eds., *Divine Presence and Absence in Exilic and Post-Exilic Judaism*, FAT 2.61 (Tübingen: Mohr Siebeck, 2013); Michael C. Rea, *The Hiddenness of God* (New York: Oxford University Press, 2018).

67. See further Ian Silverman, "Coincidence, Fate, and Happenstance in Rabbinic and Medieval Sources," *Conservative Judaism* 60 (2008): 31–49. See also Sommer, "Yehezkel Kaufmann," 237–38.

68. For explorations on related topics, see David J. Bartholomew, *God of Chance* (London: SCM, 1984); Theodore de Bruyn, *Making Amulets Christian: Artefacts, Scribes, and Contexts* (Oxford: Oxford University Press, 2017); Euan Cameron, *Enchanted Europe: Superstition, Reason, and Religion 1250–1750* (New York: Oxford University Press, 2010); Karl W. Gilberson, *Abraham's Dice: Chance and Providence in the Monotheistic Traditions* (New York: Oxford University Press, 2016); John Martin Fischer and Patrick Todd, eds., *Freedom, Fatalism, and Foreknowledge* (New York: Oxford University Press, 2015); Marvin Meyer, ed., *Ancient Christian Magic: Coptic Texts of Ritual Power* (Princeton: Princeton University Press, 1999); Kevin Taylor and Giles Waller, eds., *Christian Theology and Tragedy: Theologians, Tragic Literature and Tragic Theory* (Burlington, VT: Ashgate, 2011); Keith Ward, *God, Chance & Necessity* (Oxford: One World, 1996).

69. See further Bartholomew, *God of Chance*, 109–14; Michiko Yusa, "Chance," in *Encyclopedia of Religion*, ed. Lindsay Jones, 2nd ed., 15 vols. (Detroit, MI: Macmillan References USA, 2005), 3:1526–29.

Accidents are unknown to God, or immortal Mind, and we must leave the mortal basis of belief and unite with the one Mind, in order to change the notion of chance to the proper sense of God's unerring direction and thus bring out harmony. Under divine Providence there can be no accidents, since there is no room for imperfection in perfection.[70]

But another theological tradition, less well-known, runs from Thomas Aquinas to contemporary process theologians and theologians of science. In the crisp phrasing of Aquinas:

Now it would be inconsistent with divine providence if all things happened of necessity.... Therefore it would also be inconsistent with divine providence if there were no luck or chance in the world.[71]

In this tradition, chance is not viewed as undermining divine agency but as itself an expression of divine providence. Both necessarily *and* contingently, things proceed according to God's will (Thomas Aquinas, *Summa theologiae* 1.19.8).[72]

A New Testament warrant for this view can be found in the apostles' use of lots to choose between Joseph and Matthias (Acts 1:23–6). As the biblical passage makes clear, the divine will is understood to guide the outcome of the procedure. But why use lots at all? At various moments in the Gospel accounts, moreover, Jesus suggests that not every eventuality in human life is caused by the direct action of God, and that not every human misfortune is an expression of divine punishment. In spite of the fact that not a single sparrow falls to the ground without it being the will of God the Father (Matt 10:29–31), sun and rain come to both the just and unjust alike (Matt 5:45).[73] Bad things simply happen sometimes and are not necessarily to be interpreted as instances of divine judgment (Luke 13:1–5; John 9:3).[74]

---

70. Mary Baker Eddy, *Science and Health with Key to the Scriptures* (Boston, 1875), 424, as cited in Bartholomew, *God of Chance*, 114. This view has become firmly established in religious life in the United States and, in a more secularized form, in American civil religion.

71. Thomas Aquinas, *Summa contra gentiles* 3.74, as cited in Bartholomew, *God of Chance*, 124.

72. See further John F. Wippel, "Divine Knowledge, Divine Power, and Human Freedom in Thomas Aquinas and Henry of Ghent," in *Divine Omniscience and Omnipotence in Medieval Philosophy: Islamic, Jewish, and Christian Perspectives*, ed. Tamar Rudavsky, Synthese Historical Library 25 (Dordrecht: D. Reidel, 1984), 213–41, at 230: "According to Thomas, it is because things are eternally present to the divine mind that God can know future contingents with certainty as they are in themselves."

73. Note that this perspective is quite similar to that of Ecclesiastes.

74. See further Bartholomew, *God of Chance*, 107–8. The use of lots in the New Testament has been continued by various Christian groups down to the present day as a means of decision-making. Other divinatory practices, such as book sortilege or bibliomancy (opening the Bible at random in

This perspective need not subvert divine sovereignty and, as Aquinas perceived, can in fact be seen as intrinsic to it. So, within the Christian tradition as well, providence and chance have not always been regarded as solo dancers, each one attempting to edge the other out of the spotlight, but were sometimes understood to be dance partners performing a complicated tango.[75] Chance can still appear within contemporary Christian faith and practice—now and then, here and there—as a divine look-alike.

---

order to receive divine guidance), are also established in the Christian tradition and still practiced. See further AnneMarie Luijendijk and William E. Klingshirn, eds. (with the assistance of Lance Jenott), *My Lots Are in Thy Hands: Sortilege and Its Practitioners in Late Antiquity*, Religions in the Graeco-Roman World 188 (Leiden: Brill, 2019).

75. See Machinist, "Fate," 161: "Religious traditions, it would appear, are not governed totally either by fate or by morally guided action; the situation is normally if not always mixed, and it is the differing balances of fate and morality—the ways the two are present and play off against one another—that serve as the distinguishing mark of each tradition."

CHAPTER 12

"Can a Woman Forget Her Nursing Child?" Divine Breastfeeding and the God of Israel

Christopher B. Hays

THE E-MAIL CAME from a fellow biblical scholar: "I have a question for you. Someone in my church has been advocating that we address God as 'Mother' in worship. As part of the discussion, this person has made the claim that El Shadday means 'God, the breasted one.'" He shared a link that his fellow parishioner had used in support of the claim, adding: "Is that just a kooky idea to serious OT scholars?"

This practical question opens out into a range of issues spanning millennia; it is only the tip of the iceberg when one considers the relationship of femininity to the God of the Bible. This essay looks at images of deities breastfeeding—the *dea nutrix* or Divine Wet Nurse—that were relatively common in polytheistic ANE religions. But could YHWH have been imagined as nursing his adherents? Was that an aspect of ANE goddesses' roles that was incorporated into God's character as part of the convergence of divine characteristics that Mark S. Smith has particularly emphasized?[1] How was such imagery carried on and manifested in later Jewish and Christian traditions, and what resistance and critiques has it faced in the process? Finally, it looks at ways in which controversies over the femininity of God have continued into the present, and how we might think about the use of such imagery today.

El Shadday, Breasts, and Fertility

To begin with my colleague's specific question: The original meaning of the ancient, biblical divine epithet El Shadday is arguably beyond the ken of

---

Author's Note: I am grateful to David Petersen, John Goldingay, John Thompson, Oliver Crisp, David Downs, and Jennifer Powell McNutt for discussing issues related to this paper with me, though of course the views, errors, and infelicities herein remain my own.

1. Mark S. Smith, *The Origins of Biblical Monotheism: Israel's Polytheistic Background and the Ugaritic Texts* (Oxford: Oxford University Press, 2001), 163.

historical research, but at a minimum, one can say that it was at times associated with fertility, procreation, and breastfeeding.

There is a small handful of instances of deities being called Shadday in the ANE outside the Bible; some are in doubt, and none is particularly useful for determining the meaning of the term.[2] The most interesting comparative suggestion connects Shadday to the Egyptian Shed (*šdy*), which means "savior."[3] Used widely as an epithet of various Egyptian gods, especially Horus, Shed as a distinct god was first recognized in the Eighteenth Dynasty (ca. 1550–1295 BCE). But there is no indication of this derivation in the biblical occurrences of the name.

Numerous Semitic etymologies have been proposed for Shadday, not all of which need to weighed any longer.[4] In fact, it may not be possible to reconstruct the processes by which scribes came to the pointing *šadday*. Given that the name may long predate not only the Masoretes but perhaps nearly all the HB, and that in any case it went through various (implicitly) proposed etymologies within the Bible itself, it is best not to put too much weight on the rules of historical linguistics in this instance. The debate about the etymology of Shadday was already underway when the versions were translated.[5]

The Semitic root that provides the most likely derivation for Shadday, as was pointed out more than a century ago by Paul Haupt, is *ṭd*, "breast," which rendered the Ugaritic term of the same spelling, as well as Hebrew *šad*.[6] As for the *–ay* suffix, presumably a *nisbe* ending, the Ugaritic divine name Raḥmay (*KTU* 1.23.16, 28) seems to have been formed in the same manner from the noun for "womb." It is worth nothing that there is not only an Egyptian verb

---

2. A group of gods called the Shaddayin (*šdyn*) are mentioned as an assembly of divine judges in the Deir 'Alla Plaster Text; see P. Kyle McCarter Jr., "The Balaam Texts from Deir 'Allā: The First Combination," *BASOR* 239 (1980): 49–60. An *il šdy* is mentioned in a broken context in *KTU* 1.108.12, but G. del Olmo Lete translates "god of the steppe" (*Canaanite Religion: According to the Liturgical Texts of Ugarit*, trans. W. G. E Watson, 2nd ed., Alter Orient und Altes Testament 408 [Münster: Ugarit-Verlag, 2014], 153). Dennis Pardee translates "the god *Shaddayu*" but grants that the passage in unclear (*Ritual and Cult at Ugarit*, Writings from the Ancient World 10 [Atlanta: Society of Biblical Literature, 2002], 194, 205–6). For the others, see Aren M. Wilson-Wright, "The Helpful God: A Reevaluation of the Etymology and Character of (*ʾēl) šadday*," *VT* 69 (2019): 149–66, at 150–53.

3. D. B. Redford, *A Study of the Biblical Story of Joseph (Gen 37–50)* (Leiden: Brill, 1970), 129; Manfred Görg, "Šaddaj: Ehrenrettung einer Etymologie," *Biblische Notizen* 16 (1981): 13–15; Mathias Neumann, "(El) Šadday—A Plea for an Egyptian Derivation of the God and Its Name," *Die Welt des Orients* 46 (2016): 244–63.

4. See the review in Wilson-Wright, "Helpful God," 154–58. Wilson-Wright's suggestion that *shadday* means "the helpful (one)," based on Ethio-Semitic and Arabic *sdy*, founders for lack of support from more ancient Semitic languages.

5. G. Mushayabasa, "The Effect of Etymology on the Rendering of the Divine Epithet (El) Shaddai in the Peshitta Version," *Journal of Semitics* 19 (2010): 19–35.

6. Paul Haupt, "Die Schlacht von Taanach," in *Studien zur semitischen Philologie und Religionsgeschichte: Julius Wellhausen zum Siebzigsten Geburtstag am 17 Mai 1914 gewidmet von Freunden und Schülern*, ed. Karl Marti, BZAW 27 (Giessen: Töpelmann, 1914), 212.

šdi meaning "to save" but also one meaning "to suckle,"[7] and the two actions were often related in Egyptian descriptions of divine protection and salvation.[8] Some object that Egyptian etymologies are phonologically impossible, but this concern seems to me overstated.[9]

The other etymology from the Semitic sphere that has commanded great influence is the argument of W. F. Albright and F. M. Cross for a Proto-Semitic term that meant both "breast" and (derivatively) "mountain."[10] They pointed out that the naming of topographical features after body parts was characteristic of ancient Semitic languages; such associations are exemplified even in modern times by names for mountains such as the Grand Tetons.[11] However, the most important evidence they supplied has now evaporated.[12] It is understandable that they glossed rapidly over the meaning "breast" in favor of interpreting YHWH as "the one of the mountains,"[13] in light of the rampant associations between mountains and numerous ANE deities, including YHWH, and the fact that YHWH was

---

7. Raymond O. Faulkner, *A Concise Dictionary of Middle Egyptian* (Oxford: Griffith Institute, 2002), 273. In conjunction with other interesting similarities between Egyptian and Akkadian verbs for nursing, *šdi* may point to very ancient lexical connections among ANE terms for these basic biological phenomena. For example, the Akkadian verb to suckle is the Š stem of *enēqu* (i.e., *šūnuqu*), which can be compared not only to Hebrew *y-n-q*, but also to the Egyptian *šnq(šnḳ)*, an alternative to *šdi* for "suckle."

8. On divine suckling, protection, and salvation, see Christopher B. Hays, "'Those Weaned From Milk': The Divine Wet Nurse Motif in the Ceremony of the Covenant with Mut (Isa 28)," *Journal of Hebrew Scriptures* (forthcoming). This possible derivation is mentioned in passing in David Biale, "The God with Breasts: El Shaddai in the Bible," *History of Religions* 20 (1982): 240–56, at 249. It is possible that Ugaritic also had this verb; in the Baal Myth (1.6 IV 18), the phrase *šd yn 'n b qbt* could be understood to mean "suck sparkling wine from a goblet."

9. See the representative comments of Wilson-Wright, "Helpful God," 157. It does not seem safe to me to draw definitive conclusions from a very small number of Egyptian loanwords in Biblical Hebrew. Note that the Egyptian /d/ is used to write a number of different Semitic phonemes in the New Kingdom and Third Intermediate Period, but the most common was Semitic /d/; see James E. Hoch, *Semitic Words in Egyptian Texts of the New Kingdom and Third Intermediate Period* (Princeton: Princeton University Press, 1994), 376–80. Furthermore, on the doubling of *d* in Shadday, note that *šdi* is attested with a geminated stem: *šdd* (Leonard H. Lesko and Barbara S. Lesko, *A Dictionary of Late Egyptian*, 2nd ed., 2 vols. [Providence, RI: B. C. Scribe, 2004], 2:140).

10. W. F. Albright, "The Names Shaddai and Abram," *JBL* 54 (1935): 173–210; Frank Moore Cross, "Yahweh and the God of the Patriarchs," *HTR* 55 (1962): 244–50; Cross, *Canaanite Myth and Hebrew Epic: Essays in the History of the Religion of Israel* (Cambridge: Harvard University Press, 1973), 52–60.

11. See Eduard P. Dhorme, "L'emploi métaphorique des noms de parties du corps en hébreu et en akkadien," *RB* 31 (1922): 230–32.

12. Briefly: In Ugaritic, "breast" (*ṯd*) seems to be derived from a Proto-Semitic root distinct from Ugaritic *šd*, which was in turn cognate with Akkadian *šadû* and Hebrew *śādê*. When Cross wrote, the possibility of a Ugaritic word *ṯd* for mountain was still entertained, but in the latest edition of *DULAT* (*A Dictionary of the Ugaritic Language in the Alphabetic Tradition*, ed. Gregorio del Olmo Lete and Joaquín Sanmartín, 3rd rev. ed., 2 vols. [Leiden: Brill, 2015]), it is not.

13. Cross, *Canaanite Myth*, 55. Also Raymond de Hoop, *Genesis 49 in Its Literary and Historical Context*, OtSt 39 (Leiden: Brill, 1999), 215.

more commonly portrayed with masculine characteristics. In doing so, however, they favored the broader ANE religious context over the actual literary contexts in which the epithet (El) Shadday appears.

Significantly, one of the major theological perspectives that makes up the HB did understand Shadday as related to childbearing. David Biale points out that "all of the passages using El Shaddai in Genesis, with one exception, are fertility blessings." Thus he argues that an early Israelite tradition "understood El Shaddai as a fertility god."[14] He demonstrated the point through a survey of passages from Genesis in which Shadday occurs (17:1–2; 28:3; 35:11; 48:3–4), all of which are blessings to be fruitful and multiply.

The most significant and revealing passage, however, is Gen 49:25, from the Blessing of Jacob, which clearly plays with the etymology of Shadday. It says that Joseph will be aided

> by the God of your father,
> > who will help you,
> by El Shadday who will bless you
> > with blessings of heaven above,
> blessings of the deep that lies beneath,
> > blessings of the breasts and of the womb [šādayim wārāḥam].

Verse 26 continues, "The blessings of your father are stronger than the blessings of the eternal mountains"[15]—which, although it does not use a term for "mountain" cognate with Shadday, may indicate that even this author was playing with different etymologies for Shadday.

One might add to Biale's argument Ps 22:10–11[9–10], in which the Psalmist says to the Lord: "you kept me safe on my mother's breasts (ʿal šədê ʾimmî) / On you (ʿālêkā) I was cast from my birth." The repetition of the preposition ʿāl poetically compares the mother and God, and the use of šədê contains an echo of Shadday, in light of the parallelism.

Biale points out that, for a name as plausibly ancient as El Shadday, the etymological derivation that so engrossed Albright was almost certainly of secondary importance by the first millennium. Biale says of the biblical author:

> He inherited a language composed of words which had lost their original meanings, and his own writing was often an attempt to impose meanings

---

14. Biale, "God with Breasts," 247. Interestingly, some of Biale's argument was presaged (albeit clumsily) by J. P. Lesley, "On the Hebrew Word ShDI (Shaddai), Translated 'The Almighty,'" *Proceedings of the American Philosophical Society* 23 (1886): 303–12.

15. Assuming the widely accepted emendation *harrê-ʿad* (as Hab 3:6) for the Masoretic Text's *hôray ʿad*.

on such words as a result of his own contemporary concerns. The understanding of a biblical expression must therefore begin by adopting the point of view of the biblical author: What did he mean when he used a certain word or phrase? Only then can the search for cognates bear fruit.

If Biale is right, then when was this author who emphasized El Shadday as a fertility deity working? He argued that the El Shadday fertility tradition was very ancient. Only later, as part of the polemic against goddesses, was a new association with destruction substituted, at which point Shadday became a distant, inscrutable, and dangerous deity in exilic/postexilic theology.[16] This effort seems particularly overt in Joel 1:15, which can be understood implicitly to supply a different etymology for the divine epithet: "The day of YHWH is near, and as destruction from Shadday it comes [ûkəšōd mišadday yābô']." Occurrences of Shadday in late texts such as Job, Ruth, and Ezek 10:5 arguably reflect the same understanding, which is very different from the understanding of Shadday as a source of fertility blessings in Genesis. One could argue that this was a theological reaction to the sense of distance that the Babylonian exile created between God and the people.

Biale's explanation is elegant but also problematic in that it presupposes the antiquity of the above Genesis texts. The first four are, however, all attributed to the Priestly source, presumed to be the latest in the Pentateuch.[17] Therefore, the status and date of the Blessing of Jacob in Gen 49 becomes crucial.[18] Its sayings are generally considered to derive from independent tradition and not assigned to any of the sources, and they are "almost unanimously considered to be old."[19] The blessing has often been taken as a premonarchic poetic composition akin to Exod 15's Song of the Sea,[20] but it can no longer be confirmed as an archaic text on linguistic grounds alone.[21] Still, on the basis of its emphasis on Judah and its

---

16. Biale also pointed out that Anat might have provided a kind of background conceptual framework for the theologians who carried this off, since she was associated with both fertility and extreme violence.

17. It seems to me that the arguments of what might be called "the Hebrew University School" for the antiquity of at least some Priestly material deserve serious consideration, but the argument here does not depend on their accuracy.

18. Jean-Daniel Macchi, for example, assumed that it must follow the P references to El Shadday in Genesis (*Israël et ses tribus selon Genèse 49*, OBO 171 [Fribourg: Academic Press, 1999], 221).

19. Hoop, *Genesis 49*, 55. See also Antony F. Campbell and Mark A. O'Brien, *Sources of the Pentateuch: Texts, Introductions, Annotations* (Minneapolis: Fortress, 1993), 130n86; Richard Elliott Friedman, *The Bible with Sources Revealed: A New View into the Five Books of Moses* (San Francisco: Harper, 2003), 114; W. Randall Garr, "The Grammar and Interpretation of Exodus 6:3," *JBL* 111 (1992): 398–401.

20. E.g., Frank Moore Cross and David Noel Freedman, *Studies in Early Yahwistic Poetry*, SBLDS 76 (Missoula, MT: Scholars Press, 1975), 46–63.

21. David A. Robertson, *Linguistic Evidence in Dating Early Hebrew Poetry*, SBLDS 3 (Missoula, MT: Society of Biblical Literature, 1972).

possible allusion to Shiloh in 49:8–12, it remains a reasonable conclusion that the text was compiled and shaped during the period of the united monarchy.

Therefore, it would appear that the Priestly authors drew on an ancient tradition of El Shadday as a deity associated with breasts and fertility. (Exodus 6:3 points to the same conception of the antiquity of the name El Shadday.) This adoption may be explained by the priestly emphasis on procreation (Gen 1:22, 28; "Be fruitful and multiply, and fill the earth").

Divine Breastfeeding in the Bible, Beyond Shadday

The association of YHWH with breastfeeding is attested in other canonical texts, but these biblical instances do not transgress sensibilities opposing the *dea nutrix*, because in various ways they avoid identifying YHWH as one who breastfeeds. In the Song of Moses, YHWH's provision for Jacob is described in poetic terms: "He nursed him with honey from the rock" (Deut 32:13).

Perhaps the most striking examples, however, are postexilic passages in Isaiah that portray Jerusalem/Zion as a mother, both in labor and in nursing. For example, in Isa 49:14–15, Zion is imagined as accusing the Lord of forsaking and forgetting her. God responds:

> Can a woman forget her nursing child,
>   or show no compassion for the child of her womb?
> Even these may forget,
>   yet I will not forget you.

So, although God is compared to a nursing mother, the use of metaphor distances God from actually being considered feminine.

In Isa 60:16, God says to Zion:

> You shall suck the milk of nations,
>   you shall suck the breasts of kings;
> and you shall know that I, YHWH,
>   am your Savior and your Redeemer.

Finally, in Isa 66:10–11, Zion/Jerusalem is imagined as the nursing mother to its inhabitants:

> Rejoice with Jerusalem, and be glad for her, all you who love her;
>   rejoice with her in joy, all you who mourn over her—that you may
>   nurse and be satisfied from her consoling breast;
>   that you may drink deeply with delight from her glorious bosom.

Blending the imagery of flowing milk into that of flowing water, the passage goes on to promise that the wealth of nations will be "like an overflowing stream," inverting the negative imagery of floods as a violent threat in, for example, 30:28; 28:2, 15–18; and 10:22. God then says: "As a mother comforts her child, so I will comfort you; you shall be comforted in Jerusalem" (66:13). So this passage distances YHWH from breastfeeding imagery both through the use of simile and by projecting the divine nursing onto Jerusalem/Zion as a proxy. Nevertheless, it is difficult to ignore the effort to connect God with *dea nutrix* imagery.

The case in the New Testament is somewhat similar. The Pauline letters are prone to use nursing imagery to portray the care of the apostles for the early churches.[22] In 1 Cor 3:1–3, Paul writes: "I could not speak to you as spiritual people, but rather as people of the flesh, as infants in Christ. I fed you with milk, not solid food, for you were not ready for solid food." And in 1 Thess 2:5–8:

> We might have made demands as apostles of Christ. But we were gentle among you, like a nurse [*trophos*] tenderly caring for her own children. So deeply do we care for you that we are determined to share with you not only the gospel of God but also our own selves, because you have become very dear to us.

In both these instances, arguably, the gospel is compared to breast milk. But as with the passages from Isaiah, the idea of a genuine divine feminine is marginalized. Arguably something similar went on with Paul's claim in 1 Cor 1:24 and 30 that Christ "became for us wisdom [*sophia*] from God"—in this way Paul claimed that a male figure took on the role that had been imagined in a feminine way. But these early texts were subject to ongoing reflection, and the *dea nutrix* would reemerge vigorously in the early church and the synagogue.

Dea Nutrix in Postbiblical Traditions

Imagery of the God of the Bible as *dea nutrix* appears full-blown in the Odes of Solomon, which were Christian texts from the first or second century CE:[23]

> The Son is the cup, and He who was milked is the Father: and the Holy Spirit milked Him: because His breasts were full, and it was necessary for Him that His milk should be sufficiently released; and the Holy Spirit

---

22. For further discussion, see Beverly R. Gaventa, *Our Mother Saint Paul* (Louisville, KY: Westminster John Knox Press, 2007).

23. For discussion, see J. Rendel Harris, *The Odes and Psalms of Solomon* (Cambridge: Cambridge University Press, 1911), 116–17. English translations above are Harris's.

> opened His bosom and mingled the milk from the two breasts of the Father; and gave the mixture to the world without their knowing: and they who receive in its fullness are the ones on the right hand. (Ode 19)

> My own breasts I prepared for [those who love me] that they might drink my holy milk and live thereby. (Ode 8)

In these odes, the members of the Trinity are explicitly portrayed as nursing their worshipers, a boundary that the biblical texts were not willing to cross. Some of the major church fathers, however, explored the same territory. For example, Clement of Alexandria wrote:

> What further need has God of the mysteries of love? And then thou shalt look into the bosom of the Father, whom God the only-begotten Son alone hath declared. God Himself is love; and out of love to us became feminine. In His ineffable essence He is Father; in His compassion to us He became Mother. The Father by loving became feminine: and the great proof of this is He whom He begot of Himself; and the fruit brought forth by love is love.[24]

And Augustine wrote: "Nor did [John] alone drink at the fountain of the Lord's breast, to emit again in preaching ... those sublime truths regarding the divinity of Christ."[25] Images of divine breastfeeding such as these were clearly part of the theological milieu from the beginnings of the church.

In the medieval Christian tradition, *dea nutrix* imagery also appeared with some regularity.[26] Bernard of Clairvaux wrote: "If you feel the stings of temptation, ... suck not so much the wounds as the breasts of the Crucified. He will be your mother, and you will be his son."[27] Guerric of Igny made a particularly forceful statement: "The Bridegroom [Christ] ... has breasts, lest he should be lacking any one of all duties and titles of loving kindness. He is a father in virtue of natural creation, ... and also in virtue of the authority with which he instructs.

---

24. Clement of Alexandria, *Quis dives salvetur* 37, in *Ante-Nicene Fathers: The Writings of the Fathers Down to A.D. 325*, ed. Alexander Roberts et al., 10 vols. (Peabody, MA: Hendrickson, 1994), 2:601.

25. Augustine, *Tractates on John* 24.7 (on John 21), in *A Select Library of the Nicene and Post-Nicene Fathers of the Christian Church*, ed. Philip Schaff, 1st series, 14 vols. (Grand Rapids: Eerdmans, 1978), 7:452.

26. See, e.g. Eleanor McLaughlin, "'Christ My Mother': Feminine Naming and Metaphor in Medieval Spirituality," *Nashotah Review* 15 (1975): 228–48; Carol Walker Bynum, "Jesus as Mother and Abbot as Mother: Some Themes in Twelfth-Century Cistercian Writing," in *Jesus as Mother: Studies in the Spirituality of the High Middle Ages* (Berkeley: University of California Press, 1982), 110–69.

27. Bynum, "Jesus as Mother," 117.

He is a mother, too, in the mildness of his affection, and a nurse.... But behold, all at once the Holy Spirit was sent from heaven like milk poured out from Christ's own breasts, and Peter was filled with an abundance of milk."[28] Perhaps most famously, the great mystic Julian of Norwich wrote that "as truly as God is our Father, so truly is God our Mother"; indeed, "Jesus is our true Mother."[29] She went on:

> The mother can give her child to suck of her milk, ... but our tender Mother Jesus can lead us easily into his blessed breast through his sweet open side, and show us there a part of the godhead and of the joys of heaven, with inner certainty of endless bliss.... This fair lovely word "mother" is so sweet and so kind in itself that it cannot truly be said of anyone or to anyone except of him and to him who is the true Mother of life and of all things.[30]

Thus as Rosemary Radford Ruether noted: "We cannot conclude that female imagery for the Spirit is a later 'deviation' of heretical Christianity. Rather, we should see an earlier Christianity, which used such female imagery, gradually being marginalized."[31]

The motif of divine breastfeeding also flourished in medieval Jewish mysticism.[32] As with the Christian tradition, a number of classical Jewish sources already included theological reflections on breastfeeding. For example, the miracle of Sarah suckling children (Gen 21:7) was interpreted as a mythological explanation for the conversion of gentiles: "Sarah stood and uncovered herself, and her two breasts were pouring milk like two spouts of water.... And the nations of the world were bringing their children to Sarah so that she would suckle them" (Pesiqta Rabbati 43:4).[33]

In the Babylonian Talmud, the breasts of "the wife of your youth" in Prov 5:18–19 are interpreted as Torah: "Why are the words of Torah compared to a breast? As with this breast, that every time the child touches it he finds milk

---

28. Ibid., 122.
29. Julian of Norwich, *Showings*, ed. Edmund Colledge and James Walsh (New York: Paulist, 1978), 296.
30. Ibid., 298.
31. Rosemary Radford Ruether, *Sexism and God-Talk: Toward a Feminist Theology* (Boston: Beacon, 1983; repr. with new introduction, 1993), 59.
32. For a much more adequate treatment (to which I am indebted), see Ellen Davina Haskell, *Suckling at My Mother's Breasts: The Image of a Nursing God in Jewish Mysticism*, SUNY Series in Western Esoteric Traditions (Albany: State University of New York Press, 2012).
33. See also Genesis Rabbah 53:9 (fifth century CE), b. Bava Metzi'a 87a (fifth or sixth century CE), Pesiqta de Rab Kahana 22:1 (fifth century CE), and Pirqe Rabbi Eliezer 52 (eighth or ninth century CE); discussed in Haskell, *Suckling*, 16–20 (English translation of Pesiqta Rabbati is taken from Haskell here, as also are those of b. Eruvin and Sefer ha-Zohar the following paragraph).

in it, so it is with the words of Torah. Every time that a man reasons in them, he finds pleasure in them" (b. Eruvin 54b). But it was in the thirteenth century that this imagery flourished into a *dea nutrix*. Rabbi Ezra of Gerona commented on the Song of Songs 8:1: "You will receive suckling from ... the spirit of the living God." By the time of Sefer ha-Zohar, this became a fully realized image in which the Shekinah (i.e., "Divine Presence," one of the ten *sefirot*, or aspects, of God) was portrayed as a nursing mother: "This is the Shekinah who was in the Temple, and all the children of the world used to suckle from her.... And the Shekinah rested upon them in the Temple, like a mother covering over her children" (1:203a).

Tensions Around the *Dea Nutrix*

The preceding examples could give the impression that *dea nutrix* imagery has always been accepted as completely normal in Christianity and Judaism. The fact that such imagery is surprising and controversial to many religious adherents in the present day is one indication that this is not the case.

The polemic against *dea nutrix* imagery for God is deeply connected with the process by which Israelite religion came to focus on a single deity for whom masculine pronouns were most commonly used. The attempted exclusion of goddess worship, particularly that of Asherah (e.g., 2 Kgs 23:4–7),[34] left a psychological void for Yahwistic worshipers that continued to be filled in various ways. Monotheism was a revolutionary idea—or to put it a different way, an irregular one. It is not surprising that it was resisted; consider the backlash against the religious innovations of Akhenaten or Nabonidus. Rather, it is surprising that it endured.

The polemic against feminine imagery for YHWH arguably began with an intrabiblical reinterpretation of the etymology of Shadday in texts such as Joel 1:15 (above), which associated it with destruction rather than fertile breasts. As Biale noted: "The transformation of El Shaddai from a fertility god with feminine characteristics to a seemingly male god of war makes great theological and even psychological sense, for what better way to suppress one interpretation of a god than by substituting its opposite?"[35]

---

34. I make no attempt whatsoever here to survey the enormous amount of literature on Asherah and her exclusion, but for the present purpose, see Tikva S. Frymer-Kensky, *In the Wake of the Goddesses: Women, Culture, and the Biblical Transformation of Pagan Myth* (New York: Fawcett Columbine, 1993). Harriet Lutzky has argued that Shadday is best understood as an epithet for Asherah ("Shadday as a Goddess Epithet," *VT* 48 [1998]: 15–36), though I do not think this is as helpful as Biale's comparison to Anat.

35. Biale, "God with Breasts," 256.

There are other indications of an aversion to *dea nutrix* imagery within the HB. One example is Isa 28, in a passage that condemns the leaders of Judah for seeking diplomatic protection by making a covenant with Kushite Egypt in the late eighth century BCE. In a series of recent publications, I demonstrated that Egypt is represented by its national goddess, Mut.[36] The key to the passage is the wordplay on the paronomasia between Mut's name and the Hebrew word *mwt*, "death": the covenant with Mut becomes a covenant with Death in Isa 28:15 and 18. In the course of the oracle, Isaiah belittles the Judahite leaders as babies "just weaned from milk," who have scarcely "outgrown the breast" (28:9). The prophet asks: Is the Lord really going to "teach knowledge" or "explain the message" to such infantile bumblers?

Mut, as a mother goddess, was a quintessential *dea nutrix* figure, although the manifestations of Isis in that role are more widely known. In the Kushite period (and through a relatively wide swath of Egyptian history), Mut was portrayed precisely as suckling her worshipers, as a symbolic form of strengthening and protecting them—Kushite amulets from the Twenty-fifth Dynasty depict this act. In a slightly earlier text, a Kushite prince portrays himself as a faithful adherent of Mut's cult at Thebes by describing how he "he received her breasts of electrum, suckling her milk so that it enter[ed into him] as life and dominion, while she gave to him [her valor and] her victories."[37] Cultic breastfeeding practices also seem to have been known across a relatively wide range of ANE cultures; artifacts from Mari, Khirbet Qeiyafa, Tell Qasile, and in the Phoenician diaspora supply examples of the kinds of ritual vessels that might have been used to simulate breastfeeding, which may help to explain why Isaiah knew of them.[38] But the motif was especially characteristic of Egyptian goddesses such as Mut.[39]

Strictly speaking, Isa 28 condemns only the covenant with Mut, and not the idea of divine breastfeeding in general. But, since the prophet uses *dea nutrix* imagery to insult the Judahites, the rhetoric may well have presupposed a more general aversion to the image.

In any case, rhetoric like Isaiah's did not abolish *dea nutrix* theologies. One marker of the endurance is that "Judean pillar figurines," female statuettes made of clay and often with exaggerated breasts, appear widely throughout

---

36. Hays, "Those Weaned"; Hays, "The Egyptian Goddess Mut in Iron-Age Palestine: Further Data From Amulets and Onomastics," *JNES* 71 (2012): 299–314; Hays, *Death in the Iron Age II and in First Isaiah*, FAT 79 (Tübingen: Mohr Siebeck, 2011), 288–315.

37. Robert K. Ritner, *The Libyan Anarchy: Inscriptions from Egypt's Third Intermediate Period*, Writings from the Ancient World 21 (Atlanta: Society of Biblical Literature, 2009), 351, 354. From the eleventh year of Takelot II of the Twenty-second Dynasty (ca. 839 BCE), the text is known as The Chronicle of Prince Osorkon ("B").

38. Hays, "Those Weaned," throughout.

39. Stephanie Budin, *Images of Woman and Child from the Bronze Age: Reconsidering Fertility, Maternity, and Gender in the Ancient World* (Cambridge: Cambridge University Press, 2011), 35.

Judah from before Hezekiah's time to after Josiah's. Thus, "they appear to have been totally unaffected by reforms associated with Yahwistic orthodoxy, had such reforms taken place."[40] The significance of these remains in dispute, and one prominent theory is that they were "the physical expression of a woman's prayers for fertility and successful lactation."[41] Another is that they were related to protection or healing.[42] In either case, they seem to point to an ongoing need for and supplication of the divine feminine. Texts such as Jer 44 reflect an outright popular rejection of the ban on goddess worship. The people tell Jeremiah: "We are not going to listen to you. Instead, we will do everything that we have vowed, make offerings to the queen of heaven and pour out libations to her, just as we and our ancestors, our kings and our officials, used to do" (Jer 44:16–17). A more irenic approach was taken by the aforementioned late passages from Genesis, Isaiah, and Psalms, which attempted to emphasize YHWH's femininity.

At the roots of monotheism, then, there began a kind of theological dance in the tension between the desire to preserve female imagery for God, including the *dea nutrix*, and the denial that this is possible for a single deity who was more commonly imagined as male. This would go on through the ages. Even individual theologians were often of two minds. For example, the same Augustine who spoke of "the Lord's breast" elsewhere declared that, in "the image of God, ... there is no sex," and that the woman is not the image of God except when she is joined together with her husband.[43]

In the Reformation period, it can be argued that the closing of many convents in Europe led to the loss of spaces for women's dedicated spirituality, which had long given rise to reflection on the maternal aspects of God. Furthermore, the affirmation of clerical marriage came with a greater emphasis on the roles of women in marriage and family and a greater differentiation of gender roles that may have worked against gender-bending images of God.

Some aspects of the Reformers' theology were indeed not conducive to feminine images of the divine. The Christocentrism of the theologies of Martin Luther and John Calvin both meant that the Marian piety of the Middle Ages, which considered Mary to be the Queen of Heaven and Mother of God, was greatly restricted.[44] Even though both Reformers affirmed the doctrine of the

---

40. Erin Darby, *Interpreting Judean Pillar Figurines: Gender and Empire in Judean Apotropaic Ritual*, FAT 2.69 (Tübingen: Mohr Siebeck, 2014), 400.

41. Carol L. Meyers, *Households and Holiness: The Religious Culture of Israelite Women*, Facets (Minneapolis: Fortress, 2005).

42. Darby, *Interpreting*, 402–5.

43. Augustine, *On the Trinity* 12.5.5 and 12.7.10. For discussion and further reading, see Rosemary Radford Ruether, *Goddesses and the Divine Feminine: A Western Religious History* (Berkeley: University of California Press, 2005), 137.

44. Allison P. Coudert, "The Myth of the Improved Status of Protestant Women: The Case of the Witchcraze," in *The Politics of Gender in Early Modern Europe*, ed. Jean R. Brink, Allison P.

theotokos in principle, Calvin refused to call Mary "Mother of God," "lest it cause misunderstanding among Christians who did not understand its doctrinal basis."[45]

These same major Reformers were content to affirm feminine imagery for God, however. For example, Calvin wrote in his commentary on Isa 46:3 ("Listen to me ... remnant of the house of Israel, who have been borne by me from your birth, carried from the womb"):

> If it be objected that God is everywhere called "a Father" (Jer 31:9; Mal 1:6) and that this title is more appropriate to him, I reply that no figures of speech can describe God's extraordinary affection towards us; for it is infinite and various; so that, if all that can be said or imagined about love were brought together into one, yet it would be surpassed by the greatness of the love of God. By no metaphor, therefore, can his incomparable goodness be described.... The intention of the Prophet is to show that the Jews, if they do not choose to forget their descent, cannot arrive at any other conclusion than that they were not begotten in vain; and that God, who has manifested himself to be both their Father and their Mother, will always assist them.[46]

Calvin also dedicated this same commentary to Edward VI and Elizabeth, then king and queen of England, and did so by emphasizing that Isa 49:23 calls queens and kings to be "nursing-mothers" and "nursing-fathers" to the church. So Calvin was capable of thinking creatively about gendered metaphors.

Similarly, Luther commented on Isa 49:15: "In ... tribulations we think we have been deserted. But in the very thing in which He forsakes us He is our mother, most solicitous in cherishing and nourishing us."[47] And on 66:11:

> When the consolation of the Word comes, the breast is full, abounding in consolations.... The breasts of the Holy Spirit are full, consoling us by giving us our fill to the very depths of our heart.... The church's breasts satisfy through the Word.... Through the Holy Spirit the breasts of the church comfort many hearts with peace and security of faith.[48]

Coudert, and Maryanne C. Horowitz, Sixteenth Century Essays & Studies 12 (Kirksville, MO: Sixteenth Century Journal, 1989), 61–90, esp. 85.

45. Ruether, *Goddesses*, 221.

46. John Calvin, *Commentary on the Book of the Prophet Isaiah*, trans. W. Pringle (Edinburgh: Calvin Translation Society, 1850), 436–37.

47. Martin Luther, *Lectures on Isaiah Chapters 40–66*, vol. 17 in *Luther's Works*, ed. Hilton C. Oswald (Saint Louis: Concordia, 1972), 183–84.

48. Luther, *Lectures on Isaiah Chapters 40–66*, 408.

This last quotation shows Luther preferring to distance the feminine from God and Christ by ascribing the divine feminine to the church or to the Spirit—since, conveniently, it is grammatically feminine. In much the same way, Calvin particularly emphasized the church as mother.[49] This tendency is in line with the Isaianic authors who imagined Jerusalem (but not God!) breastfeeding. It redirects the emphasis of the divine feminine away from God, and thus stops short of fully affirming it.

In sum, it does not seem that the church fathers or Reformers whose theologies eventually marginalized female imagery were thoroughgoing misogynists. Nevertheless, they were enmeshed in deeply patriarchal cultures, and the outcome was the further marginalization of feminine imagery for God.

Toward the Present Day

Despite the closing of the convents, the spirituality of the divine feminine did not disappear in Protestant countries after the Reformation. As Ruether remarked: "[The] view of a patriarchal Protestantism with exclusively male symbols is itself too simple." She goes on to fault mainstream Protestants, however, who "have failed to recognize, and to appropriate as part of their tradition, continual waves of mystical and millennialist Protestantism from the seventeenth to the nineteenth centuries, which redeveloped the Wisdom symbol and re-created a vision of God and the human being as androgynous."[50] Indeed, the movements that would arise to emphasize divine femininity in the wake of the Reformation tended to be small sects that had limited impact on the broader culture. Often these had female leaders: Margaret Fell was known as the "Nursing Mother of Quakerism"; Mary Baker Eddy, founder of the Christian Science movement, prayed to and taught about the "Father-Mother God";[51] and Ann Lee was believed by her Shakers followers to be the second coming of Christ in the form of a woman:

> During visionary trances, [Lee] "bore for souls" by visiting and preaching the gospel to the dead, and then, like a nursing mother, she nourished them with the milk of the Shaker gospel. According to Lee, some refused to confess their sins to her, but others came like hungry infants who were eager to be nursed. As she explained to Samuel Fitch, "When the gospel

---

49. John Calvin, *Institutes* 4.1.1, with an allusion to God as a mother hen in Matt 23:37 // Luke 13:34.
50. Ruether, *Goddesses*, 9–10.
51. Leslie Harris, "God Our Father-Mother," *Christian Science Sentinel*, January 25, 1958, sentinel.christianscience.com/shared/view/2olct5vgaic.

was offered to them, they were so hungry for it, that they would come, with their mouths wide open, to receive it."[52]

Many of these movements still endure in various ways, although they had to swim upstream against the "muscular Christianity" of the late nineteenth and early twentieth centuries in America, which mirrored Theodore Roosevelt's "cult of manliness" and brought about an associated "cult of true womanhood."[53] Like earlier periods of "reform," these tended to emphasize distinct gender roles and separate spheres for men and women, and this did not support gender-bending imagery for God.

The American church continues to exist in the tension between the longing for the divine feminine and backlashes against it. The latter part of the twentieth century saw the rise of a new-age/neo-pagan Goddess movement. Prominent within it was Carol Christ, whose "Why Women Need the Goddess"[54] inspired the Unitarian Universalist minister Shirley Ann Ranck to write a Sunday-school curriculum entitled *Cakes for the Queen of Heaven*, which promoted a kind of self-help spirituality aimed at women. It became a popular success and eventually was published in book form.[55] As Ranck's embrace of Jeremiah's opponents and Christ's publication in a journal called *HERESIES* emphasizes, "thealogians" such as these tended to posit themselves over against the tradition.

Slightly closer to mainstream Christianity is Ruether, a Roman Catholic theologian. While seeking to affirm Goddess spirituality, she has criticized the naiveté of the early Goddess movement for thinking that embracing threads of prehistoric goddess worship would free it from patriarchy:

> Feminists have no perfect option from some past tradition. This means that we can choose from various options such as Judaism, Christianity, or Buddhism, or we can pursue new options by seeking to recover other ancient traditions. But as we go deeper into these traditions, we find the need to be "reformers" and reinterpreters of those traditions. A fully

---

52. Rufus Bishop, *Testimonies of the Life, Character, Revelations, and Doctrines of Our Ever Blessed Mother Ann Lee* (Hancock, MA: Tallcott and Deming, 1816), 43, 19, 231, 238; quoted in Catherine A. Brekus, *Strangers and Pilgrims: Female Preaching in America, 1740–1845*, Gender and American Culture (Chapel Hill: University of North Carolina Press, 1998), 108–9.

53. Clifford Putney, *Muscular Christianity: Manhood and Sports in Protestant America, 1880–1920* (Cambridge: Harvard University Press, 2001), 144.

54. Carol Christ, "Why Women Need the Goddess," *HERESIES: a Feminist Publication on Art and Politics* 2 (1978; *The Great Goddess Issue*): 8–13; see also C. Christ, "Why Women, Men and Other Living Things Still Need the Goddess: Remembering and Reflecting 35 Years Later," *Feminist Theology* 20 (2012): 242–55.

55. Shirley Ann Ranck, *Cakes for the Queen of Heaven: An Exploration of Women's Power, Past, Present and Future* (New York: Authors Choice Press, 2006).

pro-woman feminist theology and spirituality did not exist in the past in any clearly recoverable sense, although all these traditions contain many hints of alternative perspectives.... Feminists need to recognize that in whatever tradition we choose to stand, we are reinterpreting from our own context.[56]

Our own contexts certainly need ongoing reinterpretation of tradition. On the one hand, attempts to affirm and incorporate feminine imagery continues, including within traditional Protestant churches. For example, in a contemporary hymnal published by the United Methodist Church is a hymn entitled "In Unity We Lift Our Song," which includes this stanza:

For God our way, our bread, our rest,
Of all these gifts the Giver.
Our strength, our guide, *our nurturing breast,*
Whose hand will yet deliver.[57]

On the other hand, new eruptions of "muscular Christianity" are taking place all over the country. A documentary called *Fight Church* chronicles the stories of some of the seven hundred churches around the United States that have incorporated MMA (mixed martial arts) cage-fighting into their ministries.[58] In it, a gym owner who started his own MMA-based church says: "Mainstream or Western Christianity has feminized men [and] taken away their God-given attributes of aggressiveness and competitiveness."[59]

Another widely cited example of hypermasculine Christianity in recent years is Mark Driscoll's Mars Hill Church, which attracted more than thirteen thousand weekly attendees in more than a dozen locations before Driscoll's abuse of parishioners and misuse of church funds forced him from that pulpit in 2014. Along the way, a large part of his appeal was his theology that God is masculine, rather than "a Richard Simmons, hippie, queer Christ ... neutered and

---

56. Ruether, *Goddesses*, 5. In this context, Ruether makes clear that this critique has already been absorbed by many of the scholars who have contributed to the Goddess movement more recently.

57. Ken Medema, "In Unity We Lift Our Song," no. 2221 in *The Faith We Sing* (Knoxville, TN: Abingdon, 1994). Sung to the tune of "Ein' Feste Burg."

58. imdb.com/title/tt2118623/.

59. sacredmattersmagazine.com/jesus-never-tapped-out-a-review-of-fight-church/. The filmmakers observe: "Pastors like him feel that the church's traditional evangelizing is not resonating with young men anymore, and they are resolved to change that." See also Daniel Junge and Bryan Storkel, "Pastor With a Punch," *New York Times*, Sept. 8, 2014, nytimes.com/2014/09/09/opinion/pastor-with-a-punch.html.

limp-wristed popular Sky Fairy of pop culture that ... would never talk about sin or send anyone to hell."[60] In another instance, the Washington Post reported:

> Driscoll went on a sexist rant in an interview with a British radio host who was married to a female pastor. When the host disagreed with Driscoll's hostile analysis of female leadership, Driscoll called him a coward and asked: "Is God like a mom who just embraces everyone? Or is he like a father who also protects, and defends, and disciplines? If you won't answer the question, I think I know the answer." [61]

The movement is far from ending with Mars Hill Church's subsequent implosion. Driscoll was only tapping into the latest wave of concern about the feminization of the church.[62] Churches with similar emphases have continued to pop up regularly, and Driscoll himself quickly founded a new church.[63]

AS LONG AS A CHURCH is patriarchal, or indeed outright misogynistic, as long as it is a means for men to worship and reinforce their own power, which is often what it has been throughout history, then people will always feel a need for a goddess. If Christians are going to worship our own likenesses, then femininity is, after all, not less worthy of adoration than masculinity. As long as God the Father reinforces patriarchy, it is entirely natural that many will want to make cakes for the Queen of Heaven.

That is not, however, the end of the matter, because the notion that the God of the Bible is masculine rather than feminine is false. Despite the overwhelmingly masculine language used for God in the Bible, to extract the notion that God is male is an example of the error of the *via eminentiae*: the idea that God is like something else, only more so. In this case: *God is like a king, only much more powerful; God is like a father, but a better father than any human.* It is necessary, albeit difficult, simultaneously to affirm the metaphors as metaphors

---

60. Molly Worthen, "Who Would Jesus Smack Down?," *New York Times*, Jan. 6, 2009, nytimes.com/2009/01/11/magazine/11punk-t.html.

61. Kristen Powers, "Why Is a Popular Interfaith Website Giving a Disgraced Misogynistic Pastor a Platform?," *Washington Post*, October 20, 2017, washingtonpost.com/news/acts-of-faith/wp/2017/10/20/why-is-a-popular-interfaith-website-giving-a-disgraced-misogynistic-pastor-a-platform/.

62. For examples, see Leon Podle, *The Church Impotent: The Feminization of Christianity* (Dallas: Spence, 1999), and David Murrow's *Why Men Hate Going to Church*, 2nd ed. (Nashville, TN: Thomas Nelson, 2011).

63. Elizabeth Brueing, "The Failure of Macho Christianity," *New Republic*, February 24, 2015, newrepublic.com/article/121138/mark-driscoll-and-macho-christianity. For a recent academic analysis, see Jessica Johnson, *Biblical Porn: Affect, Labor, and Pastor Mark Driscoll's Evangelical Empire* (Durham: Duke University Press, 2018).

and to admit that they fall so far short of divine reality that they threaten to lead us astray in crucial ways.

As long as the dominant Christian church is patriarchal and misogynistic, women in particular (though also some men) will look at it and know innately that is not the true church, and that it cannot meet the needs with which their Creator created them. Only a church that recognizes and worships a God who is beyond human male and female identity is the true and fulfilling church. But we cannot avoid gendered imagery, so we must instead embrace it in all its forms, feminine as well as masculine. As Elizabeth A. Johnson put it in her influential book *She Who Is*, it is necessary to affirm feminine metaphors for God "if speech about God is to shake off the shackles of idolatry and be a blessing for women."[64]

A God beyond human gender can still be imagined in terms of gendered humans, without any rejection of tradition, as long as those images or metaphors are not reified. As such, the nursing God is as valid as any other biblical image, and it has the potential for great good. As Davina Haskell observed, it "construct[s] an emotionally positive relationship of nurture and reliance between God and human beings" and "establishes an intimate, familial bond between divinity and humanity, redefining the relationship between the two in terms of tenderness, rather than dominion."[65] As the Bible testifies, this is part of God's identity.

Efforts to discourage and stamp out goddess worship are at best useless, and at worst harmful. Christians who attempt this are already conformed to the patriarchy of this world, and they can be transformed, as Paul said, only by the renewing of their own minds. The battle that has long been waged outward against the culture must be turned inward if it is to succeed—turned toward the long self-inquiry and self-analysis required to root out the ways in which the church continues to push people away from the God of the Bible, who offers his nurturing breast to all. The resources of the tradition are rich in this area. Using feminine language and imagery for God in worship is a starting point that can create fruitful discomfort and invite worshipers to ask hard questions about God and gender that lead to good conversations.

---

64. Elizabeth A. Johnson, *She Who Is: The Mystery of God in Feminist Theological Discourse*, 10th anniversary ed. (New York: Crossroad, 2002), 243.

65. Haskell, *Suckling*, 3.

CHAPTER 13

Bulls and Horses, Gods and Goddesses: The Religious Iconography of Israel's Neighbors

P. M. Michèle Daviau

Our understanding of animal figurines and statues from archaeological excavations has a tortuous history. First identified as discarded toys,[1] zoomorphic ceramic figurines were later reevaluated when found in association with female figurines[2] and attached to cultic stands. Similar images were depicted on stelae, leading us to wonder whether there was more to these figures than what meets the eye. Are they related to religious beliefs and practices? What changes occurred during the Late Iron Age that resulted in the increased importance of animal iconography? Do these figures represent attribute animals for individual deities? Can this approach also be used to better understand comparable iconography in Israel and Judah?

Four animals appear to have been important in the southern Levant: primarily bulls and horses, and secondarily lions and rams. Serpents and birds were of less importance. In order to appreciate the meaning of these animals and their iconography and to understand the use of religious imagery, we will first examine depictions of deities and their sacred animals from Anatolia, Syria, and Egypt. Secondly, we will evaluate the influence that these cultures had on the peoples of the southern Levant and consider the material evidence from sites in Jordan in order to better identify figurines found in Iron Age towns. In this study, the focus will be on bulls and horses, by far the most numerous figures found in Transjordan.

---

1. William F. Albright, *The Iron Age*, vol. 3 of *The Excavation of Tell Beit Mirsim*, Annual of the American Schools of Oriental Research 21–22 (New Haven, CT: American Schools of Oriental Research, 1943), 8.
2. James B. Pritchard, *Gibeon Where the Sun Stood Still: The Discovery of the Biblical City* (Princeton: Princeton University Press, 1962), 121–22, figs. 88–89; Nelson Glueck, *The Other Side of the Jordan* (Cambridge, MA: American Schools of Oriental Research, 1970), 188, figs. 95–98; Grace M. Crowfoot and Eliezer L. Sukenik, "Israelite Figurines," in *The Objects from Samaria: Samaria III*, ed. John W. Crowfoot, Grace M. Crowfoot, and Kathleen M. Kenyon, Samaria-Sebaste [Reports of the Work of the Joint Expedition in 1931–1933 and of the British Expedition in 1935] 3 (London: Palestine Exploration Fund, 1957), 78.

Religious Imagery in the Near East

The dominant iconographic influences throughout the Levant come from the Late Bronze Age superpowers, Hatti and Egypt. In the Hittite depiction of deities in Chamber A at the sanctuary of Yazilikaya, Hepat, the sun goddess of Arinna, stands on a lion and faces the Hurrian storm god, Teshub (see fig. 13.1*a*). This male deity stands on mountain gods and, like the sun goddess, is flanked by a bull wearing the divine crown. Along with these great gods, we also see lesser deities, including their son (Sharruma?), who stands on a lion, and two goddesses who hover above a two-headed eagle.[3] In Chamber B, the Sword God is blended with symbol-rich animals: lion heads sprout from his shoulders and lion bodies encase his body on both sides (see fig. 13.1*b*).[4] The importance of full animal representation of the deity appears in a relief at the Hittite site of Alaca Höyük, where the king and queen are shown standing before an altar and worshiping a deity in the form of a bull standing on top of his temple.[5]

The Iron Age peoples of eastern Anatolia and northern Syria, the Urartians, Neo-Hittites, and Aramaeans, continued certain Hittite iconographic traditions. The association of deities with their supporting animals is seen at Adilcevaz, where a 3.5-meter-tall basalt relief depicts the Urartian deity Teisheba standing on a bull (see fig. 13.1*c*),[6] while on another relief, the deity is shown twice, winged and standing on a lion.[7] In the minor arts, the god Haldi standing on a lion and Teisheba on a bull are engraved on a bonze belt from Karmir Blur-Teishebaini.[8] In another medium, recumbent creatures with bovine and leonine features support horned anthropomorphic figures (semi-divine?), possibly forming the legs of a bronze Urartian chair or throne.[9]

The same combination of powerful animal symbols is seen at Carchemish, where a large basalt statue depicts a deity seated on a throne supported by flanking lions and fronted by a lesser deity with both human and animal attributes (see fig. 13.2*a*).[10] This combination of features is seen in stone-carved reliefs, especially those of a sphinx or cherub with leonine and human heads

---

3. Martha S. Joukowsky, *Early Turkey: An Introduction to the Archaeology of Anatolia from Prehistory through the Lydian Period* (Dubuque, IA: Kendall/Hunt, 1996), 283, fig. 7.40; Maurice Vieyra, *Hittite Art 2300–750 B.C.*, Chapters in Art (London: Alec Tiranti, 1955), pl. 20.

4. Joukowsky, *Early Turkey*, 283, fig. 7.46.

5. Trudy S. Kawami and John Olbrantz, *Breath of Heaven, Breath of Earth: Ancient Near Eastern Art from American Collections* (Seattle: University of Washington Press, 2013), fig. 4.7.

6. Boris B. Piotrovskii, *Urartu: The Kingdom of Van and its Art,* trans. P. S. Gelling (London: Evelyn Adams & Mackay, 1967), fig. 44.

7. Joukowsky, *Early Turkey*, fig. 9.5.

8. Piotrovskii, *Urartu*, fig. 31

9. Ibid., figs. 17 and 18.

10. Vieyra, *Hittite Art*, pl. 37.

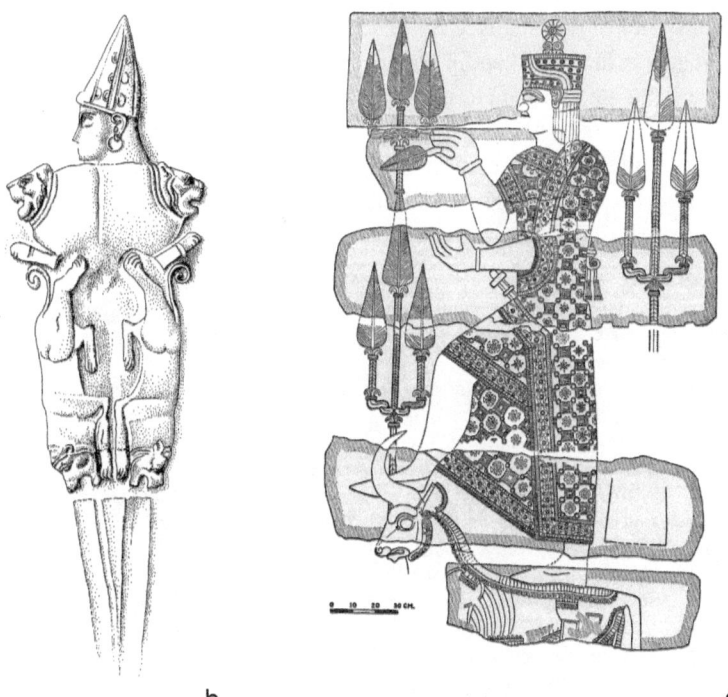

FIGURE 13.1 (a) After Martha S. Joukowsky, *Early Turkey: An Introduction to the Archaeology of Anatolia from Prehistory through the Lydian Period* (Dubuque, IA: Kendall/Hunt, 1996), fig. 7.40. Drawing by Jean Blackburn, used with permission. (b) After Joukowsky, *Early Turkey*, fig. 7.46. Drawing by Jean Blackburn, used with permission. (c) Adapted from reproduction of stone image of Urartian god Teisheba on the bull. Van Museum, Turkey, public domain.

(see fig. 13.2b)[11] and bird-headed, semidivine male figures. The combination of anthropomorphic and zoomorphic features is seen on reliefs and monuments across southeastern Anatolia, including the processional way at Karatepe with its combination of regional, Phoenician, and Assyrian styles.[12]

Along with a relief of an elongated lion supporting two deities at Carchemish,[13] the most impressive examples of deities standing on their attribute animals in northern Syria are from the temple at Tall Ḥalaf (ancient Guzana), where the storm god stands on his bull.[14] Composite figures are also seen here, as well as on the facade of the temple of ʿAin Dara[15] and on reliefs in the temple of the storm god at Aleppo.

Probably of greater importance for the southern Levant is Egyptian iconography in which gods and goddesses were known to manifest themselves first in human form, second in human form with zoomorphic features, and third in animal form. This can be seen easily in the Late Bronze Age representations of the goddess Hathor, who is shown in the Luxor Museum as a seated female with symbols of her divine status: a sun disc framed by bull's horns on her head and an ankh sign in her right hand.[16] Hathor is represented with the same symbols in a wall relief in the tomb of Horemheb, while the face of Hathor with bovine ears crowns the pillars in her shrine at the mortuary temple of Hatshepsut at Deir el-Bahari.[17] She is also shown in her complete bovine form in a gold-covered statue from the tomb of King Tutankhamun.[18] Less frequently, the goddess

---

11. Joukowsky, *Early Turkey*, figs. 8.13–8.15; Vieyra *Hittite Art*, pl. 44.

12. Irene Winter, "On the Problems of Karatepe: The Reliefs and Their Context," *Anatolian Studies* 29 (1979): 115–51, pl. XVIIa.

13. Vieyra, *Hittite Art*, pl. 49.

14. Nadja Cholidis and Lutz Martin, *Die geretteten Götter aus dem Palast vom Tell Halaf* (Berlin: Schnell & Steiner GmbH, 2011), fig. 11.

15. Ali Abou Assaf, *The Temple of ʿAin Dara*, Syrian Site Tourism Pamphlet (Damascus, n.d.), fig. 14; Assaf, *Der Tempel von ʿAin Dara*, Damaszener Forschungen 3 (Mainz am Rhein: Zabern, 1990). Bird-headed and scorpion-bodied figures serve as capitals and column bases at several neo-Hittite and Aramaean sites. See Cholidis and Martin, *Die geretteten Götter*, figs. 12, 19; M. Wahid Khayyata, *Museum Guide*, trans. Mohammad Muslim and Dorothy Stehle (Aleppo: National Museum of Aleppo, 1991); Kay Kohlmeyer, "The Temple of the Storm God in Aleppo during the Late Bronze and Early Iron Ages," *Near Eastern Archaeology* 72 (2009): 190–202, at 199.

16. Alessandro Bongioanni, *Luxor and the Valley of the Kings*, trans. Amy C. Ezrin, Treasures of Ancient Egypt (Cairo: American University in Cairo Press, 2004), fig. 33.

17. Hathor is also seen on a stele with Ptah in the temple of Ptah at Karnak (Elizabeth Frood, "Egyptian Temple Graffiti and the Gods: Appropriation and Ritualization in Karnak and Luxor," in *Heaven On Earth: Temples, Ritual, and Cosmic Symbolism In The Ancient World*, ed. Deena Ragavan, Oriental Institute Seminars 9 [Chicago: Oriental Institute of the University of Chicago, 2013], fig. 13.14; Bongioanni, *Luxor and the Valley of the Kings*, figs. 31 and 112).

18. A schist statue of the scribe Psamtek and his protector Hathor in her bovine form comes from the Late Period (Twenty-sixth Dynasty) at Saqarra (Zahi Hawass, *Tutankhamun: The Golden King and the Great Pharaohs* [Washington, DC: National Geographic, 2008], 74; Bongioanni, *Luxor and the Valley of the Kings*, fig. 31).

FIGURE 13.2 (a) After Joukowsky, *Early Turkey*, fig. 8.13. Drawing by Jean Blackburn, used with permission. (b) After Joukowsky, *Early Turkey*, fig. 8.14. Drawing by Jean Blackburn, used with permission.

appears as a female figure with a complete bovine head. Thus, the iconography of the deity is variable,[19] but it is the goddess who is divine.

Close links between a deity and his or her attribute animal were applied to Canaanite deities, who were introduced into the Egyptian pantheon during the Eighteenth Dynasty and adopted in the Nile delta as special pharaonic protectors during the Ramesside period. This included Reshef, a warrior god represented both in anthropomorphic form and in his bull figure. In addition, three female goddesses were adopted, including Anat, who appears as a warrior goddess carrying weapons and wearing an *atef* crown. Another goddess, Qudshsu/Qedeshet, is named on stone-carved reliefs where she appears naked standing on a lion,[20] while Astarte is shown on several reliefs as a warrior goddess riding naked on a horse.[21] The Egyptian depictions are of great value, thanks to the inscriptions that accompany them, naming the deity and illustrating his or her characteristics. Although Egyptian culture was influential in Canaan in the Late Bronze and Early Iron Ages and appears to have been reflected in the religious imagery of the small kingdoms of Israel and Judah in the ninth through seventh centuries, the iconography in these kingdoms is mute. We can only guess at the meaning and identification of anthropomorphic and zoomorphic images. This limitation is seen in attempts to understand the figures on the Taʿanach stand that include equids, caprids, felines, and hybrid forms.[22] The same is true of the cultic stands from Beth-shean, one of which was adorned with serpents and birds, and the other with a serpent and a human figure. Female figures in Canaanite metalwork also depict a divine figure on an animal, such as the gold plaque from Tel Lachish depicting a naked female deity standing on a horse and holding lotus blossoms[23] and, in the Walters Art Museum, a gold pendant frame in the form of a seated female warrior (Astarte?) on her horse.[24] In all of these examples, the

---

19. Erik Hornung, *Conceptions of God in Ancient Egypt*, trans. John Baines (Ithaca: Cornell University Press, 1982), 110.

20. Already in the Old Bablyonian Period, Ištar the warrior was depicted standing on two opposing lions (Kawami and Olbrantz, *Breath of Heaven*, pl. 9).

21. Izak Cornelius, *The Many Faces of the Goddess: The Iconography of the Syro-Palestinian Goddesses Anat, Astarte, Qedeshet, and Asherah c. 1500–1000 BCE*, OBO 204 (Fribourg: Academic Press; Göttingen: Vandenhoeck & Ruprecht, 2004), pl. 4.4.

22. Brian R. Doak, *Phoenician Aniconism in its Mediterranean and Ancient Near Eastern Contexts*, ABS 21 (Atlanta: Society of Biblical Literature Press, 2015), 129–31.

23. Crista Clamer, "The Pottery and Artifacts from the Level VI Temple in Area P," in *The Renewed Archaeological Excavations at Lachish (1973–1994)*, ed. David Ussishkin, Sonia and Marco Nadler Institute of Archaeology Monograph Series 22 (Tel Aviv: Emery and Claire Yass Publications in Archaeology, 2004), 1314–20, notes the assimilation of the Canaanite goddess Qudshu with Astarte, based on the horse as Astarte's attribute animal (see figs. 21.21:4 and 21.26:1, 2). See also David Ussishkin, "Excavations at Tel Lachish–1973–1977, Preliminary Report," *Tel Aviv* 5 (1978): 1–97, at 21, pl. 8.

24. Kawami and Olbrantz, *Breath of Heaven*, pl. 17.

primary iconographic representation of deities is anthropomorphic with attribute animals playing a supporting role.

Closer to ancient Israel and Judah are its neighbors in Transjordan: Gilead and the northern Jordan Valley, Ammon, Moab, and Edom. Throughout Transjordan, more than two hundred anthropomorphic figurines and statues have been published, some with clear divine attributes, such as the stone statues of males wearing the *atef* crown of Osiris from the Amman area.[25] These sculptures serve as the model for ceramic and bronze figurines representing the same deity, possibly El.[26] The figurines are concentrated in the region of Amman and surrounding Ammonite sites, with a few examples from the North, such as Tall az-Zira'a near Gadara.[27] One example of a goddess with an *atef* crown, probably Anat, appears on the Balu'a stela from central Moab.[28]

Zoomorphic Imagery in Jordan

When we turn to the zoomorphic and theriomorphic figures found in Jordan, we see the influence of Aramaean/neo-Hittite culture in the iconography of a male deity. Stelae found at Gaziantepe ('Ain Tab) in southeastern Anatolia and from sites in southern Syria near Damascus ('Awas and Tell el-Ash'ari) share similar features with the bull-headed figure on a broken stela from et-Turra in northern Jordan[29] and the well-preserved stela from Bethsaida (see fig. 13.3a).[30]

Bull Imagery: In central Jordan, a ceramic bull statue from the temple at 'Ataruz (see fig. 13.3b)[31] and a leg and body fragment from an animal statue or zoomorphic vessel found at shrine WT-13[32] appear to represent a powerful

25. Ali Abou Assaf, "Untersuchungen zur Ammonitischen Rundbildkunst," *UF* 12 (1980): 7–102.
26. P. M. Michèle Daviau and Paul E. Dion, "El, the God of the Ammonites? The *atef*-crowned Head from Tell Jawa, Jordan," *ZDPV* 110 (1994): 158–67.
27. Dieter Vieweger and Jutta Häser, "The Tall Zar'a and the Gadara Region Project in the years 2007 and 2008," *ADAJ* 52 (2008): 375–95, at 389 (fig. 17).
28. Piotr Bienkowski, *Treasures from an Ancient Land: The Art of Jordan* (Merseyside, UK: National Museums and Galleries on Merseyside, 1991), 35.
29. For a detailed study of these stelae, see Stefan J. Wimmer and Khaled Janaydeh, "Eine Mondgottstele aus *et-Turra* / Jordanien," *ZDPV* 127 (2011): 135–41, fig. 5.
30. Monika Bernett and Othmar Keel, *Mond, Stier und Kult am Stadttor: die Stele von Betsaida (et-Tell)*, OBO 161 (Fribourg: Academic Press; Göttingen: Vandenhoeck & Ruprecht, 1998).
31. Chang-Ho Ji, "The Early Iron Age II Temple at Ḥirbet 'Atārūs and Its Architecture and Selected Cultic Objects," in *Temple Building and Temple Cult: Architecture and Cultic Paraphernalia of Temples in the Levant (2.–1. Mill. B.C.E.) on the Occasion of the 50th Anniversary of the Institute of Biblical Archaeology at Tübingen University*, ed. Jens Kamlah, Abhandlungen des Deutschen Palästinavereins 41 (Wiesbaden: Harrassowitz, 2012), 211.
32. P. M. Michèle Daviau, *A Wayside Shrine in Northern Moab: Excavations in the Wadi ath-Thamad*, ed. P. M. Michèle Daviau and Margreet Steiner, Wadi ath-Thamad Project I (Oxford: Oxbow, 2017), fig. 5.2:6.

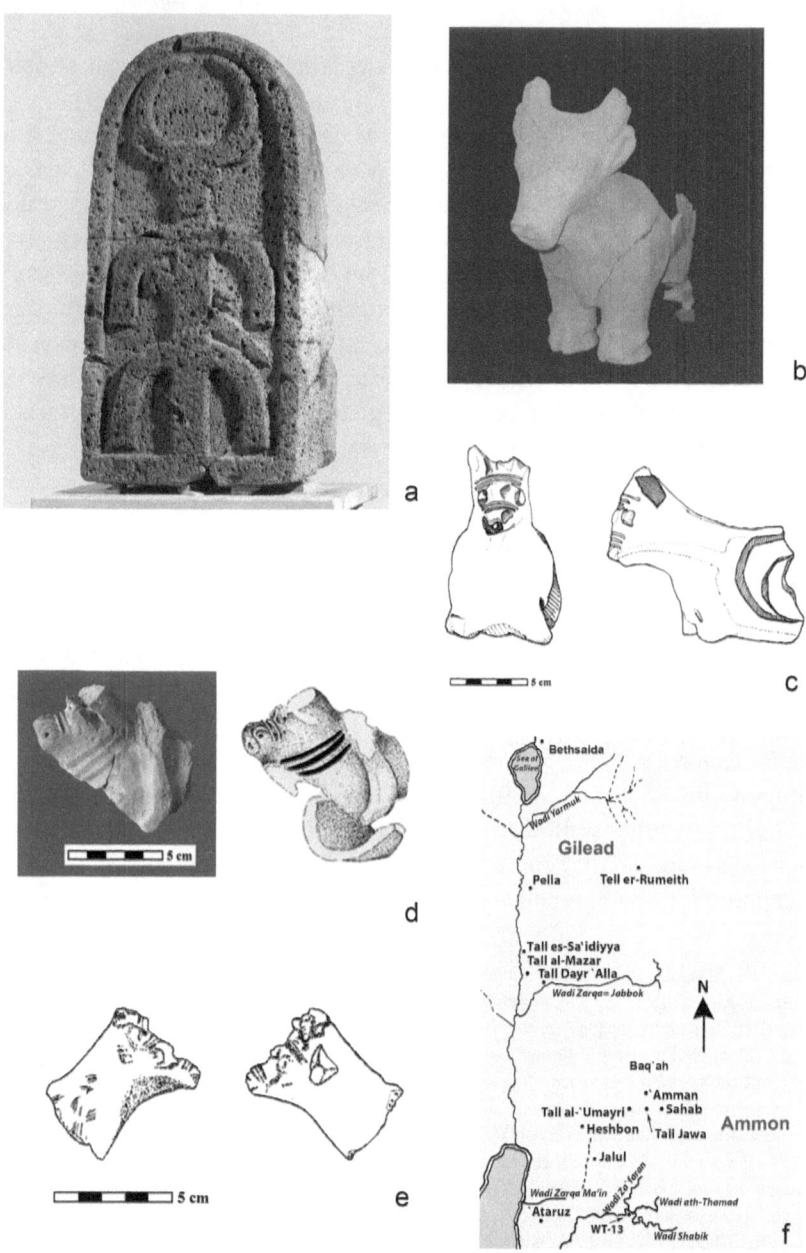

FIGURE 13.3. (a) Photo provided by Rami Arav, used with permission. (b) Photo by the author, courtesy of the Madaba Museum, Jordan. (c) After Nancy L. Lapp, "The Iron Age Figurines," in Tristan J. Barako and Nancy L. Lapp, *Tell er-Rumeith. The Excavations of Paul W. Lapp, 1962 and 1967*, American Schools of Oriental Research Archaeological Reports 22 (Boston: American Schools of Oriental Research, 2015), fig. 9.3:1, used with permission. (d–e) After P. M. Michèle Daviau, *The Iron Age Artifacts*, vol. 2 of *Excavations at Tall Jawa, Jordan*, CHANE 11/2 (Leiden: Brill, 2002), figs. 2.39:1 and 2.37:1.

male deity. The importance of bull iconography is also seen in the presence of small ceramic figurines and vessels in domestic contexts in both the northern and central sectors of Jordan, notably at Tell er-Rumeith (see fig. 13.3c), Tall Abu Kharaz,[33] Tall Dayr 'Alla, 'Amman, and Tall Jawa, where a bull-shaped vessel was recovered along with four bull figurine fragments (total of five; see fig. 13.3d–e).[34] Additional representations appear in relief on a palette from Tall Irbid,[35] on a krater from Tall Dayr 'Alla, and on a storejar from 'Ataruz, whereas a bronze bull head attachment comes from the 'Amman Citadel (AC 37).[36] Thus the distribution is concentrated in the northern half of Jordan with no known bull imagery south of 'Ataruz. This may reflect influence derived from the Aramaean expansion in the ninth century mentioned in the Tel Dan Inscription.

Horse Imagery: Horse figurines have an unusual geographical distribution, with their heaviest concentrations at Mudayna Thamad in northern Moab and, to the west, in Jerusalem.[37] The horse is distinguished from the bull by its long, nearly upright neck, a mane and forelock, and an elongated muzzle.[38] Riderless horses are represented either with or without a bridle (see fig. 13.4a–e). These ceramic figurines come from a variety of archaeological contexts: domestic, cultic, and disposal. Yet it is clear that they were meaningful to their owners and had been made with care by ceramic specialists. Although their concentration is in central Jordan, horse figurines are found as far north as Pella in the Jordan Valley and as far south as Tawilan in Edom. There is also a small concentration at Tall Dayr 'Alla, a site that had an important temple in the Late Bronze Age, and where the Iron Age Balaam inscription was located.

33. Teresa Bürge, "Appendix 1: Figurines," in Peter M. Fischer, *The Iron Age*, vol. 3 of *Tell Abu Al-Kharaz in the Jordan Valley*, Österreichische Akademie der Wissenschaften / Contributions to the Chronology of the Eastern Mediterranean 34 (Vienna: Verlag der Österreichische Akademie der Wissenschaften, 2013), fig. 462:3.

34. P. M. Michèle Daviau, *The Iron Age Artifacts*, vol. 2 of *Excavations at Tall Jawa, Jordan*, CHANE 11/2 (Leiden: Brill, 2002), figs. 2.37:1 and 2.39:1–4.

35. Four zoomorphic figures are carved around the rim of this small ivory bowl or palette from the "Ivory Tomb" in Irbid. The animals were initially identified as lions, but since each one appears to have horns and bovine hoofs (Peter M. Fischer, Teresa B. Urge, and Mohammad A. al-Shalabi, "The 'Ivory Tomb' at Tell Irbid, Jordan: Intercultural Relations at the end of the Late Bronze and the Beginning of the Iron Age," *BASOR* 374 [2015]: 209–32, fig. 6, back cover), these attachments are included here among bull figures.

36. Fawzi Zayadine, "Recent Excavations on the Citadel of 'Amman," *ADAJ* 18 (1973):17–35, pl. XIV:1.

37. Zoomorphic figurines were also common in Israel and Judah. For example, seventy zoomorphic figurines found at Gibeon in the water system were in secondary deposition and cannot be assigned with certainty to the Iron Age (James Pritchard, *The Water System of Gibeon* [Philadelphia: University of Pennsylvania Press, 1961], 17, figs. 42–45; Pritchard, *Gibeon Where the Sun Stood Still*, 121–22, fig. 89). Although a few resemble horses, many fragments cannot be identified.

38. For a detailed list of criteria, see Zeran in P. M. Michèle Daviau and Emily Zeran, "Astarte on Her Horse at Khirbat al-Mudayna in Northern Moab," in *Iron Age Terracotta Figurines from the Southern Levant*, ed. Erin Darby and Izaak J. de Hulster, CHANE (Leiden: Brill, forthcoming).

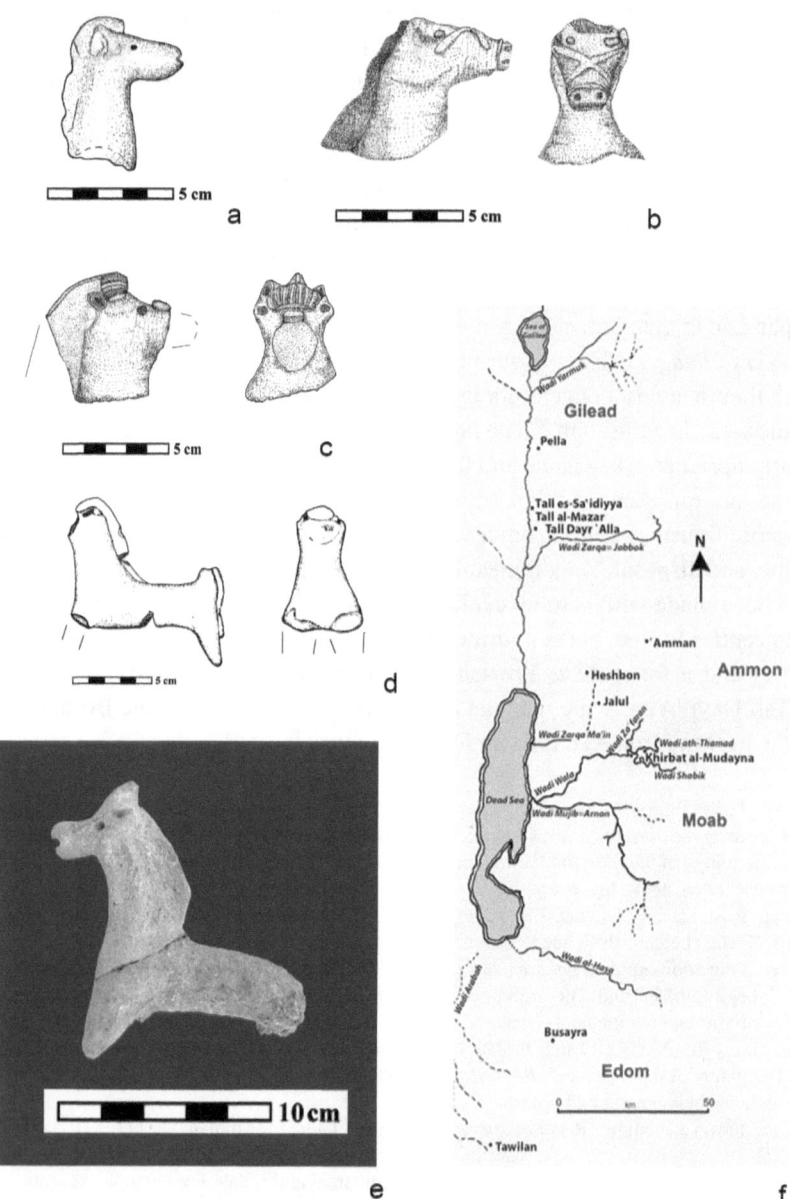

FIGURE 13.4. (a–e) Khirbat al-Mudayna Project. From P. M. Michèle Daviau and Emily Zeran, "Astarte on Her Horse at Khirbat al-Mudayna in Northern Moab," in *Iron Age Terracotta Figurines from the Southern Levant*, ed. Erin Darby and Izaak J. de Hulster, CHANE (Leiden: Brill, forthcoming).

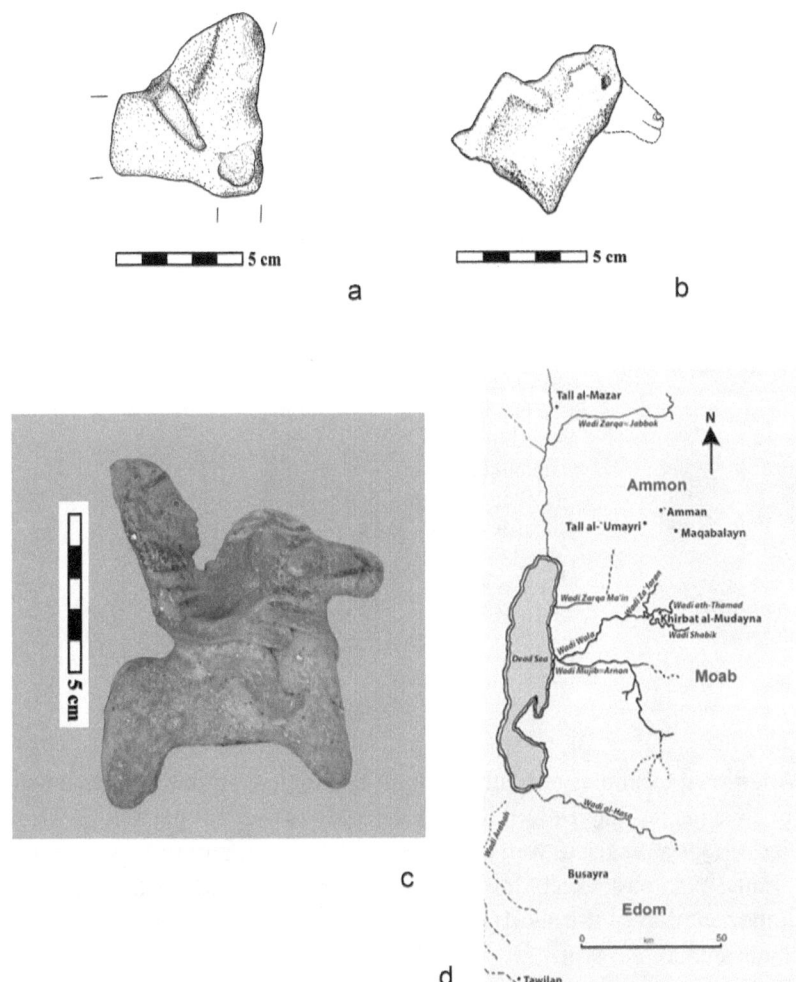

FIGURE 13.5. (a–b) Khirbat al-Mudayna Project. From Daviau and Zeran, "Astarte." (c) Photo provided by E. van der Steen and Khair Yassine, used with permission.

Horse-and-rider figurines are an interesting combination of anthropomorphic and zoomorphic figures. Such figurines cluster in the Ammonite area at Tell el-Mazar (fig. 13.5a), 'Amman, Maqabalayn, and Tall al-'Umayri, one each at the Edomite sites of Busayra and Tawilan, and eight fragments, nearly 50 percent of the corpus, at Mudayna Thamad in Moab (fig. 13.5a–b).[39]

39. These numbers vary from Thomas Holland, "A Study of Palestinian Iron Age Baked Clay Figurines, with Special Reference to Jerusalem: Cave I," *Levant* 9 (1977): 121–55, since we have clear evidence that horse-only figurines are just that and need to be understood in their own right, not

TABLE 13.1. Number of Bull Figurines and Images by Site

Site	Number
Bethsaida	1
Tall Irbid	1
Tall Rumeith	3
Pella	1
Tall as-Sa'idiyya	2
Tall Dayr 'Alla	5
Tell el-Mazar	1
Baqah tomb	1
'Amman	4
Sahab-Tombs	2
Tall Jawa	5
Tall al-'Umayri	2
Hesban and area	2
'Atarus	2
WT-13	1
Unknown	1
eṭ-Ṭurra	1
Total	**35**

Additional examples of figurines, figurine moulds, protomai/attachements, kernos elements, images in relief on ceramic vessels and painted on plaster depict various animals, as well as sphinxes. These zoomorphic images occur as individual examples, except for caprids and lions; as we saw earlier, lions were an important part of the neo-Hittite/Aramaean iconography and appear as an attribute animal in Egypt.

Religions of Jordan: We are now left with questions that ancient peoples did not have: who produced these artifacts? What did these figurines represent? How were they used? Did they represent tribal or ethnic, political, or religious groups? In this presentation, the focus is on two of these questions: what did they represent, and how were they used? The raw numbers tell us that horses by far dominate the repertoire, with 180 examples. This number does not include the eighty-six fragments mostly attributed to horse figurines or the horse-and-rider

---

as incomplete examples of the horse-and-rider type. His article was republished in Thomas A. Holland, "A Study of Palestinian Iron Age Baked Clay Figurines, with Special Reference to Jerusalem: Cave I," in *The Iron Age Cave Deposits on the South-east Hill and Isolated Burials and Cemeteries Elsewhere*, vol 4 in *Excavations by K. M. Kenyon in Jerusalem 1961–1967*, ed. I. Eshel and K. Prag, British Academy Monographs in Archaeology (Oxford: Oxford University Press, 1995), 159–89.

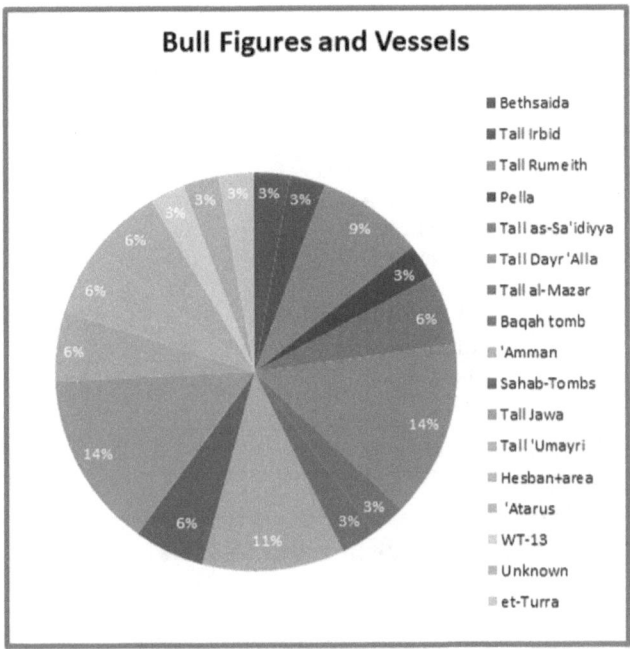

CHART 13.1. Distribution of Bull Figurines and Vessels in Jordan.

figures that add to these numbers. While bulls are many fewer in number,[40] they sometimes dominate the corpus at a given site, such as Tall Jawa, where no horse figurines were identified.

Distribution of Bull Iconography (see fig. 13.3*f*): When we look at the distribution of these zoomorphic figures, we can see that bull imagery is located at sites north of the Wadi Mujib/Arnon (table 13.1; chart 13.1). This is of interest given the presence of bulls in the iconography of the Aramaean/neo-Hittite sites to the north and at certain sites in Israel, along with the spreading influence and control of Assyria with its human-headed guardian bull statues. Reference to a powerful male deity, Bull El in Ugaritic literature,[41] suggests that the dominant cultural influence in the Late Bronze and Early Iron Ages was from the north. Also of importance was the figure of the bull in Egyptian religion, where it was also a representative of power, protection, and fertility from as early as the predynastic period, culminating in the Apis bull, the animal of Ptah of the beautiful

---

40. The numbers in tables 13.1–3 reflect a restudy of many previously published figurines but remain tentative due to continuing excavation at many Iron Age sites in Jordan. References for individual figurines, statues, and stelae are included online with the appendix.

41. Marvin H. Pope, *El in the Ugaritic Texts*, VTSup 2 (Leiden: Brill, 1955), 35–37.

TABLE 13.2. Number of Horse Figurines by Site

Site	Number
Pella	1
Tall as-Sa'idiyya	2
Tall Dayr 'Alla	23
Tell el-Mazar	3
'Amman	10
Hesban	5
Mudayna Thamad	123
Busayra	18
Tawilan	1
Jalul	3
Total	**189**

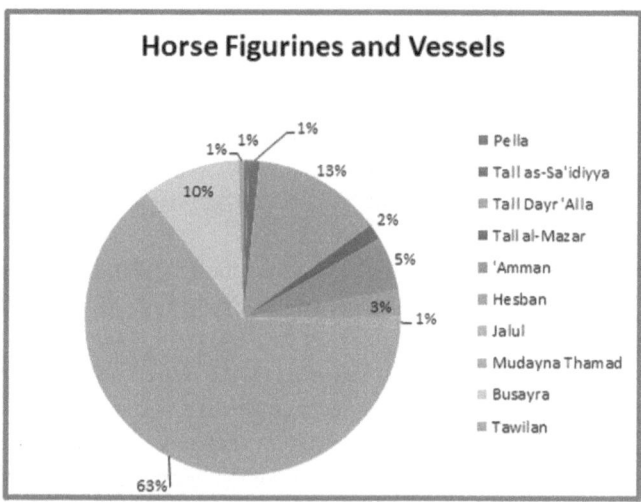

CHART 13.2. Horse Figurines and Vessels.

face. The discovery of bronze bull figures in Canaan emphasizes the importance of this animal in all levels of cultic practice.

Distribution of Horse Iconography (see fig. 13.4*f*): The presence of horse figurines overlaps that of bull figures but is more extensive, being found throughout the country (table 13.2; chart 13.2). At the same time, the heaviest concentration is at Mudayna Thamad in northern Moab (123 clearly recognizable horses, plus 55 legs). The same is true for the kingdoms west of the Jordan, where horses are found in small numbers at numerous sites from Hazor in the north to Beer-sheba in the south, with the greatest number at Jerusalem (574 clearly recognizable

TABLE 13.3. Number of Horse-and-Rider Figurines by Site

Site	Number
Maqabalayn	2
Tall el-Mazar	1
ʻAmman	4
Tall Umayri	1
Mudayna Thamad	10
Busayra	1
Tawilan	1
Total	**20**

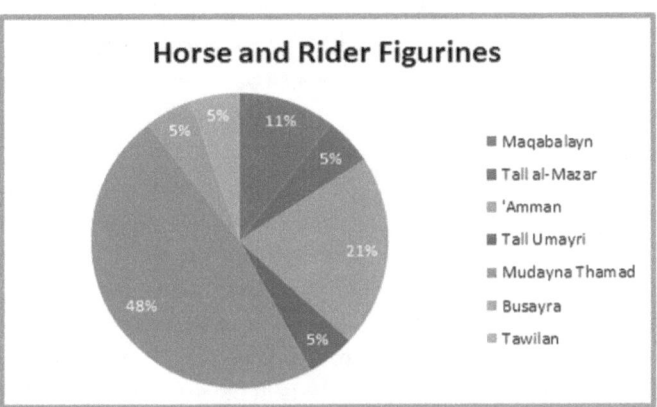

CHART 13.3. Distribution of Iron Age Horse and Rider Figurines.

figurines and 100 legs).[42] Mudayna Thamad is one of only three sites in Jordan where an Iron Age temple has been excavated, but it is not clear that the horse figurines were directly related to worship in the temple, since they were also found in other contexts.

Distribution of Horse-and-Rider Iconography (see fig. 13.5d): Horse-and-rider figures are few in number during the Iron Age (table 13.3; chart 13.3), becoming more numerous in the Persian Period. What is not clear at this stage is whether the figurines from the fifth and fourth centuries had a meaning and a function different from those of figurines from Iron Age contexts.

Function: Although the number of animal figurines in Transjordan is less than one fourth that of the corpus from Israel and Judah, the function of all of

---

42. Daviau and Zeran, "Astarte on Her Horse." The number of clearly recognizable horse figurines from Jerusalem is based on Zeran's criteria.

these figurines is most likely the same. They represent the attribute animals of major deities known throughout Syria, the Levant, and Egypt and were essential components of religious practice. Prior to the publication of town sites in central Jordan, Walter Aufrecht could claim: "There is no single known text in which they (the Ammonites) directly communicate their system of beliefs, and there is no single known artifact or feature in an Iron Age archaeological context that clearly and exclusively can be associated with the practice of religion."[43] At the same time, Aufrecht acknowledges that anthropomorphic and zoomorphic iconography reflects Ammonite religion, especially the anthropomorphic statues and figurines that represent El, and that the zoomorphic figurines may be a reflection of the beliefs, if not the practices, of these people. Ammonite personal names include two dozen divine names, among which El is dominant, with fewer occurrences of Anat, Astarte, Baal, and Milkom. In Canaanite religion, the bull was the attribute animal of El,[44] but it was adapted in Egypt as the animal of Reshef and such adaption may also be the case in Ammonite religion for Milkom.

The deities important to the Moabites are better known, thanks to the Mesha Inscription of the ninth century. The principal deity was Chemosh (or Kamish, as vocalized in the Ebla texts).[45] Controversy continues regarding a second deity mentioned in the Mesha Inscription, Ashtar-Chemosh, who is sometimes identified as the consort of Chemosh (possibly Astarte) or as another name for the male deity. Rüdiger Schmitt notes that Astarte was already known in Ugaritic texts to be related to horses as a huntress and warrior,[46] although she was then second in importance to her sister Anat. It is in the first millennium that Astarte becomes prominent as a goddess associated with kingship. In the ninth century, the status of the king of Tyre as the reflection of the god Melqart points to the link between deity and monarchy in Tyre[47] and as the power behind the trade networks of the Phoenicians in the Mediterranean (see oracles against Tyre in Isa 23 and Ezek 26–27). Astarte, the consort of Melqart, was also the lady of Sidon, and the king was her high priest. She was still considered a warrior goddess by Esarhaddon (680–669) in the text of his treaty with Baal of Tyre.[48] With

43. Walter E. Aufrecht, "The Religion of the Ammonites," in *Ancient Ammon*, ed. Burton MacDonald and Randall W. Younker, CHANE 17 (Leiden: Brill, 1999), 152–62, at 152.

44. Helmer Ringgren, *Israelite Religion*, trans. D. E. Green (Philadelphia: Fortress, 1966), 21.

45. Gerald L. Mattingly, "Moabite Religion and the Mesha' Inscription," in *Studies in the Mesha Inscription and Moab*, ed. Andrew Dearman, ABS 2 (Atlanta: Scholars Press, 1989), 211–38, at 217.

46. Rüdiger Schmitt, "Astarte, Mistress of Horses, Lady of the Chariot: The Warrior Aspect of Astarte," *Die Welt des Orients* 43 (2013): 213–25, at 216.

47. Maria E. Aubet, *The Phoenicians and the West: Politics, Colonies and Trade*, trans. M. Turton (Cambridge: Cambridge University Press, 1996), 123–26.

48. Schmitt, "Astarte," 218.

the increase in Egypto-Phoenician cultural influence on Judah and on the small kingdoms in Transjordan during the seventh century *pax Assyriaca*, Egyptian iconography and traditions had an impact on the religion of Moab, which we see in the large number of horse figurines, the attribute animal of Astarte.[49]

For Edom, the evidence is sparse; the principal deity, Qos, is known from inscriptions found in the Negev as well as in the Edomite heartland. However, at this stage in our knowledge, his attribute animal is uncertain, although a bulla inscribed with the name "Qos Gabr melek edom" has a sphinx in the central register.[50]

Zoomorphic figurines uncovered in Transjordan are only one component of the ever increasing amount of iconographic representation of deities. For a fuller understanding of the wide variety of religious beliefs and practices, we need to combine anthropomorphic, zoomorphic, and symbolic elements. Relating these finds to their context, whether it be cultic, domestic, or industrial, will certainly add to our better appreciation of the function of these figurines, as well as of the religious rituals and beliefs of the peoples of Transjordan at a time of expanded contact with Egypt, Phoenicia, and Assyria through travel, trade, and tribute.[51]

Reflections

In this short study, we saw various aspects of zoomorphic iconography in Anatolia, the Levant, and Egypt during the Late Bronze and Iron Ages that include: attribute animals as supports for the deity; animals, both individual and complex, as guardians of the deity; animals as indicators of the presence of the deity; and complex anthropomorphic and zoomorphic representations of the divine. Thus, zoomorphic iconography reflects the embodiment of the features and function of a given deity: strength, speed, violence and destructiveness, and protectiveness and care for his or her people.

The use of iconography was an important aspect of religious belief and practice in Transjordan, where archaeological excavations have yielded 347 animal

---

49. The large number of horse figurines in Jerusalem may correspond to the arrival of Israelites from the north, who brought with them religious practices influenced by Phoenician traditions. The reforms of Manasseh, rebuilding the high places, erecting altars for Baal (Melqart?) and placing an image of Asherah in the temple (2 Kgs 21:3–7) could be seen as an accommodation of the new settlers in northern Judah and Jerusalem. This could also account for the large number of horse figurines, the emblematic animal of Astarte.

50. Peter van der Veen, "The Seal Material," in *Umm al-Biyara: Excavations by Crystal-M. Bennett in Petra 1960–1965*, ed. Piotr Bienkowski, Leipziger semitische Studien 10 (Oxford: Oxbow, 2011), 79–81.

51. P. M. Michèle Daviau and Stanley Klassen, "Conspicuous Consumption and Tribute: Assyrian Glazed Bottles at Khirbat al-Mudayna on Wadi ath-Thamad," *BASOR* 372 (2014): 99–122.

figurines and zoomorphic images (table 13.4; chart 13.4). However, this leaves open the question of religious iconography in Israel and Judah, kingdoms that were an integral part of the broader Levantine culture. While the principal imagery of YHWH in religious texts is anthropomorphic, the importance of anthropomorphic and zoomorphic figurines especially in Judah and its principal cult center at Jerusalem is cause for a renewed investigation of the meaning and function of these artifacts. It is clear that these objects were produced by professional potters, often slipped or painted with the same surface treatment as high-status pottery vessels, and that they were important cultural artifacts that were meaningful to their owners. According to Ephraim Stern, horse-and-rider figurines may represent a Phoenician warrior god and not an ordinary human.[52] Karel van der Toorn suggests that these figurines represent YHWH, while for Othmar Keel and Christoph Uehlinger, they constitute members of the host of heaven.[53] Images of deities from Israelite Samaria and other Levantine sites are depicted on reliefs and mentioned in booty lists by Assyrian kings, suggesting the importance of anthropomorphic statuary at these sites.[54] So too, zoomorphic and anthropomorphic figurines found in Cave I and other areas of Jerusalem indicate their cultic relevance.[55] The varied interpretations of figurines have sparked considerable discussion, but the story remains unfinished as new excavations yield additional examples of previously unknown figurines, vessels, and stelae.

Finally, the description of the house of YHWH in Jerusalem details the features of the holy of holies, an inner room containing two gold-covered olivewood cherubim or sphinxes (1 Kgs 6:23–32), whose wings extend from one wall to the other. This is also the understanding reflected in the vision of Ezekiel, who sees YHWH resting above the cherubim, each of which has four faces: cherub, man, lion, and eagle (Ezek 1:1–14). While YHWH himself may not be depicted, his attribute animals appear as an element of Israelite religion. These references

52. Ephraim Stern, "The Phoenician Source of Palestinian Cults at the End of the Iron Age," in *Symbiosis, Symbolism, and the Power of the Past: Canaan, Ancient Israel, and Their Neighbors from the Late Bronze Age through Roman Palaestina, Proceedings of the Centennial Symposium, W. F. Albright Institute of Archaeological Research and American Schools of Oriental Research, Jerusalem, May 29–31, 2000*, ed. William G. Dever and Seymour Gitin (Winona Lake, IN: Eisenbrauns, 2003), 315; but see Jack Sasson, "On the Use of Images in Israel and the Ancient Near East: A Response to Karel van der Toorn," in *Sacred Time, Sacred Place: Archaeology and the Religion of Israel*, ed. Barry M. Gittlen (Winona Lake, IN: Eisenbrauns, 2002), 63–70.

53. Karel van der Toorn, "Israelite Figurines: A View from the Texts," in Gittlen, *Sacred Time, Sacred Place*, 45–62, at 61; Othmar Keel and Christoph Uehlinger, *Gods, Goddesses, and Images of God in Ancient Israel*, trans. Thomas H. Trapp (Minneapolis: Fortress, 1998), 345.

54. Christoph Uehlinger, "Anthropomorphic Cult Statuary in Iron Age Palestine and the Search for Yahweh's Cult Image," in *The Image and the Book: Iconic Cults, Aniconism, and Rise of Book Religion in Israel and the Ancient Near East*, ed. Karel van der Toorn, Contributions to Biblical Exegesis and Theology 21 (Leuven: Peeters, 1997), 124–27.

55. See Holland, "Study of Palestinian Iron Age Baked Clay Figurines."

TABLE 13.4. Numbers of Types of Zoomorphic Images in Transjordan

Type	Number
Bull	35
Horse	189
Horse-and-Rider	20
Other Animal	17
Fragment	86
Total	347

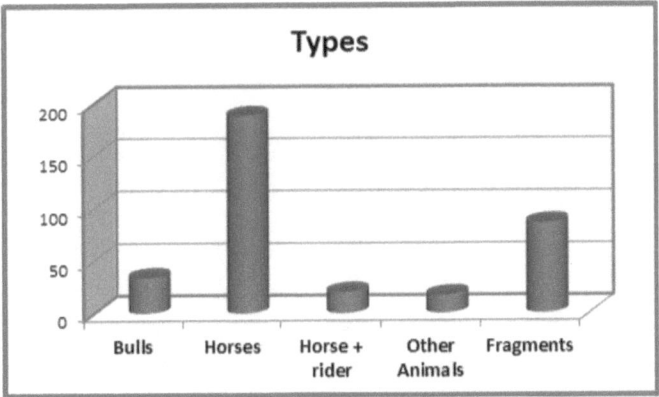

CHART 13.4. Types of Zoomorphic Representation.

evoke the iconography of Canaanite Megiddo, as seen in the ivory inlay that shows a ruler seated on a throne flanked by winged sphinxes.[56] Animal iconography is also mentioned in the description of the Jerusalem temple's walls and doors that were covered in gold with carved cherubim and floral motifs (1 Kgs 6:35). Additional furnishings, such as the panels on large stands, were carved with cherubim, lions, and oxen (1 Kgs 7:27–29). Most notable is the description of the bronze sea supported on the backs of twelve oxen (1 Kgs 7:23–25). The purpose of these zoomorphic creatures is to serve as YHWH's attribute animals, embodying his power and otherworldly being. Although there is no image of the deity, this is not unique to Israel; in the entrances to the temple at 'Ain Dara, sphinxes/cherubim frame the doorways on either side of stone thresholds marked by the oversize footprints (approx.1 meter long) of an invisible deity entering the temple.

56. Gordon Loud, *Megiddo Ivories*, Oriental Institute Publications 52 (Chicago: University of Chicago Press, 1939), pls. 4:2a, 2b.

CONTRIBUTORS

Bob Becking is emeritus senior research professor for Bible, Religion, and Identity at the University of Utrecht. His research focuses on the impact of societal changes on the construction of religious identities in ancient Israel. He was coeditor of the *Dictionary of Deities and Demons in the Bible* (Brill, 1995; 1999) and has authored many books, most recently a commentary on Ezra and Nehemiah for Peeters's Historical Commentary on the Old Testament series (2019). Ordained in the Dutch Reformed Church, he pastored two congregations from 1979 to 1989 before his promotion to professor.

Stephen B. Chapman is associate professor of Old Testament at Duke Divinity School and the director of graduate studies for Duke's PhD program in religion. He is the author of *1 Samuel as Christian Scripture* (Eerdmans, 2016) and *The Law and the Prophets* (Mohr Siebeck, 2000), as well as numerous essays. He coedited *The Cambridge Companion to the Hebrew Bible / Old Testament* (2016) and *Biblischer Text und theologische Theoriebildung* (Vandenhoeck & Ruprecht, 2001). An ordained American Baptist minister, his current project is a book on *The Theology of Joshua* for Cambridge University Press.

Collin Cornell is visiting assistant professor for the School of Theology at Sewanee: The University of the South. His interests include theological interpretation of Scripture, history of religions, and the doctrine of God. He has published articles in *Harvard Theological Review*, *Scottish Journal of Theology*, and *Zeitschrift für die alttestamentliche Wissenschaft*, and his monograph *Divine Aggression in Psalms and Inscriptions: Vengeful Gods and Loyal Kings* is forthcoming in Cambridge University Press's Society of Old Testament Studies series. He is an ordained ruling elder of the Presbyterian Church (USA).

P. M. Michèle Daviau is professor emerita of archaeology and classical studies at Wilfrid Laurier University and a member of the graduate faculty in the department of Near and Middle Eastern civilizations at the University of Toronto. Since 1996, she has been the director and chief archaeologist of the Wadi ath-Thamad project of excavation and survey in the Hashemite Kingdom of Jordan. She has been engaged in publishing the final report volumes concerning Tall Jawa (Jordan), an Iron Age and early Islamic site excavated under her direction (1989–1995). Her recent research concerns sites in the Wadi ath-Thamad survey area that date to the Iron Age (Moabite culture) and the Roman period (Nabatean and Roman settlements and forts). Dr. Daviau has a special interest in religious iconography and in the tools of various crafts and industries.

J. Andrew Dearman is senior professor of Old Testament at Fuller Theological Seminary. In addition to his early work as editor of *Studies in the Mesha Inscription and Moab* (Scholars, 1989), he has written several books, including *Religion and Culture in Ancient Israel* (Hendrickson, 1992), commentaries on Jeremiah and Lamentations (New International Version Application Commentary series, 2002) and Hosea (New International Commentary on the Old Testament, 2010), and a coauthored introduction to the Old Testament (Eerdmans, 2018). He also participated in two Bible translation projects, contributing to The Voice translation (Thomas Nelson) and serving as a translation editor for the Common English Bible (Abingdon). He is ordained as a teaching elder in the Presbyterian Church (USA).

Robert Goldenberg is Professor Emeritus of Judaic Studies at Stony Brook University in New York. He authored *The Nations That Know Thee Not* (New York University Press, 1998) and *The Origins of Judaism* (Cambridge University Press, 2007), and he recently coedited a volume of essays by Rabbi James S. Diamond for Pickwick (2019). He also has served as coeditor of *AJS Review*.

M. Patrick Graham is Margaret A. Pitts Professor of Theological Bibliography emeritus for the Candler School of Theology at Emory University. He has research interests in the interpretation of 1 and 2 Chronicles and the history of Old Testament research. He chairs the Research and Publications Committee of the Society of Biblical Literature and the Endowment Committee of the American Theological Library Association. He is the author of *The Utilization of 1 and 2 Chronicles in the Reconstruction of Israelite History in the Nineteenth Century* (Scholars, 1990) and has edited numerous other works, including several on Chronicles. Before becoming a professor and librarian, he was preaching minister of an Atlanta congregation of the Churches of Christ for several years.

Christopher B. Hays is the D. Wilson Moore Professor of Ancient Near Eastern Studies at Fuller Theological Seminary and served as President of the Society of Biblical Literature's Pacific Coast Region in 2018. He is the author of *The Origins of Isaiah 24–27: Josiah's Festival Scroll for the Fall of Assyria* (Cambridge University Press, 2019) and *Hidden Riches: A Textbook for the Comparative Study of the Old Testament and the Ancient Near East* (Westminster John Knox, 2014). His next projects include *A Handbook of Ugaritic* (Eisenbrauns) and the Isaiah commentary for the Old Testament Library series. Hays received the Manfred Lautenschlaeger Award for this first book, *Death in the Iron Age II and in First Isaiah* (Mohr Siebeck, 2011). He is an ordained teaching elder of the Presbyterian Church (USA).

Othmar Keel is professor emeritus of Old Testament and the biblical world on the Catholic theological faculty of the University of Fribourg. Among many other works, he is author of the two-volume *Die Geschichte Jerusalems und die Entstehung des Monotheismus* (Vandenhoeck & Ruprecht, 2007), as well as *Gods, Goddesses, and Images of God* (Fortress, 1998). He is considered a founder of the discipline of iconographic exegesis, and he was granted the title of honorary doctor by the universities of Bochum, Geneva, and Lund.

Jon D. Levenson is the Albert A. List Professor of Jewish Studies at Harvard Divinity School. He has a strong interest in the philosophical and theological issues involved in biblical studies, especially the comparison of premodern modes of interpretation to modern historical criticism. Much of his work centers on the relationship between Judaism and Christianity. His book *Resurrection and the Restoration of Israel* (Yale University Press, 2006) won a National Jewish Book Award and the Biblical Archaeology Society Publication Award in the category of Best Book Relating to the Hebrew Bible. His latest book is *The Love of God* (Princeton University Press, 2015).

Patrick D. Miller Jr. is Charles T. Haley Professor of Old Testament Theology emeritus at Princeton Theological Seminary. He has published numerous books, including *The Divine Warrior in Early Israel* (Society of Biblical Literature, 1973), *They Cried to the Lord* (Fortress, 2000), and *The Religion of Ancient Israel* (Westminster John Knox, 2007), as well as book-length entries on Deuteronomy and the Psalms. He coedited the Interpretation series for Westminster John Knox and edited the journal *Theology Today* for twenty years. He is ordained as a teaching elder in the Presbyterian Church (USA), and he pastored in South Carolina before transitioning into seminary professorship.

Josey Bridges Snyder received her PhD from Emory University and has published in *Ugarit-Forschungen*, the *Women's Bible Commentary* (3rd ed., Westminster John Knox, 2012), and the *Journal for Study of Pseudepigrapha*. Her research interests include reception criticism, history of religions, and character studies. She now works with the Center for Leadership Excellence in the North Carolina Conference of The United Methodist Church, and she teaches in the United Methodist Course of Study and Deaconess / Home Missioner programs.

Brent A. Strawn is professor of Old Testament and professor of law at Duke University. Prior to joining the faculty there, he was William Ragsdale Cannon Distinguished Professor of Old Testament at the Candler School of Theology and Graduate Division of Religion of Emory University. He specializes in ancient Near Eastern iconography, Israelite religion, legal traditions of the Old Testament, and Old Testament theology. He has edited many works, including *The Oxford Encyclopedia of the Bible and Law* (Oxford University Press, 2015), which won the American Library Association's Dartmouth Medal for Excellence in Reference (2016). His book *The Old Testament is Dying* (Baker, 2017) received a starred review in *Publishers Weekly*. He is an ordained elder in The United Methodist Church.

INDEX OF AUTHORS

Abma, R., 85n25
Ackerman, James S., 24n54
Ahlström, Gösta W., 23n51, 177n46
Ahn, Gregor, 18in1
Alanís, Javier, 102n3, 145n30
Albertz, Rainer, 68, 182n3
Albrektson, Bertil, 174n35, 176–78, 185n17
Albright, William F., 182n2, 203–4, 219n1
Alt, Albrecht, 16–17
Alt, Franz, 55
Alter, Robert, 175
Amir, Yehoshua, 183n6
Amit, Yaira, 72n39
Anderson, Bernhard W., 31n70
Anderson, G.W., 174n35
Anderson, James S., 82n16, 182n3
Anneler, Hedwig, 73n46
Annus, Amar, 140n6
Arav, Rami, 226
Arneth, Martin, 61n4
Arnold, Bill T., 144n28, 192n47
Assaf, Ali Abou, 222n15, 225n25
Assheuer, Thomas, 54n67
Assmann, Jan, 38n20, 54
Aubet, Maria E., 234n47
Aufrecht, Walter E., 234n43

Baines, John, 224n19
Baker, J. A., 133n20, 174n34
Barako, Tristan J., 226
Barr, James, 149n53, 178n50
Bartelmus, Rüdiger, 37n16
Barth, Karl, 11, 110–11, 149n53

Bartholomew, David J., 198nn68–69, 199nn70–71, 199n74
Barton, Dorothea, 27n61
Barton, John, 80n12, 183n4, 183n7, 184n11
Bauer, Walter, 47n46
Baumgartner
Baumgärtel, Friedrich, 12, 14, 28, 30n69
Bausani, A., 13n29
Beaulieu, Paul-Alain, 74n53
Becking, Bob, 2, 70n26, 183n4
Beckman, Gary, 183n7
Beek, M. A., 95n25, 188n32
Bellinger, W. H., Jr., 79n8
Ben-Chorin, Shalom, 50
Bennett, Deborah, 190, 191n43
Benz, Frank L., 71n32
Ben Zvi, Ehud, 72n39
Berg, Robert M. van den, 110n32
Bernett, Monika, 225n30
Bethge, Eberhard, 111n36
Biale, David, 203n8, 204–5, 210
Bianchi, U., 13n29
Bienkowski, Piotr, 225n28, 235n50
Bishop, Rufus, 215n52
Blackburn, Jean, 221, 223
Blair, Judit M., 62n6
Bleeker, C.J., 13n29
Block, Daniel I., 149nn51–52, 155n72
Blum, Erhard, 45n37, 57n77
Boda, Mark J., 85n24
Bodner, Keith, 67n21
Bohak, Gideon, 185n17
Bonfiglio, Ryan P., 104n11

Bongioanni, Alessandro, 222nn16–18
Bonhoeffer, Dietrich, 111n36
Boshoff, W. S., 81n16
Botta, Alejandro F., 72n40, 73n48
Botterweck, G. Johannes, 135n30, 189n38
Bousset, Willhelm, 8n13, 160, 175
Bowden, John, 62n6
Bowen, Nancy R., 155n72
Boyer, Pascal, 142n13
Braude, William G., 167n20
Brekus, Catherine A., 215n52
Brenner, Athalya, 66n20
Brettler, Marc Zvi, 124n14
Brink, Jean R., 212n44
Brocke, Edna, 32–33, 56
Bromiley, Geoffrey W., xn12, 106n17, 135n30, 190n38
Brown, Peter, 52n64
Brueggemann, Walter, 108n25, 143n21, 157n87
Brueing, Elizabeth, 217n63
Brumlik, Micha, 55n73
de Bruyn, Theodore, 198n68
Büchsel, Friedrich, 106n17
Budin, Stephanie, 211n39
Bultmann, Rudolf, 12, 161
Bürge, Teresa, 227n33
Burnett, Joel S., 79n7, 198n66
Bynum, Carol Walker, 208nn26–27, 209n28

Cadbury, H.J., 11n26
Cameron, Euan, 198n68
Campbell, Antony F., 205n19
Carr, David, 43n30,
Carter, Charles A., 139n3
Chapman, Stephen B., 192n46
Charles, R. H., 156n78
Charney, Davida H., 103n9
Charpin, Dominique, 75n57
Chatman, Seymour, 195n53
Childs, Brevard, 11n23, 11n26, 12n28, 103n5, 154n71, 174n36
Chisholm, Robert B., Jr., 43n31
Cholidis, Nadja, 222n14
Christ, Carol, 215n54
Clamer, Crista, 224n23
Clapham, Lynn, 177n46

Clements, Ronald E., 182n3
Clines, David J. A., 70n29
Colledge, Edmund, 209n29
Collins, John J., 92n12
Conklin, Blane, 73nn44–45
Cornelius, Izak, 183n4, 224n21
Cornell, Collin, ixn5, x, xin15, 72n40, 98, 108n23, 109n29, 138n1, 151n63, 152n64, 152n66, 157n84
Coudert, Allison P., 212n44
Courth, Franz, 43n34
Coxe, A. Cleveland, 106n16
Cross, F. L., 153n68
Cross, Frank Moore, 12, 16–19, 25nn55–56, 29n67, 72n39, 144, 146–47, 157n86, 177n46, 203, 205n20
Crowfoot, Grace M., 219n2
Crowfoot, John W., 219n2
Cryer, Frederick H., 190n42
Currid, John D., 144n23

Dalferth, Ingolf U., 78n3
Daniels, Peter T., 52n63
Darby, Erin, 212n40, 212n42, 227n38
Daviau, P. M. Michèle, 121n10, 225n26, 225n32, 226, 227n34, 227n38, 228–29, 233n42, 235n51
Davies, Alan T., 161n7
Day, John, 183n4
Dearman, J. Andrew, x, 3, 128n7, 234n45
deClaissé-Walford, Nancy, 144n26
Deissler, Alphons, 42n27
Deist, Ferdinand, 35n9, 195n58, 196, 198n65
Delamarter, Steve, 102n3, 145n30
Delitzsch, Friedrich, 7
Dempsey, Carol J., 85n24
Dever, William G., 183n4, 236n52
Dhorme, Eduard P., 203n11
Dietrich, Manfred, 39n25
Dietrich, Walter, 34n6, 45n36, 47n46, 55n72
Dijkstra, Meindert, 183n4
Dillenberger, John, 31
Dion, Paul E., 225n26
Doberstein, John W., 112n38
Donaldson, James, 106n16
Doak, Brian R., 224n22

Dozeman, Thomas B., 197n63
Dupont-Sommer, André, 70n31, 71n33, 72n39,
Dürrenmatt, Friedrich, 54n69, 57n75

Eckardt, A. Roy, 161n7
Eckert, Willehad Paul, 45n36, 49n54
Edelman, Diana Vikander, 182n3
Eddy, Mary Baker, 199n70
Edgar, William, 105n15
Eichhorn, Albert, 8
Eichrodt, Walther, 42n27, 133n20, 173, 174n34
Eidinow, Esther, 151n61
Eilberg-Schwartz, Howard, 143n19
Eissfeldt, Otto, 12
Emerton, J. A., xn12
Enns, Peter, 124n14
Epp, Eldon Jay, 162n10
Eshel, I., 230n39
Evans, Craig A., 197n63
Ezrin, Amy C., 222n16

Fassberg, Steven E., 70n30
Faulkner, Raymond O., 203n7
Finkel, Irving L., 72n39
Finkelstein, Israel, 35n10, 72n39
Finkelstein, Jacob J., 23n52, 176n45
Fischer, John Martin, 198n68
Fischer, Peter M., 227n33, 227n35
Flesher, LeAnn Snow, 85n24
Fohrer, Georg, 7nn8–9, 8n11, 9n19, 12, 19n37, 42n27
Foster, Benjamin R., 148n50
Fox, Nili, 183n7
Frahm, Eckart, 139n2, 139n5
Frankemölle, Hubert, 50n57
Fredriksen, Paula, 183n5
Freedman, Amelia Devin, 198n66
Freedman, D. N., 134n21, 205n20
Fretheim, Terence E., 197n63
Friedberg, Lilian, 39n23
Friedman, Richard Elliott, 198n65, 205n19
Friedrich, Gerhard, 106n17
Frohnhofen, Herbert, 45n36
Frood, Elizabeth, 222n17
Frymer-Kensky, Tikva S., 210n34
Fuller, Reginald, 111n36

Garr, W. Randall, 205n19
Gaventa, Beverly R., 207n22
George, Martin, 45n36, 47n46, 55n72
Gelling, P. S., 220n6
Gerstenberger, Erhard, 62n6, 63n10
Geuss, Raymond, 146n33
Gibb, H. A. R., 59n80
Gilberson, Karl W., 198n68
Gillman, Neil, 89n4
Ginsberg, H.L., 144n25
Ginsburg, David, 102n1
Gitin, Seymour, 186n23, 236n52
Gittlen, Barry M., 236nn52–53
Glueck, Nelson, 219n2
Gnuse, Robert K., 182n3
Godley, A.D., 56n74
Goedicke, Hans, 178n50
Goldenberg, Robert, 3, 90n8, 91n10
Goldstein, Jonathan A., 156n79
Gordon, Robert P., 182n3
Görg, Manfred, 58n79, 202n3
Gotthard, Axel, 69n25
Göttner-Abendroth, Heide, 39
Gottwald, Norman, 168n24
Grabbe, Lester L., 80n12, 183n6, 184n11
Graham, M. Patrick, ixnn5–6, xn10, 98, 126n1
Gras, Michel, 37n17
Gray, Patrick, 145n29–30
Green, D. E., 135n30, 190n38
Green, Garrett, 111n33
Greenberg, Moshe, 143n22
Greene, William Chase, 189n36
Greenstein, Edward L., 105n13
Gressmann, Hugo, 8
Gröndahl, Frauke, 71n32,
Guder, Darrell, 111n36
Gunkel, Hermann, 7–10, 107–8, 147

Haacker, Klaus, 47n45
Habel, Norman, 20n40, 62n8
Hadas, Moses, 186n21
Hadley, Judith, 66n20
Hagelia, Hallvard, 107n18
Hahn, Herbert F., 6n1
Haidt, Jonathan, 129–30, 135n24
Haitch, Russell, 102n3, 145n30
Halpern, Baruch, 35n10

Index of Authors

Halton, Charles, 149n52
Hamilton, Mark W., 130n15
Hamori, Esther J., 190n42
Handke, Peter, 54n67
Handy, Lowell K., 66n19
Hankins, Davis, 157n87
Hanson, K. C., 128n8
Hanson, Paul D., 174, 178
Hanson, Robin, 132n17
von Harnack, Adolph, 10
Harrington, Daniel J., 124n14
Harris, Leslie, 214n51
Harris, Marvin, 56n74
Harris, J. Rendel, 207n23
Hartenstein, Friedhelm, 78n3
Hasel, Gerhard, 109n31
Häser, Jutta, 225n27
Haskell, Ellen Davina, 209nn32–33, 218
Haupt, Paul, 202
Hawass, Zahi, 222n18
Hayman, Peter, 183n5
Hays, Christopher B., 141n9, 203n8, 211n36, 211n38
Heath, J. M. F., 152n64
Heckl, Raik, 74n49
Heinemann, J., 196n61
Heiser, Michael S., 182n1
Hempel, Johannes, 14n31
Hendel, Ronald S., 140n6
Herbener, Jens-André P., 182n1
Herdner, Andree, 58n78
Heschel, Abraham J., 89n4, 93n19
Heschel, Susannah, 55n72
Hiebert, T., 151n60
Hoch, James E., 203n9
Hoffman, Mark Vitalis, 102n3, 145n30
Hoffman, Yair, 107n18
Houellebecq, Michel, 54n67
Holladay, William L., 65n18, 67n21
Holland, Thomas A., 64n16, 229–30n39, 236n55
de Hoop, Raymond, 203n13, 205n19
Hornung, Erik, 224n19
Horowitz, Maryanne C., 213n44
Hossfeld, Frank-Lothar, 79n8
Houtman, Cornelis, 66n20
Hubbard, Robert, 192–94
Hübner, Ulrich, 61n5

de Hulster, Izaak J., 198n66, 227n38
Hurtado, Larry W., 183nn6–7
Hurvitz, Avi, 70n30

Iwry, Samuel, 192n47

Jackson, Kent P., 135n27
Jacobsen, Thorkild, 21, 22n49, 24n53, 172, 177n46
Jacobson, Rolf A., 144n26–27
Janaydeh, Khaled, 225n29
Janowski, Bernd, 38n18
Jaroš, Karl, 36n15, 64n17
Jeffers, Ann, 192n47
Jensen, Hans J. Lundager, 107n18
Jeremias, A., 7
Jeremias, Jörg, 184nn11–12
Ji, Chang-Ho, 225n31
Jindo, Job Y., 187n24
Joannès, Francis, 75n57
Johnson, Elizabeth A., 218
Johnson, Jessica, 217n63
Jones, Arun W., 102n3, 145n30
Jones, Lindsay, 198n69
Joukowsky, Martha S., 220nn3–4, 220n7, 221, 222n11, 223
Junge, Daniel, 216n59
Jüngel, Eberhard, 111n36, 112n38
Jüngling, Hans-Winfried, 24n54

Kaiser, Otto, 42n27
Kamlah, Jens, 225n31
Kampman, A. A., 9s5n25
Kang, Sa-Moon, 135n26
Kapstein, Israel J., 167n20
Kärkkäinen, Veli-Matti, 60n2
Kasper, Walter, 49
Katz, Jacob, 170n26
Kaufman, Gordon, 29n68, 30–31, 107
Kaufmann, Yehezkel, 143n22, 171, 172n33, 182n2, 186–88, 198n67
Kawami, Trudy S., 220n5, 224n20, 224n24
Kawin, Bruce F., 155n72
Keel, Othmar, ixn7, xiiin18, 2, 34n7, 38n19, 38nn21–22, 41, 43n30, 43n33, 51n61, 52n63, 54n71, 117–18n5, 139n3, 183n4, 187n24, 225n30, 236

Kehm, George H., 31n71
Kelly, J. N. D., 153n68, 154n69
Kempinski, Aharon, 35n11
Kenyon, Kathleen M., 219n2
Khayyata, M. Wahid, 222n15
Kindt, Julia, 151n61
Kinzig, Wolfram, 153n68
Kippenberg, Hans G., 185n17
Kittel, Gerhard, 106n17
Klassen, Stanley, 235n51
Klatt, Werner, 6, 7n6, 7n10, 8n15, 9n16, 9n20, 10, 107n21, 147n36
Klein, Charlotte, 161n5
Kletter, Raz, 42n29, 64n16
Klingshirn, William E., 200n74
Knapp, Andrew, 84n21
Knauf, Ernst Axel, 61n5, 62n8, 183n7
Knitter, Paul F., 141n10
Koch, Klaus, 12, 54
Köhler, Ludwig, 42n27
Kohlmeyer, Kay, 222n15
van Kooten, George H., viiin1, 110n32
Kornfeld, Walter, 135n30
Korpel, Marjo C. A., 62n7, 183n4
Kosch, Daniel, 55n73
Kottsieper, Ingo, 75n57, 182n3
Kratz, Reinhard G., 182n3, 183n4
Kraus, H.-J., 6n1, 7n10, 8n12
Krüger, Thomas, 37n16
Küchler, Max, 34n7
Kuhrt, Amélie, 72n39
Kümmel, W. G., 6n1, 8n13
Kynes, Will, 195n54

Labuschagne, C. J., 103n8, 104n10
Lambert, W. G., 139nn4–5, 140n7, 141n8, 144n24, 177n47, 188n32
Lang, Bernhard, 68n22
Lapp, Nancy L., 226
Lauterbach, Jacob Z., 167n20
Lawson, Jack N., 187–89
Layton, Bentley, 152n64
Leibig, Janis E., 162n10
Lemaire, André, 70n30, 182n3
Lemke, Werner E., 157n86
LeMon, Joel M., 117n4
Lenzi, Alan, 140n6, 149n52
Lesley, J. P., 204n14

Lesko, Barbara S., 203n9
Lesko, Leonard H., 203n9
Levenson, Jon D., xi, 34, 36n12, 150, 155n72, 159, 172n33
Levin, Christoph, 182n3
Levinson, Nathan Peter, 45n36, 49n54
Lewis, Theodore J., 63n10, 183n7
LiDonnici, Lynn R., 190n38
Lieber, Andrea, 190n38
Lieberman, Saul, 170n26
Lim, Timothy H., 92n12
Lindblom, Johannes, 14n31
Link, Christian, 34n6
Lipschits, Oded, 72n39, 136n32
Livingstone, E. A., 153n68
Lodahl, Michael, 148n49
Lohfink, Norbert, 26n60
Lohr, Joel N., 197n63
Loretz, Oswald, 39n25, 60n3, 63n10,
Loud, Gordon, 237n56
Louth, Andrew, 149n54, 150n56
Lozachmeur, Hélène, 70n27
Lubetski, Meir, 72n39
Luijendijk, AnneMarie, 200n74
Lutzky, Harriet, 210n34
Luz, Ulrich, 45n36, 47n46, 55n72

Macchi, Jean-Daniel, 205n18
Maccoby, Hyam, 164–65, 168–69
MacDonald, Burton, 234n43
MacDonald, Nathan, 60n3, 151n62, 182n1, 182n3, 198n66
Machinist, Peter, 186, 189n34, 190n38, 195n55, 200n75
Macholz, Christian, 45n37, 57n77
Maiden, Brett E., 142n13
Maloney, Linda M., 58n79
Malul, Meir, 62n6
Margolin, Ron, 105n13
Marks, John H., 150n58
Marquardt, Friedrich-Wilhelm, 50n56
Marti, Karl, 6, 202n6
Martin, Lutz, 222n14
Martin, M. F., 121n9
Martínez, Florentino García, 35n9
Mattingly, Gerald L., 127n3, 234n45
Mays, James L., 25n57
Mazar, Amihai, 64n17

McCann, J. Clinton, 144n27
McCarter, P. Kyle, Jr., 202n2
McCarthy, Dennis J., 133n19
McEntire, Mark, 155–57
McGrath, Alister, 60
McLaughlin, Eleanor, 208n26
Medema, Ken, 216n57
Melton, Brittany N., 198n66
Mencken, H. L., 111n35
Mendenhall, George E., 168n24
Mettinger, T. N. D., 78n3, 84n21
Metz, Johann Baptist, 49
Meyer, Marvin, 198n68
Meyers, Carol L., 212n41
Migliore, Daniel L., 149n53
Miles, Jack, 198n65
Miller, J. Maxwell, x
Miller, Patrick D., Jr., xn12, xi, 2, 20n42, 23n51, 78n4, 102nn3–4, 107, 112n39, 127n3, 130n14, 133n18, 136n31, 139n3, 146–48, 151n60, 157n86
Miller, Robert D., II, 143n20
Miskotte, K.H., 101, 109nn28–29, 111–14
Moberly, R. W. L., 157n86, 159, 197n62, 197n64
Moore, George Foot, 160–61, 172, 178
Moran, William L., 21n44, 140n6, 172n32
More, Henry, 182n1
Morgenstern, Matthew, 72n39
Mowinckel, Sigmund, 174
Muffs, Yochanan, 74n48
Mulack, Christa, 55
Müller, H.-P., 138n1,
Murrow, David, 217n62
Mushayabasa, G., 202n5
Muslim, Mohammad, 222n15
Mußner, Franz, 50–51

Neumann, Mathias, 202n3
Newby, Gordon D., 74n53
Niehaus, Jeffrey J., 105–6, 144n23, 149–50n55
Niehr, Herbert, 61n5, 71n36, 182n3
Nielsen, Kirsten, 62n7
Nijland, C., 95n25
Nims, Charles F., 75n55
Nissinen, Marti, 61n5, 139n3
Nock, Arthur Darby, 12n28
North, Wendy E. S., 182n1

O'Brien, Mark A., 205n19
Oeming, Manfred, 136n32, 181n1, 182n3, 183n7
Oesterley, W. O. E., 156n78–79
Oesterreicher, John, 45n35
Olbrantz, John, 220n5, 224n20, 224n24
Olmo Lete, G. del, 202n2, 203n12
Olson, Dennis, 103n5
Olyan, Saul M., 104n12
van Oorschot, Jürgen, 77n1, 184n10
Oppenheim, A. Leo, 139n5, 187n27
Osborne, Robin, 151n61
Oswald, Hilton C., 213n47
Oswalt, John N., 144n23
Otto, Eckart, 33n2, 51n60
Otto, Walter F., 186n21

Pannenberg, Wolfhart, 31, 107
Pardee, Dennis, 202n2
Parker, Simon B., 126n2, 127nn4–5, 128n9
Parkes, James, 161n7
Patai, Raphael, 23n51
Patton, Kimberly C., 142n17
Paul, S. M., 190n38
Paulus, Witold, 142n16
Pedde, Brigitte, 57n75
Penchansky, David, 192nn44–45
Perlitt, Lothar, 7n7
Petersen, David, 142n11
Petershans, Sören, 112n41
Petuchowski, Jakob J., 168n22
Piotrovskii, Boris B., 220n6, 220nn8–9
Plaskow, Judith, 41n26
Podle, Leon, 217n62
Poliakov, León, 161n7
Polzin, Robert, 91n10
Pongratz-Leisten, Beate, 182n1, 186n22
Pope, Marvin H., 231n41
Popovic, Mladen, 70n26
Porsch, Felix, 46nn38–39
Porten, Bezalel, 63, 71n35, 71n37, 157n83
Powers, Kristen, 217n61
Prag, K., 230n39
Preuss, Horst Dietrich, 36
Pringle, W., 213n46
Pritchard, James B., 219n2, 227n37
Putney, Clifford, 215n53

Quinn, Edward, 161n5

Rabanus, Maurus- Akademie, 45n36
von Rad, Gerhard, 12, 27n61, 42n27, 150
Ragavan, Deena, 222n17
Ranck, Shirley Ann, 215n55
Ray, Benjamin C., 142n17
Ray, Paul J., 121n11
Rea, Michael C., 198n66
Redford, D. B., 202n3
Rendtorff, Rolf, 12, 14, 79n6, 161n6
Reiner, Erica, 139n5
Reisner, George A., 72n39
Renz, Johannes, 64n17
Reventlow, Henning Graf, 107n18
Riemann, Paul, 20–22
Rijckmanns, J., 95n25
Riley, G. J., 62n6
Ringgren, Helmer, 12, 135n30, 189n38, 234n44
Ritner, Robert K., 211n37
Roberts, Alexander, 106n16, 208n24
Roberts, J.J.M., 178
Robertson, David A., 205n21
Robinson, James M., 151–52n64
Rollston, Christopher A., 183n4
Römer, Thomas, 146n33, 182n3
Roncace, Mark, 145n29–30
Rose, Martin, 134n22
Rösel, Martin, 84n20
Rosenzweig, Franz, 49, 110
Rosin, Hellmut, 109n28
Rothman, Eugene, 91n10
Rouillard, Pierre, 37n17,
Rudavsky, Tamar, 199n72
Ruether, Rosemary Radford, 49, 161–65, 209, 212n43, 213n45, 214–15, 216n56
Rüterswörden, Udo, 123n13

Saggs, H. W. F., 171, 177
Sanders, E. P., 160–61, 173, 178
Sanders, J. A., 157n86, 185n14
Sandmel, Samuel, 142n14, 161n7
Saner, Andrea D., 80n11
Sanmartín, Joaquín, 203n12
Sarna, Nahum M., 105n13
Sasson, Jack, 236n52
Sayce, Archibald H., 102n1
Schäfer, Peter, 185n17
Schaff, Philip, 208n25
Schenker, Adrian, 187n24

Schifferle, Alois, 38n22
Schlimm, Matthew J., 102n3, 107n19, 108n24, 148–49
Schloen, J. David, 84n23, 184n11
Schmid, Konrad, 181n1, 182n3, 183n7
Schmidt, Werner, 26n58, 27n61
Schmitt, Rüdiger, 68n23, 234n46, 234n48
Schön, David A., 154n70
Schoonover, Myles, 70n26
Schroer, Sylvia, 52n63, 53n66, 54n71, 55n72
Schultz, Richard M., 155n72
Schwiderski, Dirk, 71n35
van Selms, Adrianus, 95n25
al-Shalabi, Mohammad A., 227n35
Sharpe, Eric J., 23n51, 177n46
Siegele-Wenschkewitz, Leonore, 55n72
Silverman, Ian, 198n67
Simler, Kevin, 132n17
Smelik, Klaas A. D., 127n6, 128nn7–8
Smith, Mark S., 58n78, 77n1, 127n3, 129n10, 135n25, 135n30, 151n63, 152n65, 152n67, 182n1, 183–85, 187, 201
Smith, Morton, 95n25, 102n2, 185n15
Smith, Jonathon Z., 142
Sneed, Mark R., 195n54
Snyder, Josey Bridges, x, 116n2, 121n8, 142n12
Sokoloff, Michael, 186n23
Sommer, Benjamin D., 183n7, 186–87, 198n67
Soulen, R. Kendall, 109n28
Sparks, Kenton L., 139n4
Speiser, E. A., 177n46
Spieckermann, Hermann, 182n3, 183n4
Staerk, Willy, 38n20
Stalker, D. M. G., 90n7
Stark, Rodney, 77n2
Staubli, Thomas, 53n66, 56n74, 187n24
Stavrakopoulou, Francesca, 80n12, 183n4, 184n11
van der Steen, E., 229
Stegemann, Ekkehard W., 45n37, 57n77
Stehle, Dorothy, 222n15
Steiner, George, 54n69
Steiner, Margreet, 225n32
Steiner, Richard C., 75n55
Stendahl, Krister, 11

Stern, Ephraim, 136n32, 183n4, 236
Stern, Menahem, 33n3
Stern, Sacha, 91n12
Stewart, Zeph, 12n28
Steymans, Hans Ulrich, 32n2
Stoellger, Phillip, 78n3
Stöhr, Martin, 45n36, 49n54
Storkel, Bryan, 216n59
Strawn, Brent A., ixn7, x, 102n3, 108, 117n4, 121n8, 139n3, 142n15, 143n20, 144n28, 145n29–30, 155n72
Strich, Christian, 57n75
Stroup, George W., 108n25
Stuckenbruck, Loren T., 182n1
Stummer, Friedrich, 14n31
Sukenik, Eliezer L., 219n2
Surls, Austin, 80n11
Swartz, Michael D., 185n17

Talmon, Shemaryahu, 196n61
Tanner, Beth LaNeel, 144n26
Taylor, Kevin, 198n68
Teixidor, Javier, 37n17
Theissen, Gerd, 45n37, 46–48
Theuer, Gabriele, 38n21
Todd, Patrick, 198n68
van der Toorn, Karel, 63n10, 64n15, 73n43, 74, 75nn57–58, 76n59, 146n33, 236
Trachtenberg, Joshua, 162n12
Trapp, Thomas A., 43n33, 118n5, 183n4, 236n53
Tucker, W. Dennis, Jr., 79n8
Turton, M., 234n47
Twelftree, Graham H., 197n62

Uehlinger, Christoph, 34n7, 43, 57n76, 117n5, 183n4, 236
Uffenheimer, Benjamin, 107n18
Urge, Teresa B., 227n35
Ussishkin, David, 224n23
Utzschneider, Helmut, 37n16

Van Dam, Cornelis, 190n42
Vandenberghe, Marijn, 70n26
Vanderhooft, David S., 130n15
Van der Steen, Eveline J., 128n7
Vatke, Wilhelm, 6
van der Veen, Peter, 235n50

Vermès, Géza, 50n56
Vieweger, Dieter, 225n27
Vieyra, Maurice, 220n3, 220n10, 222n11, 222n13
Vleeming, Sven P., 74n50
Vollenweider, Samuel, 45n36, 48n49
Volz, Paul, 14n31
Vriezen, Karel J. H., 183n4
Vriezen, T., 12

Wagenaar, Jan A., 66n19
Waller, Giles, 198n68
Walser, Martin, 54n67
Walsh, James, 209n29
Ward, Keith, 198n68
Ward, W. A., 121n9
Watson, W. G. E., 202n2
Weiler, Gerda, 39
Welburn, A. J., viin2
Wellhausen, Julius, 6, 8n15
Wesselius, Jan W., 74n50
Westermann, Claus, 42, 90n7
Wetter, Anne-Mareike, 62nn7–8
Whitelam, Keith W., 134n21, 134n23
Whitney K. William, Jr., 147n37
Widengren, Geo, 13n29
Wilken, Robert Louis, 153n68
Williams, P. H., Jr., 151n60
Willis, John T., 135n30, 189n38
Wilson, John A., 73n44
Wilson-Wright, Aren M., 202n2, 202n4, 203n9
Wimmer, Stefan J., 225n29
Wimpfheimer, Barry, 91n9
Winckler, Hugo, 7
Winston, Krishna, 54n67
Winter, Irene, 222n12
Winter, Urs, 63n13, 63n15
Wippel, John F., 199n72
Witte, Markus, 77n1, 184n10
Weinfeld, Moshe, 32n2
Winitzer, Abraham, 130n15
Wöhrle, Jakob, 182n3
Worthen, Molly, 217n60
Wright, George E., 11nn26–27, 14, 24n54, 27–28, 143n22, 174–75, 185n16, 187n27
Wynne, Frank, 54n67

Yardeni, Ada, 70n30
Yassine, Khair, 229
Younger, K. Lawson, 152n67
Younker, Randall W., 234n43
Yusa, Michiko, 198n69

Zadok, Ran, 72n39
Zayadine, Fawzi, 227n36
Zehnder, Markus, 107n18
Zenger, Erich, 34n6, 49, 51, 52n62
Zeran, Emily, 227n38, 228–29, 233n42
Zevit, Ziony, 63n10, 183n4, 186n23
Zimmerli, Walther, 42n27, 109

INDEX OF SCRIPTURE

Genesis
1:1   96
1   8, 9, 10, 54, 139, 141n8, 143
1:22, 28   206
1–11   150
2   52
3   23, 92
4:26   170
9:1–7   42
9:1–17   150, 170
9:20–27   166
9:25–6   34
10   35n9
10:6–20   33
10:15–16   35
10:26   71
11   57, 139
11:10–26   34
12:3   131
14:18–24   78n4
15:2   83
15:19–21   33
17:1–2   204
18   37
19   38
19:37   118
20   37, 170
20:3   84n22
21:7   209
21:33   37

Genesis (cont'd)
28   37
28:3   204
28:10–22   34n5
31   63n9
31:13   34n5
33:20   79n5, 184n12
35:11   204
36:12   169
38   37
42:28   193n49
45:8   194
48:3–4   204
49   205
49:1–28   42
49:25   19, 42, 204
50:20   194

Exodus
1:10   193
3:1–15   80n9
3:8   34n4
3:13–15   80n11
3:15   18
3:17   34n4
6:2–3   18, 31
6:2–8   80n9
6:3   206
12:12   115
13:5   34n4
15   205

Exodus (cont'd)
15–17   134
15:3   131
15:11   103
15:18   19
17:16   168n23
17:14–16   167
20   68
20:3   81
20:3–6   134
21:2–11   51n60
21:3   84n22
22:17   34n6, 38
23:13   109
23:19   91
23:23   34, 34n4
23:28   34n4
23:28–29   34
24:3–8   34n5
32:32–33   190n38
33:2   34n4
33:19   132
34:11   34n4
34:11–17   135, 135n29
34:13   117
34:16   106
34:26   91

Leviticus
1–7   135
11:44   135

253

Leviticus (cont'd)
18   36, 166
18:1–5   135
18:3   37
18:6–18   37
18:24–30   37, 135, 166
18:28   166
19:3–37   136
19:33–34   118
23:16   91
25:2–38   51
26:3–13   42

Numbers
14   134
21:29   119
22   92
22:22–35   119
22:40–23:30   135n28
22–24   118
24:21   19
25   119
25:1–5   118, 135n28
25:10–13   155
25:18   106
32:3   133
32:37–38   96
33   166
33:55–56   166

Deuteronomy
2:16–25   108
4:19   36, 150–51
4:19–20   90
4:28   104
4:33–34   113
4:35, 39   109n28
5   68
5:7   81
5:6–21   133
6:4   60, 64
6:4–5   26, 133
7:1   34n4
7:1–5   35n9, 166
7:1–11   34n6
7:5   33, 36, 117
7:6–8   168
7:7   113

Deuteronomy (cont'd)
7:23–26   166
9:5   166
10:17   83
10:19   118
12:2–3   33
12:3   36, 117
12:31   36
13   33
13:7–12   34n6
13:15–16   135
14:21   91
15:1–18   51n60
16:21   117
17:14–20   134
18:9–12   36, 166
18:14   36
20   135
20:16–18   131
20:18   33
21:10–14   135
21:13   84n22
23:3–4   118
23:4–7   169
23:5   169
23:6   118, 119
23:8   169
23:9–14   135
23:11   190
23:16–17   51n60
25:5–10   85n26
25:17–19   167
25:19   167
28:1–14   42
28:15–68   33
20:16–18   33
20:17   34n4
29:26   151
31:29   193n49
32:6   19
32:8   69n24, 107n18
32:8–9   184
32:13   206
32:16–19   106n16
33   42
33:5   134
33:15   19
33:21   96

Deuteronomy (cont'd)
34:1   96
34:3   74n54

Joshua
3:10   34n4
3:11   83n18
7   131
9:1   34n4
11:3   34n4
11:12   135
11:20   193n49
12   131
12:8   34n4
24   133
24:11   34n4

Judges
1:16   74n54
2:11   81
3   118
3:5   34n4
3:7   116
3:24–25   118
4:9   159
5:4–5   80
10:6   119
11   107
11:24   69, 107, 119
16:23   108n27
17–18   63n9

Ruth
1   62
1:1   118
1:6   193
1:15–16   119
1:16–17   62
2:3   192, 193
2:8–9   118
4:13   193
4:18   169
4:18–22   169

1 Samuel
2:3   84
4–6   190
5   101, 108

1 Samuel (cont'd)
6   190, 192
6:4   190
6:5   190
6:9   191
6:12   191
6:16   191
6:19   191
8   134, 195
9   195
9:1–2   167n19
9:12   196
9:13   196
9:14   194, 196
9:15   194
9:16   194
9:20   194
9:23–24   194
14   131
15   63n9, 167
20:5–16   192
20:17–22   192
20:22   192
20:26   192
22:3–4   118
28   38

2 Samuel
1:13–16   167
2:8   82n17
3:4   83n19
4:4   82n17
5:10   84n21
5:16   82n17
5:20   82
11–12   132
12:7–14   134

1 Kings
2:3   134
6:35   237
7:23–25   237
7:27–29   237
9:20   34n4
8:22–61   132
11:7, 33   107, 119
11:33   79n7
18–19   25

1 Kings (cont'd)
18   89n5
18:16–46   81n13
18:39   109
22:34   197
22:38   197

2 Kings
1–3   128
3:27   135n28
5   69
5:15–19   108
6   131
8   131
16   131, 136
17   131
19:18   104
19:22   135
21   131
21:2–3   134
21:3–7   235n49
23:4–7   210
21:4–9   135, 135n29
22–23   67
23:13   104, 199
23:20   35

1 Chronicles
1:26   71
3:8   82n17
8:33   82n17
8:34   82n17
12:6   82n17, 83n19
14:7   82n17
16:26   90
29:14–19   131

2 Chronicles
12:14   134
14:2   134
14:6–7   131
23   134
24:17–26   132
25:3–4   134
28:15   74n54
30:6–9   132
32:19   vii, 104, 110
32:23   110

Ezra
5:1   70n28
6:14   70n28

Nehemiah
5:1–13   51n60
9   133, 136
13:1–2   118
13:23–27   136

Esther
2:5   167n19
3:1   167
3:1–6   53
3:7–11   53
4:14   193n49
8:9–9:10   167

Psalms
8:2   83
19   61
22:10–11   204
29   20, 144
58   61
59:6   84n21
68:5   144n28
68:7   142n15
69:7   84n21
69:29   190n38
72   61
80:8   84n21
80:15   84n21
80:50   84n21
82   18, 19, 22, 24,
     24n54, 61, 95n26
89:6–8   19
91   61
91:5–6   61
94:1   84
96:5   90
100:3   109n28
104   38
115:4   104
115:4–9   104n11
115:15   158
121:2   158
124:8   158
134:3   158

Index of Scripture

Psalms (cont'd)
135:15   104
135:15–18   104n11
137:7   169n25
146:6   158

Proverbs
5:15–23   43
5:18–19   42, 209

Ecclesiastes
1:4–9   174n35
2:14–15   195n55
3:19   195n55
7:16–18   146
7:18   146
7:20   132
9:2–3   195n55

Song of Songs
8:1   210

Isaiah
1:7, 9   38
1:21   38
1:24   84n21
2:1–4   131
4:3   190n38
6:5   83n18
7   136
10:22   207
19:18   35
23   90n8, 234
27:1   20
28   203n8, 211
28:2   207
28:9   211
28:15   211
28:15–18   207
30:28   207
37:19   104
40   64
40:18–20   104n11
40–66   85
41:2   193n49
41:6–7   104n11
43:10   viiin4, 104n12
43:12   91, 177n46

Isaiah (cont'd)
44:6   viiin4, 88n3, 89, 104n12
44:6–8   65
44:9–20   104n11
44:14–20   171
44:15, 19   104
45:5   viii, 104, 115n1
45:5–6   viiin4, 104n12
45:15   196
45:22   177n46
46:3   213
46:9   viiin4, 104n12
49:14–15   206
49:15   213
49:23   213
51:9   20
51:17, 20   193n49
53:2   113n44
54:5   84
55:8–9   190n38
60:16   206
62:4–5   85
65:11   186n23
66:10–11   206
66:11   213
66:13   207

Jeremiah
2:8   81n13, 85
2:19   84n21
2:23   85
2:27   37
3   86
3:1–5   85, 85n26
3:6–18   85
3:7–8   85n26
3:9   37
3:14   85
3:19–20   86n27
7:9   85
7:31   37
10:1–16   104n11
10:3   104
10:3–5   65
12:14   176
13:24–7   193n49
16:11   92

Jeremiah (cont'd)
18:11   190n38
19:5   85
19:6   37
28   94n24
31:9   213
31:31–34   86
31:32   86
31:33   86
34:8–22   51n60
44   65, 66, 68, 94n23, 185, 212
44:2–10   66
44:11–15   66
44:16–17   212
44:20–30   66
44:22–3   193n49
46–50   90n8
48:7, 13, 46   119

Lamentations
4:3   42
4:21–22   169n25

Ezekiel
1:1–14   236
8   185
10:5   205
16   86
16:3   35
16:8   86
23   86
23:1–49   85n24
25   90n8
26–27   234
47:16, 18   123

Daniel
10:14   193n49
10:21   190n38

Hosea
1–3   86
2   109
2:10   81n13
2:18   81, 84n22, 177n46
2:19   81
3:4   34n5
4:13   37

Hosea (cont'd)
  8:4–6 104n11
  9:14 42
  10:1 34n5
  11:1–11 86
  13:2–3 104n11

Joel
  1:15 205, 210

Amos
  1:11 169n25
  3:13 84n21
  6:14 84n21
  9:7 108

Micah
  1:3–7 85n24
  4:5 90
  5:12–13 104n11
  6:1–8 136
  6:7 37
  6:8 133

Nahum
  3 90n8

Habakkuk
  2:15 92n14
  2:18–19 104n11
  3:3–7 80
  3:6 204n15

Zephaniah
  2 90n8

Haggai
  1–2 70n28
  2:4 91n12

Malachi
  1:6 213

Matthew
  5:45 199
  6:1–18 162
  10:29–31 199
  13:32 107

Matthew (cont'd)
  23 55
  23:37 214n49
  25:31–46 170
  27:24–5 45n37, 46
  27:25 162

Luke
  12:10 46
  13:1–5 199
  13:34 214n49

John
  1:5 164
  1:19 47n46
  2:18 47n46
  2:20 47n46
  4:22 46
  5:10 47n46
  5:15–16 47n46
  5:19–47 162n11
  5:23 162
  6:27 52
  6:41, 42 47n46
  7:28 162n11
  8:19 162n11
  8:39–44 46
  8:44 162
  8:47 162n11
  9:3 199
  14:6 170
  15:18–25 162n11
  16:1–3 162n11
  21 208n25

Acts
  1:23–6 199
  5:38–9 58
  7:51–2 45, 45n37
  7:52 46
  17:16–34 149
  17:22 149
  17:31 149

Romans
  2:25–29 162
  7:12 164
  8:28 194

Romans (cont'd)
  9–11 162n9
  11 48, 166
  11:11–32 162
  11:13–24 50n57
  11:17–24 49
  11:21–22 166

1 Corinthians
  1:23 114
  1:24 207
  1:30 207
  3:1–3 207
  7:7 43
  7:28 52
  8:4–6 184n12
  10 106
  10:14 106
  10:20 106n16
  11:27 47

2 Corinthians
  3:4–6 162
  11:14 106n16

Galatians
  3:5–14 162
  3:10–11 55
  3:28 51
  4 164
  4:3 43

Ephesians
  1:20 150
  5:21–33 52

Philippians
  3:18–20 51

Colossians
  2:8 43
  2:20 43

1 Thessalonians
  1:9 viii
  2:5–8 207
  2:14–16 46, 47
  2:16 46

1 Timothy
4:1   106, 106n16
6:1–2   5in59

Philemon
1   5in59

Hebrews
11:1   93n18

1 John
3:8   47

Wisdom
13:1–7   58
13:10–19   104

1 Maccabees
2:21   155
2:23–26   155
2:26–27   155
2:39–42   156n80
2:42   155
2:48   155, 156
2:50   155
2:58   155

1 Maccabees (cont'd)
2:64   156
2:67–68   156
3:46–57   156n80
4:24   156n80
4:30   156n80
12:15   156n80

2 Maccabees
5:11–20   156n80
8:19   156
8:28   156

SUBJECT INDEX

Akkadian, 17, 74, 148, 176, 185–89, 203
Amalek, 167–69
Amherst Papyrus, 64n15, 74–76.
Anat, 205n16, 210n34, 224–25, 234. See also Anathbethel.
Anathbthel, 63
Anti-idol polemic. *See also* Idols.
Anti-Judaism. See also Antisemitism.
  in the New Testament, 44–46, 159, 161–63
  in modern scholarship, 45, 48–50, 161
Antisemitism, 44–46, 159, 161
Apocryphon of John, viin2
Aramaic, 63, 70, 74
Ares, 138n1
Asherah, 42, 64, 66–68, 76, 117, 184, 210, 235n49. *See also* Divine feminine; Goddess.
Ashtar-Chemosh, 120–21, 134, 234. *See also* Chemosh.
Ashur, 21, 22
Assmann, Jan, 38n20, 54
Augustine, 198, 208, 212

Baal. *See also* God, storm god.
  common noun, 78, 85, 122
  adoption of Baalistic features into Yahwism, 20, 29, 82, 144
  Yahwistic rivalry with Baalism, 25, 29, 81–82, 85, 109, 177
Barth, Karl, 11, 110–11, 149n53
Bibel und Babel, 7, 23, 57, 176
Breasts. *See* Breastfeeding, divine

Breastfeeding, divine, 40–42, 64, 180, 201–14. *See also* Dea nutrix; Goddess; Figurines, female.
Bull
  Bull of Jacob, 17
  bull figurines, 219–20, 225, 227, 231

Calvin, John, 213–14
Canaanite religion, 7, 16–17, 20, 25, 36–39, 117, 166, 177n46, 224
Chemosh, ix–xi, 69, 98–99, 101–2, 104–8, 111–14, 116, 118–21, 122. *See also* Mesha Inscription; Ashtar-Chemosh.
Cherubim, 19, 112, 220, 236–37
Childs, Brevard, 11n23, 11n26, 12n28, 103n5, 154n71, 174n36
Conquest of Canaan. *See* Genocide, of Canaanites.
Creation, 9–10, 39, 52, 54, 58, 139, 153
Cross, Frank Moore, 12, 16–19, 144, 146–47, 203

David, 42, 82, 118, 131, 134, 169, 192
Dea nutrix, 64, 180, 201, 206–8, 210–12. *See also* Breastfeeding, divine.
Dead Sea Scrolls. *See* Qumran.
Divine feminine. *See also* Goddess.
  loss of, in Israelite religion, 22–24, 39–43, 201, 210–12
  inevitability of, 58–59, 217–18
Divination
  belomancy (arrows), 192
  book sortilege, 199n74

259

Divination (cont'd)
  cleromancy (lots), 190, 199
  necromancy (the dead), 38
  with cows, 190–92

Egyptian. *See also* Elephantine.
  culture, 7, 37
  iconography, 222, 224, 231, 235
  jurisprudence, 73
  language, 64n15, 73, 202
  religion, 9n19, 14, 37, 150, 202–3, 211, 222, 224, 231, 235
  messianic hope, 8
El (the god), 17–18, 19–20, 78–79, 116–17, 122, 146, 225, 231, 234
Election, divine, 17, 42, 113, 132, 198–99. *See also* Grace, divine.
Elephantine, 35, 63, 71–74, 157. *See also* Egypt.
Enuma Elish, 77, 139–40, 143, 188. *See also* Ludlul bel nemeqi
Eschatology, 8, 43, 51, 53–54, 162–63
Eusebius, 7, 149
Exclusivity formulae, viiin4, 27, 64–65, 88–91, 104, 177n46

Figurines, female, viii, 23, 40–41, 64, 120–21, 136n32, 211, 219

Genocide, of Canaanites, 34, 36, 131, 159, 166, 168. *See also* Joshua son of Nun.
God. *See also* Dea nutrix; Breastfeeding, divine; Goddess
  bachelor God, x, 98, 125, 142, 158
  high god, 134n23, 177n46
  name of God, 79–80, 109, 168
  nonsexuality of, 20, 129n10, 212
  southern origin of YHWH, 18, 80, 204n15
  storm god, 20, 22, 25, 80, 141, 220, 222
  Triune God, 60, 153, 170n26, 207–9
  cult of YHWH outside of Israel/Canaan, 80, 146, 184
Goddess, 22, 23n51, 39–40, 66–67, 79n7, 117, 120–21, 180, 183, 201, 210–11, 215, 217, 220, 224. *See also* Asherah; Divine feminine; Queen of Heaven.
Grace, divine, 99, 132, 137, 148–49, 172. *See also* Election, divine.

Gunkel, Hermann, 7–10, 108, 146–47

Hadad, 17, 81n13
Hathor, 151, 222
Hegel, G.W.F, 6
Herodotus, 33, 53, 56n74
History of religions, 5, 8, 11, 113, 147
Horus, 202

Idols, viii, 27n62, 33, 65, 93, 106, 110, 133, 170
Ishtar, 120–21, 151, 188
Islam, 56, 60, 170n26

Jepththah, 69, 107
Jesus Christ, 29–31, 36, 49, 50–51, 55, 112, 122, 150, 153, 158, 162, 164, 207–9, 216–17
John Hyrcanus, 35
Josephus, 36, 39, 46–47, 92
Joshua son of Nun, 131, 168
Justice, divine, 25, 38–39, 42, 51, 58, 131–33, 172, 176–77, 194–95. *See also* Grace, divine.

Khnum, 71
Kuntillet 'Ajrud, 64, 117n4

Ludlul bel nemeqi, 139–40
Luther, Martin, 213–14

Maccabees, 155–57
Magic, vii, 38, 166, 185, 187n27
Maimonides, 56, 92n16
Marcion, 145
Marduk, 21–23, 77, 108–10, 139–40, 142, 147–48, 171, 188. *See also* Enuma Elish
Melqart, 81n13, 234, 235n49
Mesha inscription, ix–xi, 101–2, 120–21, 126–29, 134, 137, 138, 234
Mesopotamia, 6n4, 7–8, 10, 17, 21, 23, 57, 121, 139–40, 172–73, 177–78, 186–88
Midrash, 90, 95–96, 167–70
Milkom, 82, 151, 234
Monotheism
  definition, 20–21, 68, 151, 186
  convergence, 23, 77–78, 80, 82–83, 183–85

desert profile, 54, 141
monolatry, 81, 88, 94, 172
origins, 54, 181–85
relationship to fate, 186–87
Moses, 18, 25, 42, 61, 95–96, 103, 131, 166, 182, 197n62. *See also* Song of Moses.
Muslim. *See* Islam.
Mut, 211

Naaman the Syrian, 69, 109
Nabu, 70, 72n39, 75, 151
Nostra aetate, 44–45, 107

Paul, the apostle, viii, 46, 48, 51–52, 106, 149, 161–62, 164–65, 207
Papyrus Amherst. *See* Amherst Papyrus.
Philo of Alexandria, 56
Phoenician
    language, 71, 84
    religion, 6n4, 7, 37, 84, 235
Pillar figurines. *See* Figurines, female.
Prayer, 52, 95–96, 148–49, 162, 188, 212

Qaus (or Qos), 141, 235
Queen of Heaven, 64–67, 212, 215–17
Qumran, 13, 69n24, 92n14, 91n12

Rosenzweig, Franz, 49, 110
Ras Shamra. *See* Ugarit.
Ruether, Rosemary Radford, 49, 161–65, 209, 212n43, 213n45, 214–15, 216n56
Ruth, 62, 118–19, 169, 192–93

Sati or Satet (goddess), 73
Sennacherib, vii, 104, 156, 169

Second Isaiah, 20, 64–65, 84–85, 89, 91, 104, 171, 196, 206–7, 213
Schiller, Friedrich, 54
Sexuality
    celebration of, 43
    homosexuality, 37
    regulating of, 33, 36–37, 52, 166
    sin of Ham, 34–35, 166
Shadday, 16, 62–63, 202–6
Shema, 26, 60, 64, 133
Song of Moses, 69, 206
Stendahl, Krister, 11
Sumerian, 148, 176

Tammuz, 172
Temple
    the First Temple, 39, 67, 131, 135, 169, 176, 185, 210, 236–37
    the Second Temple, 46–47, 92, 155, 176, 210
    the YHW temple on Elephantine, 63, 157
    Syrian temples, 222
Tiamat, 9, 15, 23, 25, 147

Ugarit, 13, 18, 58, 116–17, 142, 202, 234
Ugaritic. *See* Ugarit.

Wellhausen, Julius, 6–7, 10
Wesley, John, 148–49
Wright, G. Ernest, 14, 27–28, 147, 174–75

Yamm, 23–24

Zeus, 56n74, 110n32, 152n64

www.ingramcontent.com/pod-product-compliance
Lightning Source LLC
Chambersburg PA
CBHW030442090526
44586CB00044B/510